The Soviet Soldier

THE
Soviet
Soldier

Soviet Military Management
at the Troop Level

Herbert Goldhamer

Crane, Russak & Company, Inc.
NEW YORK

Leo Cooper Ltd
LONDON

THE SOVIET SOLDIER

Published in the United States by

Crane, Russak & Company, Inc.
347 Madison Avenue
New York, New York 10017

Published in Great Britain by

Leo Cooper Ltd
196 Shaftesbury Avenue
London WC2H 8JL England

Crane, Russak Hardcover Edition ISBN 0–8448–0615–3
Crane, Russak Softcover Edition ISBN 0–8448–0652–8
Leo Cooper Hardcover Edition ISBN 0–85052–041–X
LC 74–26727
Copyright © 1975 The Rand Corporation

Printed in the United States of America

Contents

Tables

NOTE   Citations of *Krasnaya zvezda* and *Kommunist vooruzhennykh sil* in the footnotes are abbreviated *KZ* and *KVS* respectively. All other citations of Soviet journals and newspapers are given in full.

Preface

The understandable preoccupation of military specialists and Sovietologists with Soviet military doctrine, weapons systems, troop dispositions, and high-level personnel changes has led to some neglect of the Soviet soldier and field officer and of the administrative and control system by which the day-to-day operations of the Soviet forces are regulated. This study attempts to fill, in some measure, the gap thus created. The resulting portrait of the Soviet military establishment at the troop level has an interest well beyond the area of comparative military studies. Soviet management of the troops throws into sharp relief Soviet ideas and preferences with respect to the management of men generally, and contributes to an understanding of the civil society and the role of the Party in it.

The scope of the study and the sources used are discussed in the Introduction. A detailed table of contents also serves to define the character of the study.

I am indebted to Arnold L. Horelick, Roman Kolkowicz, Nathan Leites, Andrew W. Marshall, Theodore M. Parker, and Thomas W. Wolfe for their careful reading of the manuscript and the comments, criticisms, and suggestions that they provided. Lilita I. Dzirkals and Barbara Kliszewski provided invaluable assistance in unearthing and checking elusive data and sources. To Alyce Brewer I am indebted for her talent in transforming with great speed a disorderly manuscript into an accurate typescript.

This study was sponsored, through Project Rand of The Rand Corporation, by the United States Air Force. It does not, of course, necessarily reflect the opinions or policies of its sponsor.

HERBERT GOLDHAMER

Santa Monica, California
January 1975

The Soviet Soldier

Introduction

This study provides a portrait of the day-to-day life of the Soviet armed forces at the troop level. Obviously, in studying a military establishment there is no substitute for direct participation in it or contact with it. Nonetheless, Soviet unclassified military journals provide vivid and valuable accounts of many aspects of the day-to-day operations of the military. They permit an overall picture that may not be complete but that adds greatly to our knowledge of the Soviet armed forces. Military journals generally are noted for what they leave out as well as for what they say, and Soviet publications in particular are treated, understandably, with some reserve. Naturally, I cannot claim to have avoided all the pitfalls that such materials hold for both the wary and the unwary. Still, exposure to large amounts of these materials makes one sensitive to the probable presence of overstatements, understatements, pure rhetoric, misleading statistics, candid and accurate evaluations, and useful facts.

There is, I believe, a tendency to assume that most Soviet publications mainly provide glowing and exaggerated accounts of great accomplishments. There are, to be sure, many such expressions of self-congratulation in Soviet military journals, but the unclassified military journals are intended to perform an important pedagogical and control function and therefore are preoccupied with deficiencies and failures as well as successes. The deficiencies and failures are such, of course, relative to demands on the one hand of the Party and the political officers and on the other hand of commanders who are concerned less with ideological and disciplinary matters than with military training and operational effectiveness.

The developments traced in this study begin for the most part with 1967 and the revised form of the Law of Universal Military Service of that year. The materials investigated for the study, however, date mainly from 1970 through the autumn of 1974. The study is based primarily on translations of Soviet unclassified military journals made available in *Translations on USSR Military Affairs* issued by the U.S. Joint Publications Research Service. In addition, I have made systematic use of *Daily Report: Soviet Union* issued by the Foreign Broadcast Information Service (FBIS) and the *Current Digest of the Soviet Press* published by the American Association for the Advancement of Slavic Studies. References to Soviet materials are based on the citations given in these translations. Consequently page references are to the articles themselves and not to the particular passages quoted. I have made more incidental use of other sources that are cited in the notes.

It would have been useful to compare Soviet patterns of military management with those of other military establishments. This, however, would have required a greater knowledge of other military systems than the author can claim. Only very occasionally have I suggested comparisons. Consequently, in most instances in which I describe a Soviet propensity I do not thereby imply that it is unique to the Soviet military establishment or to Soviet society.

Chapter I

Cadres and Conscripts: Soviet Military Manpower Policies

In the early post–Civil War years Soviet military debate turned on the relative advantages and disadvantages of a permanent regular army as compared with a territorial militia system. Both the Eighth (1919) and the Ninth (1920) Party Congresses decided in favor of a peacetime army based on universal training and gradual transition to a territorial militia system. In fact, however, in the years that followed, the Soviet armed forces developed according to a mixed system, with both regular army units and territorial formations.[1] In 1934 regular army forces were greatly increased and the territorial forces were gradually reduced, so that when World War II broke out the Soviet army was in effect a regular force based on universal military service.[2]

Whether constituting a militia or a regular standing army, the Soviet forces have been a conscript rather than a professional, or volunteer, army. An

[1] *Voyenno-istoricheskiy zhurnal,* January 1970, pp. 83–91.

[2] John Erickson, "The Army, the Party, and the People," in *The Soviet Union in Europe and the Near East: Her Capabilities and Intentions* (London: Royal United Services Institute for Defense Studies, 1970), p. 16.

aversion to a professional army is understandable in a revolutionary state. Nonetheless, we shall see shortly that elements of professionalism are prominent in the Soviet armed forces and are being strongly encouraged. In the meantime it is evident, quite apart from any new measures that may be taken, that an army with professional career officers and nondraft noncommissioned officers (NCOs), especially an army in which about 20 percent of the personnel are officers, already contains a high level of military professionalism.[3]

A. USSR LAW OF UNIVERSAL MILITARY SERVICE, 1967

Basic to an understanding of the Soviet system of military service and of many specific aspects of Soviet military administration is the USSR Law of Universal Military Service of 1967.

The most striking change in the 1967 law was the reduction in the length of military service. Service in the army, the coast guard, the air arm of the navy, and the border and security troops was reduced from three to two years. Service on naval ships, vessels, coast guard combat units, and maritime units of border troops was reduced from four to three years.[4] Inductees with higher education serve for only one year.[5] It is not unlikely that the efforts of young Soviet men to be admitted to schools of higher learning are partly related to the existence of the deferments and shorter term of military service that a higher education confers.

The 1967 law reduced the age of call-up from nineteen to eighteen years, thus providing a younger and less mature set of draftees (Article 10). In addition, the call-up for active duty now takes place twice a year, in May and June and again in November and December, instead of only once a year (Article 23). These two periods of call-up coincide with the completion of

[3] John Erickson, *Soviet Military Power* (London: Royal United Services Institute for Defense Studies, 1971), p. 14, gives an estimate of 20 percent based on two main considerations: (1) taking the figure for Party membership in the military as being virtually synonymous with officer strength; (2) in Khrushchev's 1960 figures on Soviet demobilizations, 250,000 of the 1.2 million men released were identified as officers. Erickson's first consideration seems inaccurate. In 1972 only about 71 percent of all the officers in the army and navy were members or candidate members of the Party (see table 3). Erickson also does not take into account the fact that a substantial number of Soviet enlisted, that is, nondraft (and therefore older), men, generally NCOs, are Party members. Nonetheless, I have used Erickson's 20 percent estimate for officers in the armed forces largely on the basis of his second consideration, although of course there is a real possibility that the percentage of officers released was not the same as that of noncommissioned personnel.

[4] Articles 13a and 13b. The complete law is reproduced in *Current Digest of the Soviet Press* 19, no. 45, November 29, 1967, pp. 4–10. The original law of September 1, 1939, required two years of service in the army (increased to three years in 1950) and in Ministry of the Interior troops; three years service in the border troops; four years in the air force and Coastal Defense units; and five years in the navy (reduced to four years in 1955). M. A. Peltier, "Organization, Personnel and Training of the Soviet Navy," in M. G. Saunders, R.N. (ed.), *The Soviet Navy,* New York, 1958, p. 129.

[5] Article 13c.

spring and autumn intensive agricultural activity in many parts of the Soviet Union.

The reduction of military service by a full year compounded by the receipt of less mature draftees and their induction into the army twice a year created difficulties for those charged with the training of young Soviet inductees. This is especially so because most of the inductees are trained in operational forces and not in special training units (see chapter III, section B).

Soviet discussions point out that the reduction in the length of military service was made possible by the increased educational level of Soviet inductees and their resultant ability to acquire military skills that emphasize technical capabilities and the manipulation of scientific and technical instruments more swiftly. Indeed, this reason for the reduction is written into the preamble to the Law of Universal Military Service. Nonetheless, Soviet military writers make it perfectly clear that the new law imposes great burdens on them. The law has established "the bare minimum" period of service.[6] It is evident that it was not the particular stage of development of the Soviet armed forces and the instruments at their disposal that primarily dictated the reduction in length of service, but rather the demands of the economy, which also requires young, well-educated men. Despite the official line in the preamble to the law, military writers have occasionally conceded that the competition of the national economy was a factor in dictating the reduction in military service. "This law was drafted with due regard for social changes and proceeded from the needs of defense and the national economy."[7] The lowering of the age at which draftees begin their service is also a help to the economy. This change permits graduates of Soviet secondary schools to begin their military service immediately and to complete it before entering the labor force. This is more efficient than entering the labor force, withdrawing for military service, and then reentering the labor force.

The Law of Universal Military Service leaves an obvious question unanswered. How is the evident injustice—assuming that military service is not always welcomed by the individual—of inducting some draftees for two years of service and others for three years (navy and coast guard vessels) handled? Soviet journals are reticent on this question, which also applied, of course, to all the earlier versions of the law. The problem is alluded to and dismissed in Article 15b: "The USSR Ministry of Defense is granted the right, if necessary, to transfer servicemen from one branch (arm of the services) of the USSR armed forces to another, *with the corresponding change in the periods of service.*" (Emphasis added.) No statement is made concerning the initial difference in periods of service. Possibly, a sufficient number of qualified Soviet youths are eager for shipboard service. A substantial number of them who undergo

---

[6] *Kommunistas,* Vilnius, no. 4, April 1972, pp. 31–38.
[7] *Krasnaya zvezda,* February 3, 1972, pp. 2–3. Hereafter cited as *KZ.*

specialized preinduction military training (see chapter II, A) study specialties of a naval character, thus increasing the chances that they will be inducted into the navy.[8] Naval service holds the appeal of faraway places, especially now that the Soviet navy sails on all the oceans of the world.[9] This appeal is fortified by the apparently not infrequent tendency of the sons of fathers who have served in the Soviet navy to request naval service when drafted.

A second question suggests itself: how really *universal* is universal military service in the Soviet Union? According to Article 3, all men are "obligated to do active duty in the ranks of the USSR armed forces." But being obligated to do service does not necessarily mean being called up. Given the size and structure of the Soviet armed forces and of the Soviet population, current Soviet eighteen-year-old cohorts constitute almost double the number that the Soviets take into the armed forces annually as draftees. The eighteen-year-old male cohort numbered about 2.2 million when the 1967 law was passed. The cohort has now grown to about 2.5 million and will remain approximately at this level until about 1983, after which it will decline to about 2.1 million.[10] The size of the Soviet forces, including border guards and internal security troops, is estimated at 3.850 million.[11] Of these, approximately 770,-000 are officers and 400,000 are extended-service or enlisted men.[12] This yields a total cadre force of 1.170 million and consequently a conscript force of 2.680 million. Given the length of military service in the ground and naval forces,[13]

[8] However, the student's choice of a particular DOSAAF specialty program is not always voluntary. (DOSAAF is the All-Union Voluntary Society for Assistance to the Army, Air Force, and Navy.)

[9] A Soviet study of 230 young naval officers reported in 1969 that 124 had been on long cruises and 118 had been in foreign ports. *KZ,* November 25, 1969, p. 2. The number would be even greater in a comparable survey today.

[10] Based on Soviet age- and sex-specific census figures of January 15, 1970.

[11] International Institute for Strategic Studies, *The Military Balance 1973–1974,* London, 1973, pp. 5–7. The inclusion of security troops and border guards is justified here because Soviet draft-age youth enter them as well as the army and navy. "The Armed Forces of the USSR consist of the Soviet Army, Navy and Border and Internal Troops" (Article 4, Law of Universal Military Service). The Ministry of Internal Affairs (MVD) controls the security troops, and the Committee of State Security (KGB) the border troops.

[12] I have taken John Erickson's estimate that officers constitute one in five of the Soviet forces, see page 4, note 3 above. The number of nondraft extended-service personnel is difficult to estimate, but fortunately even a sizable error in this category is unlikely to alter the conclusion we reach. The derivation of this estimate is given on page 11, note 25 in this chapter.

[13] I have assumed that a half-million naval conscripts serve three years and the remainder of the conscript force serve two years. For the size of ground and naval forces, see *The Military Balance,* pp. 5–7 (see note 11 above). A more exact estimate of the number of draftees inducted annually would have to take into account an undisclosed number of women in the armed forces and the fact that men with higher education are eligible for various deferments and, if inducted, serve only one year. These two sources of error in the estimate operate in contrary directions but do not, of course, necessarily balance each other. Nor is it clear that the estimated size of the Soviet forces given by the International Institute for Strategic Studies is intended to include its women members, most of whom are in the medical services.

approximately 1.3 million draftees are required each year, that is, a little more than one-half of the eighteen-year-old cohort.

Articles 34 to 38 of the law permit draft deferments for family reasons, essentially the dependency of disabled parents or of wife and children of the draftee;[14] for the continuation of education;[15] and for reasons of health.

1. Preinduction Military Training

Two features of the Law of Universal Military Service provide, from the standpoint of the armed forces, some mitigation for the one-year reduction in the length of military service: preinduction military training for Soviet predraft youth and additional military training after personnel are released into the reserves.

The Law of Universal Military Service established procedures for providing introductory or preinduction military training for young men, primarily in the seventeen-year-old group, in schools and enterprises. Preinduction military training in the general education schools begins in the ninth grade and both here and in the technical and vocational schools is led by military instructors. The leaders of enterprises, institutions, organizations, collective farms, and educational institutions are held responsible by the Law of Universal Military Service for seeing that all boys of preconscription and conscription age receive preliminary training for active military service (Article 17). This important aspect of the Soviet military training system is discussed in detail in chapter II.

2. The Reserves

The ability of the armed forces to require additional training and service from the noncommissioned ranks who have been discharged into the reserves also compensates for the 1967 reduction in the length of service. Men remain in the Soviet armed forces reserves until they reach fifty years of age.[16] Reservists in the age group of thirty-five and under are subject to four refresher training sessions lasting up to three months each. Reservists under thirty-five who have served less than one year can be called back for refresher training sessions six

[14] Deferments for family reasons may be granted to men up to twenty-seven years of age. If by the time he reaches this age the right to deferment has not been lost, the individual is exempt from active military service and is enrolled in the reserves.

[15] Students in schools of higher education, unless they forfeit their deferment for reasons of discipline or academic failure, are deferred until the age of twenty-seven for the continuation of their schooling. Pupils in secondary schools of general education and specialized secondary schools are deferred until their graduation if they are under twenty years of age.

[16] Reservists who join the militia (police) are not liable to further military service. *Vedomosti verkhovnovo soveta SSSR*, no. 24, June 13, 1973, item 309.

times for periods lasting up to three months each time (Articles 47–50). Air reservists under thirty-five years of age are subject both to these training sessions and to refresher flying practice sessions up to five times for forty days each time (Article 52). That is, air reservists are subject to a maximum of almost nineteen months of additional training. In addition, reservists can be summoned to attend "examination sessions" for a period lasting up to ten days (Article 55). It is evident that the military retains considerable control over the amount of time noncommissioned personnel spend in the reserves.

The training time that can be imposed on reserve officers is even greater. Reserve officers under thirty-five years of age can be summoned every year for a period lasting up to three months each time, although the total amount of

Table 1
Maximum Age of Active Duty and of Reserve Status, by Rank

	Active Duty	Reserve Status
Junior lieutenants, lieutenants, and equivalent ranks	40	50
Senior lieutenants, captains, and equivalent ranks	40	55
Majors and equivalent ranks	45	55
Lieutenant colonels and equivalent ranks	45	60
Colonels and equivalent ranks	50	60
Generals and admirals up to lieutenant general, vice-admirals, and corresponding ranks	55	65
Colonel generals, admirals, and corresponding ranks, generals of the army, marshals of arms of the service, fleet admirals	60	65

SOURCE: Article 57, USSR Law of Universal Military Service, 1967.

time spent in reserve sessions is not to exceed thirty months, that is, two and one-half years (Article 59). However, "the USSR Minister of Defense has the right to detain, if necessary, reserve officers, generals, and admirals at refresher training sessions for up to two months longer than the periods established by this law, and also to increase the number of refresher training sessions for reserve officers, without exceeding the total amount of time spent at sessions" (Article 60). Reserve officers in the thirty-five to forty age group can be recalled for two sessions of up to three months each, and those over forty-five can be recalled for one session (Article 60). In addition, "commanders sessions," lasting from thirty to sixty training hours and organized by the commanders of garrisons and by local military commissariats, are held for reserve officers under thirty-five years of age once every three years. These sessions are held near the officer's place of residence.

More important, reserve officers can be assigned during peacetime to full active duty for two to three years if they are under thirty years of age. "The number of those so serving and their military service specialties are determined by the USSR Council of Ministers" (Article 61b).

Our sources do not permit an accurate estimate of how freely these rights of recall are exercised, although references in Soviet military literature make it clear that they are frequently invoked. Both officer and enlisted reserves are often brought back for refresher training during major maneuvers. During the Yug maneuvers "some of the men who were working literally yesterday at factories, on farms, and in various offices are participating in the Yug maneuvers."[17] Similarly, a political officer who was "just yesterday . . . at the factory . . . is now participating in the Yug maneuvers."[18]

The option to recall reserve officers for two to three years of active duty is exercised quite frequently. Soviet discussions of training, discipline, and other problems of the officer corps make not infrequent references to cases involving young reserve officers who resent their recall from civilian life. A reserve lieutenant called to duty wrote to *Krasnaya zvezda:* "When the battalion commander asked me to take over the company, I was quite surprised and naturally refused. I explained my refusal by pointing out that I am not a cadre officer. There is much that I do not know. I cannot be responsible for combat equipment and matériel. And now I have been punished for no reason whatsoever." *Krasnaya zvezda* comments: "In fact, it appears that the lieutenant was punished for questioning an order. The lieutenant is complaining that he, an officer called up from the reserve, is being compelled (he stressed the word) to serve on a par with cadre officers."[19] These young officers recalled from the reserves for two to three years constitute an appreciable portion of Soviet technical or engineer officers. Their recall from the reserves frequently inter-

---

[17] *Trud,* June 12, 1971, p. 3.
[18] *KZ,* June 13, 1971, p. 3.
[19] Ibid., January 25, 1970, p. 2.

rupts a professional engineering career in civil society. Officers with specialties that are in high demand and others who have had no prior active military service are also likely to be called up.[20] The latter are presumably persons in specialized secondary and higher schools who have studied in the program for training reserve officers (Article 35c).

The negative attitudes of young reserve officers to their recall are unfortunate for the military establishment, which seeks to encourage reserve officers to stay in the armed forces as professional soldiers. "Individuals who have been reactivated are in particular need of constant assistance. Many reactivated reserve officers express the wish to make a career out of it. Such thinking should be encouraged in every way."[21] "The extent to which officers who have been called up from the reserves express a wish to remain among the troops depends a great deal on the colonel and the time he devotes to them. . . . Colonels who treat their reserve officers as if they were on temporary duty will not encourage them to stay with the military. . . . Good living conditions help a great deal in getting officers to remain as career military."[22]

3. Extended-Service (Enlisted) Personnel, Ensigns, and Warrant Officers

In addition to conscription for two or three years, the Soviets provide for "extended military service" on a volunteer basis. Soldiers, sailors, sergeants, and master sergeants about to be discharged into the reserves, as well as those already in the reserves, could until 1972 enlist for periods of two, four, or six years. Although these conditions are not specified in the law, extended military service was available to well-disciplined soldiers who had had at least seven years of schooling and for soldiers in the reserves who were not more than thirty-five years of age. Women who are unmarried, childless, between the ages of nineteen and twenty-five, and physically fit, and who have received an education for not less than seven years, may enlist for a period of not less than two years "as a soldier, sailor, sergeant, or petty officer." The selection of women for military service is conducted by the military commissariats. The number selected and the military specialties for which they are selected are determined by the Ministry of Defense.[23] Servicemen on extended duty are assigned to all arms and services. "They serve as aviation specialists and boatswains, administrative managerial workers, chiefs of workshops and re-

[20] *Kommunist vooruzhennykh sil,* no. 14, July 1971, pp. 84–86. Hereafter cited as *KVS.*
[21] *KZ,* January 20, 1970, p. 2.
[22] Ibid., April 15, 1972, p. 2.
[23] *Ekonomicheskaya gazeta,* February 1973, p. 16. Article 16, Law of Universal Military Service, provides different specifications: "Women nineteen to forty years of age who have medical and other specialized training can be taken into military service in peacetime, recruited for refresher training periods, or admitted as volunteers for active duty." Presumably these specifications were subsequently changed.

pair shops, specialists in the medical service, musicians in orchestras. . . . They are sergeants and petty officers."[24]

It is difficult to estimate the number of enlisted or extended-service personnel in the Soviet forces. A crude estimate suggests that there may have been about 400,000 such servicemen in the army and navy in 1971.[25] Whatever the correct estimate is, it appears that Soviet inducements did not suffice to draw into the military the requisite number of NCO long-term cadres to compensate for a shortage of junior officers and the extra training burdens imposed by the reduction of conscript service. In any case, a new measure was taken.

In November 1971 the USSR Supreme Presidium issued a decree (effective January 1, 1972) in accordance with which the grade of serviceman on extended service was replaced by the grades of ensign and warrant officer. This decree was clearly an attempt to upgrade the status of enlisted or extended-service personnel. By the decree, the rank of ensign (*praporshchik*) is used in the Soviet army, in coastal units, in the air forces of the navy, and in border and internal security troops. The rank of warrant officer (*michman*) is used on ships, boats, and coastal security units of the navy and in border-troop seagoing units.[26]

These new grades are not viewed simply as NCO grades of a higher level. "It is wrong to view the change as simply one of terminology. The new ranks represent a new detachment of professional military personnel closely associated with the officer corps. It is for good reasons that under certain conditions the rank of officer can be conferred upon ensigns and warrant officers."[27] The two new grades are given shoulder boards with two gold stars. "Comrades'

---

[24] *KZ*, September 6, 1973, p. 1.

[25] This estimate is arrived at as follows. In 1972, 22 percent of the army and navy were said to be members of the Party (table 3, line 33). Using the 1971 estimate of the army and navy size (3.375 million), this gives 742,000 Party members. We assume every fifth member of the army and navy to be an officer (p. 4), giving us 675,000 officers. Seventy-one percent of the officers were members of the Party in 1973 (table 3, line 16); this gives us 479,000 officers who are members of the Party. There are, then, 742,000 − 479,000 = 263,000 noncommissioned Party members. Of these, we estimate 30,000 to 40,000 to be drafted personnel (see p. 265). Subtracting these, we then have 230,000 extended-service personnel who were members of the Party in 1971 prior to the institution of the warrant officer and ensign grades. Given the emphasis on political reliability of cadre personnel and their higher age, it is likely that the proportion of extended-service personnel who were Party members in 1971 was substantial. If 50 percent were Party members, it would follow that there were about 460,000 extended-service personnel. If 70 percent were Party members, the estimate of extended-service personnel would drop to about 330,000. A reasonable guess would be 400,000 for the number of extended-service personnel. The foregoing calculations are confined to the army and navy and do not include the border guards and the internal troops. This is unavoidable because available Soviet data on Party membership refer to the army and navy and not to the armed forces.

[26] *Translations on USSR Military Affairs* uses the translation "warrant officer." *Michman*, however, is derived from "midshipman." *Praporshchik* and *michman* were originally junior officer ranks in the army and navy of Peter I. *Michman* later became a senior NCO rank in the Soviet navy.

[27] *KZ*, January 6, 1972, p. 1.

courts of honor" (see chapter V, section C, 2), similar to those established for officers, have been created for them.[28] "The state has allocated considerable resources . . . for the material support of ensigns and warrant officers. They and their families are entitled to a number of privileges and advantages," including housing, sanitoria, and resthouse privileges similar to those of "their senior comrades," the officers.[29] The warrant officer rank can only be awarded by naval officers holding the rank of flotilla commander and above. This also distinguishes the new rank from the NCO level. In line units of the ground forces, the ensigns are frequently platoon commanders.[30]

Ensigns and warrant officers volunteer initially for five years and then may volunteer thereafter for periods of three or five years. They may remain in service until the age of forty-five and in the reserves until age fifty.[31] After five years of service, ensigns and warrant officers who have successfully passed examinations are granted the rank of lieutenant or its equivalent. The same rank can be granted without examination to those who have served for ten or more years and have been assigned officer duties. Ensigns and warrant officers who transfer to the reserves after ten years of service become automatically "reserve lieutenants."[32]

Those accepted for the new ranks are drafted personnel who have completed their terms of service and those who are already extended servicemen. The grade of ensign or warrant officer may be granted to a soldier either without his taking special courses or after he has completed them, depending on his qualifications. Servicemen on extended service who did not want to or could not serve as ensigns and warrant officers were to remain on duty in the armed forces until the expiration date designated in their original orders.[33]

The Soviet military were explicit in acknowledging that the new grades were "associated with the greater requirement placed on command personnel and the need to train competent soldiers in a shorter period of time. . . . Ensigns and warrant officers will be found primarily in combat formations."[34] However, a later statement says that ensign and warrant officers are assigned not only to command but also to technical and Komsomol (political) work.[35]

[28] *KVS*, no. 21, November 1973, pp. 37–42.
[29] *KZ*, November 20, 1971, p. 2.
[30] *Starshina serzhant*, October 1973, pp. 2–4.
[31] Ibid., January 1971, pp. 15–16.
[32] *KZ*, November 20, 1971, p. 2. Article 44 (presumably still in effect) of the 1967 Law of Universal Military Service permitted soldiers, sailors, sergeants, and master sergeants with a higher or secondary education who passed prescribed examinations to attain officer rank upon their discharge into the reserves. The 1971 decree makes this accessibility to officer rank easier by giving soldiers the opportunity to enter into the two new quasi-officer grades while on active service and at the same time by providing for their movement into full officer rank after a prescribed period of time has elapsed.
[33] Ibid.
[34] Ibid., January 6, 1972.
[35] Ibid., April 5, 1972, p. 1.

Unit commanders have been busy talking with the extended servicemen and recommending "the more worthy" for the new ranks.[36] As befits the selection of cadre personnel, "political organs and Party organizations must participate actively in the selection of candidates."[37]

It is evident that the two quasi-officer ranks did not attract a sufficient number of former extended-duty (enlisted) servicemen or recruits. The regulations bearing on promotion to full officer status were soon changed to enable ensigns and warrant officers to become officers after three (instead of five) years of service by entering higher military schools, and to become reserve officers automatically, without examination, after five (rather than ten) years of service.[38] In addition, various benefits have been increased. Ensigns and warrant officers serving "in the remote areas of the nation"—presumably the far east —are given special leave privileges similar to those of officers.[39] Higher pay, family travel privileges, and various transfer privileges similar to those provided for officers are accorded to ensigns and warrant officers serving under "unfavorable meteorological and climatic conditions" in remote areas "in the high mountain regions of our country." Cash subsistence was raised 40 percent for students in warrant officer and ensign schools.[40]

The provision of more attractive conditions has been supplemented by a recruitment program. Military units urge appropriate military personnel who are being discharged to reenlist as ensigns and warrant officers. Military commissariats are told to talk to discharged personnel who register with them when they return home and to suggest enlistment for ensign and warrant officer training.[41]

The Soviets clearly have an unfilled demand for cadre personnel. In addition to incentives for ensign and warrant officer enlistment, a little more than a year after the process of phasing out extended-duty servicemen began, this category of personnel was reintroduced by a decree of the Presidium of the Supreme Soviet of May 10, 1973.[42] Several factors may have influenced this interesting decision: (1) The military may have found it impossible to recruit

---

[36] Ibid., January 6, 1972, p. 1.

[37] Ibid.

[38] *KVS*, no. 18, September 1973, pp. 87–88; *Starshina serzhant*, October 1973, pp. 2–4.

[39] Ibid.

[40] Ibid. To increase the prestige of ensigns and warrant officers, opportunities have been provided for them to take examinations of secondary military schools in absentia. Preparation for these examinations require "self-education and rational use of every hour of working time and non-working time." *Znamenonosets*, no. 10, October 1974, pp. 18–19.

[41] Ibid. Some commissariats have a rather casual attitude toward their responsibilities in this matter. *KZ* complains that too many misfits, drinkers, and people with bad records have been sent to warrant officer and ensign schools. *KZ*, August 5, 1974, p. 4.

[42] *Vedomosti verkhovnovo soveta SSSR*, no. 20 (1678), May 16, 1973, p. 301.

and train enough warrant officers and ensigns to replace the extended-duty personnel being phased out. An insufficiency of warrant officer and ensign replacements could in its turn be due to (a) the inability or unwillingness of the older, less well-educated extended-duty NCOs to acquire or live up to warrant officer and ensign standards; and/or (b) an inability to interest inductees in remaining in the army, especially to serve "in remote areas," or an inability to raise them to a high enough level to justify their new quasi-officer rank. (2) The military establishment may have found that in separating the senior NCOs more sharply from the inductee ranks by means of a quasi-officer status, they made noncommissioned leadership of the inductee ranks more, and not less, difficult. Such separation also, very probably, made Party and KGB (Committee of State Security) supervision of the inductee ranks harder. (3) The junior officers who had spent four years of hard work at officer cadet schools may have resented the wholesale transfer of large numbers of ill-prepared extended-duty personnel and recruits into a military status rivaling their own.

The armed forces provide a number of privileges for regular enlisted personnel. Men who enlist for extended service may indicate the military unit in which they wish to serve and are granted the rank of junior sergeant or petty officer second class simultaneously with their entrance into service.[43] They may stay on active military duty until the age of fifty and receive a regular annual leave of thirty days that increases with the years of service to a maximum of forty-five days annually. Like warrant officers and ensigns, men on extended service who serve "in isolated areas" are given certain leave privileges. "Housing for personnel on extended service and their families is made at their place of service on an equal footing with warrant officers, ensigns, and officers."[44] Finally, like officers, ensigns, and warrant officers, the enlisted men, too, have their comrades' courts of honor.[45]

The reintroduction of the extended-duty serviceman is a continuation of the Soviet emphasis on career or cadre components of the army and provides for two categories of noncommissioned cadres instead of one. This has facilitated another change. The extended-service personnel were, in previous years, an older and not very well educated group of NCOs, many of them men with World War II experience. The temporary phasing out of this category in 1972 apparently had the effect of hastening the departure of the older enlisted NCOs and introducing a new contingent. The extended-service personnel are now described as "youngish."[46]

[43] *Sovetskiy voin,* no. 2, January 1974, p. 4.
[44] *KVS,* no. 23, December 1973, pp. 84–86.
[45] *KZ,* September 6, 1973, p. 1.
[46] Ibid.

B. JUNIOR OFFICERS

Soviet military literature stresses that, besides the high level of technical competence and education of its officer personnel, they are increasingly a young group.[47] A frequently cited figure is 65 percent of regimental officers are in the age group under thirty.[48] More than two-thirds of regimental officers have not had any war experience.[49] Another statement affirms that young officers, without specifying the age group embraced by this term, account for two-thirds of all officers at division level and below.[50] Writers point out that it is no longer a rarity for a company or a battery to be commanded by an officer under the age of twenty-five or for a battalion to be commanded by someone who is twenty-eight or thirty years old. In a number of units every second or third officer promoted to a company and battery commander slot is twenty-five years old or younger. A major commanding an airborne unit who received his command at the age of thirty-two is cited.[51] The rapid promotion of young officers creates problems among older officers: "Of course, in attach-

Table 2
Prior Occupation of One Thousand Soviet Army Lieutenants

	Percent
Students	
General secondary schools 27	
Technical schools 7 }	37.0
Suvorov army schools 3	
Production workers	27.0
Army servicemen	20.0
Agricultural workers	5.0
Employed in Komsomol	0.9
Schoolteachers	0.7
Reactivated reserve officers	10.0

NOTE: "The last figure—10 percent—of course does not reflect the actual situation. The number of lieutenants called up from the reserve—100 men—we questioned intentionally in order to have a more complete impression of these young [reserve] officers." *KZ,* April 5, 1969, pp. 3–4.

[47] The senior officers, on the other hand, have largely been men in their sixties with World War II experience. However, in some military districts there has been a substantial turnover of senior personnel and their average age has been reduced. *KVS,* no. 5, March 1971, pp. 37–41.

[48] *KZ,* August 5, 1971, p. 2.

[49] *Soviet Military Review,* no. 9, 1971, p. 5.

[50] *KZ,* December 2, 1969, p. 1.

[51] Ibid., January 20, 1970, p. 2.

ing great importance to the bold promotion of the younger officers, we should also deal with our more experienced cadres attentively and sensitively."[52]

On the other hand, we are also told that in the Odessa Military District during 1971 every tenth young officer was promoted, and this does not seem to imply an unduly rapid rate of promotion.[53]

Approximately one-third of the Soviet officers have served as privates or NCOs.[54] Many of them are clearly middle- or senior-grade officers who served in World War II in the noncommissioned ranks. Among the young officers a little more than 20 percent have come from the ranks.[55] Almost all the officers in the junior ranks are graduates of military academies and specialized schools of one sort or another. This, however, does not mean that they had not served in the ranks before being admitted to the military academies.[56] "Particularly fine results" are obtained at cadet schools by those who enter after serving as soldiers rather than entering directly from school.[57]

About 85 percent of the young army officers are the children of manual and office workers, and about 15 percent are the sons of agricultural workers. However, only 4.6 percent actually had agricultural occupations before becoming lieutenants.[58] Between 40 and 48 percent of the students in command, military-political, and engineering schools are the sons of workers.[59] On the other hand, among generals and admirals the situation is very different. Twenty-four and four-tenths percent are the children of workers, 21.3 percent the children of office workers, and 54.3 percent the children of peasants.[60] This marked difference in the social origins of younger and older officers reflects, of course, the increase in urbanization and industrialization of the Soviet Union that occurred between the two generations and the increasing importance of educational qualifications in the military. In 1973 more than 41 percent of command personnel had attained a higher education—a striking shift from the 10 percent in 1953.[61]

---

[52] Ibid.

[53] *KVS*, no. 5, March 1972, pp. 25–30.

[54] *Bloknot agitatora*, no. 11, June 1971, pp. 1–5.

[55] This is based on the Soviet study "One Thousand Lieutenants," *KZ*, April 5, 1969, pp. 3–4. The figure cited by the study for junior officers with previous service in the ranks is an underestimate, since the sample included, in order to provide more information on them, a disproportionate number (100) of lieutenants recalled from the reserves. See note to Table 2.

[56] Enlisted men and NCOs who have served with distinction may be given the status of reserve officers when placed in the reserves. Soldiers who have received a higher education may take a test for the rank of reserve officer after completing their one-year period of service. If recalled into service, these reservists would also contribute to the number of officers who at one time served in the ranks. *Bloknot agitatora*, June 1971, pp. 1–5; *Sovetskiy voin*, June 1971, p. 13.

[57] *KZ*, March 3, 1972, p. 1.

[58] "One Thousand Lieutenants" (see note 55 above). Since it is not possible to judge how the sample of 1,000 lieutenants was drawn, figures cited in this study should be regarded with caution.

[59] *KVS*, no. 13, July 1972, pp. 9–15.

[60] Ibid., no. 4, February 1971, pp. 27–34.

[61] Ibid, no. 4, February 1974, pp. 9–17.

Soviet writers emphasize that a substantial proportion of young officers come from families that have a tradition of military service. If this means that many of their fathers served in World War II the statement is trivial but the same claim seems to be implied in the case of professional military service. In the Soviet study of 1,000 young army lieutenants only about 3 percent are graduates of Suvorov military schools.[62] But other Soviet studies suggest that about one-third of the officer cadets come from families with a "tradition" of military service.[63]

A study of young naval officers indicates that among 230 junior and senior naval lieutenants, 202 completed higher naval schools and 13 civilian higher schools. Of these officers, 89 entered naval school from civilian schools, 93 from industry, 14 from agriculture, 58 from naval military service, and 17 from the army.[64] Eighty percent were married, as compared to 75 percent of the army lieutenants.[65]

The Soviet military journals, especially *Krasnaya zvezda,* periodically announce openings in various officer cadet training schools.[66] Frequently these announcements indicate that specialties within the school's major field of study can be chosen by the applicant if he is accepted. Generally the schools accept military personnel who are serving their initial enlistment, those on extended service who are less than twenty-one years of age, and civilian personnel between seventeen and twenty-one. Applicants must have completed their secondary education, be healthy, and pass the entrance examination at a secondary school level in mathematics, physics, and Russian language and literature.[67] The requirement for Russian language and literature may discrimi-

---

[62] *KZ,* April 5, 1969, pp. 3–4. The Suvorov army schools and Nakhimov naval schools for the sons of Soviet officers were founded as exclusive cadet schools in 1943 and accepted officers' sons at the ages of eight and nine years. Raymond L. Garthoff, *Soviet Military Policy* (New York, 1966), p. 37.

[63] *KZ,* October 24, 1973, p. 2.

[64] These figures add up to 271 instead of 230, possibly because of duplications.

[65] *KZ,* November 25, 1969, p. 2.

[66] The announcements in the March 1, 1972, issue of *KZ* of openings in cadet schools covered six engineering schools (three years instruction), two tank schools (four years), two construction-technical schools (three years), two chemical command schools (four years), three motor vehicle command schools (four years), one rear service school (four years), one railroad and communication school (four years), one topographical school (four years), one civil defense school (three years), one communication school (study period not specified), one engineering-fuels school (four years), one financial service school (three years), and one engineering technical school for service to "the organs of capital construction of the Ministry of Defense" (five years). Ibid., March 1, 1972, p. 4.

[67] Ibid., April 20, April 21, and April 29, 1971. In addition to military schools for young cadets, there are, of course, military schools for officers already in the military forces who are accepted for graduate study. High educational qualifications are generally required. Thus, a higher military engineering technical school announced that it is accepting applications from army and navy officers provided they are not over forty years old, have completed a higher engineering education, and have had at least two years of practical work. The applicant's commanding officer must approve the application. Ibid., December 25, 1969, p. 4.

nate against soldiers of non-Russian nationalities. This could be interpreted as an attempt to discourage applications from non-Russian nationalities, but more likely it is based on the requirement that an officer speak fluent Russian, since Soviet minority nationalities do not serve in units formed of their own conationals. In Estonia "shortcomings exist in the teaching of Russian in schools employing Estonian as their teaching language. This makes service in the ranks of the Soviet army more difficult for young men and constitutes an obstacle to their entry to military schools."[68]

Most schools provide a two-week winter and a thirty-day summer vacation with free transportation at the end of each academic year.[69]

It is difficult to say which of the military specialties are the most appealing to cadets, although there is some indication that flying leads in popularity. In the Kursk region, 36 percent of the young Russians who went to cadet schools chose a flying school, 22 percent a combined arms school, and 12 percent a naval school.[70] This pattern of choice is consistent with the findings of Soviet studies of occupational prestige, in which pilots came out very high on the list; there is virtually no reliable difference between their status index and that of physicists (see p. 23 below).

In March 1972 new rules for admission to higher institutions in the Soviet Union were introduced. In conformity with this change, both higher and secondary military schools now give greater emphasis to "points" earned by the previous record of the individual and less emphasis to his qualifying examination marks.[71] This change seems to be related to an interest in exercising greater political control over the selection of students for military schools.

USSR Minister of Defense Marshal A. A. Grechko pointed out in 1972 that more than 50 percent of the young officers entering the forces had higher education.[72] The percentage with higher education varies considerably among the services. Thus, 45 percent of the army and navy officers are said to be engineers and technicians, but for missile force officers this figure is 75 percent.[73] All the officers of a nuclear missile (apparently Yankee-class) submarine have received a higher education.[74] Between 1967 and 1972 the number of officers with a higher military or special education doubled. An above-average proportion of officers with a higher education in some services or sectors means

[68] *Sovetskaya Estoniya,* July 5, 1972, p. 3. For further discussion of the effect of language differences and associated nationalist sentiments on the Soviet military, see chapter VI, sections C6 and D3 and chapter VII, section B8.

[69] *Kryl'ya rodiny,* March 1971.

[70] *Soviet Military Review,* March 1971.

[71] *KZ,* May 24, 1972, p. 4.

[72] *Pravda Ukrainy,* March 2, 1972, p. 4. At the outbreak of World War II only 7 percent of the Soviet officers had received a higher education, although 63 percent had either secondary or higher military education. *KZ,* January 20, 1970, p. 2; *Soviet Military Review,* no. 9, 1971, p. 5.

[73] *KZ,* February 1972, pp. 2-3. See also *Bloknot agitatora,* June 1971, pp. 1-5.

[74] *Voyennyye znaniya,* April 1971, pp. 8-9.

a lower proportion of such officers in other sectors. Thus, among troops stationed in East Germany in 1971, it appears that only one out of every five of the officers had a higher education.[75] This probably implies a higher average age level of the officers serving in East Germany.

A few years ago the Soviets were having great difficulty recruiting a sufficient number of junior officers. This is clearly indicated by a provision of the 1967 law permitting junior lieutenants and lieutenants to remain on active duty up to the age of forty—an increase of ten years over preceding legislation. "It is now possible *and necessary* upon reaching [the former] maximum age to leave certain officers on active military duty."[76] (Emphasis added.) Senior lieutenants, captains, and majors had their periods of service extended by five years.

The Soviets seem to have alleviated their severe shortage of junior officers. Since 1968, military instructors in Soviet secondary schools, teaching in the preinduction military training program, have provided the armed forces with a valuable recruiting agency for the cadet academies. In 1972 there were six applicants for every opening at a military aviation school.[77] In 1973 there were "several applications" for each vacancy at the naval cadet academies.[78] Nonetheless, a concern to increase recruitment to the academies still exists.

Students who apply for admission to a cadet academy often know little about the various types of military skills and careers, and after a period of time find that they are in the wrong field. "Such students comprise a considerable portion of those dismissed from military schools."[79] Local military commissariats are frequently charged by the military authorities with irresponsibility in recommending ill-prepared youths and persons "with low moral qualities" to the cadet academies.[80]

Soviet military authorities warn against a passive attitude to recruitment. They point out that the formation in secondary schools of groups that bring together sharpshooters, parachutists, signalmen, topographers, and so forth provides an excellent basis for officer cadet recruitment. A survey in one section of Moscow in 1973 showed that schools in which the majority of tenth-grade students were active in military groups provided twice as many future officers as schools where only a minority of the students participated in such groups. Schools whose students were given opportunities to visit and spend time with military units provided almost three times as many students for the cadet academies as did schools where such visits were not arranged.[81]

[75] *KVS,* no. 9, May 1971, pp. 39–44.
[76] Ibid., no. 24, December 1969, pp. 43–47.
[77] *Voyennyye znaniya,* no. 8, August 1973, pp. 4–9.
[78] *Sovetskiy patriot,* April 28, 1974, p. 3. See also p. 57 below.
[79] *KZ,* September 18, 1973, p. 2.
[80] Ibid., March 3, 1972, p. 1.
[81] Ibid., October 24, 1973, p. 2.

C. INDUCTION

Induction is the responsibility of the local draft commission.[82] Annually, during February and March, young men who have turned or will turn seventeen during the year must register with the military commissariat and bring along with them certain required documents.[83] Twice a year, in May-June and November-December, the local draft boards assemble the draftees of their districts and select those whom they will take to fill their quotas. Draftees may indicate their preferred form of service, and very often they choose one in which their preinduction training, especially military specialty training, will be advantageous. The draft board assigns draftees to a particular service on the basis of these and other considerations. At the *oblast* [regional] assembly point a final selection of draftees is made, and some selected by local commissariats may be rejected.[84]

Both at the local level and at the *oblast* assembly point, the inductees are given a sendoff at which local dignitaries make speeches, soldiers' songs are sung, and war veterans talk to the draftees about "heroes, about banners steeped in glory."[85] On the occasion of the spring induction of 1972, a *Krasnaya zvezda* editorial urged local commissariats to insure that the induction was "a radiant and moving event that touches young hearts. . . . Let ceremonial meetings of collectives be held everywhere. . . . Let the people express their wishes to the future soldiers at these meetings. . . . Let farewell ceremonies . . . become a striking display."[86]

Both at the local military commissariat and at the *oblast* level, considerable information about the draftees is available in terms of which decisions can be made about selection and assignment. Generally, files exist on the individual's past education and habits, and fairly detailed records are available about his preinduction military training and his relations with the Komsomol and with various sport and "civic" organizations.[87]

Inductees who enter service from an enterprise rather than from a school

[82] The local draft commission is under the chairmanship of the head of the district or city military commissariat. The commission is composed of representatives of the district Soviet executive committee and of Party and Komsomol committees, together with the head or assistant head of the district militia (police) and a physician. Decisions of the draft commission are adopted by a majority of votes. Article 27, Law of Universal Military Service. Physicians are sometimes absent from draft commission examinations, and when present often certify as fit men who have to be returned to their homes because of physical disabilities. *KZ*, September 4, 1973, p. 4.

[83] Articles 21–22, Law of Universal Military Service.

[84] *KZ*, December 3, 1969, p. 4.

[85] Ibid., November 30, 1969, p. 2.

[86] Ibid., April 14, 1972, p. 1. The commissariat sometimes fails to do its duty. One group of draftees had to wait for more than an hour before the commissariat arrived in a drunken condition. No motor vehicles were available, and the draftees had to go tens of kilometers on foot. Ibid., November 30, 1969, p. 2.

[87] Ibid., December 3, 1969, p. 4.

receive a termination allowance, generally equivalent to two weeks' pay.[88]

When the young inductee arrives at his regiment, a traditional billeting ceremony takes place in the barracks. Sometimes the new soldier is placed next to the cot of a second-year soldier, often one from his own geographical area. He will thus be able to learn from his "senior comrade."[89]

Soviet military literature points out that induction boards have more human material than they require to fill their quotas and that they choose the best in terms of education and preparation in preinduction training.[90] Difficulties nonetheless do occur. Units sometimes receive inductees who, for reasons of health or family circumstances, should not have been accepted. At the same time, complaints are made about deferments being granted without sufficient basis and contrary to regulations. Adequate attention is not always paid to the assignment of recruits. Youths having an industrial skill or military specialty acquired in preinduction training are sometimes assigned to units where their knowledge or specialty cannot be fully used. "It is emphasized that these and other deficiencies must not be repeated during this present call-up."[91] However, the same complaints were lodged exactly a year later: "Young men were not subjected everywhere to a thorough medical inspection. . . . Instances occur of individual citizens being unjustifiably granted a deferment. . . . Correct solutions have not always been found for the question of where . . . to send a given draftee. . . . A young man who has certain professional skills or who has obtained a military specialty . . . ends up in a unit where his knowledge cannot be utilized."[92]

Soviet emphasis on and pride in the high educational level of the Soviet soldier ("the best educated in the world"; "the best read army in the world"[93]) is in part a reaction to the rapid change in the educational composition of the troops, but it also seems to be a reaction to the old image of the Russian soldier as an untutored peasant with little or no experience of the world. In 1971 every second serviceman in the forces had completed a full ten-year secondary or higher education.[94] In the same year 80 percent of those inducted had received either a higher, secondary, or incomplete secondary education.[95] For 1972 the figure rises to "more than 90 percent."[96]

[88] *Starshina serzhant,* November 19, 1970, p. 37.
[89] *KZ,* April 15, 1971, p. 2.
[90] Ibid., December 3, 1969, p. 4.
[91] Ibid., April 15, 1971, p. 1.
[92] Ibid., April 14, 1972, p. 1.
[93] *KVS,* no. 4, February 1974, pp. 9–17.
[94] *Soviet Military Review,* no. 9, 1971, p. 4.
[95] *Starshina serzhant,* September 1971, pp. 2–3. In the Soviet Union primary education is eight years and secondary education two years.
[96] *KVS,* no. 1, January 1973, pp. 76–83.

As in the case of officers, the Soviets send a higher percentage of their better-educated inductees into the more technical military services. In naval and aviation subunits, 70 percent of all the inductees have completed either a secondary or a secondary technical education.[97] A submarine crew is said to have an average education of ten grades among its nonofficer personnel.[98] All the sailors and petty officers of a missile submarine have had either a general secondary or a technical secondary education.[99]

Given the concentration of the best-educated inductees in the highly technical services, it follows that the other services receive a larger proportion of the less well educated soldiers. How much larger this proportion is, is suggested by the fact that in a study of 1,000 inductees in motorized infantry units, the ratio of inductees who came from production units (that is, who were working in plants or on farms) to students (that is, inductees who came directly from school) was 5 to 1.[100] We can probably assume that the inductee-workers were less well educated than the inductee-students. In any event, given the 5 to 1 ratio, it follows that in the infantry sample only 17 percent of the inductees came directly from school, whereas in the army as a whole it appears that "more than half of the men arrive in their training regiment directly from school."[101]

The induction of well-educated youth is facilitated by the rapidly increasing level of education of the younger members of the Soviet population. Even in the countryside more than half of the rural population is said to have had a higher or secondary education, as compared to only 6 percent before World War II.[102] This now makes it possible for the army and navy to recruit "well-educated young representatives of the peasantry."[103] "With each call-up we notice more changes in the new recruits. During the thirties and forties rural youth were only rarely assigned to servicing complicated naval equipment, but today they are mastering in a short period of time very modern shipboard technical equipment."[104]

Military educational requirements will presumably be met even more easily in the future. The Soviet educational system is supposed to make a

[97] *Leningradskaya pravda,* May 28, 1971, p. 3.

[98] *Voyennyye znaniya,* April 1971, pp. 8–9.

[99] *Sovetskiy voin,* July 1971, pp. 8–12.

[100] The study of 1,000 infantry inductees (*KZ,* April 18, 1972, p. 4) showed that 57 percent of working inductees had predraft training, 39 percent of student inductees had predraft training, and 54 percent of the total group had preinduction training. We have, then, where W is for working inductees and S is for student inductees:

$$57W + 39S = 54 \ (W+S)$$
$$\frac{W}{S} = \frac{5}{1}$$

[101] *KVS,* no. 10, May 1971, pp. 30–34.

[102] *KZ,* February 3, 1972, pp. 2–3.

[103] Ibid.

[104] *Sel'skaya zhizn',* July 25, 1971, p. 3.

transition to universal ten-year education during the ninth five-year plan (1971–75). In 1970 the Soviet Union produced 3.2 million high school graduates who had completed a ten-year education. Universal ten-year education will require the annual graduation of 4.5 to 4.7 million students by 1975.[105] The Soviets induct about 1.3 million persons annually; already there are 1.6 million male ten-year graduates available annually, from whom the inductees will be selected, with a prospect of 2.3 million ten-year male graduates, perhaps by 1975 but more likely several years later. Of course, those who receive deferments must be subtracted from these numbers.

D. ATTITUDES TOWARD THE MILITARY AND MILITARY SERVICE

The Soviets have taken steps to increase the receptivity of inductees to military training and the incentives of young people to join the military forces on a permanent professional basis. They have tried to improve living standards, especially for junior officers, and have increased efforts to surround military life with rituals and appeals that associate the virtues of heroism, national service, and adventure with military life. They have tried to build a better image of the military in a very literal sense by providing better-fitting and more attractive uniforms and placing great emphasis on a smart appearance.

The Soviets are sensitive to the importance of occupational prestige in recruiting personnel for different occupations. Retail marketing managers complain that the low prestige of sales personnel interferes with the recruitment of sales clerks. Just like military writers, marketing managers try to increase the prestige of sales clerks by emphasizing that in certain department stores almost all the sales personnel have had a secondary education.[106] A 1969 Soviet study shows that in terms of prestige sales people rated only 1.8 on a 10-point scale. In the same study, professional military people (presumably officers) received a scale value of 4.3. This placed the military forces below scientific and technical occupations such as physicist, engineer-radio technician, medical scientist, engineer-geologist, mathematician, chemist, radio technician, aircraft pilot, engineer in chemical industry, biologist, and physician. These occupations ranged from a maximum of 6.6 down to 5.3 (for physicians). Below physicians came writers and artists at 5.2, university teachers at 4.5, professional military at 4.3, and "social scientists in philosophy" at 4.2 (probably Party ideologists). Primary school teachers ranked 2.5, and housing maintenance workers were among the lowest-ranking, at 1.2[107] This ranking

---

[105] Soviet Minister of Education Mikhail A. Prokofyev, at the Twenty-fourth Party Congress, cited in the *New York Times,* June 26, 1971.

[106] *Izvestia,* December 1, 1971, p. 3.

[107] Zev Katz, "Sociology in the Soviet Union," *Problems of Communism,* May-June 1971, p. 37.

of the military on the occupational prestige scale, if it accurately reflects opinion in the Soviet Union, is probably not very acceptable or flattering to the top military whose self-image would almost certainly require a higher rating. In the mid-fifties Soviet officers were reacting angrily to what they considered to be a negative image of Soviet military men in Soviet literature.[108] On the other hand, it is possible that Party and government authorities find a not-too-high rating of the military in public prestige much more acceptable.

There is apparently considerable variation in the prestige of the different arms and services. Although firm evidence is lacking, it appears that the navy benefits from a certain esprit and reputation resulting from a relatively heavy infusion of the sons of former officers into this service. *Pravda* notes a rebirth of "the hereditary tradition of naval service by successive generations."[109] The navy benefits also, because, as a service that has expanded the scope of its operations over much of the globe, it holds a certain appeal. When a group of atomic submarines of the Soviet navy left their base to circumnavigate the globe, the naval chief, Admiral Gorshkov, addressed all personnel with the words: "You will sail through oceans and seas in which Russian sailors have not traveled for more than 100 years." Soviet naval personnel, particularly officers, probably derive considerable satisfaction from this expansion of the Soviet naval presence. Public attention is frequently called to the fact that Soviet ships visited and called at twenty-six different countries in 1968, thirty-eight countries in 1969, and forty-seven countries in 1970.[110] In 1972 this number dropped to forty,[111] and in 1973 to thirty-six.[112]

Although the Soviets have made a considerable effort to make the military more attractive to young inductees, many of them are not enamored of military life, with its strict subordination. A questionnaire addressed to 1,000 young motorized infantry recruits who had just completed their first six months of military life reveals that only 26 percent found military life to be what they had expected. The discussion surrounding this figure makes it clear that the remainder found military life worse or more rigorous than they had anticipated.[113] The prestige of the military among young people has also apparently been affected by the early course of World War II. A deputy minister of defense asks: "Why is it, then, that in the initial period of the war our armies were forced to retreat? This question bothers many, especially young people."[114]

[108] *Economist* (London), October 20, 1956, p. 226.
[109] *Pravda,* March 30, 1972, p. 6.
[110] Ibid.
[111] *Sovetskaya kul'tura,* February 23, 1973, p. 1.
[112] *KVS,* no. 13, July 1974, pp. 33–37. In the past five years Soviet naval vessels paid 2,000 visits to ninety-seven ports in more than sixty countries.
[113] *KZ,* April 19, 1972, p. 4.
[114] *Voyennyye znaniya,* no. 2, 1971.

1. Military Living Conditions

Soviet military authorities recognize "that a gap exists between the conditions in which students live at home and those of military service. This disparity is often the reason for the difficulties of young soldiers. Therefore, it is necessary to devote attention [in civilian organizations] to familiarizing youth with the demands placed upon them by military service."[115] It is characteristic of Soviet thriftiness to try to escape the cost of reducing the discrepancy between civilian and military standards of living by preparing youth for the worst. However, the military have also tried to improve the living conditions of both enlisted men and officers, especially the junior officers.

The conditions of life in the military depend not only on what the soldier is provided by the military establishment, but also on what he can buy with his military pay. The pay of the conscript soldier is extremely small and indeed is usually referred to as an allowance. Recruits receive only three to five rubles per month, with the pay varying according to the particular type of job performed, that is, according to the specialty of the soldier and his rank.[116] Soldiers who have completed the required period of service and enter the extended-service (enlisted) troops receive an increase in pay.[117]

The small allowance that soldiers receive frequently leads parents to send money orders to their sons in the army. The army complains that such money is apt to be spent on alcohol. Besides, a Party newspaper points out, it is now quite unnecessary for parents to send money to young soldiers because their living conditions have improved so much.[118]

Unlike the inductee, the army officer, who is a professional soldier, receives one-third more pay than he would receive in civilian life for similar qualifications. A senior lieutenant receives 140 rubles, a full colonel 500 rubles, and a marshal up to 2,000 rubles per month.[119]

Soviet military authorities acknowledge that officers are paid "a fitting remuneration" for the duties they perform. They affirm, however, that Soviet youth know well that it is not the material benefits offered by the military profession that attract them to officer training schools. One military writer points out that a questionnaire showed that 85 percent of Soviet young officers were motivated by "profound ideological convictions" and only 9 percent associated the officer's profession with high pay. This is contrasted with American studies, which show, it is said, that the principal motivation for entering military service is "the opportunity to earn money."[120]

---

[115] *KZ,* October 5, 1971, p. 4.

[116] *Starshina serzhant,* October 1971, pp. 13–15; Erickson in *The Soviet Union in Europe and the Near East,* 1970, p. 22.

[117] Ibid., November 1970, p. 37.

[118] *Bloknot agitatora,* no. 12, June 1971.

[119] Erickson in *The Soviet Union in Europe and the Near East,* 1970, p. 22.

[120] *Soviet Military Review,* no. 8, 1971, p. 28.

The validity of these figures, which imply an indifference to pay, may be questioned. A study of the aspirations and attitudes of Estonian third-year higher education students is also said to show that their interest in material gain is far less than among U.S. students investigated in a comparable study. An examination of the tabular data shows, however, that in response to the statement "A profession must offer the possibility of making a good living" the percentages of Estonian and American students agreeing with it are almost identical.[121]

Soviet military authorities raised the soldiers' rations from 3,800 calories in 1961 to 4,112 calories in 1971.[122] Special efforts have been made to make the food interesting and palatable, especially in services where individuals are under considerable stress, as in submarine duty. A writer points out that the food on submarines is not only excellent, but is the same for sailors and officers.[123] To improve the quality of the basic military rations, troop units are encouraged to develop kitchen gardens and raise animals. A remote base far from any sizable town has a mess that is "equipped no worse than an average restaurant." The base has a PX store that sells fresh pastries, dry wines, whole milk, and apples.[124] Efforts are continually being made to ensure that mess halls provide a pleasant atmosphere.[125]

Despite efforts to improve the food situation both in terms of quality and dining environments, it is apparent that the difficulties the Soviets experience in catering to civilian tastes and preferences exist equally in the army. An article on food in the military points out that in a soldiers' tearoom one will sometimes find everything to eat and drink except tea. It turns out that tea is a low profit item and therefore "does not enter into the plan."[126] A *Krasnaya zvezda* editorial points out that despite improvements, many messes are poorly

[121] Vladimir Shubkin, "The Occupational Pyramid: Low- and High-Status Jobs," *Soviet Life*, September 1971, pp. 20–21 and 40–41. The exact data are:

		Most Impor- tant	Very Impor- tant	Fairly Impor- tant	Un- impor- tant	No An- swer
A profession must offer the possi- bility of making a good living	Estonians	9.1	40.2	51.1	7	1.7
	Americans	10.0	39.0	48.0	13	—

Note: *Soviet Life* does not explain why these figures add up to more than 100 percent.

[122] *Starshina serzhant,* October 1971, pp. 13–15.
[123] *Sovetskiy voin,* July 1971, pp. 8–12.
[124] *Trud,* January 8, 1971.
[125] *KVS,* no. 24, December 1969, pp. 3–8.
[126] *KZ,* October 27, 1971, p. 2.

equipped and have old, wood-burning stoves. Hygienic conditions are poor, dishes are often not washed, and the food is monotonous and not attractively prepared. Even the dining halls run by the PX system for the extended-duty (enlisted) personnel and for the officers are not adequate. There are long lines, food is monotonous, and the service is poor. The new five-year plan, according to the editorial, calls for new dining halls, cafés, and tearooms in military garrisons, "but so far builders are not fulfilling their assignments." Nor is it at all clear whether the managers of the new tearooms will find the serving of tea sufficiently profitable for it to "enter into the plan."[127]

Barracks, at least for the NCOs and soldiers who are on extended service, have been renovated, and new barracks are being built. The new barracks are said to "have all the conveniences." Rooms are set aside for washing and pressing clothes.[128] Officer apartments in a remote base are described as having balconies, modern furniture, television sets, and shelves filled with the latest books and journals.[129] In writing about an isolated garrison in the southern desert where life is harsh, a writer describes the officers' quarters as cottages that the officers had surrounded with orchards and vineyards. The article refers to small swimming pools in many of the yards permitting the officers, after a hard day's work, to take a swim in cool water.[130]

Apparently, however, everything is not going so well for the young officers. Speaking of bachelor officer quarters, *Krasnaya zvezda* points out that "it is no secret that the quarters given to young officers constitute an important component of their attitude and subsequently their professional success. Unfortunately, some people fail to consider this fact. We visited the bachelor officer quarters. The building was well constructed but the rooms were dreary, crowded, and depressing. When the lieutenant came home in the evening, there was no quiet place where he could read, write a letter, or prepare for classes." However, part of the blame is placed on the lieutenants themselves, and part is placed on their immediate superiors, the company and battalion commanders who are quartered separately. The young lieutenants are blamed for not keeping the barracks clean and in proper order, and the company and battalion commanders are blamed for rarely visiting the dormitories and having no idea of the conditions under which their junior officers are living.[131] Similar accounts appear quite regularly.

[127] Ibid., June 26, 1971, p. 1.
[128] *Bloknot agitatora,* no. 12, June 1971.
[129] *Trud,* January 8, 1971.
[130] *Soviet Military Review,* no. 7, 1970, p. 35.
[131] *KZ,* January 25, 1970, p. 2.

Since the great majority of young officers marry early (see p. 17 above), the conditions of life for a young military couple are important. A political officer points out that the Komsomol would be well advised to take more interest in the families of young officers. The wives often encounter unfamiliar and difficult conditions when they come to live at a post. They are alarmed by the problem of fitting into the group. Further, insufficient attention is given to the family situation and to the importance of a harmonious and happy family life to enable the officer better to devote himself to the Soviet motherland. In some garrisons recreational evenings for the families of young officers are held, but frequently there is little for the family, especially the wife, to do. This is particularly true at the more remote garrisons, where wives find it difficult to get jobs and earn money. Commanders and Komsomol committees at such garrisons are urged to establish the wives in various available positions in military clubs, dining halls, PX stores, schools, and headquarters buildings. The problem is aggravated by the fact that most of the wives of young officers have received a secondary or higher education. This education can be partially put to use by inviting them to give lectures and talks to soldiers about literature, art, and medicine, and by doing extra school work with children.[132]

Some officers prefer not to bring their wives to distant garrisons but spend their time and their wives' time trying to get transferred to garrisons in cities or close to cities.[133] The army is trying to make the conditions of garrison life more agreeable; this is apparent not only from general statements to this effect, but also from the fact that in 1969, 22 percent more money was spent on the construction and routine repair of barracks and quarters than in 1965.[134]

Some categories of soldiers seem to receive less adequate attention than others. Construction troops which may have a relatively large proportion of soldiers with a low level of education have complained bitterly that they do not receive their mail or even telegrams, that newspapers do not arrive, and that in general living conditions are miserable. An investigation by *Krasnaya zvezda* confirmed that these complaints were very largely true.[135]

For officers and NCOs and the enlisted men who have money to spend, the adequacy of post exchange facilities affects the standard of living. The post exchange system is run by Voyentorg, the directorate of the trade establish-

---

[132] *KVS,* no. 4, February 1971, pp. 70–74.
[133] *KZ,* March 2, 1971, p. 2.
[134] *KVS,* no. 24, December 1969, p. 7. This concern does not seem to apply to the design of military systems. Modern Soviet naval vessels are said to provide sailors with half the living space of American ships and apparently do not provide amenities such as air conditioning, which would make service in hot climates such as Cuba, the Mediterranean, or the Indian Ocean more agreeable.
[135] *KZ,* March 10, 1971, p. 2.

ment for military personnel. In the eighth five-year plan, capital expenditures for military trade were 122 million rubles; in the ninth five-year plan (1971–75) they were planned to exceed 200 million rubles. In 1971, capital investments were 43 million rubles, as compared with 31 million in 1970. Three-fourths of these funds were earmarked for warehouse construction, and the remainder for large stores, restaurant-cafés, personal service centers, and living quarters for military trade workers.[136]

Changes in Soviet troop deployment to the East and an emphasis on better PX facilities for isolated garrisons are reflected by the fact that in 1970 the sale of merchandise increased by 40 percent in remote garrisons, as compared with an average growth of 10–12 percent for the military trade system as a whole.[137] In 1971 the growth in trade turnover was 12–20 percent in border districts and small remote garrisons, as compared with a 9.5 percent overall trade turnover growth.[138]

The effort to make consumer goods more generally available to the military, especially to officers, led to increases in the sales of consumer durables during the five-year period 1967–72: an increase in the sale of television sets of 18 percent, of radios 20 percent, of washing machines 57 percent, of wrist watches 60 percent, motorcycles and motorscooters 36 percent, furniture 65 percent, small automobiles 300 percent, and household refrigerators 400 percent.[139] A major effort has been made to facilitate the purchase of goods by mail. In the first half of 1971 the new military book-by-mail department processed forty-eight thousand letter-orders.[140]

Self-service stores have been introduced into the armed forces to expedite and rationalize service. By mid-1971 there were 200 such stores, and all army and navy stores are scheduled to be converted ultimately to self-service.[141]

Despite all the improvements, Soviet authorities still severely criticize the post exchange system. Administration is highly variable in its effectiveness: at one garrison, customers may be grateful for air shipments of early vegetables to their snow-covered region, while in another store it is impossible to find a single box of matches.[142] In self-service stores, wrapping paper and weighing

[136] *KVS*, no. 16, August 1971, pp. 32–38.

[137] *KZ*, June 29, 1971, p. 4.

[138] Ibid., March 14, 1972, p. 4.

[139] Ibid., March 26, 1971, p. 3. These increases in officer purchases of consumer durables are in most cases about four times greater than the increases in civilian purchases in the corresponding period. There are, however, two exceptions: the increase in civilian radio purchases was a little bit more than for officers, and increases in civilian purchases of TV sets was about double that of officer purchases. Total USSR sales taken from *Narodnoye khoziaistvo SSSR v 1968 g.*, p. 594; *1970 g.*, p. 562.

[140] *KZ*, September 28, 1971, p. 4. Some 40 million books each year are distributed through the military book trade.

[141] Ibid., June 29, 1971, p. 4.

[142] Ibid.

scales and other materials for the packaging of goods are not available.[143] Not only daily necessities, but even military items like shoulder boards and insignia are often not procurable. In many post exchange shops the tailoring services are poor, and there is a tendency either to overstock or to understock. "Waste and misappropriation still occur, principally because Party principles in the selection of personnel are violated. Because of this, unreliable and dishonorable people penetrate the trade organizations. The turnover of personnel is also great."[144] The Party has tried its hand at improving military trade centers, but it has defended its inability to do very much by pointing to the necessity for political workers to travel hundreds of kilometers to cover the various centers and shops.[145]

An important aspect of living conditions for soldiers is freedom from worry about their parental families or about their wives and children. Wives who live in urban areas each receive a very small monthly allowance of fifteen rubles for the first child and twenty-two rubles for two children. Those who live in rural areas and are connected with agriculture are paid seven and a half rubles for one child and twelve rubles for two or more children.[146] Allowances are also provided for the children of officer candidates and students at military educational institutions. Complaints are continually made about the failure of family allowances to be paid.[147] It seems that such complaints are acted upon with considerable vigor. The military authorities appear anxious to ensure that their soldiers get what is coming to them and that they are not cheated out of various perquisites by civilian agencies. Housing privileges for the families of military personnel are particularly prized, and the complaints often have to do with them. Article 70 of the Law of Universal Military Training forbids the eviction of families of military personnel from their living quarters. Article 32d instructs local officials to enroll the children of inducted soldiers in nursery schools within one month of their application.[148]

Special attention is given to a person who enlists for the six-year term, and his right to his former living space is retained. Inductees, too, may demand that the premises on which they lived before induction be vacated upon their return

[143] Ibid. The military trade organization is looking forward to the end of the present five-year plan (1971–75), when industry is supposed to supply about 55 percent of retail goods in small prepacked form. Ibid., March 14, 1972, p. 4.

[144] KVS, no. 16, August 1971, pp. 32–38.

[145] Ibid. Difficulties in the PX system, not surprisingly, seem to be greater the further one gets from the center. Among the areas where problems seem most acute are the Transbaykal, Ural, and Central Asian Military Districts. KZ, March 14, 1972, p. 4.

[146] KZ, August 9, 1973, p. 2.

[147] Ibid., June 18, 1971, p. 4, and June 21, 1972, p. 2.

[148] Starshina serzhant, November 1970, p. 37.

to civilian life. They must, however, demand this right within six months after their release from service. If the occupants refuse to release the premises, they are subject to eviction by the courts.

Soldiers who have completed their terms of service are accepted on a noncompetitive basis in secondary special educational institutions.

Applications and complaints of servicemen and members of their families are supposed to receive rapid attention. Soldiers' letters are received and sent without charge.

Time spent as a serviceman is considered as a part of one's overall labor service in his record. Local soviets and the heads of enterprises are obliged to offer jobs to people who have been discharged into the reserves no later than one month after they apply. Persons who formerly worked in enterprises and organizations retain the right to have a job at the same enterprise.[149] As Soviet writers point out, it is important that "soldiers and sailors who defend the homeland have peace of mind."[150]

"Peace of mind" also depends on the draftee's relations with his officers and with older soldiers. Soviet higher military authorities are aware that any abuse of inductees by officers, NCOs, and older soldiers, or of junior officers by senior officers, is damaging to their attempt to make military life professionally attractive to inductees. Although they are firm in their requirement that "exactingness" be demanded of inductees, they are also firm with respect to the "exactingness" required of higher-ranking personnel in their behavior toward lower ranks. This is discussed more fully in chapter VI, section C3.

2. The Romance of Military Service

In its attempt to make military service attractive to young people and particularly to potential officers, Soviet military spokesmen have emphasized the romantic nature of military life. "The romance of exploits has always attracted youngsters. . . . The profession of a military man has always been for youngsters one of a romantic and attractive nature. What lad does not dream of becoming a tanker, pilot, sailor, or missile man?"[151] Speaking of a missile-carrying submarine, an officer writes, "Ours is a very romantic service."[152]

For Soviet spokesmen, the romance of military service does not mean seeing far-off places such as India or Cuba; rather, romance is inherent in the conflict with nature, in the ability to overcome discomfort and danger, as well as in seeing places that may be far off in the Soviet East and North, but whose romantic component derives not from their distance but from their climate.

[149] *Sovety deputatov trudyashchikhsya,* no. 5, 1971.
[150] Ibid.
[151] *KZ,* October 5, 1971, p. 4.
[152] *Voyennyye znaniya,* April 1971.

"The harsh and unusual nature of the Arctic makes that region romantic. Like a powerful magnet it draws to the North people who seek the new and the unknown, who thirst for adventure and conflict. Everyone here joins in the romance of our region."[153]

A writer, comparing the Soviet or desired Soviet attitude toward military service with that of the bourgeois countries, points out that in modern warfare the role of the heroic is especially great. In bourgeois writings, on the contrary, the opinion is widespread that war has been completely deglorified. To the Soviet writer, such assertions are not evidence that romance and heroism have disappeared from war, but rather are a confession that bourgeois military figures lack confidence in the human material of their armies.[154]

Despite, or perhaps because of, the insistence with which the theme of "the romance of an officer's life" is repeated in Soviet military journals, a young officer, taking his courage in his hands, wrote to *Krasnaya zvezda* that, "I work from morning to night and fail to detect any sign of beauty or romance in my work."[155] This letter led to an outburst by a general who responded to the young officer's letter with a lengthy statement in *Krasnaya zvezda*. "It seems to me that you have still not understood that romance that said to you, 'Leave the easy paths, happiness is found on the steep and thorny ones.' Yes, he who serves our Soviet society wholeheartedly experiences real happiness. The happiness that is found in books does not exist. Neither the comfort of large cities, nor the comfort of restaurants, nor endless pastimes make up the romance of a normal, full-blooded life. Romance is born in faraway garrisons where mad storms wander, where all around you is the taiga or semidesert which, in another era, only a plane could reach. In my opinion, romance lives unique, light, and pure in the hearts of those who subordinate everything to the formula—myself, my collective, my motherland. This formula gives birth to heroes. Subordinate the personal to the collective, live for the motherland. Remember always that no matter what you might do, the collective has formed you and the motherland has given you happiness. . . . The romance of service as a Soviet officer led me to harsh times on the soil of revolutionary Spain. It led me through the fiery battles of World War II. It lives even now in peaceful days."[156]

Nonetheless, in the last several years this type of lyrical description of the romance in military life seems to have declined. Indeed, one began to find in 1971 admissions that not all forms of military service are necessarily romantic. This line is clearly established in a statement directed toward political officers: "In their imagination, youth paints army life in the beginning in romantic colors. But a little time passes and it turns out that though it is interesting there

[153] *KZ*, December 19, 1969, p. 4.
[154] *KVS*, no. 21, November 1971, pp. 18–25.
[155] *KZ*, December 28, 1969, p. 2.
[156] Ibid., December 21, 1969, p. 2.

are few adventures and more day-to-day monotony and much hard work. The teacher must foresee this and direct the youth and romantic yearnings of young soldiers into the current of day-to-day matters, primarily toward raising combat readiness. All military service is permeated with romance. It is just necessary to help youth to see this and to learn to obey, understanding a commander's order with heart and mind."[157] It is characteristic that the romantic image of army life so sedulously cultivated by the army and the Party is now blamed on the callowness of youth.

Quartermaster officers and others concerned with rear services can now wryly point out that military personnel whose specialties involve cooking and storekeeping are not generally doing work that is viewed as romantic. Nonetheless, by pursuing a thrifty attitude in the expenditure of state materials and money, they can earn respect and recognition.[158] The head of the Soviet rear service, however, insists that "We, too, have our romance and our heroes: the romance and heroism of selfless labor in the name of the motherland."[159] An admiral describing a submarine crew is compelled to acknowledge that "in the military and in peacetime much seems, at first glance, to be rather dull and routine." However, "we must bear in mind that we must be prepared at all times to deliver a powerful, devastating return blow to the enemy."[160] It is now admissible that some military work is not only not romantic but can be "monotonous and fatiguing."[161] It seems that those engaged in developing an appropriate image of the Soviet military have been persuaded that a greater degree of realism needs to be introduced in trying to make military service attractive. It is likely that the new schools of Soviet personnel psychology and sociology are beginning to have their effect.

3. Appearance

Soviet military journals and newspapers constantly inveigh against persons who fail to maintain the appearance proper to a Soviet soldier. Soldiers and sailors in Moscow, very often on leave from other areas, are seen "wearing improper uniforms and dirty shoes, and evidently in dire need of haircuts. . . . Young and even senior officers are committing so-called minor disciplinary infractions: wearing nonregulation neckties, unpressed uniforms, brightly colored socks, and worn-out shoes, and smoking in public."[162] Sailors in Lenin-

---

[157] *KVS,* no. 10, May 1971, pp. 30–34.
[158] *Starshina serzhant,* October 1971, pp. 4–12.
[159] *Nedelya,* September 2, 1973, p. 5.
[160] *Kazakhstanskaya pravda,* October 28, 1971, p. 4.
[161] *KVS,* no. 21, November 1971, pp. 18–25. However, the theme of the romance of military life has not been entirely displaced. "The romance of army life" and "the romantic life of an officer" are still referred to. See, for example, *Sovetskiy patriot,* April 28, 1974, p. 3.
[162] *KZ,* January 12, 1971, p. 2.

grad are charged with "changing their official clothing in order to conform to what they consider to be the transient whims of fashion."[163] One officer is praised because he has never been seen "unshaven, in a baggy blouse, or a dirty jacket."[164] The connection that is made between improper care of one's appearance and a lack of discipline is indicated in the case of a junior sergeant whose "untidy hair, combined with his dandified whiskers, showed his disrespect for army orders" and whose appearance is viewed as the visible sign of the inner collapse that ultimately led him to appear for disciplinary action.[165]

The relation between outer appearance and inner states of mind is emphasized by a writer discussing submarine crews. It is sometimes thought on long trips submarine crews need not be concerned about appearance and may be allowed a certain amount of sloppiness in dress. On the contrary, "without outer smartness, there cannot be that psychological climate that is imbued with exactingness."[166]

Soviet concern with the appearance of officers and men is shared by most military establishments, at least in the western world. That the uniform is "uniform" for particular grades and services reflects the military interest in the subordination of individuality to particular functions. Breaches of appearance are breaches of regulation and are an indication of a refractory will. In the Soviet armed forces this source of concern is all the greater since in the Soviet view serious offenses often begin with minor offenses such as infractions of uniform regulations (see chapter V, section B).

There are, however, also other reasons for the considerable concern that the Soviet military leadership has shown for the appearance of officers and men. Professional pride and self-esteem are wounded by the image of the Soviet fighting man as a peasant in uniform. The recruitment of well-educated officer personnel is made more difficult by the officer corps' mediocre level of prestige and this is hardly improved by the poor appearance of many Soviet soldiers. The emergence of the new well-educated type of inductee has also necessitated a lessening of the gap between the officers and the men in the ranks. To these ends, the Soviet military in 1970 introduced new uniforms for both enlisted men and officers.[167] The new uniforms were introduced in Moscow, Leningrad, the capitals of the union republics, and several overseas garrisons in 1970, but the change was not completed until 1972.[168]

Soldiers and officers now have four types of uniform: parade, semidress, service, and field. The parade uniform is worn during ceremonial occasions and parades; the semidress uniform is worn at the theater, at receptions, on

[163] Ibid., July 7, 1971, p. 2.
[164] *Pravda,* May 21, 1971, p. 6.
[165] *Starshina serzhant,* October 1971, pp. 34–35.
[166] *KZ,* February 5, 1971, p. 2. The same point is made in connection with small isolated garrisons or posts.
[167] Ibid., June 7, 1970, p. 1.
[168] Ibid.

holidays, on days off, and during vacations.[169] Judging from Soviet photographs, it would appear, at least by western standards, that the navy officers have come off best with their everyday two-tone summer uniforms with white jackets.[170] Noncommissioned personnel have received uniforms that not only improve their appearance but also provide greater warmth and dryness. Privates now have full-dress uniforms made from "good woolen fabrics."[171] "For the first time in the history of our army an open parade dress uniform is available to servicemen on extended duty. A new artificial fur is now used for the fur cap with the ear flap."[172]

The new uniforms have increased the emphasis in Soviet military literature on the importance of "a smart, dashing appearance" and "elegance" as qualities that elicit respect for the officer who exhibits them. A properly turned out officer stands out among other people because of his "fine, severe, elegant uniform."[173]

Naturally, an "elegant-looking" officer is best suited to supporting the image of the officer corps as constituting a "romantic" career. But this will be even more the case if his wife is equally attractive. A military writer describes an ideal military couple: "The wife was tastefully and well attired and beautifully behaved, and beside her was such a smart and dashing military man. This involuntarily aroused admiration." Unfortunately there was another officer "whose wife was like a queen," but he was "carelessly dressed, had unduly familiar manners, waddling in front of his wife who could barely keep up with him while carrying a full shopping bag."[174]

E. PROFESSIONALISM AND CONSCRIPT FORCES

It is evident from the introduction of the ensign and warrant officer grades, the reintroduction of the extended service category shortly after its elimination, the stepped-up campaigns to recruit personnel into these sectors of the

---

[169] Ibid.

[170] *Soviet Military Review,* no. 12, 1969, pp. 27–29.

[171] *KVS,* no. 24, December 1969, pp. 3–8. Nonetheless, four years later we learn that "the quality of the fabrics continues to improve." *KZ,* March 6, 1973, p. 4.

[172] *Bloknot agitatora,* June 1971.

[173] *KZ,* December 3, 1970, pp. 1–3, and April 28, 1971, p. 2; *KVS,* no. 24, December 1970, pp. 64–69. Not only military uniforms are elegant. An article dealing with customs officials describes them as going out into the examination hall at the airport "elegant in their gray uniforms." *Leningradskaya pravda,* March 19, 1972, p. 3. Children parading in a newly invented ceremony replacing religious confirmation are described as appearing in their "smart black coats."

[174] *KZ,* April 28, 1971, p. 2. The emphasis on "smart, dashing" officers is reminiscent of Czarist traditions of the young aristocratic officer. But it is also reminiscent of the 1930's, when Soviet officers were taught French, polo, and dancing. Many officers during this period divorced their proletarian wives to marry young women who could be "beautifully behaved." The Soviet air force has been particularly noted for its lieutenants in "sharp uniforms," and its "smart, elegant colonels at Sochi." See Raymond L. Garthoff, *Soviet Military Policy: A Historical Analysis* (New York, 1966), pp. 36–37, on the past striving for elegance in the Soviet military.

military and into the officer cadet academies, and the attempts to build up the prestige of the military officer and to make his appearance and living conditions conform to the desired image of a professional military man, that the authorities are determined to strengthen the cadre or professional components of the armed forces.

Despite this intent to enhance the appeal of the military as a career choice, other considerations intrude that erode the professional status of Soviet military cadres. Of major importance in this respect has been the increasing insistence of the Party on its role as the leader in all military matters. All the victories of the Soviet military forces—all their doctrinal, technical, and other accomplishments—are due to wise Party leadership. Further, the Party insists with ever-increasing emphasis that the primary duty and accomplishment of a military officer lie not in his military skills but in his promotion of troop loyalty to the Party. Insistence that the officer is first and foremost a political, rather than a military, leader necessarily diminishes the status of the officer.[175]

The fact that the officer-engineer called up from the reserves often does not consider himself a military man erodes further the professional status of the military. These and other young officers often have to endure living conditions little consistent with a professional military status; this reduces the professional standing of the military still further. The mediocre prestige of the Soviet officer reflected in the study that was summarized earlier (p. 23) is, no doubt, partially the result of these different factors, which undermine the efforts of Soviet military and Party authorities to give the career military man a high status.

Soviet efforts to upgrade the cadre components does not mean a reduced interest in universal military service. One of the great advantages of universal military service over volunteer, career forces is that in the former a larger number of men receive military training. Of course, if conscripts lose much of their military skill after their return to civilian life, this advantage is to a corresponding degree lost. However, the recall of reserve soldiers and officers for relatively prolonged periods of retraining ensures that a substantial part of the special advantage of universal military service is retained. The ability to train successive cohorts of young men and thus to build up large reserves of trained soldiers is important to the Soviets, who have a high regard for the value of large numbers of men and of their immediate availability, especially since the long period of compulsory service, reserve training, and the very large cadre component provide at the same time many of the advantages of a volunteer, career force. Universal military service, with its negligible pay for conscripts, is also, of course, economically attractive.

There is an additional reason why the Soviets must almost necessarily opt for universal military service. The idea that an obligation to the state as major

---

[175] For a detailed discussion of Party-commander relations, see chapter VIII.

as military service should be at the option of the individual rather than of the state is inadmissible to Soviet leaders who view the change to a volunteer force in the United States as a confession by the government of its inability to enforce mass acceptance of military training. This does not exclude some envy of a United States purely professional or career army, especially given its greater combat experience. About two-thirds of Soviet regimental officers are without wartime service.

Chapter II

Preinduction
Military Training

The reduction in 1967 in the length of compulsory military service imposed severe burdens on military training programs in the Soviet armed forces and on the maintenance of a high operational level. This chapter discusses one of several means intended to reduce these difficulties: compulsory preinduction military training of Soviet youths in the two years prior to their call-up.

A. DOSAAF (THE ALL-UNION VOLUNTARY SOCIETY FOR ASSISTANCE TO THE ARMY, AIR FORCE, AND NAVY)

The 1967 Law of Universal Military Service provides for introductory or preinduction military training "to be conducted for young men of preconscription and conscription age everywhere, without interrupting production and studies" (Article 17). This training is to be conducted at all secondary schools —general, specialized, and technical-vocational—and, for those not in school, at training points set up at enterprises, institutions, organizations, and collective farms.

The leaders of schools and enterprises are held responsible for seeing that all boys receive training for active military service. The law also authorizes the training of specialists for the armed forces in educational institutions of DO-SAAF and in technical-vocational schools (Article 18).

Both preinduction military training and the training of specialists "are conducted under the leadership of the USSR Ministry of Defense" (Article 19). The necessary training and material base, the selection and training of military instructors, and the organization of military training is a joint responsibility of the Ministry of Defense, other "appropriate ministries and departments," and the Central Committee of DOSAAF (Article 19).

DOSAAF's responsibility for preinduction military training and for the provision of instruction in military specialties does not by any means date from the law of 1967. Already in 1962–63 some DOSAAF organizations had begun to develop training points that, with public support, prepared youths for military service.[1] When the 1967 law was passed, a substantial number of such training points had already been established, but the reduction in length of active service increased the need for predraft training and gave these activities a state, compulsory form. Similarly, DOSAAF activities in organizing military technical sports and in providing youth with instruction in military specialties had already developed in the fifties and were given further authorization and support in a resolution of the USSR Council of Ministers in May 1966, a year and a half before the Law of Universal Military Service was enacted.[2] It is not surprising, therefore, that in discussions of predraft training DOSAAF has always loomed very large, especially in the provision of training material and procedures. A change, however, has been taking place.

In 1971 *Krasnaya zvezda* noted "a general strengthening of Party supervision over this [DOSAAF] work." In addition, "ties between DOSAAF and military commissariats must be especially strong. Military commissariats constantly select directing personnel for DOSAAF organizations. The selection of reserve officers to head *rayon* [district] and city committees of DOSAAF is a common practice."[3] In early 1972 a much more vigorous statement appeared in *Krasnaya zvezda:* "The military commissariats have been entrusted with the direct management of predraft military training. They participate in organizing and conducting all measures jointly with the organs of people's education

[1] Predraft military training, however, goes back even farther. "The study of applied military science in secondary schools was given great emphasis in prewar years. Almost every draftee had acquired one or two defense-oriented specialties before induction; many had sports ratings, badges as Voroshilov sharpshooters, were ready for medical assistance for defense, air and chemical defense badges, etc." *Sovetskaya pedagogika,* February 1972, pp. 60–63. For an account of still earlier Soviet organization of civilians in support of the military, see William E. Odom, *The Soviet Volunteers: Modernization and Bureaucracy in a Public Mass Organization* (Princeton, N.J.), 1973.
[2] *Sovetskiy patriot,* December 20, 1970, p. 3; *KZ,* May 25, 1971, p. 2.
[3] *KZ,* August 26, 1971.

and the leaders of schools, educational institutes, and enterprises; they select the military instructors, the chiefs of training points, and the instructors, and together with the DOSAAF committees they organize their methodological training, furnish assistance in creating the required equipment base, and exercise control in various areas."[4] In this interesting passage, DOSAAF is mentioned rather late and in a restricted role. To be sure, a little later, *Sovetskiy patriot*, the newspaper organ of DOSAAF, printed a statement by Minister of Defense Marshal A. A. Grechko that affirmed the important role in predraft military training that is delegated to DOSAAF by the Communist Party,[5] and two years later Marshal of Aviation Pokryshkin, chairman of the Central Committee of DOSAAF, asserted that "the training of youth to carry out its holy duty to defend the socialist fatherland is effected by DOSAAF organizations in close interaction with the Leninist Komsomol and with trade unions."[6] This hardly precludes the possibility of a downgrading of DOSAAF relative to the military commissariats.

The significance of these various statements is not easy to determine. It is by no means clear whether they are to be interpreted in terms of a conflict between a military and a civilian (DOSAAF) bureaucracy, or between the military and the Party, or between the Party and the DOSAAF bureaucracy.[7] The increased role of the military commissariats may reflect a dissatisfaction with DOSAAF administrations and an intent to give greater importance to the predraft program and to extract greater military value from it. In any case, possible rivalry over major responsibility for predraft military training does not seem to apply to DOSAAF's role in training youths in technical military specialties; here DOSAAF appears to maintain full control. DOSAAF's own regulations make it clear that it exercises more control in the latter than in preinduction training. "In accordance with the law of the USSR 'On Universal Military Obligations' [DOSAAF] *conducts* the training of specialists in the training organizations of the society from among youths of predraft and draft ages for the armed forces of the USSR and *participates* in the creation and operation of training points for primary military training of the youths."[8] (Emphasis added.)

---

[4] Ibid., March 3, 1972, p. 2.
[5] *Sovetskiy patriot*, March 29, 1972, p. 1.
[6] Ibid., May 19, 1974, p. 3.
[7] Although it was organized to give assistance to the armed forces, DOSAAF's newspaper made it abundantly clear that "the main content of the agitation, propaganda, and mass political work in the DOSAAF organization should be a convincing and clear demonstration of the role of the Communist Party as the leading and directing force of Soviet society," *Sovetskiy patriot*, May 30, 1971, p. 1. DOSAAF regulations require members to promote "love and respect" for the armed forces, but "boundless devotion" to the Communist Party. DOSAAF Regulations, 25a, ibid., January 12, 1972, pp. 1–2.
[8] DOSAAF Regulations, 14j, ibid.

DOSAAF is a mass organization in the fullest sense of the word. It is open to all citizens of the USSR fourteen years of age and older. The entrance fee is an insignificant ten kopecks and annual membership dues are ten kopecks for schoolchildren, teachers, and housewives, and thirty kopecks for others.[9]

The basic element in the DOSAAF organization is the "primary organization." Primary organizations are found in schools, in industrial plants, in offices, in farm establishments, and in enterprises of all types. In July 1971 DOSAAF claimed "tens of millions of DOSAAF members active in more than 300,000 primary organizations."[10] In the Kirghiz Republic there were in July 1971 about 3,000 primary DOSAAF organizations with more than 600,000 members. This yields an average membership in the republic of about 200 per primary organization. In Tallinn, Estonia, in early 1972 there were 113,000 members in 572 primary DOSAAF organizations, and this figure also yields an average of 200 members per organization.[11] In Uzbekistan there were in 1974 more than 4 million members in about 15,000 primary organizations, that is, an average of about 265 in each primary group.[12] Soviet schools are the locus of 80,000 primary organizations with about 11 million teacher and student members. This averages to a little fewer than 140 members per school primary organization. If we assume that the average number of members in all the primary organizations fell somewhere between 140 and 200, we might then suppose that the "tens of millions" of DOSAAF members was equivalent to approximately 40 to 60 million members. In 1974 DOSAAF had 315,000 primary organizations and claimed that more than half of the adult population of the country were members. Half of the population 20 years of age and over is roughly 75 million. This together with nonadult members implies a membership of about 80–85 million.[13] In 1971, 70 percent of all Komsomol members belonged to DOSAAF.[14] In some republics, membership is clearly far below the average. Thus, in 1972 only 31 percent and 20 percent of the eligible population in the Kirghiz and Kazakh Republics were members of DOSAAF.[15]

The variability of membership among local areas is high. In one *rayon* 90 percent of the adult population were in the ranks of the society. On the other hand, at a certain motor transport base only 25 percent of the workers were members of DOSAAF primary organizations.[16] At the Estonian State

[9] DOSAAF Regulations, IX, 53, ibid.
[10] *KVS,* no. 14, July 1971, pp. 90–91.
[11] *Kommunist Estonii,* April 1972, pp. 63–71.
[12] *Sovetskiy patriot,* June 12, 1974, p. 1.
[13] Ibid., September 22, 1974, p. 1.
[14] *Za rulem,* May 1971, pp. 1–2.
[15] *Kazakhstanskaya pravda,* July 5, 1972, p. 1.
[16] *Voyennyye znaniya,* November 1969, pp. 10–11.

Agricultural Design Institute only 7 percent of the personnel participate.[17]

Above the primary organizations stands a complex set of DOSAAF bureaucrats who are organized in municipal and district committees, *oblast* [regional] committees, and republic and *kray* [territorial] committees, led by the all-union committee under the chairmanship of a high military figure. In addition to the DOSAAF administrative bureaucracy there is a substantial number of additional personnel engaged in producing DOSAAF magazines and newspapers. A single edition of the various DOSAAF magazines and the DOSAAF newspaper *Sovetskiy patriot* amounts to about 3.5 million copies. In addition to *Sovetskiy patriot,* DOSAAF publishes the magazines *Voyennyye znaniya* (Military Knowledge), *Za rulem* (Behind the Wheel), and *Kryl'ya rodiny* (Wings of the Motherland). *Voyennyye znaniya,* published in part for civil defense workers, has a circulation of more than 300,000. In 1970, DOSAAF's publishing house issued more than 12 million books and pamphlets.[18]

Between 1967 and 1970, DOSAAF constructed 560 buildings for military training and military sports activities. This represented two and one-half times more construction than DOSAAF had achieved during the four years preceding the enactment of the Law of Universal Military Service. In 1973, DOSAAF had 9,000 buildings and other facilities. The current DOSAAF five-year plan (1971–75) allocated 150 million rubles for the construction of 570 training buildings and installations.[19] In Armenia these buildings are standard three-story structures with provisions for garages, technical military courses, rifle ranges, and laboratories.[20]

Military and technical training materials—weapons, ammunition, parachutes, planes, small ships, diving gear, motor vehicles, and electronic and other equipment—represent major expenditures. Military units have been encouraged to supplement what DOSAAF itself has bought by lending or donating military matériel to primary organizations and higher committees of DOSAAF in their neighborhoods. To aid in this process, military units are encouraged to "adopt" DOSAAF technical schools or clubs or preinduction military training points in their areas and to provide them with material and moral support. In its aviation schools "DOSAAF now has everything necessary at its disposal: excellent aircraft, wonderful training classes, [ground] trainers, and experienced instructors."[21]

The managers of plants and other enterprises and the directors of schools

---

[17] *Sovetskaya Estoniya,* June 30, 1972, p. 4. Perhaps this is an indication of Estonian "resistance."

[18] *Sovetskiy patriot,* December 23, 1970, p. 1; *Voyennyye znaniya,* May 1971, pp. 38–39.

[19] *Za rulem,* February 1973, pp. 4–5. The current five-year plan originally called for the construction of 800 new buildings. See *Sovetskiy patriot,* August 4, 1971, p. 1.

[20] Ibid.

[21] Ibid., August 19, 1973, p. 1.

also have some responsibility for providing equipment, and this fragmentation of responsibility leads in many instances to chaotic conditions—possibly one of the reasons for the increased responsibilities of the military commissariat. Higher authorities do not agree that all the equipment and the various teaching aids required in predraft training should be issued from a central point. "A great amount of equipment must be produced locally. . . . This equipment can be produced with the aid of the students, patronizing military units, enterprises, and institutes. This will aid in developing creative initiative on the part of the students and the teaching staff, and will make the military study groups the pride of the school."[22]

Another major cost is the pay of the retired and reserve officers who act as instructors in the predraft training programs. Soviet publications avoid stating who pays these salaries, although it seems that Soviet schools and enterprises carry the financial burden of them. Originally the state had achieved savings by virtue of the reduced pensions that were paid to retired officers who were employed as instructors. But a dearth of officers for the expanding preinduction training program led on December 1, 1970, to a new rule permitting a full pension to be paid to officers regardless of pay they had received as instructors.[23] This new regulation attests to the seriousness of the support given to the preinduction training program, as do also the official pay rates "comparable to those for school deputy directors for academic affairs."[24] At schools with only three or fewer classes in the ninth and tenth grades, payment is fixed at half the regular rate.[25] Some schools share the same instructor. Although DOSAAF does not pay the salary of these military instructors, it probably does pay the instructors and personnel of its own military technical schools and clubs out of its own budget.

DOSAAF, with its millions of members, must necessarily have substantial administrative expenses. DOSAAF leaders in various provincial, city, and other committees are alleged to expand their staffs and to spend money unnecessarily. But "the solution of problems is not to be based on increasing staffs, paying more wages, or making new capital investments, but rather on qualitative factors—improving the leadership, strengthening discipline, and achieving involvement of political activists in the work."[26]

How are the DOSAAF military specialist and preinduction training programs funded? To the extent that they are funded by DOSAAF itself, funds are derived from the following sources:

1. Membership dues, of which the primary organization keeps 30 percent

[22] *Voyennyye znaniya,* August 1971, pp. 27–28.
[23] *KZ,* April 28, 1971, p. 2, and July 2, 1971.
[24] Ibid., May 24, 1972, p. 4.
[25] Ibid.
[26] *Sovetskiy patriot,* December 20, 1971, p. 3.

and higher-level committees keep the rest.[27] Given the rate of dues, the ratio of school members to adults, and the estimated membership, a rough guess of annual dues would be 25 million rubles.

2. DOSAAF lists income from its publishing activities, although it is not clear whether this income exceeds publishing expenses.

3. DOSAAF provides chargeable services to enterprises and repair shops by its specialist training groups (see pp. 55–57 below). Thus, for example, its divers seem to be one of the main sources for underwater work needed by construction and other enterprises.[28] Another profitable DOSAAF service is its dog-training and breeding clubs, which supply qualified dogs to the army, border troops, government ministries, and farms.[29] DOSAAF also provides courses of instruction in certain technical and sports activities for individuals and enterprises that pay instruction fees.[30] "The Zhitomir Distinguished Automotive Club gets 40,000 rubles a year net profit from its self-supporting enterprises, and 10–15,000 rubles in payment for training specialists for the nationalist economy."[31] In 1971 dozens of DOSAAF enterprises and shops "put out millions of rubles worth of products."[32]

4. DOSAAF receives financial contributions from economic, trade union, sports, and other organizations interested in its development.

5. The principal financial support of DOSAAF comes from the general population in the form of the purchase of lottery tickets. DOSAAF operates two lotteries annually. The scale of the lottery is still growing and the seventh lottery (spring 1972) provided twice as many prizes as the sixth. The spring 1972 lottery had sold 30 million tickets (apparently at two rubles per ticket) by April 1972.[33] DOSAAF sold a total of 432 million rubles worth of tickets in its first six lotteries.[34] The cash and material prizes awarded in these six lotteries were worth 216 million rubles.[35]

The amount of money raised by DOSAAF organizations does not necessarily coincide with the amount actually available for DOSAAF work. In

---

[27] DOSAAF Regulations, IX, 50, ibid., January 12, 1972, pp. 1–2.

[28] According to DOSAAF, "it is difficult to overestimate the military significance of this kind of work." Income from underwater work enables DOSAAF clubs to acquire various types of expensive diving equipment. *Voyennyye znaniya,* October 1971, p. 45.

[29] Ibid., p. 45. In 1971, DOSAAF had 115 dog-breeding clubs with 61,000 members "working on a full profit and loss accounting basis." These clubs are sometimes criticized for neglecting the service or working qualities of the dogs as a criterion for breeding, and lapsing into dog-show criteria.

[30] The fee for a radio master, shortened course, is fifty-four rubles; for a motorcycle driver's course, thirty rubles; and for a "nonprofessional driver" course, it "should not exceed fifty-two rubles." Ibid., September 1971.

[31] *Sovetskiy patriot,* June 18, 1972, p. 1.

[32] Ibid., July 16, 1972, p. 2.

[33] Among the principal prizes in the sixth lottery were 20,000 automobiles; 180,000 motorcycles, motor scooters, and motor bikes; and 100,000 radios and tape recorders. Ibid., April 23, 1972.

[34] Ibid.

[35] Ibid., June 28, 1972, p. 1.

DOSAAF literature, considerable emphasis is placed on DOSAAF auditing commissions to monitor the system of collecting membership dues and, even more important, the sale of DOSAAF lottery tickets, both of which provide opportunities for large-scale peculation. The higher levels of DOSAAF recommend that, in addition to the regular audits, other audits should be made when a "signal" exists that dictates the need for one. "A surprise audit can serve to prevent abuse, excessive expenditures, and violations."[36] The situation is sufficiently serious to have led to auditing commissions to audit the audits. In announcing the second issue of the sixth lottery, the authorities gave warnings to the auditing commissions to turn over money promptly to the Gosbank and to guard against pilferage of lottery tickets and misappropriation of money.[37] Despite the activity of the auditing commissions, "the society continues to experience shortages and misappropriations of money and materials."[38] In any case, audits presumably cannot disclose misappropriations that are due to the selling of lottery tickets "at higher prices than the instructions permit."[39]

DOSAAF's total income and expenditures, even if one could estimate them, would not be an estimate of the cost of Soviet preinduction and military specialist training. It would be necessary to add the costs noted earlier for instructors' salaries, equipment provided by others, and facilities provided by enterprises and schools. Besides, not all DOSAAF activities are directly related to military training itself. DOSAAF engages in a considerable amount of civil defense work, training for some civil occupations, and general mass patriotic indoctrination.

The income devoted to preinduction and specialist military training and the expenditures incurred on behalf of them are, of course, of interest not only for the sake of descriptive completeness, but also because information on these matters would provide an estimate of at least some of the amounts of money devoted to direct military preparedness that do not show up in the USSR military budget. The preinduction military training of students might cost less if it were performed by the military during the regular period of military service. For this reason, and since complete expenditures are not available in any case, the "military worth" of the preinduction and specialist military training programs probably should be judged by estimating what it would have cost the armed forces to bring the inductees up to the level of military skill acquired from the predraft programs by the time of their induction. This can, at best, be estimated only crudely, but even a crude estimate first requires a fuller account of the training programs, the skills acquired, and their evaluation by the armed forces. We defer, therefore, the question of "military worth" until we have completed our account of the training programs and activities.

[36] Ibid., October 13, 1971, p. 3.
[37] Ibid., August 4, 1971, p. 1.
[38] Ibid., June 20, 1971, p. 2.
[39] Ibid., April 23, 1972, p. 4.

B. PREINDUCTION AND SPECIALIST TRAINING

1. Growth

The transition in 1967 from a more or less voluntary to a compulsory predraft training program developed slowly. It was not until May 1968, some five months after the passing of the Law of Universal Military Service of 1967, that the first predraft training program was developed and approved.[40] The law made no mention of any areas, schools, or enterprises that were to be temporarily excused from conformity with it. Yet it was evident that the introduction of a training program in thousands of Soviet secondary schools, industrial enterprises, rural establishments, and urban offices required an extensive organization and bureaucracy; the mustering of facilities, training materials, and instructional personnel; and the introduction of control systems. In fact, the Party and the state had no intention of providing these, at least on the scale and with the speed that even a modest conformity with the law would have required. Given the fragmentation of responsibility, and the insistence on minimizing costs by maximizing local effort, often of a volunteer character, the program was bound to lag enormously and to result in highly varied levels of performance and the failure of many schools and enterprises to undertake any training activities at all.[41]

The USSR Ministry of Education, recognizing these limitations, proposed that in the 1968–69 school year only schools that had qualified instructors available should introduce a training program.[42] This does not seem to have been calculated to impress school administrators with the urgent need to look for instructors, and it may have represented a less-than-enthusiastic welcome by the ministry of the new responsibilities thrust on the specialized and general secondary school systems. In any event, three years later, in the 1971–72 school year, predraft training programs had been provided at just somewhat "more than one-half of all the secondary specialized training schools throughout the country."[43]

By the beginning of the 1971 school year, only 7,665 secondary schools and pedagogical institutes had preinduction training programs; 16,000 additional schools were to adopt programs in the 1971–72 school year; and the remaining 18,000 schools in the 1972–73 school year.[44] However, in mid-1972 it was stated that "in 1972 [perhaps meaning the school year 1972–73] military

[40] *KZ*, August 1971, pp. 27–28.
[41] The administrative rationale for this great discrepancy between law and reality is discussed in chapter IX.
[42] *Uchitel'skaya gazeta*, October 19, 1971, and December 25, 1971.
[43] *Sredneye spetsial'noye obrazovaniye*, April 1972, pp. 13–16. In addition to the general education schools, there are technical and vocational schools, entrance to which is possible after completion of primary school.
[44] *Narodnoye obrazovaniye*, no. 7, 1971, pp. 2–9.

training will be introduced completely everywhere in the country."[45] Basic
training, it is asserted, now exists in 60 percent of the schools and "next year
[1973–74?] will be introduced in the remaining 40 percent. Many of them will
be distant rural schools." A late 1973 statement affirms that "beginning with
this year [1973–74] a 140-hour course in preinduction military training, including civil defense, became mandatory in all general education institutions
and in training institutions of professional technical education.[46]

Given the slow rate of development of predraft training between 1968 and
1971, the acceleration planned for 1972–74 suggests some pressure, perhaps
by the military establishment, to get fuller conformity with the Law of Universal Military Service and thus to receive more of the compensation promised
by the law for the one-year reduction in the length of military service. However, it is reasonable to suppose that some of the acceleration is due to increasing experience, better facilities, and indoctrinational pressure, as the initial
years of local fumbling and resistance to central authority recede.

The fact that only a fifth of the general secondary schools had programs
by the end of the third year does not mean, of course, that only a fifth of the
secondary-school ninth and tenth graders received predraft training. It was to
be expected that fewer of the smaller secondary schools, especially in rural
areas, would have programs, and indeed this is confirmed by USSR Deputy
Minister of Education Shtykalo. "Although before now introductory military
training had been introduced mainly in city schools, in the coming school year
[1972–73] it will be introduced primarily in underdeveloped country
schools."[47] In 1971, 54 percent of a sample of motorized infantrymen had had
predraft training.[48] It is likely that ground force inductees represent a less well
educated and less urban group than those in the more technical services (such
as the missile forces, the air force, and some naval branches). The percentage
of inductees with preinduction training in these technical services in 1971 was
probably well above the 54 percent in the motorized infantry sample. Seventy
to eighty percent of the current Soviet inductees are now said to have received
preinduction military training. This, of course, does not mean that a corresponding percentage of all Soviet youth have received preinduction training,
since those with preinduction training are more likely to be inducted.

The extension in 1971–72 and 1972–73 of the preinduction training program to the remaining secondary schools probably imposed a severe strain on
the program, requiring as it did a fivefold increase over the level achieved in
general secondary schools between 1968 and 1971. In addition, extensions
were planned in the types of production enterprises required to provide train-

[45] *Sovetskiy patriot,* July 16, 1972, p. 3.
[46] *Smena,* November 1973, pp. 16–19.
[47] *Uchitel'skaya gazeta,* December 25, 1971.
[48] *KZ,* April 18, 1972, p. 4.

ing programs.[49] This probably referred to rural and smaller enterprises that had not yet been incorporated in the program. The managers of production enterprises are supposed to ensure that their young workers receive predraft training, and to do so without production losses. At some plant "the exercises with the inductees at the training centers are held without leaving production, once or twice a week in two- to three-hour sessions. The young men reach the training center tired after a multi-hour shift. At certain plants the [future] inductees are completely released from work twice a month [and] study for seven hours at the training centers. Obviously such an organization of training should be legalized. . . . In some areas they have an incorrect understanding of the role of the military sports camps and endeavor to use them instead of exercises at the [production] training centers. . . . Such a situation cannot be accepted."[50] Young workers trained as specialists by DOSAAF are permitted five to seven working days off without loss of pay in order to take examinations at DOSAAF training centers.[51]

Given the difficulties the program has faced, it is unlikely that the ambitious objectives for 1972–74 were met. Still, there is little doubt that a push is on and that the predraft training program now conforms much more closely to the objectives specified in the Law of Universal Military Service. The extension of predraft training to most schools and enterprises may benefit especially the ground forces and the other less technical services, since the missile forces, the air force, and the navy are probably already getting the better-educated students with the fullest predraft training.

2. Instructors

The expansion of the predraft program has required a sizable increase in the number of military instructors. The 40,000 secondary schools and the 50,000 industrial establishments would alone require 90,000 military instructors if one were to assume the presence of one instructor for each school and each industrial establishment. Some smaller training points share the same instructor, but others are probably large enough to require more than one. It is likely that the prescribed program, including rural enterprises, could easily require 100,000 military instructors employed in full- or part-time duties.

In 1973, 72 percent of the military instructors in the general secondary and teacher-training schools were reserve officers.[52] The greatly increased need for military instructors is reflected in the fact that "the most promising military instructors among the reserve sergeants undergo special training . . . and

[49] Ibid., April 1972, p. 4.
[50] *Sovetskiy patriot,* January 17, 1973, p. 2.
[51] *Sovetskiy voin,* September 1973, pp. 34–35.
[52] *Sovetskiy patriot,* November 19, 1973, pp. 1, 3.

receive the rank of officer in the reserves."[53] Military instructors who are reserve officers are required to wear uniforms.[54] In enterprises, responsibility for recruiting instructors is divided between the military commissariat and the director of the industrial establishment.

The military instructors are required to provide summer field exercises for ninth-grade students as a supplementary part of predraft training. Just as the students themselves contribute part of their free time to preinduction training, so the military instructor manages a military library, organizes and leads civil defense groups, and shows films on military patriotic themes in his spare time. "For performing these duties he receives no pay."[55]

The increasing seriousness with which the preinduction training program is taken is reflected in the emergence of courses given to instructors in order to improve their pedagogical skills. Also, at the beginning of each academic year, a "familiarization meeting" is held for newly appointed military instructors.[56] In order to improve instruction the Ministry of Education has developed departments of predraft military training for military instructors in many of the advanced training institutes for teachers.[57] However, at least 50 percent of the reserve officers in the cities are said to have had a higher military or pedagogical education, and 70 percent are Communist Party members.[58]

Initially the military instructor appears to have been viewed as an interloper in the school, but the regularization of his activities and the support provided for him and his activities have increased his status more and more. Nonetheless, military journals still refer to problems that suggest that the military instructor is not always received with open arms. "The [school] director is the direct chief and mentor of the military instructor. A military instructor is equal to a deputy director . . . only with respect to his salary. Naturally he is not actually a deputy director."[59] "The military instructor is completely on a par with the other members of the faculty of the school. He conducts all his work in close contact with the other instructors. He must achieve full mutual understanding with them."[60]

[53] Ibid., November 12, 1973, p. 1.

[54] *KZ,* May 24, 1972, p. 4. According to a later statement, "an absolute majority of military instructors conduct classes in their officer's uniforms and this has an important significance in the military training and education of youth." A.I. Averin, [*Basic Military Education in the General Education School*], Moscow, 1973.

[55] *KZ,* May 24, 1972, p. 4.

[56] Ibid. For the time of this meeting the instructors are paid a small per diem of one ruble and thirty kopeks, a quarters allowance of eighty kopeks per day, and the cost of travel to the place of meeting and return.

[57] *Uchitel'skaya gazeta,* October 19, 1971.

[58] *KZ,* May 27, 1971, p. 1. Another writer states that 70 percent of the reserve officers who teach are members of the Party or Komsomol. Ibid., April 28, 1971, p. 2. The two estimates are not as different as they may seem, since relatively few reserve officers would still be members of Komsomol.

[59] *Voyennyye znaniya,* August 1973, pp. 37–40.

[60] *KZ,* September 14, 1971, p. 1.

Some military instructors have taken pleasure in subordinating Soviet secondary-school youths to a strict military regime. This enthusiastic militarization has led to warnings that "the schools should not be converted into a sort of military subunit."[61] The military instructor is appointed and relieved by the educational authorities, but only with the consent of the district military commissariat. It is not surprising that some military instructors go beyond the officially defined training program, since the authorities sometimes specify far-reaching objectives. Thus, the goal of preinduction military training is, according to one military writer, to prepare the inductee "from the first day of his service for competent and decisive action under the conditions of modern battle."[62]

Friction between military training officers and school authorities developed out of the opinion of some military officers that they have "disciplinary rights over students. In their opinion the military training officer is not simply a teacher. He is a commander and, moreover, in military uniform. Therefore, he may not only persuade but also demand, and sometimes employ certain measures of punishment."[63] Special disciplinary rights for military instructors in the schools were, however, firmly rejected by the chief of the preinduction program. "It is our opinion that there is no need to establish additional disciplinary rights for military instructors or for the chiefs of training points."[64]

Although school directors now seem resigned to the increasing role of military training, some resistance is still suggested by occasional complaints of military instructors that the school directors plan the military training classes for the last hours of the day when it is already growing dark and is inconvenient for tactical training and parade drills.[65]

3. The Preinduction Military Training Program

The original programs introduced into the early preinduction training points in the schools and industrial establishments varied considerably according to the ideas of the military instructors, the availability of different types of facilities such as firing ranges, and the ability to procure training materials of various sorts. Although there appears to have been a recommended program, the degree of latitude and the variability in facilities rendered this pretty much a dead letter. Some military instructors developed overly ambitious programs, and these collapsed in the light of a realistic assessment of matériel availability. The attempt of some military instructors to introduce relatively advanced forms of tactical training ran up against the increased time that this took and

[61] *Sovetskiy patriot,* August 16, 1972, p. 3.
[62] Ibid., July 16, 1972, p. 3.
[63] *Voyennyye znaniya,* June 1971, pp 25–26.
[64] *KZ,* August 1971, pp. 27–28.
[65] *Voyennyye znaniya,* June 1971, pp. 25–26.

the distractions imposed on the schools and on the industrial establishments. In any event, the program for preinduction training was reviewed at a high level and "in 1970, the military commissariat, jointly with the organs of public education, the state committees for professional technical education, DOSAAF committees, and civil defense staffs, and with the participation of military instructors from various areas, developed proposals for partially changing the program. The proposals were reviewed by the predraft military training directorate of the USSR Ministry of Defense, jointly with the interested ministries and departments."[66]

Some of the more ambitious aspects of the original program were altered. Thus, all tactical exercises lasting longer than six hours were eliminated from the regular program and reserved for practical training during summer vacations in the field. Similarly, certain ambitious weapons training programs were eliminated, such as gunnery training and the study of the jet-propelled antitank grenade thrower. An additional four hours were allotted for drill—which suggests that the original program had sacrificed basic military training for more technical matters. The new program also emphasized military discipline and a knowledge of military formations. Of the time saved from activities that were reduced, six hours were allotted in the new program for military topographic studies, presumably map reading and related exercises, and an increased amount of time was made available for the study of military regulations. In 1970–71, more than a half million copies of the combined arms regulations were produced for predraft military training. In addition, a first allotment of 300,000 copies of a textbook for preinduction military training was issued in response to demands for central help in providing teaching aids.

The revised training plan called for increased training of military technical specialties. The largest military occupation is that of motor vehicle operator, and a great many schools have vehicle clubs that produce people qualified to fill this job.[67] Twenty-five percent of all training time is now devoted to a technical military specialty. Some instructors resent this and want the time to be given to drill, firing, and tactical training, but *Krasnaya zvezda* insists that military specialty training is essential.[68]

The revised program introduced greater uniformity into military training preinduction programs, but considerable variability still exists.[69] Nonetheless, the core of the training program is now a 140-hour program spread over one

---

[66] Lieutenant General A. Odintsov, Chief of the Predraft Military Training Directorate of the USSR Ministry of Defense, *KZ*, August 1971.

[67] *Sovetskiy patriot*, May 12, 1974, p. 2.

[68] *KZ*, June 9, 1974, p. 2.

[69] Some schools, at their own discretion, change the content of lessons and neglect practical training. No doubt this is in part due to the absence of adequate practical training materials and facilities, but perhaps is due also to the tendency to find classroom instruction much more convenient than larger-scale activities. *Uchitel'skaya gazeta*, December 25, 1971.

and a half and sometimes two academic years. Descriptions of the program vary somewhat but generally run as follows: learning the mission of the armed forces; acquiring a good knowledge of regulations, automatic weapons, light machine guns, and grenades, and practicing the firing of these weapons; and the acquisition of a military technical specialty such as driver, motorcycle operator, radiotelephone operator, or electrician.[70] Another account states that the program includes "the study of the organization, character, and regulations of the Soviet armed forces; tactical, firing, and drill training; and military topography."[71]

The ability to train predraft youth in military specialties is clearly greater in the technical and vocational schools than in the general education schools. In technical schools, military specialties involving electrical engineering, radio electronics, and motor vehicles are stressed. Thus in the 1970–71 training year the Rostov Electrical Engineering Technical School trained not only 154 qualified riflemen and 237 marksmen, but also 90 motorcycle operators, 68 "driver enthusiasts," 166 radio-telegraph operators, and 15 parachutists.[72]

It appears that better organization and the complaints of military instructors who have particularly deplored the lack of rifles, carbines, and light machine guns have made needed equipment more freely available. However, "almost no attention has been given to equipping the training areas used for providing practical instruction to the students: areas for drill training and for preparation for firing and sighting, for the throwing of grenades, and for studying the duties of sentries. Owing to the lack of training areas, classroom exercises have become the principal form of training, and this has served to reduce the quality of military training and the physical hardening of the students."[73]

Some indication of what the program aims at is provided by the description of a predraft training point in an industrial plant that won a banner for outstanding work in predraft training. This training point "contained well-equipped military study groups, classes for military technical training, a parade ground for drill exercises, and a 50-meter firing range for small-arms firing. Its chief is a reserve colonel." This particular training group supplemented its military training activities with various military-patriotic measures, which no doubt also helped it to win the banner that distinguished it.[74]

The preinduction military training program is primarily for young men, but there is also a program for training girls in medical auxiliary work.[75]

The 140 hours of compulsory predraft military training provided in the

[70] *KZ*, March 3, 1972.
[71] *Izvestia*, January 20, 1972.
[72] *Sredneye spetsial'noye obrazovaniye*, April 1972, pp. 13–16.
[73] Ibid.
[74] *Voyennyye znaniya*, July 1971, pp. 32–33.
[75] *Sovetskaya Estoniya*, October 12, 1971, p 1.

school or plant training point are supplemented by summer camps where registered draftees undergo field training.[76] These camps are frequently referred to as "military sports camps," but they are operated on a military basis with the campers divided into squads, platoons, and battalions. Administration of the camp follows military regulations. The authorities prefer that the students bivouac close to a regular military unit and follow the same routines as the troop unit.[77] The program of activities is often organized by the local military commissariat together with DOSAAF committees. The length of the camping period is frequently referred to as seven to eight days, but the revised program described by General Odintsov referred to military camp periods of ten to fifteen days.[78]

It appears that those who resent the interference of military training with plant production and school education would prefer that all predraft military training be moved out of the factories and schools into summer camps. General Odintsov pointed out, however, that "it is our opinion that these camp assemblies pale in comparison with predraft military programs that last from one to one and one-half years. The camp can furnish military knowledge . . . but it is impossible to instill in a young man high moral and psychological qualities . . . in a period of ten to fifteen days. . . . This is why we believe that military athletic camps serve as a supplement and as a crowning stage in the training of youth for service in the armed forces."[79]

How many of the students who complete the 140-hour basic program also attend the military sports camps? In 1970 in one *oblast* 90 percent of the prospective conscripts were said to have attended military sports camps. In a number of other instances the percentages ranged from 70 to 80.[80]

Young men who do not have training points at accessible distances, usually because they live in rural areas, attend camps that last for three to four weeks. Presumably the extension of the predraft program to many rural schools and rural enterprises that was planned for 1972–74 reduced the frequency with which these camps are required. Some camps are organized by the local councils of workers' deputies, with the heads of enterprises and farms directing the actual work. The funds for the camps are provided by educational departments, trade-union committees, enterprises, and rural establishments. DOSAAF generally provides small-bore rifles, cartridges, targets, various

[76] Field training has also been substantially increased by the introduction of military or war games for Soviet youth—Summer Lightning *(Zarnitsa)* for the Young Pioneer age group (ten to fifteen years) and The Eaglet *(Orlenok)* for Komsomol-age youth. These military games and additional military training and indoctrination both below and above the ninth and tenth grades are discussed in chapter III.

[77] *Sovetskiy patriot,* April 4, 1973, p. 2.

[78] *KZ,* August 1971, pp. 27–28.

[79] Ibid.

[80] *KVS,* no. 10, May 1971, pp. 30–34.

teaching aids, and other training materials.[81] Many of the camps have been built with help from units of the Soviet armed forces.[82] Trainees who come from training points where firing ranges and weapons have not been available get their first experience in firing live rounds from automatic weapons and their first experience in military marches at these camps.[83]

Special schools are sometimes established in which rural young men can get their predraft training. In Khabarovsk a DOSAAF naval school provides two months of naval school training for preconscription youth living in the outlying rural areas. These students, who come mostly from farms, timber camps, and other rural establishments, are supposed to receive 50 percent of their average earnings during the period that they are in camp. This money is not always paid by the employer.[84]

4. Military Specialist Training

It is not always easy to distinguish, in DOSAAF accounts, the work the organization does in preinduction military training from its activities in military specialist training that lie outside of the preinduction training program proper. Part of this difficulty is due to the fact that the equipment and courses in technical and vocational schools permit a ready organization of predraft military training centered around skills that have both a military and a civilian vocational significance. Since about half of the secondary-school students in the Soviet Union attend schools of a vocational and technical character, it is apparent that a substantial number of Soviet draft-age youth are in educational institutions where the predraft training prgram can be organized around military technical specialties. The same possibility may soon apply to students in the general secondary-education schools, since the present tendency in Soviet educational policy is "to develop and perfect the general-education school as a labor and polytechnical school."[85]

There are military specialties that are not always easy to teach within the framework of a general or special secondary school. It is particularly these specialties that DOSAAF teaches in its own special schools and in its various military and military sports clubs.

Typical of this form of specialist training are the DOSAAF aviation clubs and schools, which have had a major responsibility for seeing to it that the Soviet Union has led for so many years in aviation-type sports. In 1971 the

[81] *Sovetskiy patriot,* December 20, 1970.
[82] *KZ,* May 27, 1972, p. 1.
[83] *Sredneye spetsial'noye obrazovaniye,* April 1972, pp. 13–16.
[84] *Sovetskiy patriot,* December 16, 1970, p. 3.
[85] *Pravda,* June 25, 1972, p. 1.

Soviet Union held 320 out of 771 world records registered with the International Aviation Federation.[86] The Soviet all-union Federation of Aviation Sports noted that in 1971 approximately 66,000 different sports competitions had been held during the preceding four years. More than one million persons participated, including "hundreds of thousands of pilots, parachutists, helicopter operators, glider pilots, and builders of model airplanes."[87] That DOSAAF aviation clubs operate on a fairly high level was indicated in 1971 when the clubs began to switch from piston aircraft to jets. In the DOSAAF air clubs, members first study the theory of flight and aviation equipment and then learn to fly sport aircraft. In 1971 many clubs acquired L-29 jet training planes.[88] In the same year each of the second-year members of DOSAAF aviation clubs flew more than ten hours in trainers.[89]

DOSAAF clubs have made a specialty of parachute jumping, although this is not confined entirely to specialist training and has been adopted as a part of instruction in some general preinduction training points. Thus, an industrial plant in Vilna reported that in the course of preinduction military training twenty-six persons were trained as parachutists and nineteen as aqualung swimmers, although the great majority (1,070) received training as riflemen.[90]

Some military commissariats classify future conscripts, when they register, by the type of military service they are likely to be sent to when they are later inducted. This facilitates preinduction specialist training. In the time between registration and induction, a number of youths are given training at DOSAAF training points in the military specialty indicated by the military commissariat.[91]

DOSAAF specialist training not only prepares youth for military service but also provides technically trained persons for the civilian economy. Some skills cannot be allocated to one or the other of the two sectors, since both could benefit from them. DOSAAF claims to have trained, between 1965 and 1970, 8 million truck drivers, bulldozer operators, radio operators, skin divers, and other specialists.[92] Between 1966 and 1973, the number of participants in military, technical, and motorized forms of competition increased from .9 to 3.5 million.[93] In 1972 in the Ukraine 140,000 persons received training in the operation of motor vehicles and motorcycles.[94] According to a DOSAAF report, 92 percent of all trainees now pass examinations of the state motor

[86] *KVS,* no. 14, July 1971, pp. 28–33.
[87] *Kryl'ya rodiny,* July 1971, pp. 2–3.
[88] Ibid., August 1971, pp. 2–3.
[89] Ibid., July 1971, pp. 8–9.
[90] *KZ,* October 22, 1971, p. 2.
[91] *Smena,* November 1973, pp. 16–19.
[92] *Voyenno-istoricheskiy zhurnal,* July 1971, pp. 96–100.
[93] *Sovetskiy patriot,* October 3, 1973, p. 1.
[94] *Za rulem,* February 1973, pp. 4–5.

vehicle inspectorate on the first try, whereas in 1966 this figure was only 77 percent.[95]

DOSAAF specialist training received a new impetus from the 1967 Law of Universal Military Training. By 1971, one out of every four men inducted into military service had acquired a military specialty. By 1973 this had increased to one inductee in three.[96] In addition, about 70 percent of all draftees now acquire some degree of military technical specialization in their regular preinduction military training.[97]

5. Military-Patriotic Education

Predraft training is not only intended to provide young people with military skills. It also aims to "ease entry into an unaccustomed army situation and make it possible to subordinate oneself more rapidly to a high level of discipline."[98] It should contribute to "preparing students psychologically and physically for service in the armed forces."[99]

Entry into officer candidate schools is open to students of predraft age. Predraft training thus comes at an opportune time, when students are preoccupied both with the question of career choices and with the early prospect of induction. Given the Soviet need for junior officers (see chapter I), the predraft program as a center for cadet recruitment is an important asset. Military writers indicate that where secondary schools have developed good predraft military training programs, entrance into military cadet schools has substantially increased. "Thus in Leningrad among all graduates of secondary schools in which military training was initiated in 1968, one out of four entered a military school in 1969."[100] In 1968 in Voronezhskaya Oblast only 830 middle school graduates applied for admission to a military institute as compared with more than 4,000 applicants in 1973. And in Moldavskaya SSR applicants increased from 880 in 1970 to 2,500 in 1973. These increases are attributed to the preinduction training program. "The same situation more or less obtains in other republics and *oblasts.*"[101]

Krasnaya zvezda points out that military instructors can arrange, especially during vacation periods, for military cadets to engage the secondary students in "lively but relaxing conversations" that will help the pupils of the older classes to select the profession of officer. In some schools "future officer

---

[95] *Voyennyye znaniya,* October 1971, pp. 1–3.

[96] *KZ,* April 3, 1974, p. 1, and April 25, 1974, p. 3.

[97] *KVS,* no. 16, August 1972, pp. 9–16.

[98] *Voyennyye znaniya,* no. 2, 1971, pp. 1–3.

[99] Ibid., October 1971, p. 9.

[100] *KZ,* April 28, 1971, p. 2.

[101] *KZ,* December 10, 1974, p. 2. See also p. 19 above.

clubs" are organized with the aim of giving a clearer picture of the officer profession.[102]

6. Resistance

According to the Law of Universal Military Training the leaders of enterprises and educational institutions are required to assure that draft-age persons under their control receive appropriate predraft military training. Their cooperation and their zeal are, therefore, of prime importance in determining the effectiveness of the whole system of preinduction training. It is apparent from the Soviet literature that in many places considerable resistance was offered to the program, and to a lesser extent still is, especially by the directors of enterprises who "did not understand their responsibilities"—or, probably, understood them only too well.[103] Even in 1972 there were still enterprises "where everyone is waiting for someone else to organize predraft military training."[104]

Complaints were quite regular, especially in the earlier period, that directors of enterprises were not making sufficient space available in their plants or were not arranging for other locations in which training could be conducted. Where space was allocated, it often was of little use, since facilities were not provided for cleaning it up or making it suitable for military training purposes. DOSAAF complains bitterly of the failure of many plant directors to provide the necessary equipment and to supervise the selection of instructors.

The directors of educational institutions seemed to be less able to resist the pressure to provide training facilities. DOSAAF committee reports suggest a greater compliance on their part, perhaps because they are generally under closer bureaucratic supervision than plant directors. In addition, school principals may have less reason to oppose the introduction of military training, since their "production schedules" and their incomes are not as sensitive to the use of resources for military training purposes as are those of the managers of an industrial plant.

Farm leaders seem to evade their responsibilities quite as much as urban industrial plant directors. They often fail to provide transport for the young people to areas where military exercises are to be conducted. Further, no serious attempt is made to ensure attendance.[105]

The cooperation of persons not directly involved in DOSAAF preinduction military training is also not all that is desired. Thus DOSAAF patriotic films are sent to industrial plant movie halls, but it seems that the plant movie

---

[102] Ibid., September 14, 1971, p. 1, and *Kazakhstanskaya pravda,* February 18, 1971, pp. 2–3. For more on the military-patriotic education of youth, see chapter III, pp. 72–74.

[103] *Leningradskaya pravda,* August 25, 1971, p. 2.

[104] *KZ,* March 3, 1972, p. 2.

[105] *Voyennyye znaniya,* July 1971, pp. 32–33.

clubs avoid showing these films and simply "ship them off to some rural settlement where they are never heard from again."[106]

Although the directors of plants and rural enterprises now seem to cooperate more effectively, even if unwillingly, perhaps because of the increased initiative of the military commissariats in attending to the selection of reserve officers as instructors, they still express a distaste for the responsibility that has been forced upon them. The proposal to have predraft training shifted to summer camps (see p. 54 above) was an attempt on the part of factory directors and perhaps some educational leaders to separate predraft training from civilian institutions. Some plant directors evade their responsibilities by shipping their draft-age youth to unified training points that are intended to train draftees who work in enterprises too small to have their own predraft program. Quite sizable plants have adopted this procedure "even though a sufficient number of draft-age youths are available" in their own plants.[107]

The enterprise directors are prepared to make financial sacrifices if they can be relieved of the responsibility for the program. The director of one enterprise protests: "We are civilians, we have our plan to follow. Our aim is to fulfill this plan. We are criticized if we do not create a training point and we are penalized if we do not fulfill our plan. Let our military comrades organize the exercises. We will furnish the money and facilities."[108] Another enterprise director states: "Predraft military training is a military matter. Thus, the military commissariat should be responsible for the training of draft-age and predraft-age youths."[109] *Krasnaya zvezda,* however, firmly points out that the Law of Universal Military Service says that directors of plants and schools will be held responsible for the training of persons in their organizations. Article 17 of the law states that predraft training in enterprises and schools is to be accomplished "without disruption of production or studies." Some managers have attempted to interpret this article as requiring them to curtail or postpone predraft training since it would "disrupt" their work.[110]

The authorities are persistent in bringing pressure to bear for program fulfillment. What seems to be a tighter check on preinduction programs is indicated by the following statement: "A number of ministries and departments have still not introduced the duties of inspectors of basic military training (the Ministry of Agriculture USSR, the Ministry of Health Protection USSR)."[111] This presumably refers to youths working in establishments under the direction of these ministries. Control is also exercised by an elaborate

---

[106] *Sovetskiy patriot,* July 28, 1971, p. 2.
[107] *KZ,* March 3, 1972, p. 2.
[108] Ibid.
[109] Ibid.
[110] Ibid., October 10, 1973, p. 2.
[111] *Sovetskiy patriot,* July 16, 1972.

reporting system: "A year or two ago we literally could not catch our breath from the endless checks and reports. . . . Even now there are many of them. I would find it hard to say whether they cause greater benefit or harm."[112]

C. EVALUATION

Although Soviet discussions of the predraft training program comment frequently and candidly on the resistance of plant directors, very little appears concerning the responses of the young trainees themselves. It appears that attendance at DOSAAF clubs tends to drop off sharply when spring comes and the first warm days appear. "Club leaders have to take measures to see that students do not cut classes. They must maintain close contact with military commissariats, enterprises, and parents."[113] DOSAAF has urged its local committees to organize parents' meetings in order to raise the attendance of trainees at classes.[114] A DOSAAF radio club that was reprimanded for its poor work had an attendance of fifteen to twenty out of a group of thirty-five. A large number of the club's students failed to complete their courses.[115]

Young people have their own preferences as to what they want to learn at the clubs and in preinduction training, and these preferences do not always correspond with military priorities. Thus many of the youth try to avoid joining radio clubs and say they want to join a motor vehicle or motorcycle club instead.[116] Discussions concerning the right of military instructors to impose military discipline (see p. 51 above) suggest some restiveness among the students, but this is far from clear.

A study carried out among inductees to get their opinions on what they lacked most in their predraft military training revealed that familiarization with nuclear weapons was well in the lead. This is not easy to interpret. Perhaps inductees found themselves required to take part in nuclear tactical exercises that they failed to understand, or perhaps nuclear weapons are ignored in some predraft training centers and yet, because of their dramatic qualities, attract student attention. Predraft trainees do receive civil-defense training, more in fact than their military instructors would like.[117] Perhaps, too, an interest in assignment to the high-prestige rocket forces motivates this desire to learn more about nuclear weapons. On the whole, the students did not indicate a need for additional weapons training. Their preferences were largely along the lines of making sports a requirement for everyone, conduct-

[112] Ibid., April 4, 1973, p. 2.
[113] *KZ*, May 27, 1971, p. 4.
[114] *Voyennyye znaniya*, February 1972, pp. 40–41.
[115] *Sovetskiy patriot*, April 26, 1972, p. 3.
[116] *KZ*, May 27, 1971, p. 4.
[117] *Sovetskiy patriot*, April 4, 1973, p. 2. See also *Voyennyye znaniya*, June 1972, pp. 14–15.

ing military job orientation, learning how to write summaries of lectures, and getting more instruction in physics, mathematics, radio, and electronics.[118] However, another writer states that inductees do complain of insufficient firing of weapons, especially the automatic rifle.[119]

The failure to treat equipment with the care necessary to keep it in proper maintenance is an old complaint in all branches of the Soviet economy. DOSAAF clubs and training centers do not escape this problem, either. An article on DOSAAF naval clubs that criticizes the failure to service expensive equipment and its resultant breakdown is typical. Equipment so lost is then written off with no further accountability for it. It is subject to cannibalization and can be transferred to individuals or other organizations. Naval clubs, especially, have expensive equipment, such as decompression chambers, many of which, however, do not function because of technical failure. Generally the chiefs of naval DOSAAF schools and clubs simply wait for the end of a certain operating period and write them off as scrap metal. Similarly, training vessels are not painted and rust is not removed. Efforts are made at the earliest opportunity to write off the yawls instead of repairing them. Property stored in storehouses is organized poorly and some of it is just stored in heaps without tags.[120] Similarly, in classrooms where the use and repair of motors are taught, the motors often are not in operating order and the room is so filled with exhaust gases that it is impossible to work.[121] Thus the inefficient use and care of equipment exacerbates a problem already created by the scarcity of some types of matériel required for the training classes.

Local DOSAAF committees are not always responsive to the priorities of higher DOSAAF committees, which are more sensitive to the choices made by military authorities. When the editors of Kryl'ya rodiny received a letter complaining that there were no facilities for parachute jumping in Zhitomir, the editor sent an investigator. The reason that the local DOSAAF committee doesn't organize this important type of military sport is that it just "doesn't want to be bothered."[122]

Complaints are frequently made that even when officially required activities are pursued they are dealt with in so lackadaisical a fashion that very little is accomplished. Speaking of military training in a summer camp, one critic remarks that "these were rather mass cultural measures in the fresh air rather than training."[123] Another critic, referring to student training maneuvers in the field carried out with weapons that had no live cartridges, asks, "How can he [the student] possibly be a future soldier if he has not carried a combat rifle?"[124]

[118] Sovetskaya pedagogika, February 1972, pp. 60–63.
[119] KZ, April 18, 1972, p. 4.
[120] Voyennyye znaniya, October 1971, pp. 42–43.
[121] Sovetskiy patriot, May 5, 1971, p. 3.
[122] Kryl'ya rodiny, January 1971, p. 27.
[123] Sovetskaya Estoniya, July 9, 1971, p. 1.
[124] Uchitel'skaya gazeta, December 25, 1971.

Impressive statistics are sometimes cited concerning the number of young people who have acquired the skill of radio operator, parachutist, or rifleman, or who have acquired the Ready-to-Defend-the-Motherland Badge, which involves passing certain physical and sports norms. Only occasionally does one find a reference to what one suspects is an important element in interpreting these statistics. One writer, with unusual candor, condemns "the pursuit of numbers, the striving to define impact in terms of the number of lessons or activities conducted without regard to effectiveness."[125] Similarly, an army captain complains that young men possessing the Ready-to-Defend-the-Motherland Badge often arrive in the army and navy with capabilities that are not up to the implications of the badge. "The reason for this is not hard to find." One chairman of a physical culture council at a large plant, who certified the physical training of preinductees, had them go out to a stadium and go through some of the less difficult tests and then certified them. "These certifications were then continuously signed by people higher up in various echelons."[126] As a result of this disclosure, DOSAAF activists were given increased responsibility for physical training for the badge-holders, thereby relieving plant personnel of responsibility for overseeing this activity. The same lack of "quality control" is frequently mentioned with respect to training in summer camps.[127] Speaking of the figures from a certain *oblast* [region] on those who passed the Prepared for Labor and Defense "complex," *Krasnaya zvezda* remarks: "In the *oblast* commissariat few people believe these figures, even though they have been refined to an accuracy of one-tenth of a point." At the *oblast* championship marksmanship contest only fifteen of forty-two contestants passed the norm, although only those expected to do so were sent.[128] An officer complains that two graduates of a DOSAAF motor vehicle club received in his unit experienced great difficulty when required to adjust the brakes of an army vehicle. One, who had graduated with a grade of "outstanding," was unable to regulate the idling of an engine. Two other inductees who had earned the Ready-to-Defend-the-Motherland Badge were unable to pull themselves up on the horizontal bar even once. An inductee who had received a grade of "outstanding" at a radio club was able to become a third-class radio-telegraph operator only toward the end of his two-year period of service.[129] A naval officer who, on the whole, finds the training in a DOSAAF naval club satisfactory, nonetheless deplores the poor administrative arrangements whereby trainees complete their training about five or six months before induction and consequently are likely to lose their theoretical knowledge and practical apti-

[125] *Bakinskiy rabochiy,* November 2, 1971, pp. 2–5.
[126] *KZ,* August 20, 1971, p. 4.
[127] *Voyennyye znaniya,* July 1971, pp. 32–33.
[128] *KZ,* March 22, 1974, p. 4.
[129] Ibid., June 18, 1972, p. 2.

tudes in the interim, a concern that, if justified, suggests that this training is not particularly rigorous.[130]

Despite the evident difficulties of a program requiring the cooperation of thousands of persons whose efficiency and good will can hardly be counted on, it would be a mistake to suppose that the predraft training program in the Soviet Union is entirely ineffective. There are some indications that military personnel now have greater confidence in draftees with preinduction training than they formerly possessed. A colonel in a radar regiment writes that formerly he and his colleagues felt that the best thing to do with the inductees who came from preinduction training was to treat them as schoolboys and give them a complete course in every subject. Now, however, they feel that recruits are really coming in with useful knowledge and that it would be a waste of time to start them from scratch. Indeed, many of the young men have mastered the principles of radar in preinduction training and "come to us with training on a par with that of third-class specialists."[131] A mortar specialist reports that a mortarman rating is earned faster by young soldiers who, prior to induction, received training in DOSAAF organizations. A major general affirms that the new recruits who come to him "enter operations very quickly and can be trusted with complicated equipment during their first months of service" because of their training prior to entering the army.[132] A commander of a PVO (air defense) unit states that DOSAAF training has not yet reached its full potential, but he and his colleagues are quite happy with the program in their *oblast.* He refers to cases in his unit where, after appropriate verification and testing, new men were put on the line only a week after their arrival. His inspection showed that indeed these electricians and radio and radar operators were all performing adequately, although they had just arrived at the unit.[133] Despite the dissatisfaction that commanders experience with some graduates of DOSAAF radio clubs, other graduates rapidly become first-class specialists, "aces of the atmosphere."[134] Experience is said to show that youths from DOSAAF academic organizations complete their basic training faster and carry out their military duties more efficiently.[135] A Soviet study of one thousand inductees showed that among those with preinduction training 30 percent received an overall evaluation of "outstanding," whereas among those without preinduction training only 20 percent received this grade.[136] This difference

---

[130] *Voyennyye znaniya,* February 1972, pp. 40–41.
[131] *KZ,* February 3, 1971, p. 2.
[132] *Za rulem,* November 1971, pp. 4–5.
[133] *Pravda Ukrainy,* November 4, 1971, p. 4.
[134] *KZ,* June 18, 1972, p. 2.
[135] *Kommunistas,* Vilnius, no. 4, April 1972, pp. 31–38.
[136] *KZ,* April 18, 1972, p. 4.

might, of course, be due to differences between inductees who get and do not get predraft training, rather than to the training itself.

One way to judge the value of DOSAAF specialist and preinduction training is to try to do so as much as possible on the basis of more or less indisputable facts, rather than of judgments made by persons whose motives are not always clear. Thus, if one examines DOSAAF training in the field of parachute jumping, it is apparent that no matter how inefficient the program may be, the existence of large numbers of trainees who have taken parachute jumps prior to induction clearly accelerates training activity in airborne and paratroop units. Again, although it is difficult to know how adequate the theoretical and practical training of DOSAAF flying clubs and naval clubs are, nonetheless a substantial number of DOSAAF club members do fly airplanes, navigate small boats, and manipulate other forms of maritime equipment. That a great deal of Soviet industrial underwater diving and repair work is done by DOSAAF trainees on a commercial basis clearly indicates that DOSAAF training in this area provides the navy with specialists who are ready to undertake work as soon as they enter the naval forces. During the Yug maneuvers that began on June 12, 1971, a paratroop lieutenant colonel complained that when the maneuvers began the majority of the paratroopers involved were young men *who had been inducted in May.* He added, with great disappointment, that half of them had never jumped before. Evidently this is viewed as an inadequate result of preinduction training, but to most military forces in the world it would seem extraordinary for a paratroop unit to receive inductees of whom half had already made jumps.[137] Again, even if a DOSAAF auto club graduate cannot adjust the brakes of his military vehicle or regulate the idling of his motor, the ability to drive is itself an important accomplishment that the inductee brings to the armed forces in a country where this accomplishment cannot be taken for granted, as it is in the United States. And it may be true that few DOSAAF radio specialists are proficient on the telegraph key, but this is not the same as having to train such persons from scratch. In any event, in 1972 every fourth man called to active military service possessed one of the specialties needed by the army—he was, for example, a vehicle operator, motorcycle signalman, telegrapher, radio repairman, diesel mechanic, parachutist, or scuba diver—[138] and two years later every third man inducted was said to have a military specialty acquired in DOSAAF schools.[139]

The effectiveness of general (that is, nonspecialist) training is probably increasing simply because its scope has become more modest. Parade-ground drill, study of the military regulations, mounting of the guard, and inspection require little equipment and can readily be taught even in the more backward

[137] Ibid., June 27, 1971, p. 2.
[138] *Kommunistas,* Vilnius, no. 4, April 1972, pp. 31–38.
[139] *KZ,* April 3, 1974, p. 1, and April 25, 1974, p. 3.

training points. These skills, together with firing on the range and a certain amount of map work, will probably become, as they already are at many training points, an acceptable minimum for those predraft trainees not taking military specialist courses.

Is it possible to give a more compact and, perhaps, precise evaluation of the Soviet predraft military training program than the discursive account of their negative and positive features provided in the foregoing pages? Attempts at greater precision risk going too far beyond the available evidence. Nonetheless, even an order-of-magnitude estimate can be helpful. A rough estimate, based on imperfect information, of the annual training value of the general and specialist predraft programs suggests that they are equivalent to approximately one million man-months of basic training and .9 million man-months of specialist training in the Soviet forces. A very rough estimate of the annual saving to the Soviet military budget is approximately one-quarter of a billion rubles.

These rough estimates are arrived at as follows. Assuming that about 1.3 million youths are inducted annually and that 80 percent have received predraft training, a little more than one million inductees will have received preinduction military training.[140] This training is still highly variable in different schools and establishments, but we take its value, together with summer camp periods and the Orlenok military games (see chapter III,A), to be equivalent, on the average, to one month of basic training in the military. This, then, provides approximately one million man-months of basic training. We also take one-third of the inductees as having had training in a military specialty in DOSAAF schools and clubs. We take this training to be equivalent on the average to two months of third-class specialist training in the forces.[141] This provides approximately 700,000 man-months of specialist training annually. In addition, a substantial number of the remaining inductees, perhaps about one-half, who do not take specialist DOSAAF courses, get some specialist training in their regular preinduction basic training centers. This is particularly true of those who attend technical schools. We add 200,000 more man-

---

[140] Given both current DOSAAF claims and the rapid expansion of the program planned for the school year 1973–74, it is likely that this 80 percent rate, if not already reached, will shortly be attained, and if already reached, will shortly be surpassed. Note that a figure of 80 percent of Soviet inductees having had preinduction training is not in any way inconsistent with a substantially smaller percent of Soviet draft-age youth having had predraft military training. Little more than half of Soviet youths are inducted, and the draft boards are more likely to select those with predraft training.

[141] In the Soviet military it takes six months to produce a third-class specialist and another six months to move to each higher level in the same specialty. *Bloknot agitatora,* May 1971, pp. 21–23. Our estimate thus equates the average level of skills of a DOSAAF specialist when he arrives in the armed forces at "one-third" of the level of a third-class specialist. Since DOSAAF claims that its specialist schools graduate third-class specialists, our assumption is conservative, especially since a certain undetermined number of graduates of advanced DOSAAF schools achieve second- and first-class specialist ratings.

months for this group, bringing us to .9 million man-months of specialist training.

Taking into account the negligible pay of Soviet recruits, the spartan living standards of young soldiers, and the pay scale of the officers and NCOs who train them, as a crude estimate we might take basic training costs to be about 70 rubles a month and specialist training costs at the third-class level to be about 200 rubles per month. This gives us approximately a quarter of a billion rubles saved to the armed forces budget. It is more likely that this is too low rather than too high an estimate. By way of comparison, West German forces estimated in 1971 that a first-year recruit cost 900 German Marks (DM) per month (roughly $300 at 1971 exchange rates), of which 400 DM (roughly $135 at 1971 exchange rates) is accounted for by pay.[142] The annual cost of a French recruit in 1973 was 4,307 francs (roughly $860) of which 44 percent went for food, 34 percent for pay, and 7 percent for training and transport.[143]

The compulsory preinduction military training program has advantages for the Soviet military other than preparing conscripts for service in the forces, and these should be taken into account even though their ruble value can hardly be estimated: (1) The predraft training points have become valuable recruiting centers for military officer cadet academies and in addition save some of the training costs of these institutions. (2) The use of reserve officers as instructors provides a sizable number of reserve officers with continuing military activity while in a civilian status. (3) Predraft training provides basic military training for the roughly 50 percent of Soviet youth that is not called up. This is an important contribution to the Soviet interest in "a nation in arms" (see chapter III). (4) The preinduction program is, in part, intended to inculcate military-patriotic sentiments and Communist Party discipline and values in the youth population. Political indoctrination is an important part of military training in the Soviet forces, and the predraft and associated patriotic programs prepare youth in the political creeds appropriate to a Soviet serviceman.

Any evaluation of Soviet predraft training programs should take into account their future prospects. It is clear from the Soviet sources that the programs are expanding in terms of the number of predraft youth that are reached and that these programs are improving with respect to effectiveness. Whatever military worth is accorded to the programs currently, it must almost

---

[142] Calculated from data in *Wehrgerechtigkeit in der Bundesrepublik Deutschland,* Wehrstruktur-Kommission der Bundesregierung, Bonn, 1971, p. 79. In 1973, monthly personnel costs were for conscripts 972 DM, for NCOs 1,855 DM, and for officers 3,025 DM. *The Security of the Federal Republic of Germany and the Development of the Federal Armed Forces,* Federal Ministry of Defense, Bonn, 1974, p. 66.

[143] *Le Monde,* July 2, 1974. In 1975 the pay of a French conscript was increased from sixty cents a day to $1.80. *Time,* March 17, 1975, p. 47.

certainly be assumed that this will increase in the coming years. There is no evidence of top-level political or military disillusionment with the program. Indeed, all the measures taken in the last year or two and projected for the future indicate a top-level intent to expand and rationalize the programs. It is evident now that the unwillingness in 1967–68 to commit large resources to the new program and to centralize direction, and the willingness to tolerate the most varied degrees of conformity and progress were in no way an indication that the program was not fully supported at top Soviet levels. These apparently haphazard procedures and the uncertain progress of the program were rather the result of Soviet administrative preferences in initiating mass programs. A similar form of administrative behavior and a similar program development can be traced in another mass program of military importance, the Soviet civil defense program. The significance of these administrative practices is discussed more fully in chapter IX.

Chapter III

A Nation in Arms

Soviet military manpower policy does not content itself with the combined advantages of a volunteer career army and compulsory military service. A third level of military preparation has become increasingly important in the Soviet Union—mass military defense. We have seen that given the present Soviet force size, only about 50 percent of the Soviet eighteen-year-old male cohort is inducted. The half that is not inducted does not escape military training. Most youths in the Soviet Union participate from an early age in various forms of military training and military exercises, in mass defense activities such as civil defense, in various military patriotic assemblies, marches, and rallies, and in physical training programs with direct military applications. A large part of the adult population is also involved in mass defense work, especially as members of civil defense detachments. All of these measures taken together show a steadily increasing drift in the Soviet Union toward the realization, psychologically and physically, of "a nation in arms."

In addition to preinduction training in the ninth and tenth grades of Soviet secondary schools, the authorities have managed to introduce a fair amount of military training in levels both below and above these grades. In higher schools and technical institutes, the student has an opportunity to take what is in effect an ROTC course leading to reserve officer status. However, additional steps have been taken to increase the military knowledge of higher education students, whether they take the reserve officer training program or not. "The role of military training in higher school faculties must be upgraded."[1]

In some higher education institutions, courses with titles like "History of Wars and the Art of War" were introduced during the 1970–71 academic year. Efforts were made not only to turn these courses into a form of military-patriotic education, but also to utilize them to provide military training. The historical journal *Voyenno-istoricheskiy zhurnal* points out that in order to understand military history it is necessary to know some of the elements of military science. The department of military history in at least one higher institute planned to have its courses preceded by a study of the fundamentals of tactical training and the terminology of Soviet military art. In some higher educational establishments, classes are divided into training platoons. The journal points out that lectures overloaded with detailed factual accounts of historical events and that numbers indicating the sizes of forces and casualty figures are not very interesting to students. On the other hand, the study of combat operations, descriptions of methods used to achieve victory, and accounts of heroism encourage aspirations among the students to increase their knowledge.[2]

A. *ZARNITSA* AND *ORLENOK*

DOSAAF and the Soviet authorities have introduced military training and military indoctrination not only upward into the higher schools but also downward below the ninth and tenth grades. These younger age groups receive military training and military indoctrination not stipulated by the Law of Universal Military Service. We find, for instance, an article on DOSAAF organizations in the schools that affirms that "many examples could be cited of how, during their free time, students are able to use the facilities of DOSAAF primary and training organizations and sports technical clubs to study their equipment and small arms, and to learn how to fire accurately and to operate motorcycles. . . . Improvements are constantly being introduced into the methods for conducting mass defense work with students *in the fourth through seventh grades.* They are attracted more to participating in military games and passing the norm for the badges 'young riflemen,' 'marksmen,' 'young radio enthusiasts,' and 'young sailors.' "[3] (Emphasis added.)

[1] *Sovetskaya Estoniya,* July 5, 1972, p. 3.
[2] *Voyenno-istoricheskiy zhurnal,* no. 10, October 1971, pp. 94–97.
[3] *Sovetskiy patriot,* October 27, 1971, p. 2.

Military training of children in the ages preceding their compulsory pre-draft military education is not left to individual impulses. Sixteen million Young Pioneers (ages ten to fifteen), under the direction of Marshal I. K. Bagrmayan, participate each year at summer camps in the military game Summer Lightning (*Zarnitsa*).[4] Here the children are introduced to the elements of military discipline, guard duty, military regulations, civil defense, and maneuvers in formation. The All-Union Summer Lightning game has acquired a "mass character" and is now "one of the most important forms of military-patriotic indoctrination of youth."[5] Patron army and navy units often provide leadership and facilities for Summer Lightning military exercises. In the Vladivostok area detachments of Young Pioneers participated in assault landings and in the repulse of a naval assault force. At the end of the exercise, 6,500 Young Pioneers from fifty detachments passed in ceremonial review before a vice admiral.[6]

Summer Lightning is the "little sister" of a new military game for youth. "The first year of the All-Union Komsomol military sports game Eaglet (*Orlenok*) is coming to a close. Eaglet is a continuation of the Young Pioneer game Summer Lightning. In Summer Lightning the children only begin to familiarize themselves with 'army' subjects, while in Eaglet they seriously study military regulations and familiarize themselves more thoroughly with army life."[7]

Major General of Aviation and cosmonaut G. T. Beregovoy, chief of the Eaglet game, commenting on a visit to an Eaglet camp, remarks, "Bravery, steadfastness, and the ability to overcome difficulties cannot be taught under hothouse conditions. . . . We were soon convinced that [the camp] is run in an almost army fashion."[8] The tendency to refer to Eaglet in terms of a summer-camp military exercise tends to overlook that Eaglet participants are trained throughout the year for the final tactical exercises and are members of continuing Eaglet military units.[9] Thus, their affiliation with a military formation continues throughout the year. The order of the day for Eaglets issued by General Beregovoy on August 28, 1973, commanded the secondary school students to organize elections of staff, to create subunits in the highest two grades of the schools, and to appoint platoon leaders from among former participants in Summer Lightning.[10] Eaglet headquarters personnel are ordered to hold meetings with their consultants and counselors (military instructors, reserve soldiers, etc.) and to establish permanent sponsorship over de-

[4] Ibid., November 29, 1972, p. 2.
[5] Marshal A. A. Grechko in *Molodaya gvardiya*, February 1972, pp. 13–14.
[6] *Voyennyye znaniya*, October 1971, p. 9.
[7] *Komsomol'skaya pravda*, February 13, 1973, p. 1.
[8] *Voyennyye znaniya*, September 1972, pp. 14–15.
[9] Ibid. See also *Komsomol'skaya pravda*, February 13, 1973, p. 1.
[10] *Sovetskiy patriot*, August 29, 1973, p. 1.

tachments of the Summer Lightning game.[11] According to General Beregovoy, in addition to studying Soviet armed forces regulations, Eaglets are trained in sentry duty, repelling an attack, grenade-throwing, infiltration, dealing with contamination, map and compass work, firing the carbine and the machine carbine, and civil defense.

The Komsomol, whose membership includes about 75 percent of Soviet youth over fifteen, runs Eaglet with the active assistance of reserve officers, military units that adopt Eaglet detachments, and the Ministry of Defense. Eaglet, however, is not confined to Komsomol members. The participants in Eaglet "are Komsomol members and the students of the senior classes in secondary schools, vocational and technical training establishments, and technical schools, in addition to our working youth. Young people's clubs and military and technical associations also take part."[12]

It is apparent, then, that discussions of Soviet premilitary training that concentrate on the ninth and tenth grades of the secondary schools, as suggested by the Law of Universal Military Service, tend to overlook the substantial amount of military training that goes on in both younger and older age groups. Indeed, this extension of training in military discipline and preparedness, as we shall see shortly (pp. 79–81 below), has now been carried down to the second grade.

The various Soviet predraft military programs are associated with intensive military-patriotic education of students. At an important all-union conference held in Vladivostok, the military-patriotic education of students, "one of the most important elements in the entire system of Communist education," was defined as embracing the ideological and moral-political education of students and their physical, military-technical, and predraft military training. The conference emphasized the need for a purposeful program for all students from the "first through the tenth grade to defend the homeland."[13]

The population of border areas, particularly the school population, has been trained to be especially alert and to operate as the "combat friends" of the Soviet border troops. "All an unidentified person has to do is to appear in the border area and the border guardsmen learn of him from their combat friends. . . . The high political vigilance of the local population is the result of painstaking indoctrination."[14] As Soviet concern with military preparedness

[11] Ibid.

[12] *Voyennyye znaniya,* September 1972, pp. 14–15.

[13] *Narodnoye obrazovaniye,* January 1972, pp. 111–114. "It was by no means an accident that Vladivostok was chosen as the site for the . . . All-Union . . . conference. The maritime krai is a legendary land. . . . "

[14] *KZ,* July 15, 1972, p. 2.

has grown, it has become the duty not only of the military forces but of the entire nation to attain a state of combat readiness.

The process of developing military-patriotic fervor involves visits by students to "combat glory museums," to "hero cities," and to various battle sites. The Young Friends of the Soviet Army, the Red Pathfinders; clubs of young aviators, artillery men, sailors, and tankers; military sports games, military "glory evenings," and meetings with heroes of the Revolution and of World War II—"all this helps to create high patriotic feelings."[15]

The Znaniye Society carries on lectures and meetings popularizing military knowledge among young people. The Society reports that in 1970 in the Moscow region alone it gave 10,000 lectures to conscript and preconscript youths and held 12,000 discussions and lessons on "courage." The Leningrad branch outdid the Moscow branch by organizing more than 15,000 lectures. In Archangel in 1970 the organization conducted 6,000 lectures, reports, and discussions and held 1,200 meetings with war veterans.[16] Similarly, the Komsomol Central Committee and the Committee of Soviet War Veterans have organized huge patriotic rallies. At the first rally in Brest 1.5 million people participated in a tour of military sites. A second rally was held in Moscow with 10 million participants, a third in Leningrad with 15 million, and a fourth in Kiev with 22 million participants. "The last tour of young men and women to places of combat glory was concentrated in 330 museums and 1,200 rooms and corners of glory." Commemorative tablets were set up when the names of more than 35,000 "unknown heroes" were discovered.[17] Soviet statistics in these matters are best interpreted as representing administrative pressure and should not be taken too literally.

Schoolchildren are encouraged to participate in the creation of gardens near common graves of World War II, the creation of monuments to military heroes, and the erection of memorial plaques.[18] In November 1973 an all-union conference on military-patriotic education of schoolchildren was held in the Moscow Pioneer and Schoolchildren's Palace. This conference was attended by "leaders in the education ministries and representatives of the USSR Ministry of Defense, DOSAAF, and the Academy of Pedagogical Sciences."[19]

The fifty-fifth anniversary of the Soviet armed forces became the occasion

[15] *Izvestia,* January 20, 1972, p. 5, and *Kazakhstanskaya pravda,* February 18, 1971, pp. 2–3. *KZ* describes a school visit by a group of officers, including generals, senior officers, and heroes of the Soviet Union, all in uniform and with many medals on their chests. "These visitors told of the courage of Soviet fighting men so that the children might be men of the same type and model their lives after these heroes. The children spent the entire forty-five minutes of one class period with these front-line soldiers." Ibid., December 5, 1969, p. 3.

[16] *Voyenno-istoricheskiy zhurnal,* June 1971, pp. 101–102.

[17] *KZ,* October 2, 1971, p. 3.

[18] *Sovetskiy patriot,* November 12, 1973, p. 1.

[19] *KZ,* November 14, 1973, p. 4.

for a month-long special campaign of all-union mass defense work that supplemented the continual patriotic outpourings of DOSAAF, Soviet civil defense groups, the Party, various mass organizations such as the trade unions, and the Soviet media. Since there is an endless series of special events and anniversaries—Lenin's 100th Anniversary Celebration, the Twenty-fourth Party Congress, the Fiftieth Anniversary of the USSR, the Fifty-fifth Anniversary of the Soviet Armed Forces—special occasions are not lacking on which Soviet propagandists can intensify military-patriotic indoctrination.

The military-patriotic predraft training programs contain an additional theme that responds to a somewhat different concern. This is to form "a juvenile's deep conviction of the historic justice of the ideas of communism and the indisputable advantages of the socialist system over the capitalist system."[20]

B. CIVIL DEFENSE[21]

1. Attitudes

In the early sixties, the following story circulated in Moscow:
    "What should one do in case of a nuclear attack?"
    "Wrap yourself in a white sheet and crawl very slowly to the nearest cemetery."
    "Why very slowly?"
    "So as not to start a panic."[22]
    This cynical attitude toward the possibility of defense against nuclear weapons and therefore toward the value of civil defense training created a problem for the Soviet authorities responsible for civil defense training. "Unfortunately," despite civil defense programs and intensive indoctrination measures, "people are still [1971] encountered who give it all up as a bad job: 'Why teach,' they say. It makes no difference; there is no defense against nuclear weapons. This is an incorrect attitude. It is very important that each worker

---

[20] *Voyennyy vestnik,* October, 1971, p. 9.

[21] This section aims primarily to bring together materials related to recent trends in Soviet military preparedness and management. It does not attempt to give a systematic account of Soviet civil defense doctrines, procedures, or physical installations or their evolution. On these and other problems of Soviet civil defense see Leon Gouré, *Civil Defense in the Soviet Union* (Berkeley and Los Angeles, 1962), and by the same author, *Soviet Civil Defense Revisited 1966–1969* (The Rand Corporation RM–6113–PR, Santa Monica, California, 1969); *Soviet Civil Defense 1969–1970* (Center for Advanced International Affairs, University of Miami, 1971); *Soviet Civil Defense: Urban Evacuation and Dispersal* (Center for Advanced International Affairs, University of Miami, 1972). I am indebted to Leon Gouré for comments on a draft of this section. He is not, of course, responsible for its contents.

[22] Nicole Chatel, *Carnets russes* (Paris, 1971), p. 26.

and each Soviet person be imbued with faith in the effectiveness and reliability of the means of protection against weapons of mass destruction."[23] And again, although "the entire Soviet people" are preparing for protection against weapons of mass destruction, "even now [1972] we can encounter people who have a flippant and frivolous attitude toward civil defense. As a rule, they erroneously assume that there can be no protection against nuclear weapons and if war should happen, everything living allegedly will perish. Such reasoning can bring nothing but harm, irreparable harm."[24]

Given the existence of such attitudes, Soviet civil defense faces a difficulty, probably common to civil defense programs the world over: how to paint the seriousness of nuclear attack realistically enough to be useful in training and to impel people to take the necessary training and precautions, and at the same time not to picture it so grimly that it destroys morale or discourages willingness to take civil defense training and to accept civil defense discipline.

Some Soviet articles have painted grim pictures of nuclear war—the destruction of entire zones, the contamination of food and water, the isolation of areas from each other.[25] This is now frowned upon and, while it is acknowledged that people must be made aware of the power and destructive force of modern weapons, the "principal task is that of informing people that protection can be obtained against the effect of any weapon."[26] Civil defense lecturers and authors are criticized for painting outdated and overly dark pictures and for not being sufficiently convincing in describing the means of defense. Nuclear weapons, it is agreed, are not "a paper tiger," but civil defense propagandists must make clear that reliable means of protection are provided by both the armed forces and the entire state system of civil defense.[27] According to General A. Altunin, chief of Soviet civil defense, "the task of [civil defense] propaganda is to strive to ensure that every Soviet person is firmly convinced that there is protection against any weapon, even the most modern."[28] And a year later General Altunin repeated that "all available forms of propaganda should be employed for convincing the population of the high effectiveness of the measures proposed by us for protecting them against modern weapons."[29] Not enough attention is given in civil defense to "the decisive role played by our armed forces in protecting the Soviet people."[30]

The relevance of civil defense is defended by stressing the availability of

[23] *Sovetskaya Moldaviya,* November 18, 1971, p. 4.
[24] *Voyennyye znaniya,* April 1972, pp. 18–19.
[25] See, for example, *Kommunist Tadzhikistana,* November 20, 1970, p. 4, and *Voyennyye znaniya,* Feburary 1971, pp. 14–15.
[26] Ibid., August 1971, p. 11.
[27] Ibid., June 1971, pp. 10–11.
[28] *KZ,* October 4, 1972, p. 2.
[29] *Sovetskiy patriot,* November 1973, p. 2.
[30] *Voyennyye znaniya,* no. 2, February 1974, pp. 25–26.

warning. In military indoctrination literature, warning is sometimes taken to mean strategic (prehostility) warning that permits preemption of the enemy.[31] In civil defense literature the likely amount of warning time is generally left vague. An elaborate civil defense exercise involved freeing people who were buried by debris in a shelter. This implies that they had warning prior to the simulated nuclear strike.[32]

Whether or not the Soviet people believe that the threat of nuclear war is serious or that one can do anything useful about it should it occur, there is, as one would expect, a good deal of resistance or resentment among them to engaging in the time-consuming and inconvenient activities of civil defense training. The civil defense literature is full of complaints about urban and rural enterprise directors who carry out civil defense training and exercises in a "routine and cursory fashion."[33] In particular, exercises that involve the use of masks and other equipment and require measures more fatiguing than simply listening to a lecture or watching a movie seem to be executed without enthusiasm, and to be regarded as nuisances.[34]

This resistance and foot-dragging occur both among those with responsibilities for civil defense training (but who are not themselves professional civil defense workers) and among those who are to be trained. The two groups are not necessarily distinct. An enterprise director and his chief subordinates or a school principal and his teachers will generally be responsible for assuring adequate civil defense training for their workers and students, but just because of this, they themselves may have to take special civil defense training in preparation for their responsibilities.

Urban and rural workers and students have reasons other than their attitudes toward nuclear war for viewing civil defense training with little enthusiasm. Like so many other civic activities organized by Soviet authorities, civil defense training exploits the nonworking—but not necessarily free—time of students and workers.[35] "It is well known that the mandatory program of minimum universal [civil defense] training is studied during free time."[36] Teachers find that civil defense classes during school hours compete for time in an already crowded schedule that they are responsible for completing. And when civil defense exercises and civil defense lessons are held after class hours, they equally compete with a whole series of other "free"-time activities imposed by the Party and educational authorities.

[31] See, for example, *Nedelya,* July 10–16, 1972, p. 4.
[32] *Sovetskiy patriot,* November 14, 1973, p. 3.
[33] *Sovetskaya Kirgiziya,* May 11, 1971, p. 2.
[34] *Voyennyye znaniya,* November 1969, pp. 6–7.
[35] Brezhnev, in his March 1972 address to the Fifteenth Trade Union Congress, took special pains to draw attention to the need for an effective use of leisure time: "Frequently this time is frittered away pointlessly. . . . "
[36] *Voyennyye znaniya,* September 1973, pp. 22–23.

A similar imposition on private time applies to enterprise managers and other administrators, but a more important consideration enters in their case: civil defense training employs resources of the enterprise (space, time, labor, equipment) with a consequent loss to production and income. The director of a major civil defense exercise complains—in much the same language that managers have used in speaking about the preinduction training program—that "in addition to implementing a great volume of civil defense measures," he had at the same time to ensure fulfillment of the production schedule.[37] Officials insist, nonetheless, that civil defense exercises in plants and institutions be carried out without loss of production. One writer with the characteristic exaggeration of the Party propagandist instructs managers that a well-coordinated training program not only need not interfere with production, but on the contrary can increase it.[38] This leads to a certain amount of ingenuity on the part of some plant managers. "Sometimes normal economic work is carried out under the guise of [civil defense] exercises. . . . It is perfectly clear that such an attitude toward defense measures is intolerable. . . . Certain responsible comrades should not be allowed to denigrate by their actions the significance of defense work with the population."[39]

As the civil defense program and especially civil defense exercises become increasingly elaborate, the fiction that civil defense need not interfere with production is progressively harder to maintain. During exercises at the Gorizont Electrotechnical Association in Minsk "all the [plant civil defense] command personnel were assigned to the execution of civil defense measures, even though it involved interrupting their production work." On the other hand, the association's management "found an opportunity to provide for the conducting of classes without reducing the enterprise's productive activities."[40] An exercise in Sevastopol was not supposed to interfere with normal work in the port, but "since the operations in the port continued as usual and ships were being loaded and unloaded, this presented certain difficulties with regard to controlling the personnel. A decision was thus made to halt temporarily the movement of port transports and to terminate work aboard the ships."[41]

Civil defense programs are most readily organized for collectives, that is, for workers in urban and rural enterprises and offices, and for students. Nonworking people, however, also receive practical training through the civil defense activities of village and settlement soviets. This is in line with Soviet intentions to bring civil defense training to the "entire Soviet people."[42]

[37] *Sovetskaya Belorussiya,* August 6, 1971.
[38] *Voyennyye znaniya,* September 1973, pp. 22–23.
[39] *KZ,* December 14, 1972, p. 1.
[40] *Voyennyye znaniya,* September 1973, pp. 28–29.
[41] Ibid., November 1971, pp. 16–17.
[42] *Pravda Ukrainy,* August 31, 1971.

Civil defense "today is becoming both a political and a strategic factor," and still higher levels of "combat readiness" for civil defense are required.[43] The range of organizations mobilized to promote this higher level is indicated by those represented at an important three-day USSR civil defense conference: the Central Committee of the CPSU; the All-Union Central Trade Union Council; the Central Committee of the Komsomol; the Ministries for Culture and Education of the USSR and the RSFSR; the State Committees for Television and Radio, Press, and Cinema of the Council of Ministers of the USSR and of the RSFSR; the Central Committee of DOSAAF; the All-Union Znaniye Society; the League of USSR Red Cross and Red Crescent Societies; the Committee of War Veterans; the League of Writers, Journalists, and Cinema Experts; and the editorial boards of major newspapers, journals, and book publishing houses.[44]

Soviet organizations keep up an intensive drumfire of publicity concerning civil defense. Of course, when a local society in an Estonian city with a population of 70,000 reports civil defense agitprop activities for 1970 as comprising 250 lectures and reports, more than 400 film shows, 40 broadcasts on the local radio, and 24 articles in the local newspaper, the accuracy of these numbers, and their significance for effective civil defense training even if accurate, are open to question.[45] On the other hand, these numbers reflect with some accuracy the pressure of higher authorities for more intensive indoctrination on civil defense. A 1971 directive from the chief of civil defense for the USSR required trade-union clubs, houses and palaces of culture, parks, libraries, and Red Corners to maintain civil defense displays. The "civil defense corner" may ultimately acquire some of the ubiquity of the "Red Corner" or the "Lenin Corner." The civil defense corner contains six main sections: news of advanced workers who excel in civil defense; socialist competition in civil defense and the results of competition and exercises; civil defense signals and the responses to them; the organization of different civil defense formations such as rescue teams; the tasks that the various civil defense formations are to perform; and problems of dispersal and evacuation.[46] In remote parts of the country where fewer facilities are available, mobile civil defense vehicles are sometimes employed.[47]

In 1971 *Voyennyye znaniya* published a list of civil defense films obtainable on a rental basis. Not counting new films released in 1970, forty-one different civil defense films were available.[48] The basic civil defense pamphlet,

[43] *Voyennyye znaniya,* April 1971, pp. 11–13, and *Sovetskaya Moldaviya,* August 1971, p. 4.
[44] *Voyennyye znaniya,* August 1971, p. 11.
[45] *Sovetskaya Estoniya,* September 15, 1971, p. 1.
[46] *Voyennyye znaniya,* January 1972, p. 20.
[47] Ibid., pp. 10–11.
[48] Ibid., April 1971, pp. 20–21.

This Must be Known by Everybody, has been issued in all the languages of the USSR in an edition of more than 60 million copies.[49] Larger works are published in very sizable editions. Thus, *The Organization and Conduct of Training Exercises in Civil Defense at National Economic Enterprises,* 128 pages, was published in Moscow in 1971 in 100,000 copies, and P. T. Egorov et al., *Civil Defense,* 544 pages, was published in Moscow in 1970 in 500,000 copies.

Nationwide mass education on civil defense is supplemented by technical courses for civil defense officials and for the commanders of the specialized civil defense detachments in factories and other establishments. The military provides the most highly trained specialists in civil defense. The USSR Military School of Civil Defense in Moscow trains officers who are commissioned as lieutenants following a three-year period of instruction for service with civil defense units of the army.[50]

While the foregoing indicates a substantial, long-standing interest of Soviet authorities in civil defense, there are more recent developments that provide evidence of the increasing earnestness with which the Soviet authorities view civil defense. These are: (1) the introduction of civil defense training into the second grade of Soviet primary schools; (2) the introduction of compulsory civil defense research in studies of higher technical institutes; and (3) the emphasis on "combat training," "combat realism," and military preparedness of the population through civil defense exercises and practical training in permanent civil defense detachments, as opposed to reading pamphlets and listening to lectures.

2. Civil Defense in the Second Grade

In November 1970, a program of experiments was undertaken in Moscow, Leningrad, the Moscow Oblast, and in eight of the Union Republics to investigate and test civil defense training programs for the first four grades of the primary schools. As a result of these experiments a directive of the USSR Ministry of Education and the USSR civil defense chief on January 4, 1971, created a civil defense program for second-grade children. In addition to civil defense exercises in the classroom, fifteen ten-minute training sessions outside of the class were introduced.[51] In 1974, training in civil defense in the second grade was said to take five to six hours of class time and several fifteen-minute training periods outside of the class.[52]

The lowering of the age for civil defense training from the fifth to the second grade is not without its proper material support. Soviet industry pro-

---

[49] Ibid., June 1971, pp. 10–11.
[50] *KZ,* July 27, 1971, p. 1, and February 25, 1971, p. 4.
[51] *Narodnoye obrazovaniye,* December 1971, pp. 34–36.
[52] *Voyennyye znaniya,* no. 1, January 1974, pp. 33–34.

duces gas masks, respirators, and other protective equipment designed for children of these ages.[53] In addition to the program for second-grade students, the 1971 directive further stipulated that students in the third and forth grades were to develop their skills in civil defense during nonschool hours at Young Pioneer camps, at municipal summer camps, and at similar organizations. Summer Lightning (see pp. 70–72 above) also provides eight hours of civil defense problems. The work with third- and fourth-grade students should, as a rule, be conducted during nonschool hours.[54] Thus, Soviet children learn at an early age that leisure time should not be "frittered away pointlessly" (see note 35, p. 76).

The surprisingly brief period of two months between the initiation of what is presented as an extensive program of experimentation in the first four grades of schools in eight Union Republics and the issuance of the civil defense directive (November 1970 to January 4, 1971) suggests that a decision had already been reached before the experiments were initiated and that the experimental program may have, at the most, been used to decide lesser matters, including, perhaps, whether civil defense training should be begun in the first or the second grade. The speed with which the directive was issued is all the more striking in view of the opposition among both teachers and parents to the lowering of the age for civil defense training from the fifth to the second grade. *Voyennyye znaniya* concedes that "perhaps a majority were opposed to the program,"[55] a striking departure from the time-honored formula of "unfortunately, there are a few [some] who. . . . "

Teachers objected to a further crowding of the school schedule and some felt that civil defense training might have a bad physical and mental effect, a view that was said to be rebutted by the experimental program. Some teachers apparently found it distasteful to refer to war and weapons and to teach the use of gas masks and respirators. "Teachers . . . generally did not touch on weapons of mass destruction in their explanation of the lesson. They talked simply about harmful substances and gases in the air. Children were satisfied with this."[56] Teachers also resented having to take special courses on civil defense in order to improve their civil defense instruction. A civil defense writer suggested that probably the best way to handle this problem was to provide increased civil defense training in teacher training schools, since civil defense is "not a one-time campaign or a fleeting episode, but a serious state matter."[57]

Parental concern is also a problem. "After the very first lesson it will be

[53] *Narodnoye obrazovaniye,* September 1971, pp. 47–48.
[54] *Voyennyye znaniya,* April 1971, pp. 14–15.
[55] Ibid., May 1971, pp. 14–15.
[56] Ibid.
[57] *Narodnoye obrazovaniye,* December 1971, pp. 34–36.

known at home that Masha, Petya, and Olya donned a gas mask today. It is necessary to enlist the support of parents." Teachers and principals are urged to have discussions with parents to avoid "overly emotional reactions."[58]

Civil defense programs increasingly take on a broader dimension of military-patriotic indoctrination and general mass military preparedness. This dimension now clearly reaches down to the second grade. Thus, during the classroom drills on civil defense, educational authorities are encouraged to provide the children with "skillfully selected stories on military-patriotic themes." "Thus the instructional and educational functions of the lessons are united in a single whole." "Civil defense lessons in school must not be set apart from the general task of military-patriotic education of children and young people. . . . In fact, one cannot talk about the methods and means of protection against weapons of mass destruction in classes with the fifth and ninth grades and not mention our armed forces, their combat might, and the heroism and courage of Soviet fighting men. Even in the second grade the civil defense lesson is transformed in some measure into an essential part of the process of military-patriotic education. . . . The very ritual of the lesson—precise commands and the elements of military discipline—sets the appropriate tone for the pupils. According to the testimony of elementary school teachers, civil defense lessons as well as *Zarnitsa* promote the inculcation of organization and discipline in children."[59] To enhance the military overtones of civil defense training, the second-grade children get their civil defense classes in the school's military room.[60]

3. The Continuity of Production

Concern for the "stability" of production and for the safeguarding of equipment and resources under the conditions of nuclear war now go beyond earlier measures for individual survival and the earlier programs for major plants. Soviet authorities are insistent that persons of high educational and scientific attainments apply their specialized knowledge to questions of civil defense. Engineers and scientific workers sometimes avoid civil defense responsibilities on the grounds that they do not possess specialized civil defense engineering knowledge. This plea is rejected by the authorities, who insist that such persons ought to do more than merely study the pamphlet *What Everyone Must Know*.[61] Thus, rail-transport engineers are required to consider how rail operations can best be restored after a nuclear attack and how resistant different types of materials used in rail transport are to nuclear effects. A similar

[58] Ibid.
[59] Ibid., December 1971, pp. 34–36.
[60] *Voyennyye znaniya,* no. 1, January 1974, pp. 33–34.
[61] *Vyshka,* July 7, 1971, p. 3.

emphasis on technical requirements of the economy, rather than individual survival, is reflected in civil defense films like *Repairing Damage to Electric Power Substations and Electrical Transmission Lines in the Center of Nuclear Destruction.*[62] Special films and literature on problems of rural civil defense, particularly the possible contamination of livestock and fodder and the equipment and procedures required to deal with this problem, receive considerable attention.[63]

Of particular interest in this context is the campaign to ensure that graduates of higher scientific and technical schools and of secondary technical schools are made to include civil defense as a significant part of their training. This does not mean that they should know their civil defense obligations in the sense that an ordinary Soviet citizen does, but rather thay they must learn to use their technical or scientific specialties for the solution of civil defense problems. A program introduced in 1969 following "important and timely" directives of the Ministry of Higher and Secondary Special Education and of the USSR chief of civil defense concerned the inclusion of civil defense problems in student graduation theses.[64] Some civil defense teachers insisted on including problems of civil defense in every thesis written in such institutions, but "defenders of this extreme point of view have . . . become fewer in number," as have also the defenders of the opposite position that thesis writing on civil defense is "trumped-up and impractical."[65] It appears that most students are expected either to deal in their theses with the civil defense aspects of their specialty or devote, if they wish, an entire thesis to this subject. In the Siberian Technological Institute only a few students included problems of civil defense in their theses in 1969–70. "However, in the following year problems dealing with engineering and technical measures to increase production stability were reflected in practically all theses." At the Leningrad Technical Institute of the pulp and paper industry the problems of civil defense are "treated in the graduating theses with complete seriousness." In the Vladimir Polytechnical Institute "a student working on a thesis should provide an evaluation of existing models [of the machine, device, or process] with consideration for their operation in time of war and should propose an improved type or better process. . . . The stability of operation, when acted on by a nuclear weapon

[62] *Vestnik vysshey shkoly,* May 1971, pp. 30–32.
[63] See, for example, *Voyennyye znaniya,* December 1968, p. 48, and July 1971, pp. 22–23.
[64] Ibid., January 1972.
[65] Ibid. It is clear from the cited article that there were arguments over who should exercise control in the writing of graduation theses by students—the civil defense teacher or the person responsible for the substantive area. It is not at all clear, however, that civil defense teachers sought to have primary supervision power. On the contrary, it appears that at a number of institutes engineering and science teachers were only too anxious to pass this work on to the civil defense teachers, who in turn refused to accept this responsibility on the grounds that their scientific and engineering training was inadequate to determine whether the student's application of his technical knowledge to civil defense was satisfactory or not.

and its possible secondary action, should be given in design theses. The limit of stability is defined and recommendations are given to increase stability under the influence of electromagnetic pulses and radioactivity arising in a nuclear explosion." A civil defense official points out that it is desirable for students doing such theses to consult with engineering workers in relevant enterprises. Another civil defense official summarizes the new program as follows: "The most important tasks of civil defense are to appraise the stability of national economic projects under the influence of the damaging factors of nuclear explosion, to determine the most efficient engineering and technical measures to increase stability, and to seek out . . . alternatives for the operation of an enterprise under the threat of enemy attack."[66]

The emphasis on ensuring the stability of production may have gone too far. The chief of Soviet civil defense, Colonel General A. Altunin, found it useful to state: "It must be stressed here that protection of the population is the main task. . . . An important question is ensuring steady work of the national economy."[67]

4. Training and Exercises

The core of civil defense for the general population is a mandatory twenty-hour program. Descriptions of Soviet civil defense sometimes fail to note that "this means that each citizen is obligated to spend twenty hours of his own time on it *every year.* "[68] (Emphasis added.) Persons with special responsibilities study in special programs. Thus plant and institution commanders of civil defense formations study in a thirty-five-hour program.[69] This, of course, is in addition to their duties as formation commanders.

Marshal Chuikov, former USSR chief of civil defense, pointed out that there was "an overemphasis on theoretical instruction at the cost of practical instruction." Not enough exercises are conducted in winter and at night, and this departure from "combat realism" was condemned. In addition, he complained that there is an insufficient number of joint exercises of civil defense personnel with troop units.[70]

These criticisms have certainly been taken to heart, and civil defense training as a process of reading pamphlets, watching movies, listening to lectures, and studying displays in the civil defense corner is clearly on the way out. "Even during a twenty-hour mandatory program, time must be made

---

[66] Ibid. In 1974 the Institute of Railroad Transport Engineers reported that 10 percent of the work done by students on their diploma projects dealt with civil defense subjects. *KZ*, November 23, 1974, p. 2.

[67] *KZ*, October 4, 1972, p. 2.

[68] *Voyennyye znaniya*, September 1973, pp. 22–23.

[69] *KZ*, September 15, 1973, p. 2.

[70] *Voyennyye znaniya*, February 1971, pp. 4–5.

available for the practical preparation of a simple type of protective installation (covered trench, slit trench) or for training in the practical use of the various types of protective equipment. Practical exercises provide more benefit than countless discussions."[71] To the deputy chief of civil defense, "it is gratifying to note that in a number of republics, *krais*, and *oblasts* a switch has been made to practical training."[72] It is evident that the new program will require practical training well beyond the construction of slit trenches. It will have to ensure "that each individual [knows] how to use a gas mask, close and open airtight doors and shutters . . . remove casualties from under rubble and transport them out of the disaster area and render first aid."[73]

The population has increasingly been incorporated into civil defense formations, many of them specializing in various functions, such as reconnaissance, rescue work, erecting prefab and other emergency shelters, and predicting the movement of radioactive clouds.[74] They are trained to cooperate with military civil defense units and regular army units.[75] "A formation is a shock detachment that must be ready for action at all times." Its duties are dispersal, evacuation, taking cover in shelters, and conducting rescue and emergency recuperation operations. "When necessary, all residents of the country will participate without exception, independent of age or occupation."[76] The civil defense authorities increasingly insist that these formations or detachments must be taught by their formation commanders, trained by them, and engage in exercises led by them. The authorities do not want the formations to receive their training by civil defense staff workers or by means of civil defense courses given by civil defense authorities. They are clearly determined to make each civil defense formation responsive to the direction, control, and orders of its commander. The civil defense formations have become, in this sense, quasimilitary units organized both in establishments of all types and on a territorial basis.[77]

Despite the rapidity of recent changes, "this year [1974] an entire complex of important changes will take place in connection with the civil defense systems for control, communication, warning, and technical equipping of units. . . . The basic principles underlying the protection of the population and the national economy against nuclear weapons will be reevaluated from a modern standpoint. Decisive changes have taken place with regard to making maximum use of all available engineering installations in the interests of

[71] *Sovetskiy patriot*, November 21, 1973, p. 2.
[72] *Voyennyye znaniya*, October 1973, pp. 6–7.
[73] Ibid., January 1973, pp. 24–25.
[74] Ibid., October 1973, pp. 6–7.
[75] *Sovetskiy patriot*, November 21, 1973, p. 2, and *Voyennyye znaniya*, no. 12, December 1973, pp. 4–5.
[76] Ibid., January 1973, pp. 24–25.
[77] *Sovetskiy patriot*, November 21, 1973, p. 2.

protecting the population. At the same time, the search continues for the best and most efficient methods for evacuating and dispersing the population."[78] Currently, urban evacuation exercises use a combination of evacuation procedures. Evacuation on foot of columns of 500 to 1,000 persons is not uncommon.[79] This does not preclude a considerable emphasis on permanent and emergency shelters. "Even during peacetime they are being built in all of the large cities and at national economic installations that are expected to continue operations during wartime."[80]

Soviet officials increasingly organize ambitious training exercises, which are particularly complex because Soviet civil defense doctrine calls for the maintenance of production by a portion of the working population for whom urban shelters are available and the evacuation of the rest of the population.[81] Given the demand for realism, considerable effort is required to shift people about. An exercise at one industrial plant involved the assembly of those workers who were to remain on the job, the dispatch of the remaining workers, together with their families, into a zone outside the city, the reorganization of the shop work, and protective measures for the most valuable equipment.[82] Joint exercises by military units and civil defense formations sometimes involve the destruction of a mock-up of a settlement. After the "nuclear" strike, civil defense formations specialized in reconnaissance, fire-fighting, radiation measurement, rescue, decontamination, and other functions go into action. Such exercises are made "as real as possible."[83]

There is, of course, a considerable disparity between the goals of the Soviet civil defense program and its current accomplishments. Many Soviet workers and managers are able to evade some of the demands made upon them, being facilitated in this by the inefficiency and lack of zeal of some of the officials responsible for implementing the program. As in the case of the preinduction military training program, the rural areas lag badly.[84] Nonetheless, like the preinduction training program, the civil defense program clearly improves from year to year in both the scope and quality of its training and in the numbers of persons reached. When one takes into account that it begins in the second grade, continues throughout the years of Young Pioneer and Komsomol membership, intensifies in preinduction military training and dur-

---

[78] Ibid.

[79] Evacuees are told to take with them passport, military service card, documents on education and specialty, birth certificates of children, their evacuation certificates, money, warm clothing (even if the weather is warm), individual civil defense protective clothing, toilet objects, bedding, medicines, food for two to three days, and essential dishes. *Voyennyye znaniya*, no. 3, March 1974, pp. 28–29.

[80] Ibid., no. 5, May 1974, pp. 34–35.

[81] Ibid, April 1971, pp. 20–21.

[82] *Sovetskaya Belorussiya*, August 6, 1971.

[83] *Sovetskiy patriot*, November 14, 1973, p. 3.

[84] *Voyennyye znaniya*, January 1973, pp. 32–33.

ing service in the armed forces, and then continues to some degree year after year when the individual has returned to civil life, it is reasonable to estimate that the twenty-five-year-old urban worker who served in the army will probably have had anywhere from fifteen to thirty full days of civil defense training depending on the level of his responsibility.

C. PHYSICAL TRAINING

Soviet interest in mobilizing the population for more effective performance of defense obligations is reflected in the set of physical training programs and norms established for the various age and sex groups. The emphasis on physical training and physical fitness begins for the Soviet citizen at a relatively early age, well before he enters military service. Official Soviet fitness standards now exist for all age groups from ten to sixty. These standards and the propaganda and pressure employed to get people to adhere to them are openly related to the needs of military service and civil defense as well as of labor discipline. The all-union program published in January 1971 extended the physical training "complexes" for the different age and sex groups down to the ten-year-old group.[85]

Of greater significance in the present context is the Ready for Labor and Defense of the USSR complex, which applies to young men and women in the sixteen- to eighteen-year-old group, that is, to those at the age level immediately preceding military induction. DOSAAF makes strenuous, if not always successful, efforts to get young people up to the performance levels of this complex during the course of their preinduction training.

Three levels of accomplishment (minimum, good, and outstanding) are specified for each activity in the complex. The 1971 norms for the sixteen- to eighteen-year-old male group required performances as follows: for the running of the 100 meters, 15.4 seconds, 14.5 seconds, 13.2 seconds; cross-country run of 1,500 meters, 6 minutes, 5.4 minutes, 5.15 minutes; throwing the 700-gram grenade, 31 meters, 35 meters, 42 meters; 5-kilometer ski race, 30.5 minutes, 27.5 minutes, 24.5 minutes; swimming 100 meters, 2.5 minutes, 2.25 minutes, 1.55 minutes. In addition there are various supplementary activities, such as long-distance hiking and rifle firing.[86]

Physical activities are increasingly defined in terms of "military sports" or "sports with military applications," for example, parachute jumping and the firing of weapons. In addition, "It is desirable that the physical training exercises . . . introduce the language of command and a terminology close to

[85] The lowering of civil defense instruction in the primary schools from the fifth to the second grade also occurred in January 1971 (see p. 79 above).

[86] *Sovetskiy patriot,* January 17, 1971, p. 3.

exercises in military affairs."[87] "Military multiple events" analogous to the Olympic Pentathlon and Decathlon have been organized. The military multiple event includes the firing of small-calibre weapons, grenade throwing, swimming, figure driving of a motor vehicle, and cross-country running. In 1970 a winter military multiple event was added that includes, in addition to firing and similar military "sports," ski racing and other winter activities.[88] The introduction of a set of explicit military sports is in line with a principle enunciated by General I. J. Pavloskiy, deputy minister of defense, who affirmed that "at the basis of all forms of physical training should lie an applied military orientation."[89] In conformity with this, the Ready for Labor and Defense norms now contain a civil defense section that applies to all persons ten years of age and over. In May 1974, new norms were established that included wearing a gas mask while engaging in physical work, speed and agility in the use of protective equipment, and administration of first aid to oneself and others.[90]

This emphasis on "sports with military applications" extends to age groups other than the sixteen- to eighteen-year-old preinduction cohorts.[91] Military-technical forms of sports "should be looked upon as a most important state matter." Vehicle, motorcycle, radio, aircraft, parachute, small-arms, and water sports and tournaments of military sports train sportsmen who "form a wonderful reserve . . . for the Soviet army and navy."[92] DOSAAF, the trade unions, and the Komsomol committees "must achieve the mass development of military-technical sports in the enterprises. Motor sports should be essentially cultivated at the automotive plants and radio sports at radio plants. From 1973 to 1975 we must achieve the establishment of military-technical sports clubs in specialized enterprises and in the institutions of higher learning. It would be desirable for the press, radio, and TV to describe competition in military-technical forms of sports with the same enthusiasm as is given to hockey, soccer, basketball, etc."[93]

In addition to sports that involve great physical effort and utilization of one's own physical resources, Soviet terminology recognizes "mechanized sports," such as motorboat and automobile racing. When statistical reporting of rated athletes and masters of mechanized sports was dropped from Soviet tabulations of athletic accomplishments, a letter in *Pravda* argued that "it is

---

[87] Ibid., April 4, 1973, p. 2. At one Moscow school when the military instructor proposed that command language be introduced, "none of the teachers supported him."

[88] Ibid., March 24, 1971, p. 4.

[89] *KZ*, August 12, 1972. General Pavloskiy added, "I would particularly like to stress the significance of swimming as an absolute requirement for each soldier."

[90] *Voyennyye znaniya*, no. 9, September 1974, pp. 28–29.

[91] Ibid., November 29, 1972, p. 3.

[92] *Voyennyye znaniya*, July 1973, pp. 3–4.

[93] Ibid.

wrong to neglect the development of mechanized sports in the millions of physical-culture collectives and rely on DOSAAF's sections and clubs alone." This letter was signed, among others, by a major general and a rear admiral, and suggests a military interest in maintaining public support for these activities.[94]

Clearly, these various programs enable youth to pass immediately, when inducted, into strenuous military training without loss of time. They also contribute to the military skill of both the youth and the adult population.

While relying principally on its professional and conscript military forces, the Soviets certainly have not neglected the military potential of the general population. This is consistent with the view that only in communist societies is it possible to exploit fully the military capabilities of the people.

The substantial military training in the preinduction training program of even those youths who are not inducted, the incorporation of predraft youth into the military detachments of the Eaglets, the increasing incorporation of the adult population into permanent civil defense detachments with specially trained commanders, the training of these detachments with both military civil defense troops and regular units, and the extension of military discipline to the earliest grades of the primary school, taken together with the enormous outpouring of military-patriotic propaganda intended to lend these programs an emotional aura that will help to sustain them and justify the priorities accorded to them, certainly suggest that the Soviet leaders are increasingly thinking in terms of "a nation in arms." The Soviets are not said to have a militia[95] as do the Chinese, who have an estimated five million men and women in paramilitary units.[96] But the Soviets do not hesitate to use the term "paramilitary" in speaking of the Eaglets.[97] These detachments and those of the civil defense apparatus, comprising millions of young and adult Soviet citizens, would require little transformation to justify the term militia in its western sense.

---

[94] *Pravda,* May 26, 1972, p. 6. The statement quoted in the text also suggests some annoyance with DOSAAF. On this point see pp. 40–41 above.

[95] The Soviet term "militia" refers to police forces.

[96] Charles H. Murphy, "China: An Emerging Military Superpower," *Air Force Magazine,* July 1972, p. 54. According to a TASS statement (1974) the Chinese People's Volunteer Corps numbers six to seven million. *New York Times,* September 29, 1974. *Sovetskiy voin,* citing Chinese press reports, gives a figure of 12 million. *Sovetskiy voin,* no. 12, June 1974, p. 47.

[97] *Sovetskiy patriot,* November 12, 1973, p. 1. "The number and quality of the population and its readiness for modern warfare represent an extemely important factor in defense readiness." *KVS,* no. 20, October 1974, pp. 68–75.

Chapter IV

Military Training

Military training in the Soviet forces may largely suggest an account of how Soviet recruits and young officers acquire the rudiments of military regulations, a knowledge of basic military skills, and a progressive command of their military specialties. To Soviet military and political authorities, however, military training means much more—the production of a Soviet soldier. This is a process that embraces the development of correct ideological and political views; a high state of discipline and a capacity for self-sacrifice; unquestioning subordination to commanders and total loyalty to the Party; complete dedication of body and spirit to a never-ending struggle to improve one's own performance and the ability of one's unit to exceed prescribed norms; unflinching courage in the face of adversity and danger; and uncomplaining endurance of prolonged deprivation and extreme physical and psychological stress. Most of these are virtues that are esteemed in all armies. In the Soviet armed forces they are not simply esteemed, nor are they faintheartedly pursued. Military training is, in considerable measure, a determined process to develop them. It is these virtues that make conventional military skills and knowledge both possible and useful. It is characteristic that when Marshal A. A. Grechko, Soviet minister of defense, reviewed the six demands made upon cadre officers, he emphasized that "the first and chief demand is to be ideologically convinced and politically mature . . . an active champion of Party policy." It was not until the marshal arrived at the sixth and last demand that he got around to mentioning such mundane matters as "high general military and technical efficiency."[1]

Soviet doctrine does not view military training as being primarily concerned with junior personnel. Training is required at all levels and never ceases. The Soviets fear the evanescent character of skills that are not constantly exercised. They have a strong conviction that man's potential limit is never reached, and that the frontiers of accomplishment can (and must) always be pushed a little further. There are, in effect, only two states of being for a military man—either he is fighting or he is training. And even these two states are not to be sharply separated. Soviet articles on training not infrequently make reference, especially in connection with flying skills, to the continual training and practicing of Soviet airmen while on active combat duty during World War II. There is little distinction between training forces and operational forces. Operational forces are constantly training and most forces in training have operational functions.

At the troop level, then, a very large part of the day-to-day life of the Soviet forces is embraced by the phrase "military training." This will only be partly reflected in this chapter. The great breadth of what is included in Soviet military training requires us to divide the subject matter. This chapter will deal largely with military training in the narrow or conventional sense of training in basic skills and in the acquisition of military specialties.

A. OBJECTIVES

1. Overcoming the Reduction in Length of Military Service

The reduction in 1968 of military service from three to two years in the army and from four to three years in the navy severely affected military training in the Soviet forces. A principal objective of current military training programs and procedures is to overcome the consequences of having one year less in which to bring troops up to their peak of operational effectiveness. The Law of Universal Military Service made "it . . . necessary to reorganize the entire system of combat and political training."[2] In 1971 the last of the draftees inducted prior to the enactment of the new Law of Universal Military Service

---

[1] *KZ*, March 24, 1972, pp. 1–3.
[2] *Pravda*, February 20, 1970, p. 3.

were released into the reserves. A military writer notes that the process of improving the training process had succeeded and that the transitional period of converting from a three- to a two-year (and a four- to a three-year) period of military service had ended.[3] Nonetheless, Soviet discussions on training continue to show a preoccupation with the effects of the reduced period of service.

The 1967 law replaced a single annual period of induction with two periods. This created problems for the Soviet forces almost as great as the reduction in service time. The twice-yearly reception of new recruits upsets the operational efficiency of Soviet units just at a time when the recruits who were received six months before are beginning to adapt themselves to their new duties. The reception of a second group of new recruits each year also imposes a strain on Soviet training resources. In both late spring and late autumn, when new recruits are being received, one reads in Soviet military journals that "a rather difficult situation [has] developed."[4] Or, "the Soviet armed forces are again seeing the onset of a difficult time of regular partial replacement of personnel."[5]

The fall period is particularly strenuous, since the graduates of the military schools, the young officers, as a rule arrive in their units during the same autumn period when the new recruits are arriving. Under these conditions, when both the young officers and the recruits are inexperienced, "mistakes and loss of confidence often occur."[6] The problem is further aggravated by the arrival of reserve officers who are "in particular need of constant assistance."[7]

2. New Weapons and Technology

A second objective of the training process is to teach the use of modern weapons and a great mass of highly technical equipment. The problem of accomplishing this objective is sometimes said to have been resolved by the high educational level of current recruits and officers, but it is evident that this by itself does not entirely ease the training situation. Marshal Grechko points out that combat equipment "has now become far more complicated. Strictly speaking, we have almost nothing left of what we fought with in the years of the Great Patriotic War. If one trains people according to the old manner, this means that one is inefficient."[8] Nor is it sufficient to train officers and men to handle the modern equipment that science has made available to the Soviet forces. "When we train officers we are not looking at today nor at tomorrow,

[3] *KVS*, no. 6, March 1971, pp. 3–8.
[4] *KZ*, January 11, 1970, p. 1.
[5] Ibid., October 13, 1971, p. 1.
[6] *KVS*, no. 24, December 1969, pp. 42–47.
[7] *KZ*, January 20, 1970, p. 2.
[8] Ibid., March 25, 1970, p. 1.

but, as you might say, the day after tomorrow. We are trying to anticipate trends in the development of military affairs and to foresee the future that awaits a lieutenant just beginning service.[9] It is necessary for him to be prepared for this future."[10] Some writers are impressed by the rapid pace with which technology affects military possibilities. "Cosmic space" has become a new arena of possible combat action, and "new major military organisms . . . with completely independent trends in military science and in the art of their employment" have appeared.[11]

3. Combat Readiness

A third objective of Soviet military training, and perhaps the most important, is to achieve a high level of combat readiness. Military establishments generally and nuclear powers particularly have emphasized the importance of being able to respond swiftly to military and political contingencies. Still, there is probably no major military establishment where the theme of combat readiness appears with such insistence and pervasiveness in military doctrine, in training, and in operational practice as in the Soviet Union. Constant readiness, a capability for immediate and swift action, is emphasized at every stage of the training process and in every sector of military activity. Minister of Defense Marshal Grechko, in an important speech in January 1972, pointed out that in spite of past emphasis on combat readiness, "a [further] rise in combat readiness in the future remains our main task . . . so that the Soviet people can be confident that at any time of the night or day the army and navy are ready to repel an enemy attack, no matter from where it might come."[12] Marshal Grechko spells out more fully the meaning of combat readiness. "On any day or at any hour it [combat readiness] should be on a level that would make it possible immediately to begin and conduct the most decisive and effective actions in the event that the aggressors should start a war, and to rapidly change from one type of combat to another."[13]

This passage would take on an ominous significance were one to omit the phrase "in the event that the aggressor should start a war." The clear implica-

---

[9] This outlook also affects civilian education: ". . . for a young specialist graduated in the 1970s to be ready and able to solve the scientific and technical problems of the year 2000 — problems whose nature we cannot even guess at present — it is necessary that his basic scientific training be expanded. It would be more rational to spend more time and effort studying the basics of scientific knowledge, rather than the frequently changing 'superstructure.'" *Izvestia,* August 30, 1972, p. 3.

[10] *Nedelya,* July 10–16, 1972, p. 6. This article points out that 45 percent of all officer slots are occupied by engineers and technicians. "Today it turns out that an officer will need to study more than thirty engineering, humanities, and military disciplines and pass about seventy examinations and tests when he enters a higher combined-arms command school."

[11] *Morskoy sbornik,* December 1969, pp. 32–37.

[12] *Sovetskiy voin,* January 1972. The last phrase refers, no doubt, to China.

[13] Ibid.

tion of preemptive action that the statement would then carry is perhaps conveyed in any case to Soviet readers who appreciate the need to "forestall the enemy's opening fire."[14] The reference to rapid change from one type of combat to another is no doubt intended to include a Soviet or enemy initiative in moving from conventional to nuclear weapons, and, perhaps, from border fighting to larger-scale action. It is, in Marshal Grechko's opinion, the character of modern weapons—presumably missiles and planes—that imposes the need for all troops, without exception, always to be ready for immediate action. Combat readiness requires excellent weapons, highly trained specialists, and the strictest discipline and organization, all of which are closely dependent on each other.[15] Combat readiness also involves precise computations of time, a feature that helps explain why the stopwatch is an ubiquitous instrument in Soviet military training.

Combat readiness as speed of response receives special emphasis in air defense (PVO) units and the rocket forces. "Constant combat readiness is the most important peculiarity determining the life and activity of missile forces. The combat missilemen stand watch around the clock."[16] In the rocket forces "particular stress is placed on combat readiness. Only a few seconds are required for an order issued by the high command to reach literally each and every combat crew."[17]

Soviet operational and training literature and practices give added emphasis to combat readiness by utilizing phrases that suggest that the soldier or the unit is operating in a war situation. Thus an important political exercise for the troops instructs the political officer that "during the lecture [political lesson] each soldier, sailor, and sergeant should be made to understand that the standing of combat watches during peacetime is synonomous with carrying out a combat task."[18] An admiral, speaking of the Soviet naval squadrons, points out that "even in peaceful circumstances many Black Sea sailors are in fact living by the norms and laws of battle conditions."[19] Political officers are

---

[14] " . . . closely related to the development of modern machinery [is] this area I would call the battle for seconds. The mission here is to prepare for battle as rapidly as possible and forestall the enemy's opening fire. Forestall it by just a few seconds? Some will perhaps think a few seconds cannot be of great significance. Let us recall, however, that the modern supersonic aircraft will cover almost an entire kilometer in a second, and a missile will go much further." General A. Altunin, chief of the main directorate of personnel, Ministry of Defense, in *Nedelya,* July 10–16, 1972, p. 4.

[15] *Sovetskiy voin,* January 1972.

[16] *Trud,* November 19, 1971, p. 4.

[17] *Sovetskaya Moldaviya,* November 18, 1970, p. 4. A writer, defending conventional artillery, points out that in addition to the unsuitability of some targets for nuclear weapons, conventional artillery permits "constant readiness to open fire immediately without any special preparations," perhaps referring here to political control over the use of tactical nuclear weapons. *KZ,* January 5, 1972, p. 3.

[18] *KVS,* no. 20, October 1971, pp. 68–74.

[19] *Pravda Ukrainy,* March 19, 1972, p. 3.

reminded that "in many instances the modern requirements for discipline have approached wartime requirements."[20] A eulogist at the funeral of General Krylov, former chief of the rocket forces, praised the general for having done "everything necessary to raise the combat readiness of the troops under him to the last days of his life. He lived and died a soldier on combat duty."[21]

The seriousness of peacetime combat duty is instilled with all the emotion that ritual can arouse. "The very ritual of going on combat duty helps to instill high morale and psychological qualities in the men. The solemnity of the ceremony of going on duty, the brief and precise words of command, the sounds of a military march, and the measured pace in formation—this focuses into a single whole the thought, feelings, and will of the soldiers taking over the responsible combat watch."[22]

Combat readiness, however, is not simply a matter of will, indoctrination, or dedication. Military authorities have enlisted science, especially psychology, to raise the level of combat readiness. Research on the stability of attention and the reaction time of soldiers and sailors as a function of their level of responsibility and their length of time in the service has been conducted.[23]

4. Military Specialties

Soviet military training is intended, as is training in most modern armies, to produce not "just a soldier," but a specialist.[24] In World War I there were only about fifteen to twenty military specialties in the Russian army. By World War II this number had grown to 160, and by 1952 to 400. In early 1972, 2,000 technical skills were distinguished in the Soviet armed forces.[25] The chief of the political directorate of the missile forces, General Gorchakov, points out that in many subunits of the missile forces almost every fighting man has a specialization that is different from others in his subunit.[26]

The Soviet military distinguishes within any given specialty three levels of skill—third-class, second-class, and first-class, the last being, of course, the

[20] *KVS,* no. 4, February 1972, pp. 36–43.

[21] *KZ,* February 13, 1972, p. 3.

[22] Lieutenant Colonel E. B. T. Badmayev [*An Important Factor of Combat Readiness*], Moscow, 1972.

[23] Ibid. Research has determined that attention on combat watches weakens right after coming on watch and 30 minutes before replacement. Attempts have been made to correct this by giving brief physical exercises before going on watch and providing hot tea or hot coffee during the last hour of the watch.

[24] As is often the case in the Soviet Union, military and civilian practices have their parallels. The Twenty-fourth Party Congress and the ninth five-year plan both emphasized that the young in the Soviet Union should become specialists before going to work. Executives of enterprises have been reprimanded for accepting young workers who have not yet acquired a specialty and have been told to stop hiring youths who have not completed their vocational-technical education. *Pravda,* July 4, 1972, p. 3.

[25] *Starshina serzhant,* September 1971, pp. 2–3, and *KZ,* February 3, 1972, pp. 2–3.

[26] *KZ,* April 14, 1972, p. 2.

highest level. The production of a third-class specialist seems to take about six months, with an additional six months to move to each higher level in the same specialty.[27] Not all inductees have to start from scratch to acquire their third-class specialist ratings, since, as we have seen, a substantial number of draftees receive some specialist training during preinduction military training or at a DOSAAF school or club.

Soviet training objectives go beyond teaching each soldier one particular skill. Pressure is exerted to get soldiers and officers to acquire a second specialty as well. Nor is this viewed as the maximum of which a soldier is capable. In the rocket forces, "of particular importance is the struggle being waged by personnel to master two to three specialties, for in modern battle great importance is attached to interchangeability of crew and detachment members."[28] Marshal of the Soviet Union M. Z. Zakharov recommended that a rule be established requiring that a driver-mechanic be able to fire a cannon just as well as a gunner, and the latter in turn be able to operate a tank. The marshal added that Soviet missile personnel especially have accomplished a great deal with respect to acquiring multiple specialties.[29] Statements urging soldiers and sergeants to qualify as specialists as soon as possible often add that they should learn to use not only their own weapons, but also those assigned to their platoon, company, or battery, and thus that they should qualify in two or three allied specialties.[30]

Data in Soviet military articles indicate that in the highly technical services close to 100 percent of all servicemen are qualified specialists. In the navy the figure is 90 percent, and in the air defense troops (PVO) 95 percent.[31] These figures suggest that a substantial number of draftees in the PVO and the navy have already acquired a specialist rating in DOSAAF before induction. In the less technical services the percentage is probably not as high, but it still must be sizable, since at any one time at least three-quarters of the ground troops have been in the army six months or more and consequently should have acquired at least a third-class specialist rating.

Second-class ratings occur much less frequently. In the engineering division of a destroyer, only about 25 percent of the seamen had second-class specialist qualifications and even fewer were first-class specialists. A partial explanation might be that many of the sailors had not yet served long enough, but this explanation is rejected by a Soviet writer because there were sailors

[27] *Bloknot agitatora,* May 1971, pp. 21–23.
[28] *Kommunist Tadzhikistana,* November 19, 1970, p. 3.
[29] *Starshina serzhant,* September 1971, pp. 2–3.
[30] *KVS,* no. 1, January 1971, pp. 18–26. Komsomol and Party activists in the military sometimes play a major role in getting servicemen to take their specialty examinations ahead of schedule. Ibid., no. 2, January 1972, pp. 52–56.
[31] *Sel'skaya zhizn',* July 30, 1972, p. 3; also *Voyennyye znaniya,* June 1972, pp. 6–7, and July 1973, pp. 6–8. In 1974, 97 percent of the Strategic Rocket Forces were qualified specialists. *KVS,* no. 21, November 1974, pp. 28–33.

on the destroyer who had been serving for several years without acquiring a higher qualification.[32] The 25 percent of seamen on the destroyer who had second-class specialist qualifications contrasts with an objective set for a submarine chaser of 45 percent of seamen with second-class qualifications and 32 percent with first-class qualifications. However, several officers aboard the submarine chaser expressed doubts that the objective could be attained on a vessel of this type.[33] Eighty-five percent of the personnel of the cruiser Groznyy, which won a rating of "excellent" six years in a row, have first- and second-class specialist ratings.[34]

In the air force, "at the present time more than 80 percent of . . . personnel are first- and second-class specialists. . . . Almost all flight personnel have had engineering training."[35]

As one would expect, the crews of nuclear submarines are highly trained and are under great pressure to develop first-class qualifications. On one nuclear submarine one-third of the crew were first-class specialists.[36] The troops of the rocket forces are also a highly trained group. Approximately 66 percent of missile soldiers are said to be first- and second-class specialists.[37]

The high technical rating of the rocket and PVO forces also shows up in the number of soldiers who have allied specialties. In the missile forces more than half are said to have at least a second specialty, and in the PVO about 75 percent are said to have mastered allied specialties.[38]

Perhaps one reason why some servicemen are unwilling to make the effort to improve their specialist ratings is the failure of the appropriate authorities to issue certificates to them after they have qualified and, more important, the failure to provide the extra pay that the specialist certificate confers.[39]

5. Initiative and Fear of Responsibility

A major objective of Soviet military training, but especially of the command training of officers, is the development of initiative and creativity. When Mar-

---

[32] *KZ*, April 4, 1972, p. 2.

[33] *KVS*, no. 24, December 1970, pp. 40–45.

[34] *KZ*, November 30, 1973, p. 2.

[35] *Sovetskaya Litva*, August 19, 1973, p. 2. One air regiment reported that it was striving to have 70 percent of its personnel qualify as first- and second-class specialists. *KZ*, November 1, 1973, p. 2. This does not necessarily conflict with the figure cited in the text, but the latter may be an exaggeration. It is evident, in any case, that the distribution of specialist ratings in a unit will vary greatly depending on whether it is taken just before or just after the reception of new inductees.

[36] *KZ*, July 30, 1972, p. 2. In addition to the one-third who are first-class specialists, there appears to be even a higher category comprising 15 percent of the crew who are "masters of military affairs."

[37] Ibid., November 19, 1974, p. 2.

[38] *Voyennyye znaniya*, June 1972, pp. 6–7.

[39] *Starshina serzhant*, November 1970, p. 37.

shal Grechko listed the six requirements of a cadre officer, the third requirement was initiative and independence. "These qualities are compulsory for a military man."[40]

Soviet military forces have long been criticized for their failure to give officers sufficient freedom of action, and for an even greater restriction on the freedom of the lower ranks to act according to the requirements of the moment. Part of this is traceable to the role played by political commissars in the earlier development of the Soviet forces and to the adverse effects on the careers of officers whose initiatives ended in failure.[41]

"Today initiative is being given great encouragement,"[42] but problems still exist, and Soviet military literature, particularly when it deals with the command training of officers, contains many passages dealing with the question of initiative, the assumption of responsibility, the need for creativity, and the fear of being criticized.

Recent Soviet concern with the ill effects of restrictions on officer independence and their consequent fear of responsibility is certainly related to longstanding problems of military leadership, but a new note of urgency stemming from the existence of nuclear weapons can be detected in Soviet discussions of how much freedom should be allowed officers. An editorial in *Krasnaya zvezda,* speaking of the nuclear age in the indirect language often employed ("in connection with the revolution in military science," "under present-day conditions," "in complicated and tense situations") makes it fairly clear that there is a relationship between the desire to give greater initiative to officers and the possibility of nuclear war. "In connection with the revolution in military science there is an even greater increase in the significance of initiative and independence. Under present-day conditions a commander cannot count on receiving exhaustive instructions from a senior commander at all stages of the battle. In complicated and tense situations, under conditions created by unexpected and sharp changes in the situation, the commander will have to make responsible decisions on the basis of the overall concept of action."[43]

Despite an intent to encourage initiative and independence, few Soviet writers recommend their exercise without adding some qualifications. Cases are, however, occasionally discussed in the military journals where an officer who took an initiative is praised for his independence. Thus the commander

[40] *KZ,* March 24, 1972, pp. 1–3.

[41] On the restraints placed upon the initiative of officers, especially during World War II, see Raymond L. Garthoff, *Soviet Military Doctrine,* Glencoe, Illinois, 1953, chapter XIII.

[42] *KZ,* December 23, 1970, p. 2.

[43] Ibid, June 3, 1972, p. 1. This passage probably refers to tactical initiatives that may be required in the field during disruptions of communication or sudden changes in the conventional or nuclear status of a war, and not to major decisions such as the use of strategic or tactical nuclear weapons, the rules of whose employment are hardly a fit subject for a *KZ* editorial.

of a Soviet air force plane found that because of a mechanical refueling difficulty he would have to drop out of a group operation. After consultation with his navigator, flight engineer, and second pilot he decided to rely on his reserve fuel and complete the task set for the flight. "This was an example of true creativity and not haughty willfulness." The action of the commander in ignoring a firm flight rule was viewed as "intelligent initiative, decisiveness, and knowledge" and resulted, after analysis of the flight, in changes being introduced into flight rules.[44] This case is striking because usually Soviet military writers avoid saying anything that suggests that firm regulations can be flouted. A similar case is that of an artillery commander who in a field exercise made the unconventional decision to launch an artillery attack against the enemy directly from march formation. "His decision did involve a certain risk, but under the circumstances, when there was extremely little time to organize artillery support . . . and little information on the enemy, it would have been useless to operate on the basis of a conventional scheme."[45]

Soviet air force flyers, "especially young ones, see a contradiction between the need unwaveringly to fulfill flight tasks that have been worked out in detail on the ground and approved by the commander, and decision-making on flight changes according to their personal evaluation of the developing situation. The obvious fact of the matter is that some commanders view the manifestation of initiative only as a violation of the flight tasks. . . . Evaluating it as a lack of discipline is easiest but far from the best, and not always the proper method to struggle against violations of flight regulations. . . . In order for the pilot to always act decisively and with initiative, he must be confident that this will be understood as a necessity, that his desire to do something better will be accepted."[46] Young naval officers are also encouraged to develop independence, and *Krasnaya zvezda* urges senior officers to encourage them in this direction. With an eye on the timidity of students who fear the consequences of unwise actions, a military writer urges them "to display creativity and to have no fear of undeserved reproaches for having made a bold decision," thus incidentally conceding that undeserved reproaches may indeed follow a bold decision.[47]

There is an ambiguity in Soviet discussions of initiative that frequently seems quite intentional. Some statements, as we have noted above, seem unequivocally to recommend initiative and independence for officers, but most discussions of the subject show an ambivalence that can hardly fail to be transmitted to the reader. Thus, "there have been instances in which . . .

[44] Ibid., July 13, 1972, p. 2.
[45] Ibid., May 20, 1972, p. 2.
[46] *Aviatsiya i kosmonavtika,* August 1972, pp. 11, 35.
[47] *Voyennyy vestnik,* January 1971, pp. 2–12.

officers have acted listlessly and without initiative in complex situations. . . . In developing their initiative they must be reminded that it must be directed at the best possible execution of their combat mission, that it must be based on firm knowledge of and *undeviating adherence to regulations and instructions.*"[48] (Emphasis added.) This writer makes no effort to resolve the dilemma of how to develop independence and initiative while adhering undeviatingly to instructions and regulations. Instead of trying to resolve the dilemma, one Soviet solution is to deny that any conflict is involved, indeed to affirm that the two terms of the dilemma support each other. "On what does the effectiveness of creativity on the battlefield depend? It depends on a firm knowledge of the regulations."[49] Another writer assures officers that "if he has a firm knowledge of the regulations, a commander will never become confused and will be able to extricate himself from any difficult situation."[50]

A political officer has found a different way to assure officers and soldiers that initiative is not proscribed, indeed that it is important and individuals must not shrink from responsibility. "If he has a good Communist conscience, he has nothing to fear and there is no reason for him to avoid making a decision."[51] Unfortunately, there probably are a substantial number of officers and soldiers who do not have good Communist consciences and who in any case are not convinced that their superiors will agree that they are entitled to have one. In Party affairs, the "extraordinarily important provision" of collective leadership creates conditions for developing fearless initiative. If people observe this Leninist principle strictly and without compromise, they are guaranteed against "erroneous decisions," which in this context means decisions for which they can be reproached. Unfortunately, in this case, too, one hand takes away what the other hand has offered. "Along with this, there is no relaxation of the personal responsibility of each Party member for the sector assigned to him."[52] This statement, directed not only to political officers but to all officers who are members of the Party, that is, to the great majority of Soviet officers, does not provide strong encouragement to take an initiative that, if it goes wrong, will hardly permit an officer to hide behind the principle of collective leadership even if he has first consulted Party activists in his unit.

An editorial in *Krasnaya zvezda* assures commanders that they need have no fear in accepting a risk in the interests of achieving their goals, but continues with the statement, "We have in mind here intelligent and decisive actions and not reckless and foolish ones!"[53] The question is precisely, of course, what will

[48] *KZ,* August 24, 1972, p. 1.
[49] Ibid., June 2, 1971, p. 2.
[50] *Voyennyy vestnik,* January 1971, pp. 2–12.
[51] *KVS,* no. 1, January 1971, pp. 65–70.
[52] Ibid., no. 16, 1971, pp. 25–31.
[53] *KZ,* April 8, 1972, p. 1.

be viewed as intelligent and decisive and what as reckless and foolish. Soviet military writers show little inclination to establish guidelines for distinguishing between the two.

Flying personnel might be happier to be accorded increased independence if at the same time they were not warned that "it is impermissible to risk flight safety. However, risk and initiative are far from the same thing."[54] Pilots may not be convinced that the two are so completely unrelated. Initiative and determination do not mean "reckless daring, but sober calculation."[55] To an officer faced with the need to make a quick decision, the ability to defend his action as resulting from sober calculation may seem rather limited—all the more because the right to take reasonable risks is only appropriate in the case of an officer who has "mastered all the subtle details of his profession," a qualification that many officers may feel they have not yet attained or have not had attributed to them. Nor does it seem likely to inculcate a great love of initiative to be told that an officer should have the courage of a leader and be capable of adopting a bold plan, "sometimes *even* resorting to a reasonable risk" (emphasis added), and, of course, "taking full responsibility for his plan."[56]

Disregarding traditional military principles is hazardous, since, as one writer candidly acknowledges, any evidence of independence may terminate with "an order being issued by a senior."[57] An independent paratroop general, engaged in risky parachute experiments in which many soldiers were involved, acknowledged that "afterwards I could neither eat nor sleep."[58] Although the writer who reported this seems to provide cautious support for the general, he points out that decisions that set aside tried military principles can be made by commanders only in exceptional cases. Here again, the question for any commander is precisely whether his case will be judged exceptional or not.

In addition to the ambivalence expressed toward initiative and independence in individual Soviet military writings, further ambivalence and ambiguity are introduced by contradictory appeals made in different writings. In the same month (August 1972), Soviet air force pilots could read in their journal, *Aviatsiya i kosmonavtika,* the appeal for greater boldness quoted on p. 98 above, and in a *Krasnaya zvezda* editorial the following: "The laws of flight duty are severe and inexorable. Any violation of them can entail severe, frequently irreversible consequences. This is a specific feature of flying. . . . The pilot is indoctrinated in a spirit of the strictest observance of discipline generally, and flight discipline in particular."[59]

[54] *Aviatsiya i kosmonavtika,* August 1972, pp. 11, 35.
[55] *KZ,* February 16, 1971, p. 2.
[56] *Nedelya,* July 10–16, 1972, p. 6.
[57] *Smena,* March 1971, pp. 20–23.
[58] Ibid.
[59] *KZ,* August 17, 1972, p. 1.

It is not surprising, then, that officers continue to show reluctance to demonstrate as much initiative and independence as apparently is desired by senior military authorities. The case of a PVO launch control officer who had lost contact with his commander is typical. The target being used in the exercise entered the detection zone of the missile guidance station, and not a second was to be lost if the target was to be destroyed. But the launch control officer kept trying to communicate with his commander to receive authorization to fire. When the raid was over, the inspecting officer asked the PVO officer why he had acted in this manner and received the reply, "I had to know if the commander approved the target that I had selected." The inspecting officer concluded that a superficially trained launch officer will be unable to display creativity and decisiveness in combat.[60]

Although junior officers seem to have apprehensions concerning the exercise of initiative and the assumption of responsibility, it appears that it is the older officers who are least willing to make risky decisions.[61] Possibly the older officers have a lot more to lose. Perhaps also their recollections, observations, and experiences more clearly suggest that initiative is frequently penalized.

The concern of older officers to avoid charges of irresponsibility leads them to subject junior officers to a series of trivial duties, such as conducting soldiers to the bathhouse or acting as duty officer in the dining room. Although this makes the NCOs less self-reliant, junior officers continue to be assigned to these trivial duties in order to provide security and insurance for the commander. "If a bad situation develops, the commander could then say, I am not at fault. I had assigned officer so-and-so to this subunit."[62] This not only places the junior officers in a humiliating situation, but also affects the NCOs who are squad commanders. In their combat exercises the NCOs often react to a changing situation by simply awaiting an order from one of the officers.

That junior officers sometimes lack initiative is not simply due to a fear of taking risks. It is evident from Soviet discussions that senior officers, anxious to have their units make a good showing, surround their subordinate officers with so much attention and so many instructions that they fetter their initiative and inculcate in them the bad habit of awaiting orders.[63]

The navy urges senior commanders not to indulge junior officers and oversimplify their work for them. Senior officers should not monitor the actions of the young officers too closely for fear of destroying their ability to perform independently.[64]

The Soviet air force insists that the principle of flight personnel inde-

---

[60] Ibid., March 31, 1972, p. 2.
[61] Ibid., June 18, 1971, p. 2.
[62] Ibid., December 25, 1970, p. 2.
[63] Ibid., June 29, 1971, p. 2.
[64] Editorial, ibid., March 28, 1972, p. 1.

pendence is wholeheartedly followed in many squadrons. Wholehearted independence, it turns out, is "combined with daily indoctrination and mandatory verification by superior officers who, however, do not substitute thereby for their men and do not restrict their intelligent use of initiative."[65] However, those who are concerned with flight accidents are inclined to be a little less liberal with respect to the independence of air force pilots. A colonel whose duty it is to investigate flight accidents points out that bold decisions may have to be made in battle but that in training and practice flights caution should be observed. "Intelligent caution should not be construed as overcautiousness." People who neglect to follow the regulations and their flight documents are gambling and taking unjustified risks.[66]

Personal initiative in flight training in the Soviet air force is severely restricted until the final stages of training are reached. In teaching air combat, the elements of battle are played out in a stipulated maneuver in which the actions of attacker and attacked are clearly specified. Later the pilot is permitted a certain amount of free maneuvering, but it is only in the concluding stage of training and combat maneuvering that pilots can take personal initiative in the role of the attacker. A commander responsible for pilot training is not likely to concede a great deal of initiative to his pilots, since he is fully accountable for the maintenance of flight safety in the training exercises.[67]

More generally, every commander in the armed forces "is responsible for the actions of his subordinates as well as his own."[68] The commander, therefore, has a strong incentive to restrict the initiative and independence of his subordinates if he can thereby decrease the chances of the latter making major errors for which he will be held responsible. The commander may very well hesitate to follow the advice of *Krasnaya zvezda* to trust the young officer and to support "reasonable initiative."[69]

6. Physical Hardening

A major objective of Soviet military training is to ensure that officers and men have the physical resources to perform their military duties not only in periods of relative peace and quiet but also under conditions of sustained physical and psychological stress. As we shall see later, the Soviet emphasis on combat realism during training, especially in military exercises, is intended to provide the types of stress that will test the physical hardening and endurance of the troops and that will provide incentives for adherence to physical conditioning

[65] *Aviatsiya i kosmonavtika,* February 1971, pp. 11–12.
[66] *KZ,* May 11, 1972, p. 2.
[67] *Aviatsiya i kosmonavtika,* June 9, 1972, pp. 1–3.
[68] *KVS,* no. 17, September 1972, pp. 49–54.
[69] *KZ,* September 16, 1972, p. 2.

procedures and norms. A new statute effective in the forces on November 1, 1973, requires all military personnel to pass the military sports complex (VSK) before the end of the first year of training. This complex, first introduced in 1965, the counterpart to the civilian GTO complex, and apparently identical with the fourth level of that complex, includes mandatory norms for five events: ascent and revolution on the parallel bars, 100-meter run, 1- or 3-kilometer cross-country run, 100-meter free-style swim, and 10-kilometer ski race or 6-kilometer forced march.[70]

The recruit in the military forces has a period of physical exercise right after arising. It seems that this period was originally thirty minutes long, but it has been increased, at least for some troops, to one hour. One specialist recommends that the daily physical training hour be divided as follows: fifteen minutes for gymnastics, twenty minutes for the obstacle course, and the remaining time for cross-country running. Another variant is to start the physical training hour with the obstacle course, then work on unarmed combat procedures, and end with a 3-kilometer cross-country race.[71] Unlike the enlisted men, officers are permitted to do their morning exercises independently at home.

The Soviet practice of taking every opportunity to make progress in one activity without cost to competing activities also applies to physical hardening. A much-recommended form of physical hardening in the Soviet forces is to require units going to areas where combat training exercises are to take place, or to the range or other duty areas, to do so by a forced march over as difficult terrain as the situation permits. A tank lieutenant who was urged to use such devices to harden himself and his men objected: "Are they really necessary? After all, we are not infantry personnel. We can reach any place in our tanks." This attitude was strongly condemned by *Krasnaya zvezda* and, of course, understandably so, since the point of the forced march was not necessarily to train people for forced marches over difficult terrain, but to produce a certain state of physical fitness.[72]

Soviet physical-training officers and military writers point out that running or making forced marches while en route to a training area is by no means the only way to make use of unproductive time for productive purposes. The soldier's free time can be made available for lifting weights or moving combat equipment. Another means of improving physical fitness is to encourage officers to take group vacations in ways that provide physical training, such as mountain climbing, hiking in the mountains, or going on ski trips in the winter.

The stress on endurance is understandable, given the frequent references

[70] *Sovetskiy voin,* no. 4, February 1974, pp. 26–27.
[71] *KZ,* July 21, 1972, p. 4.
[72] Ibid., March 31, 1972, p. 4.

to soldiers and officers who were unable to stand the hard pace during the course of tactical exercises and maneuvers. Soviet stress on combat training under highly realistic conditions and the frequent exercising of military skills in the field seem to reveal, more than may be the case in more indulgent armies, the benefits from and, very frequently, the lack of adequate physical hardening.

Soviet military writers also stress the usefulness of exercise and athletic events as "an aid in reducing nervous and mental strain. They produce positive emotions, such as joy, inner satisfaction, and pride in having successfully completed a task."[73] Physical training and athletic competitions permit people to develop "endurance, self-mastery, courage, and even competitive aggressiveness." An officer or an enlisted man who has not earned the military athletic badge is an incompletely trained soldier. For some types of soldiers this lack can be particularly serious. Soldiers who need to have some means of easing "nervous and emotional excitement," for example those being trained for the first time in flight operations, especially require the psychological benefits of intense physical training.[74] In addition, the Soviets have considerable respect for the enormous psychological and physical stress that may be imposed by nuclear war and believe that only soldiers who are at the peak of physical perfection will be able to withstand such stresses.

It is difficult to avoid the conclusion, after reading Soviet materials, that physical hardening, athletic competition, and physical skills are also viewed as a form of disciplining individuals and as a means of improving stamina not only of a physical but of a moral nature. Difficult athletic accomplishments or difficult exercises have the virtue of getting people to undertake difficult things and committing them to a successful performance of them. The soldier who is not properly conditioned physically is not only an incomplete soldier but, one infers from Soviet materials, is really not a totally loyal soldier. He has failed to acquire the capacity for the loyal performance of his duty, a duty that requires him to devote his body as well as his mind to the homeland. The relation of physical fitness to discipline and loyalty is partly reflected in the fact that the officer responsible for ensuring a proper level of physical fitness among the troops and for producing a prescribed number of military athletes in the unit, is often the political officer. Naturally the interpretation of physical fitness as a test of loyalty reinforces the tendency to impose additional physical training on the free time of both the soldier and the officer.[75]

[73] *Aviatsiya i kosmonavtika,* May 1971, pp. 40–41.

[74] *Kryl'ya rodiny,* June 1971, p. 18.

[75] The Soviet military has a special regard for the competitive edge that physical fitness provides. Physical fitness enables an individual to outperform a more skillful competitor who is not as adequately fit physically. The Soviet hockey team that almost succeeded in defeating the Canadian team of professionals in September 1972, and which was essentially the team of the Soviet Central Army Sports Club, came as close as it did to victory by having a higher degree of physical conditioning than the Canadian players. For an account of the intense physical training

B. MEANS

1. The Course of the New Soldier

Many Soviet inductees do not go to a military school or a training regiment for an extended period of basic training. The inductee is generally assigned to an operational unit and there, together with his fellow inductees, he is segregated into "the course of the new soldier." The length of this course appears to vary from a few days to several weeks, perhaps three or four. The brevity of the course of the new soldier is made possible by preinduction military training, which has taught most of the soldiers the rudiments of military formations, military regulations, and the handling of light weapons. Even those inductees who got little systematic preinduction training are likely to have received some military training as Young Pioneers and Komsomols, particularly in their summer military games.

Some Soviet recruits are sufficiently well trained to be assigned to operational companies from virtually the very first days. This seems to be especially the case among recruits who have received specialist training in DOSAAF clubs and schools. In a tank regiment the new recruits, although still engaged in the course of the new soldier, were already assigned to a tank unit and introduced to their tanks and other weapons.[76]

2. Individual and Group Learning

Uncertainty as to whether to train soldiers primarily by inculcating individual skills or by coordinated crew operations produces a certain tension in Soviet training doctrines and practices.[77] The emphasis on producing specialists in various military skills tends toward a corresponding emphasis on individual training. This is reinforced by a pedagogical principle of increasing importance in Soviet military training, namely that "each individual is different." Stress on individual supervision and instruction is particularly strong in Soviet air force pilot training. In an outstanding squadron a "strictly differentiated approach is taken in the training and indoctrination of each pilot, taking into account the individual characteristics of each."[78] Individual training is also encouraged in some units by assigning each new recruit to a cadre member, who then assumes responsibility for being his mentor and instructor.[79]

---

of these Central Army Sports Club hockey players, not only on the ice but in cross-country running, volleyball, soccer, weight-lifting, etc., see the *New York Times,* September 30, 1972. On the use of sport to serve foreign policy objectives, see James Riordan, "Soviet Sport and Soviet Foreign Policy," *Soviet Studies,* 26 (3), July 1974, pp. 322–343.

[76] *Pravda,* February 20, 1970, p. 3.

[77] *KZ,* November 3, 1971, p. 2.

[78] *Aviatsiya i kosmonavtika,* February 1971, pp. 11–12.

[79] *KZ,* October 21, 1971, p. 2.

Despite agreement that individual training has an important role, there appears to be an increasing requirement that more military training be carried out through coordinated group activity. Experience has shown that officers and men who get high marks in individual-duty tests often fail in military exercises due to a lack of proper coordination of the participating individuals. Coordination is taught in large-scale exercises, but this is not viewed as sufficient. The coordination of individual tasks, according to a number of Soviet writers on military training, should be taught in the training sessions themselves and practiced as such. Obviously, this procedure also conforms better with Soviet interest in combat realism. Practicing precise and rapid coordination of complex movements is especially important, because it helps to overcome a tendency on the part of persons trained in various military specialties to attend only to their own equipment and duties during the course of a military exercise and not to pay enough attention to the battle as a whole.[80] Antiaircraft missile units, while having to provide considerable time for individual specialist training, particularly depend on comprehensive practice sessions with coordinated crew operations.[81]

Beginning with the new training year in late 1970, the interest in group training and group learning led to an increase in field exercises that brought together men of all specialties and categories. This increase in field training was also thought desirable because it provided more opportunities for command training and improved the level of its performance.[82]

The emphasis on group training has been felt not only in the teaching of professional skills, but also in ideological and political training.[83] Experience indicates to Soviet air force writers that under today's conditions the focus of political indoctrination must also be shifted to the air crew, the flight, and the group, although it is granted that the foundation of indoctrination must be with the individual.[84]

3. Theoretical and Practical Training

The tension between individual and group learning has a parallel in a similar tension between the advantages of theoretical and practical training. Theoretical training in many instances consists of individual study and training, whereas practical training is more readily adaptable to groups, although it is not exclusively a group activity. Just as group learning is encouraged because

---

[80] Ibid, June 29, 1971, p. 2.
[81] Ibid.
[82] Ibid.
[83] *Aviatsiya i kosmonavtika,* February 1971, pp. 11–12.
[84] Ibid.

of its value in promoting combat realism, so practical training also receives an impetus from the argument that it increases combat realism in training and develops the skills required for combat readiness.

Practical training tends to impose greater demands on the officers themselves, and this in itself is an advantage. The proponents of practical training are insistent that whether the officer is using actual military matériel, some type of simulation device, or another form of training equipment in teaching his soldiers, he should make use of "the remarkable principle of training: 'do as I do.' " The principle of "do as I do" is the principle of eliminating most verbal and especially theoretical explanations and demonstrating the required act by one's own performance. Clearly, the officer who has to demonstrate, rather than simply to instruct orally and "theoretically," has to be able to perform well, both to win the confidence of his students and to demonstrate what it is they are supposed to do. Thus, this principle of practical, as opposed to theoretical, training has the virtue of providing training for both the trainee and the trainer.[85] Practical training has been extended in the military academies at the expense of academic training. At the Frunze Military Academy students now get on-the-job training in the forces as part of their curriculum.[86]

It is apparent in Soviet discussions that an emphasis by the authorities on one skill or mode of action does not relieve the individual of responsibility for its opposite. Although the emphasis on practical training is strong, officers who do not also have a theoretical understanding of their subjects are reproved. Without being aware of them, a certain air commander used excellent psychological principles in training his pilots. However, a writer points out that this is not sufficient and that his theoretical knowledge was inadequate. Although the commander's practical insight enabled him to train his subordinates and to take their peculiarities into account, his lack of pedagogical theory prevented him from training them to train others.[87]

4. Drill

Soviet training literature stresses the importance of drill. In one sense, drill refers to military formations, that is, to parade-ground drill. This type of drill, in the view of Soviet writers, develops discipline, alertness, the habit of fulfilling commands, and a sense of collectivism that makes it possible to unify the efforts of all the men in a general mission. In a second use of the word, drill refers to "practice makes perfect." Soviet military writers on training seem to have little confidence in any military specialist skill unless it has been learned

---

[85] *KZ,* September 10, 1971, p. 2. See also *Voyennyy vestnik,* January 1971, pp. 2–12.
[86] *KZ,* April 20, 1974, p. 3.
[87] Ibid., October 28, 1971, p. 2.

by repeated drilling and also is prevented from deteriorating by continuing drill.[88]

The belief that practice makes perfect is particularly important for personnel who perform complex operations. "The rapid professional coming of age" of young officers in the Soviet air force is due to the fact that the total number of flight hours logged today by a pilot in one year is two to three times greater than it was a decade ago.[89] Insistence on continual drill and the refurbishing of old skills is strong in the air force, where the deterioration of unpracticed skills is believed to be rapid and to be a threat to flight safety. Pilots who have been away from flight duty or flight exercises for only a short time are nonetheless required to go through drills both in a simulator and in the cockpit of a plane before being permitted to fly again.

Naval writers also emphasize the importance of continuous training. The incorrect execution of orders that sometimes results in a ship at sea getting into great difficulties is attributed to a failure to demand continuous training. Naval regulations specify that regular training exercises in each individual's occupational specialty are to be held throughout the entire period of combat training, a period that includes the time a ship is in base as well as the time it is at sea.[90] Apart from the regular training exercises that take place during a cruise, long cruises in themselves are viewed as an important form of training in endurance and in the development of appropriate reactions to rapidly changing climatic and oceanic conditions. The emphasis by the Soviet navy on the value of long cruises for training commanders and seamen suggests that the motives for the increased Soviet naval presence in the seven seas are not entirely political and in part are dictated, or at least supported and justified, by training considerations. "Ocean cruises have become the main means of training our Red Banner fleets. In cruises of vigilance the naval men get a general review of their learning, acquire sound knowledge and naval tempering, and practice solving operational training tasks under complex conditions of the seas and oceans."[91]

Both Soviet military and civilian authorities are convinced that there is an unlimited potential that is inherent in persons, which can be capitalized on if they are pushed sufficiently hard. This provides another strong incentive for continual drilling as a means of approaching the never-quite-attained level of ultimate perfection.

---

[88] Ibid., May 7, 1972, p. 2.

[89] Ibid., January 21, 1970, p. 2.

[90] Ibid., October 14, 1971, p. 2.

[91] Fleet Admiral V. A. Kasatonov, first deputy commander-in-chief of the USSR Navy, Moscow Domestic Service, July 29, 1972. When naval cadets were divided into two groups, one of which did much of its training at sea on long voyages and the other at the naval school, the former received higher grades on an examination that was given to both groups. "Long ocean voyages have now become a regular phenomenon for the cadets." *KVS,* no. 17, September 1972, pp. 17–23. See also "Ocean Voyages—A School for Conditioning Naval Personnel," ibid., no. 11, June 1974, pp. 30–37.

5. Combat Realism

Soviet training doctrine and practice emphasize that military training is for performance in war. The state of being combat-ready means the ability to perform one's duty both as an individual and as a unit under the stressful conditions of combat. Consequently, training exercises should emphasize and provide the conditions that will simulate the difficulties and dangers that occur in actual combat. "It is an imperious command of the times that troops be trained under conditions similar to those that they will encounter in actual combat."[92]

Most military establishments attempt in one degree or another to provide conditions that will simulate the stresses of combat. The Soviets, however, seem to pursue this objective in training more vigorously than most. Erickson attributes the "peculiar rigor" of Soviet training programs and their emphasis on maintaining an operational atmosphere to the Soviet lack of war experience and operational activity since World War II.[93] This no doubt contributes to Soviet motives for maintaining a high level of combat realism in training, but there are other motives as well. Soviet training doctrine is much preoccupied with the particular stresses of nuclear war, which involves many factors "that act negatively on the mind."[94] A principal problem of military training is to cultivate in the Soviet soldier steadfastness and fearlessness, so that he can resist the psychologically disabling effects of nuclear weapons.[95] Correct psychological training provides fighting men with qualities that make them capable of executing combat missions "under any threat."[96] According to Army General Kulikov, combat operations in the course of a future war will be distinguished "by tremendous tension and will be accompanied by colossal destruction and mass losses of people and equipment."[97] Those soldiers who have specialized in civil defense activities must "cultivate psychological stability under the most strenuous and dangerous conditions."[98]

Soviet training doctrine gives additional impetus to combat realism by emphasizing that under mental stress intellectual and motor abilities are subject to destructive influences, even when the stresses involved are considerably less than those that might be expected in a nuclear war. Soviet military psychologists have concluded that the first skills to suffer impairment are intellectual abilities, such as the performance of calculations and the ability to analyze and make decisions. Next comes a deterioration of motor abilities. Even the

[92] Ibid., no. 11, June 1971, pp. 3–8.
[93] John Erickson, *Soviet Military Power* (London: Royal United Services Institute for Defense Studies, 1971), p. 83.
[94] *KZ*, July 22, 1971, p. 2.
[95] *Nedelya*, July 10–16, 1972, p. 6.
[96] *KVS*, no. 12, June 1972, pp. 45–51.
[97] *Voyennyye znaniya*, no. 5, May 1974, pp. 2–4.
[98] *KZ*, May 5, 1972, p. 1.

ability to drive a combat vehicle, fire weapons, and perform similar routine military duties are affected. Only experience in realistic battle situations can enable soldiers to adapt to these stresses.[99]

An additional motive that seems to lie behind the Soviet stress on realism and rigor in training cannot be easily documented, but Soviet discussions seem to imply that any failure to face and experience the real rigors and difficulties of life and battle is a betrayal of the spirit of communist devotion. The maximum service of a Soviet soldier and a communist can only be achieved under conditions of great physical stress and fear. Such situations provide, in the Soviet view, good opportunities for producing "ideologically hardened" soldiers. Under conditions resembling actual combat, a soldier is afforded an opportunity to fulfill his obligations, to display honor and courage, and to demonstrate to his commanders that he has become "ideologically hardened."

A further motive for combat realism applies in particular to officers and NCOs. This is the commander's need to habituate himself to risks involved in making quick decisions in which the attempt to outwit the enemy involves the officer's prestige and good name. Training exercises must provide opportunities for cadres to get accustomed to dangers of this sort, as well as to dangers of a more physical character.[100] It is not possible to get habituated to the stress of making command decisions when the enemy exists only on paper; making these decisions is quite another matter when two intellects clash in battle.[101]

We have already noted the use of "combat" terminology to help induce the desired state of combat readiness. The stretching of the Soviet military vocabulary to describe ordinary operational and training activities as "combat" assignments seeks to lend an air of combat realism to these routine activities. Speaking on Aviation Day, an air force spokesman points out, "Our pilots and navigators are now carrying out with tremendous patriotic enthusiasm complex combat assignments."[102] Personnel entrusted with strategic and antiaircraft missiles, supersonic fighter interceptors, and similar types of matériel are generally spoken of as being on "combat alert duty."[103]

A favorite device for maintaining the tensions appropriate to wartime conditions is to impose sudden alerts at a time when they are least expected. Thus, after a submarine exercise had just been completed and the rocket launching crew was beginning to relax, a sudden call to battle stations was

---

[99] Ibid., September 7, 1971, p. 2. Soviet military psychologists working in PVO installations report that when the temperature level is raised from 26° to 28° C the effectiveness of operations begins to fall off. At a temperature of 36° effectiveness is only 45 to 70 percent of the basic level, and mistakes increase about sixfold. Loud noises increase mistakes and reduce productivity by 40–60 percent. Ibid., January 30, 1971, p. 2.

[100] Ibid., September 7, 1971, p. 2.

[101] Ibid., July 31, 1971, p. 2.

[102] *Kryl'ya rodiny,* no. 8, 1972, pp. 2–4.

[103] *KZ,* August 24, 1972, p. 1.

made, and the launch crew had to go again into immediate action. This is viewed as providing necessary "psychological hardening," the psychological counterpart of the desired physical hardening.[104] In a PVO unit the announced plan of an exercise involved the detection and handling of two targets that were to appear more or less simultaneously. However, the exercise umpire changed the scenario of the training session and eliminated the second target. The PVO officer in charge was thus led to look for a nonexistent target, and he was criticized for his failure to adapt adequately to the unexpected change of situation.[105]

Although surprise alerts and similar devices provide the atmosphere of tension desired by Soviet military trainers, the principal training under conditions of combat realism and the major effort to develop psychological hardening occur in exercises and maneuvers. Combat realistic procedures are not just for occasional use, but are insisted on as an integral aspect of most exercises. It is not sufficient for an individual to be placed just once or twice in a dangerous or strenuous situation in order to become battle-hardened. These experiences need to be repeated and soldiers should, so to speak, be drilled in experiencing dangers.[106] Soviet military writers warn against the tendency in exercises to place more physical and psychological stress on the soldier than on the officer, which is viewed as inimical to correct training. In addition to frequent field exercises of varying degrees of combat realism, recent years have seen the largest maneuvers in the history of the Soviet military forces— Dnieper, Dvina, and Okean. To these should be added the Brotherhood of Arms maneuvers with other socialist states in October 1970.[107]

Naturally, the ability to introduce the conditions of actual warfare in the course of exercises and maneuvers is limited, but the Soviets go as far as they can within these limitations. Particularly regretful from the standpoint of some Soviet military authorities is the inability to simulate nuclear explosions realistically enough. "Certainly, as much as we might wish, we are not able to demonstrate the full effect of nuclear explosion and its consequences, or to 'accustom' the men to the effect of its injurious factors in the exercises. But in the future, it is essential to improve these simulators. . . . The soldiers and sailors must be ready to accept unexpected complex and dangerous situations."[108] The Soviets have not been entirely unsuccessful in simulating some aspects of nuclear warfare. In conformity with the principle that troops must experience a real sense of danger (even though they are actually being protected) is the procedure followed in an exercise in which the signal for radiation

[104] Ibid., July 1, 1972, p. 2.
[105] Badmayev [*An Important Factor of Combat Readiness*], Moscow, 1972.
[106] *KZ*, September 7, 1971, p. 2.
[107] *Voyenno-istoricheskiy zhurnal*, January 1971, pp. 3–8.
[108] General of the Army A. Yepishev, Head of the Political Directorate, writing in the Introduction to Badmayev [*An Important Factor of Combat Readiness*], Moscow, 1972.

danger was given. "This announcement resulted in smiles. . . . Before long one of them [soldiers] noticed that his dosimeter was indicating radiation. Others checked their dosimeters only to arrive at the same conclusion. The smiles disappeared immediately. . . . Actually, there was no radioactive contamination in the area. Special technical 'devices' had been used to simulate radiation."[109]

There are other reasons for "fooling" troops in a training exercise. Faced with the requirement for combat realism and, at the same time, the danger of accidents, the Soviet solution has been to induce a real sense of danger by misleading the soldiers while reducing the risks. Thus, the trainee is often unaware that the danger is much less than it appears to be to him. The Soviet air force has found it possible to reduce the risk of accidents in flight training by controlling elements of danger that nonetheless seem very real to the trainee. The experienced commander is in a position to come to the rescue. "It is sometimes useful for psychological training if the pilot being trained does not know what insurance exists."[110] Another writer, referring to a commander who has taken all precautions, asks, "But should his personnel be aware of these measures?" He answers, "Not in all cases."[111]

Exercises with live fire particularly provide realistic conditions, but at the same time create considerable risk. "The creation of real fire density entails a certain risk. . . . Of course, everything must be done so that the safety measures are observed with great strictness. And only the commander should know and be confident that absolute safety has been provided. But the soldiers must experience danger and become excited."[112] Despite the risks involved, "it has become a rule in tactical exercises for a bombing strike to be carried out by the air force in immediate proximity to the troops. Then at the same time weapon and tank fire is conducted in spaces between combat formations. . . . Tank roll-overs of the soldiers are practiced along with live grenade-throwing."[113]

Soviet military literature, while constantly referring to risks involved in combat realism, carefully avoids an explicit discussion of instances where the attempt to simulate battle conditions led to actual casualties. However, occasional discussions seem to refer to cases where casualties were suffered, especially when planes bombed a target and the bomb fell on or much too close to supporting troops.[114] Naturally, it is not only the troops subject to an error in bombing but the pilots, too, who are in a state of considerable apprehension. Young officers especially are taught to engage in these attacks, and it is evident

[109] *KVS*, no. 1, January 1971, pp. 65–70.
[110] *Aviatsiya i kosmonavtika*, October 1971, pp. 9–11.
[111] *KZ*, May 13, 1971, p. 2.
[112] Badmayev [*An Important Factor of Combat Readiness*], Moscow, 1972.
[113] *KVS*, no. 12, June 1972, pp. 45–51.
[114] *Aviatsiya i kosmonavtika*, September 1971, pp. 6–7.

from the discussion of this practice that commanders experience difficulty in overcoming the fear pilots have of hitting their own troops.[115]

Soviet air force pilot-training programs seem especially to stress realism in training. This, of course, applies to air combat as well, and not only to bombing and strafing of ground targets. An air force general says, "In my opinion a training flight should be arranged so that it differs very little from an actual combat flight."[116] Another air force general states that practically all units of the air force train personnel under conditions close to combat and that this has become the principal method of training.[117]

In conformity with the Soviet desire to accustom personnel to sudden changes in situations, pilots in their training flights often find themselves faced with unexpected commands and with emergencies that are imposed without warning. This type of training is viewed as particularly important, since Soviet air force training doctrine holds that a rapidly changing situation along with the existence of an opponent are the two elements that impose maximum psychological and physical strain.[118]

Soviet sensitivity to the deterioration of performance under conditions of physical and psychological stress has led to considerable efforts to subject PVO units to a great deal of simulated battle action. Radar operators are sometimes trained to exercise their functions while battle noise simulators are exploding outside their radar cabins and smoke is pouring in through the hatches. These and various other measures are taken in order to develop an ability to concentrate under stress.[119] However, Soviet training discussions have been critical of the use of simulation devices that simply generate a lot of noise and smoke but do not provide in other respects the degree of realism required for combat training. Thus, the analysis of a PVO exercise points out that the commanding officer used a great deal of "scenery and sound effects." He had even introduced radioactive "contamination." Explosive charges and smoke pots were going off all over the place, and the entire performance reminded the Soviet analyst "of a skilled stage presentation." However, the most essential part of the exercise, namely dealing with the aircraft in the air, was ineffective because simulated aircraft were on the radar screen instead of live targets. The analyst concludes, "It is no wonder, then, that with live targets under conditions of jamming, these units often show up to have poor scores."[120]

A similar difference in performance is reported for troops that had to clear out a mine field. They performed flawlessly and cleared the field well within the established time norm. However, when the field had to be cleared during

[115] *KVS,* no. 24, December 1969, pp. 42–47.
[116] *Aviatsiya i kosmonavtika,* February 1971, pp. 4–5.
[117] *KZ,* December 10, 1970, p. 2.
[118] *Aviatsiya i kosmonavtika,* February 1971, pp. 4–5.
[119] *KZ,* January 30, 1971, p. 2.
[120] Ibid., November 3, 1971, p. 2.

the course of a tank exercise involving live firing, they did very poorly. Apparently, then, concludes the Soviet writer, training that does not involve tactical pressures and dangers of warfare is not adequate.[121]

Soviet ground forces use elaborate training fields with mock-ups of urban areas including streets with two- and three-story buildings, railway stations, and similar installations. The approaches to the "city" have various types of labyrinths, entanglements, and trenches. Some unrealistic conditions are noted as unavoidable, for example, blank training mines. However, the "city" has to be taken under assault while it is going up in flames and "in this exercise the fire is real fire . . . and you could easily get burned. . . . This makes it possible to combine tactical training with instilling strength, endurance, boldness, and resourcefulness. It is difficult to overestimate the significance of such a training base."[122]

Soviet military training specialists have developed special demonstration exercises to give regimental and battalion commanders an opportunity to develop uniform methods of holding exercises. These demonstration exercises were used originally in connection with complex combat tasks. Now demonstration exercises are also conducted for small units by regiment and battalion commanders in order to give the less experienced lower-ranking officers examples of correct training exercises. In these demonstration exercises "great attention is given to soldiers experiencing the maximum moral and physical stress."[123]

Some services of the army have failed to contribute their full share to the promotion of combat realism in exercises. Many rear service units move in supplies during an exercise without taking into account the tactical situation, and act as if there were no battle taking place. Some units provide supplies only on paper or on the night before the exercise, and in effect do not participate in the exercise. This departure from combat realism is strongly condemned.[124]

A special danger that troops, but particularly officers, must learn to face in the course of military exercises and maneuvers is enemy deception. Particular importance is attached to studying decisions of the enemy that indicate the "base and deceitful methods" he has employed.[125] However, the Soviets do not hesitate to urge the maximum use of deception as a means of attaining military objectives cheaply. "One form of military creativity is military deception." The author of this statement points out that in World War II, deception in the form of false defense lines, false tank parks, and false airfields was common.[126] In the same vein, an article on field engineering commends officers who, in tactical

---

[121] Ibid., May 19, 1972, p. 1.
[122] *Sovetskiy voin,* May 1972, pp. 8–10.
[123] *KZ,* May 17, 1972, p. 1.
[124] Ibid., August 19, 1972, p. 2.
[125] *KVS,* no. 1, January 1971, pp. 65–70.
[126] *Voyenno-istoricheskiy zhurnal,* May 1971, pp. 95–100.

exercises, use a feint for the purpose of confusing the enemy about their basic strategy or use false defense areas and false firing positions.[127] A conference of the military journal *Voyenno-istoricheskiy zhurnal* produced a number of suggestions for improvement, one of which was the following: "It would be a good thing if the editors printed more articles about the combat operations of units that by employing military cunning achieve success in battle with little bloodshed. . . . In all wars, troops resort to deceptive operations. And, of course, it is necessary to teach our commanders this art."[128]

Defense against enemy deception and one's own capacity for deception are closely related to reconnaissance. Reconnaissance, according to one writer, is not dealt with adequately in many training exercises, and its treatment represents one of the worst types of oversimplification. Good use and proper execution of reconnaissance are an important index of a good officer. Reconnaissance can be taught most effectively during two-sided exercises (that is, exercises in which there is an enemy), but even in one-sided exercises commanders have the opportunity to train forces in the conduct of reconnaissance operations and thus to provide the exercise with a greatly increased air of realism.[129]

Because of the pressure for realistic training, the striving for realism has sometimes to be kept in check. A writer, referring to the training of personnel for sentry duty, points out that officers who inspect the performance of sentries are now forbidden to approach them stealthily and to attempt to disarm them. "Such actions can have very tragic results."[130]

In addition to accidents there is another, related motive for placing bounds on combat realism—thrift. Soviet military administration is insistent that a thrifty regard for military matériel always be observed. Given the Soviet emphasis on realism in training, the adoption of a thrifty attitude toward the expenditure of ammunition, shells, and missiles is perhaps a little surprising. It is, however, never really surprising to find a Soviet administrative apparatus striving to maximize two values simultaneously. It is not unexpected to find a writer complaining, about a particular unit, that "high results in firing have been achieved at the expense of using live rounds for shells."[131] Not enough use was made in this unit of various instructional procedures and devices that would have permitted learning to proceed without a heavy expenditure of matériel. "Firing with live rounds should be the outcome or result of intensive and careful training."[132]

Flight training is particularly expensive and despite the emphasis on

[127] *KZ*, July 20, 1972, p. 1.
[128] *Voyenno-istoricheskiy zhurnal,* June 1971, pp. 98–101.
[129] *KZ*, June 24, 1972, p. 1.
[130] *Starshina serzhant,* August 1971, p. 11.
[131] *KZ*, November 26, 1970, p. 1.
[132] Ibid.

increased pilot time in the air and combat realism in flight assignments, the air force is also insistent, both for technical and thrift reasons, on the use of simulation equipment. Air force writers point out that pilots sometimes resist the intensive use of flight simulators and consider them of little value. However, air force doctrine stresses "the absolute importance of simulated flying training."[133] Training instructors sometimes side with the pilots, show a lack of enthusiasm for ground trainers, and complain that they are not provided with enough real targets. Some air force officers who have managed to arrange training according to their preferences boast that their particular units have trained mostly in the air with real targets. Some opposition to drilling on ground trainers arises from their failure to keep up with changes in flight equipment. One article concedes that these trainers are sometimes obsolete, but insists, nonetheless, that certain types of training (for example, dealing with the sudden failure of an important gauge) can still be usefully conducted with them.[134] The voice of officialdom and "compromise" comes from an officer who points out that simulation equipment is also capable of providing realistic training.[135]

6. Socialist Competition and the Grading System

Socialist competition has been a long-established device of Soviet society for motivating people to greater effort and productivity. The miner Stakhanov and the Stakhanovite movement declined in importance after World War II and especially after the death of Stalin. Stakhanov, now in his sixties, recently stated that the type of impetus that he gave to mining production and to general industrial productivity by his example of exceeding norms was no longer the most important way of attaining high productivity. Nonetheless, the use of socialist competition to drive people to surpass norms and to compete for ever greater effectiveness continues both in Soviet military administration and in civil life. Defense Minister Marshal Grechko, in a general review of military problems, lent his weight to socialist competition as one of the most powerful means for mobilizing personnel to carry out combat training missions.[136] This was in conformity with a resolution of the Central Committee of the Party ("On Further Improving the Organization of Competition"), which in turn was in conformity with the Twenty-fourth Party Congress's emphasis on the need to develop socialist competition further and to improve its organization.[137]

[133] *Aviatsiya i kosmonavtika,* February 1971, pp. 20–22. Simulation training in the cockpit of actual planes (not mock-ups) accounts for about 15 percent of total time alloted to preflight training. Ibid.

[134] *KZ,* September 14, 1972, p. 2.

[135] Ibid., December 25, 1970, p. 1.

[136] *Sovetskiy voin,* January 1972.

[137] *Pravda,* September 5, 1971, pp. 1–4.

There is no aspect of military training or military administration that cannot be improved through socialist competition. *Krasnaya zvezda* provides an impressive list of objectives that can be served by it. Socialist competition "should be directed toward improving combat readiness; fulfilling combat training and political training; instilling ideological convictions and high moral qualities; improving combat expertise and field, flight, and naval training; and the ability of personnel to perform outstanding guard and administrative duties, strengthening discipline, uniting military groups . . . improving daily routine and leisure activities, ensuring proper upkeep of military camps, and improving the training equipment base. Obligations may also be concerned with moral-ethical norms, with improving the external appearance of soldiers, with struggling to achieve honor, dignity, and faultless behavior on the part of soldiers, and with improving their political and cultural levels."[138] Of these objectives, those listed as most important are ensuring high quality competition in combat training, using training time efficiently, reducing the amount of time required to prepare a subunit for combat, mastering the operation and maintenance of combat equipment, and training outstanding and first-class specialists.[139]

Socialist competition is easiest to organize, monitor, and assess when it involves, as it often does, activities that lend themselves to quantitative measurement. Thus such accomplishments as the number of soldiers in a unit who have received specialist ratings, firing performances on the range or in exercises, or the reduction in the consumption of gasoline per kilometer driven, readily lend themselves to a grading system that permits the ranking of units or individuals. In many instances, grading is a question of the stopwatch that determines whether a tank has been put in motion rapidly or slowly, or whether an antiaircraft missile has been prepared for firing more or less quickly. The Soviet navy holds regular competitions for the championship of the navy in finding and destroying enemy submarines in the shortest amount of time. Air defense units are rated according to their speed and success in spotting and bringing down targets. A tank company able to decontaminate its combat equipment and treat contaminated personnel in one-third less time than was called for under prevailing norms "demonstrated its ability to pass another intense stage of socialist competition."[140] Similarly, an outstanding submarine exceeded the norm for tracking an enemy submarine by two and one-half times.[141] Performance on a whole series of measurable dimensions may lead to an overall grade that records the general level of a unit or an individual. In 1969, in the Moscow air defense district, socialist competition

---

[138] *KZ,* May 21, 1971, p. 1.
[139] Ibid. Note that promoting socialist competition has become a principal objective of socialist competition.
[140] Ibid., February 9, 1971, p. 1.
[141] Ibid., February 2, 1971, p. 1.

almost doubled the number of outstanding units. In addition, almost every second air defense serviceman in the district won the title of "outstanding soldier."[142]

Soviet ratings mostly make use of a four-point system that translates into verbal grades of poor, satisfactory, good, and excellent.[143] Given the intensity of the demands made upon Soviet units and soldiers, it hardly needs to be added that a "satisfactory" grade is viewed as barely tolerable.

In the last two or three years, a new emphasis has emerged on using socialist competition to promote objectives and activities that do not readily lend themselves to quantitative measurement. Whereas one can calculate "with an accuracy up to 1/100th of a percent" the percentage of soldiers who become first-class specialists or who pass certain athletic norms, the percentage who become "morally hardened" during socialist competition is not so easily determined.[144] One consequence of this fact was that "until recently we acted rather timidly as far as introducing obligations aimed at improving organizational ability and observing moral norms."[145] *Krasnaya zvezda,* in reprimanding a newspaper for its inadequate discussions of socialist competition, particularly takes it to task for having failed to deal with the uses of socialist competition in improving "military discipline, model outward appearance . . . norms of communist morality . . . struggle for thrift and economy everywhere."[146] *Krasnaya zvezda* returned to the same theme in an editorial a few months later when it praised a regiment that had introduced obligations and competition "in the fields of ethical norms, soldierly smartness, and outward bearing, and in the field of moral conduct." The editorial expressed annoyance with the failure of more articles to appear on these important areas of socialist competition.[147] Perhaps as a result of *Krasnaya zvezda's* campaign, socialist competition for best watch performance in each twenty-four-hour period on a submarine "took into consideration not only technical indices but also the level of discipline and crew member participation in volunteer work. The latter, by the way, is quite important."[148]

Socialist competition includes the acceptance and fulfillment of individual obligations. The latter term applies to a pledge by individual officers and soldiers to improve their performance with respect to some skill or norm of behavior, such as smart appearance or total conformity with regulations. The term "socialist competition" commonly refers to the performance of an entire

[142] Ibid., January 15, 1970, p. 3.
[143] Ibid., February 10, 1971, p. 1.
[144] Ibid., December 27, 1969, p. 2.
[145] Ibid., December 23, 1970, p. 2.
[146] Ibid., March 2, 1972, p. 2.
[147] Ibid., June 27, 1972, p. 2.
[148] Ibid., September 7, 1972, p. 2.

crew or unit. Since the performance of a unit depends upon the willingness of its individual members to perform with maximum effectiveness, "the basis for socialist competition must continue to be the acceptance and fulfillment of individual obligations."[149] In principle, individual obligations are similar to an athlete running against the clock, and socialist competition to racers competing with each other on a track. Since all units are capable of gaining the title of "outstanding unit," it is possible for all of them to win in socialist competition. Competition is called socialist "precisely because at its base there is a healthy competitiveness in which the pace-setters lead the remainder and help them obtain overall sucess for the group."[150]

Commanders are responsible for organizing socialist competition in their units, but it appears from much of the Soviet military literature that the political officer, the unit Party bureau, and Komsomol serve as active initiators and monitors of socialist competition. They furnish "assistance" to commanders, an assistance that in many instances amounts to a push to conform with higher headquarters and Party requirements for socialist competition. Characteristic of the role of Party personnel is one report on socialist competition on a submarine chaser. Here the goal was set to have 78 percent of all personnel rated "excellent" in combat and political training and to have a third of the crew rated "first class specialists" and a little less than half "second class specialists." Several officers openly expressed doubts about the feasibility of attaining these goals. "However, the senior political worker and a member of the ship's Party bureau as well . . . maintained that all this was possible."[151]

Commanders and Party activists are not necessarily in conflict over socialist competition. The commander's own position vis-à-vis higher commands depends in no small part on the success of his unit in socialist competition. He is, therefore, "completely aware of how important it is for [him] to receive support from the Communists and members of the Komsomol."[152]

Soviet military training and administration is accompanied by continuous testing, surveillance, inspecting and, in general, monitoring of individuals and groups. Socialist competition and individual pledges greatly increase the already enormous scope of this inspection and grading system.

Some commanders require ratings on a daily basis. In one army unit, mandatory daily summaries of the results of combat exercises held by each platoon commander had to provide, in addition to other information, the grades that each person in the platoon had achieved on that particular day.[153] On a Soviet submarine, a daily quiz is given over the public address system

---

[149] Ibid., December 23, 1970, p. 2.
[150] Ibid., December 19, 1969, p. 2.
[151] *KVS,* no. 24, December 1970, pp. 40–45.
[152] Ibid., no. 2, January 1972, pp. 52–56.
[153] *KZ,* December 23, 1970, p. 2.

on matters pertaining to general ship technical problems. Seamen in all parts of the ship must answer the quiz and the compartment commanders bring the answers to a central post where they are graded.[154] Among security troops, whose vigilance is of maximum importance, the work of each military detachment is often summarized every day and each soldier is assessed on "how vigilantly he fulfills his tasks. . . . This makes it possible . . . to draw attention to every, even the most trivial, fact of carelessness."[155]

It is not only the ranks that are subject to intensive checking on performance. The Soviet system provides for examinations by high-ranking officers who travel about and test the competence of commanders. At a PVO missile unit the visiting examiners tested not only the troops but also the top-level commanders. The chief of staff turned out to have excellent knowledge of formations, duty rosters, and internal order, but received extremely low grades on technical questions pertaining to missiles. *Krasnaya zvezda* points out that other officers of similar rank and age had managed to acquire a good technical knowledge through correspondence courses or by studying at military academies. The chief of staff had not done so and was transferred to other duties, where his failure to assimilate technical matters could not do any harm.

It is characteristic of the intensity with which the Soviets apply their methods of control that they often produce undesired effects. The self-interest of commanders and political officers in promoting socialist competition, whether because of the continuing demand for it or because of special competitions in honor of Lenin's 100th Anniversary, the Twenty-fourth Congress, or the Fiftieth Anniversary of the Soviet Union, has given rise to some rather odd and sometimes costly forms of behavior. The commander of a military hospital decided to introduce daily evaluations of each doctor and nurse on a five-point system. It was not at all clear how these determinations were to be made, and "it is a good thing that they quickly reconsidered."[156] Under the title, "Behind the Halo of Sham Innovation," a lieutenant describes socialist competition in a motor pool. Here, those in charge of socialist competition devised an elaborate scheme of positive and negative points for fuel consumption, lubrication jobs, filling out travel sheets, expenditures on upkeep, and so forth. This rating system was so complex that a whole team of soldiers working under an officer was kept busy constructing boards and making entries for each soldier in the motor pool on each factor. Hundreds of squares and many graphs were required to summarize the data. After several months most of the required

[154] Ibid., September 19, 1971, p. 2.
[155] Ibid., November 17, 1970, p. 2.
[156] Ibid., December 16, 1969, p. 2.

entries on the summary sheets were still empty. Some officers complained that a special office should be created for such extensive work.[157]

Socialist competition sometimes induces commanders who are anxious to make a good showing to take measures that are more useful to this end than they are to effective training and operational efficiency. Some regimental commanders transfer a number of their best people to their first battalion. By skimming off the cream of the trained troops and concentrating them in the first battalion, they increase the chances of having at least one battalion achieve high grades and make a good showing in socialist competition before headquarters staffs. This generates negative effects both in the first battalion, where the oldtimers feel that they are not trusted to be good enough by themselves, and in the other battalions, whose ranks are depleted of their best men. A writer, criticizing this not uncommon ploy, points out that "a socialist competition is best conducted on even terms. It is not an end in itself, but rather a means of creating an atmosphere full of creativity. . . . Or does the regimental tank commander hope to win battles with the first battalion alone?"[158] This technique for improving the chances of getting a good score has filtered down to the military game Summer Lightning, which is played by Young Pioneers. "We must not tolerate a situation wherein a special detachment is singled out at the beginning of the training year and prepared for the district Summer Lightning finale. This privilege must be extended to all of the detachments."[159] Of course, what critics do not say is how, given the system of rewards in socialist competition, commanders can be made to conform more to the requirements of military proficiency, rather than to those of personal advancement.

Socialist competition sometimes leads to departures from the proper operational sequence set down in training plans. Some commanders develop "harebrained schemes . . . to make certain jobs go faster."[160] In many instances, a relaxation of requirements occurs involving the disregard of quality for the sake of speed, which happens to be much more readily measured in socialist competition. One PVO crew, in order to be the fastest to launch a missile, ignored operating instructions and climbed up on the mobile launcher and the missile without benefit of the appropriate ladders. This led to some damage to the missile. Speaking of another antiaircraft missile unit, a writer says, "Let us say that there are rumors that the senior commander is coming with a stopwatch to check the launch crew. The battalion ignores everything else— a launch crew practices day and night. They place all their bets on how fast they can ready the missile for firing. Such things as accuracy and other features

---

[157] Ibid.
[158] Ibid., September 21, 1971, p. 2.
[159] *Vospitaniye shkol'nikov,* no. 4, 1971, pp. 19–24.
[160] *KZ,* December, 27, 1969, p. 2.

of the performance are forgotten, and they forget all about comprehensive practice sessions and coordination."[161]

The importance of good grades, both for promotion and other rewards, gives instructors and commanders an incentive during exercises to provide their protégés with special advantages. In PVO exercises it has not been unknown for instructors or commanders to provide units with the coordinates of enemy planes. Instructors sometimes give assistance to the firing personnel while the exercise is in process. "Certainly it is easier to obtain high grades in such a friendly atmosphere."[162] Another writer points out that since the grades of "poor" and "excellent" are rarely given and most persons get "satisfactory" or "good," many commanders hesitate to take risks or to deviate from stereotyped procedures, because regardless of how well they do they are still likely to receive only a "good." A mistake, on the other hand, can irreparably damage an officer's reputation and prevent further advancement in the services.[163] A cadet, commanding a battery firing in a competition, could determine the range either by establishing a bracket or by firing directly and then making the necessary precise correction. He used the latter method and was reproved by an officer who advised him to use the first method, which, although slower, would result more certainly in the high score so necessary to a team in competition.[164]

It is not surprising, in the light of the foregoing, that commanders take precautions to omit from exercises those officers and men who they think may bring down the score. A battalion commander left a new officer out of an important exercise because the commander was uncertain what he would do and "the exercise will be [our] final mark for the year."[165]

Nor is it surprising that outright cheating occurs. Reports are submitted of classes conducted and grades achieved (especially "fives") when the officers involved were not even present at the examination session.[166] Since disciplinary problems reduce the chance of a unit to achieve a high overall rating, they are often concealed. "In this dishonest way they attempt to create the impression of complete order, hide the drop in the percentage of outstanding men among the personnel, and retain the title of 'outstanding' by the military collective at any price."[167] In one unit, during an exercise, soldiers were advised to take gas masks one size too large. This enabled them to breathe more easily and operate more effectively than other platoons.[168] Individual records in military units

---

[161] Ibid., November 3, 1971, p. 2.
[162] Ibid., May 20, 1971, p. 1.
[163] Ibid., February 10, 1971, p. 1.
[164] Ibid., February 9, 1971, p. 2.
[165] Ibid., February 20, 1971, p. 2.
[166] Ibid., February 13, 1971, p. 2.
[167] Ibid., March 12, 1971, p. 2. Political officers, and not just commanders, are sometimes implicated in these cases.
[168] Ibid., June 12, 1971, p. 3.

sometimes show that scores of "two" or "three" have been changed to "four" and "five." This "rounding off" brings the grades of individuals in line with pledges made in the course of socialist competition. Sometimes no competition in combat training takes place but the platoon register later shows entries that indicate that the competitive events took place and that grades were assigned.[169] Given the existence of biases of a quite conscious as well as unconscious nature, it is understandable that some Soviet writers on the military grading system prefer objective control techniques to "personal impressions" or "subjective judgments." When control instruments are used for rating performances, ratings generally go down about one grade.[170]

Socialist competition is often riddled with "formalism." This generally means that socialist competition goals have been accepted, speeches have been delivered, and individual obligations have been assumed, after which everything is quietly forgotten.[171] Formalism is well illustrated by a Soviet enterprise with more than 500 workers where socialist obligations were assumed by printing "so-called individual pledges" with identical texts. "All that the workers had to do was enter their surname and sign it."[172] The pursuit of numbers and the striving to define impact in terms of numbers of lessons or activities conducted without regard to their effectiveness is a common manifestation of formalism.[173]

The strains and stresses induced by socialist competition are substantial. "Perhaps the most dramatic moment was the company tactical exercise. The tanks went into battle . . . visibility was extremely bad. I sat in the vehicle with the referee and was nervous. If the company didn't cope with its mission, the whole regiment would receive a low rating."[174] It is not surprising, therefore, that some officers "hold to the opinion that combat training and combat readiness are one thing and competition is something else."[175] Units that have won the rank of "outstanding" in socialist competition are under pressure to retain the title, since the loss of this distinction is viewed as a serious failure to assume their obligations. One officer, discussing the stress of having to retain a title of "outstanding" said: "We've had enough. We tested the burden of glory for its weight and it was heavy for us."[176] His unit did poorly, because the strain of maintaining a rating of "excellent" apparently led even the Communist and Komsomol members in the unit to be indifferent toward achieving an outstanding performance.

[169] Ibid., July 18, 1971, p. 2.
[170] Ibid., May 27, 1971, p. 2; *KVS*, no. 24, December 1970, pp. 40–45.
[171] *KVS*, no. 1, January 1971, pp. 18–26.
[172] *Sovetskaya Belorussiya*, March 3, 1972.
[173] *Bakinskiy rabochiy*, November 2, 1971, pp. 2–5.
[174] *Pravda*, February 20, 1970, p. 3.
[175] *KZ*, September 11, 1971, p. 2.
[176] Ibid., June 3, 1971, p.2.

The induction of new men twice a year imposes an additional strain. Just after a unit may have received high grades for its performance in exercises or in special surprise tests, new recruits are received and the rating of the unit almost inevitably falls, although it may recover its former level after a month or two.[177]

The Soviet passion for testing, surveillance, note-taking, grading, and all of the other administrative features of socialist competition inevitably imposes something that in any case in contemporary military structures is a highly developed activity, a great deal of paper work, and the generation of an enormous number of reports. Record keeping is "an important means of control and analysis."[178] One military writer complains that sometimes when new replacements are still at the reception center and have not yet taken their military oath, higher headquarters are already requesting reports on the socialist obligations that the new men have assumed. How, protests this writer, can commanders provide these reports when they have not even seen the new men yet?[179] Socialist obligations and their level of fulfillment usually have to be reported twice a year, together with special reports on the eve of important holidays and at some other special dates. The amount of reporting often overwhelms unit officers. One officer complains that a reporting form for which he is responsible requires almost 400 entries.[180]

The record keeping and reporting imposed by socialist competition is exacerbated by the fact that in addition to ordinary logistic and housekeeping reporting and bookkeeping, there is another area in which an enormous amount of paperwork is required—unit Party records and activities. In taking into account some of these less evident costs of socialist competition, one must also include the additional administrative time required to transfer, absorb, analyze, and pass on to still higher headquarters the contents and significance of this mass of paper work.

7. Unlimited Potential

Soviet leaders responsible for military training and civil administration act as if haunted by a fear of not getting everything that can be got out of the human material that they direct. The fear that this potential will not be fully realized is all the more acute because human potential is viewed as essentially limitless. It is not agreeable to the Soviet Communist temperament to accept the existence of limits or to permit individuals under their direction to act as if a limit

[177] *Pravda,* February 20, 1970, p. 3.

[178] *KZ,* January 10, 1970, p. 6; *Aviatsiya i kosmonavtika,* no. 11, 1971, p. 28.

[179] *KZ,* September 11, 1971, p. 2. Since the new recruits are already included in troop totals, the numerical indices of unit competition scores would be sharply reduced were no score assigned for them. The effect of this on reported scoring is not difficult to imagine.

[180] Ibid.

can be placed on their ability to pursue Party objectives. Improvement is always possible. This, indeed, is what distinguishes man from a machine. "It is no secret that there are limits to the tactical parameters of a combat complex. However, no limits are placed upon human potential." Even a machine, however, must have its limited capabilities pushed to the farthest point by the unlimited potential of its operator.[181] "Perfecting combat readiness is a limitless process. Any positive results should be considered only as a basis for achieving new and higher indicators."[182] Another writer expresses the same thought in more lyrical words: "There is no limit to military improvement. It is just as limitless as the blue of the sky on a clear August day."[183]

Political officers must make soldiers understand that "it should not be thought that some sort of limit exists on being able to master equipment,"[184] and a general, speaking of the troops in Germany, agrees that "no limit has been placed on how far we can improve expertise, combat readiness, and the qualifications of our specialists."[185] A writer on the training of flight personnel points out that "as is well known," there is no limit to the perfection of a person's expertise. Thus, after a soldier has received a first-class rating, he has by no means completed the development of his full potential.[186] Indeed, one of the main problems in socialist competition is that obligations undertaken by individual soldiers often are not at all up to the limit of their full capabilities.[187] Another writer objects to the allegation that "the time of the Stakhanovs is over." It only seems so "because working at the limit of one's ability has become a standard of behavior for millions of people."[188]

Given the limitless potential of human material, it is natural that training objectives should embrace the "infinite." Thus, the aim of "ideological tempering" is to produce soldiers who are "infinitely loyal."[189] Similarly, the graduates of military political schools should be "boundlessly" devoted to the cause

---

[181] *Aviatsiya i kosmonavtika,* December 1970, pp. 6–7.

[182] *KVS,* no. 20, October 1973, pp. 67–73.

[183] *Kryl'ya rodiny,* no. 8, 1972, pp. 2–4.

[184] *KVS,* no. 21, November 1970, pp. 73–78.

[185] *Sovetskiy voin,* January 1971, pp. 2–4.

[186] *KZ,* January 27, 1971, p. 1. The high demands placed on the individual are well exemplified by Brezhnev, who, speaking at a student rally, defined the qualities of a Soviet specialist. "The Soviet specialist today is a man with a good command of the fundamentals of Marxist-Leninist doctrine, a clear insight into the political objectives of the Party and the country, a broad scientific and practical training, and a perfect command of his specialty. The Soviet specialist today is a skillful organizer, capable of applying the principles of the scientific organization of labor. . . . He knows how to work with people, values collective experience, heeds the views of his comrades, and is critical in assessing achievements. Of course, the Soviet specialist is a man of high culture and broad erudition; in general he is a real intellectual of the new Socialist society." *Sovetskaya Belorussiya,* February 4, 1972.

[187] *KZ,* February 2, 1971.

[188] Ibid., August 13, 1971, pp. 2–3.

[189] *KVS,* no. 23, December 1968, pp. 53–55. Indeed, we find it affirmed that Soviet soldiers in fact are "infinitely loyal." Ibid., no. 20, October 1971, pp. 68–74.

of communism.[190] Soviet hyberbole is nicely exemplified in a discussion of the military oath. It appears that "literally every letter"—and not simply every word—is filled with profound meaning.[191]

Soviet military literature acknowledges that some officers have been critical of the tendency continually to revise norms of performance upward. However, "it turns out that with the desire, it is possible to find those reserves (and they always exist!) that make it possible when necessary even to 'jump higher than oneself.' "[192]

There is, nonetheless, one area in which Soviet personnel specialists grudgingly concede that difficulties may exist in the way of ever-increasing perfectability. The strength of a commander is not his knowledge alone or his technical skills. He must possess high moral qualities and strength of will. But "it is almost impossible to shape character in just a few months."[193] In fact, character is very resistant to alteration. One practical consequence of the difficulty in changing character is that closer attention must be paid to the process of selecting personnel, especially NCOs. Although Soviet leaders have had considerable confidence in their ability to make human material fit into the system, there appears to be an increasing recognition that suitable selection techniques can better provide some types of personnel than can a total reliance on training.

8. Time and Free Time

Soviet military writers are keenly aware that time is one of the most important resources that individuals and organizations possess. Soviet military leaders are even more sensitive to this, since the training period available to them has been shortened. "Especially now that the term of service of soldiers and sergeants has been shortened . . . it is necessary to redouble the value of each minute of study time."[194] An article addressed to political officers points out that "attention must also be paid to such a characteristic trait of our days as the unprecedented growth of the value of time. . . . That is, the value of a day, an hour, and even a minute."[195] Emphasis on the efficient use of time is not only a military attitude. The importance of time is emphasized in all areas of Soviet life and was given particular stress in a directive of the Twenty-fourth Party Congress concerning the "productive utilization of every minute of

---

[190] Ibid., no. 23, December 1970, pp. 33–38.
[191] Ibid., no. 19, October 1971, pp. 60–65.
[192] *KZ,* September 21, 1971, p. 2.
[193] Ibid., February 10, 1971.
[194] Ibid., December 19, 1969, p. 2.
[195] *KVS,* no. 21, November 1971, pp. 59–64.

working time."[196] The insistence that "each hour should be strictly accounted for"[197] is tempting because it seems to permit increased productivity without an increased use of other resources.

When the Twenty-fourth Party Congress called for the productive utilization of every minute of *working* time, they meant, of course, every minute of *free* time as well. Brezhnev pointed out in a major speech (see p. 76) that frequently leisure time is frittered away pointlessly and needs to be directed into activities useful to the state and the Party.

The exploitation of free time has been institutionalized in the Soviet Union in the *subbotnik*, the practice of Soviet citizens donating a day off at least once a year to uncompensated work.[198] The Party continually presses Soviet citizens to participate in various civic activities in their free time or to pursue their political training or their education in technical matters. They are asked to aid the Soviet militia (police), which safeguards public order, by participating in volunteer units that work in cooperation with the militia. They are asked to participate in many types of committee meetings, rallies, and of course civil defense activities, during their free time. These demands are often so frequent and so onerous that enterprise directors, out of sympathy or necessity, sometimes schedule them during working hours, a practice that leads Party and state officials to protest vigorously.[199]

Krasnaya zvezda, in conformity with the Twenty-fourth Congress and Brezhnev's Trade Union Congress speech, affirmed that "free time becomes a social wealth only when employed in the interests of augmenting the material and spiritual potential of society. Can we say that the free time granted to Soviet people is employed everywhere for these purposes? Unfortunately, we cannot yet say so. Frequently this time is spent to no purpose, thoughtlessly, and sometimes to the detriment of man himself and those who surround him, and, in the final analysis, of social interests."[200] "As Karl Marx noted," *Krasnaya zvezda* reminds its readers, "every economy in the last analysis comes down to an economy of time."[201] In agreement with this, an air force journal affirms that "by eliminating losses of working time it is possible to improve the training process. Here are our reserves."[202]

The Soviet sense of the unlimited potential of human material rests in part

---

[196] *Izvestia,* August 5, 1971, p. 4.

[197] *KZ,* October 21, 1971, p. 2.

[198] The *subbotnik* appears to have been instituted in 1919 by Moscow railway men.

[199] See, for example, *Pravda,* March 3, 1972. One advantage of being a commuter is that in some instances train schedules to the suburbs require the commuter to leave his factory and the city and return home prior to the holding of after-work meetings that he would otherwise be required to attend. Ibid., February 29, 1972, p. 3.

[200] *KZ,* August 10, 1972, pp. 2–3.

[201] Ibid., September 15, 1972, p. 2.

[202] *Aviatsiya i kosmonavtika,* May 1972, pp. 8–9.

on the ability to crowd more and more activity into both working time and free time to the point where the latter can hardly be said to exist. A young Soviet recruit, speaking of his reaction to military life, states, "I did not expect that discipline would be so great that the soldier's every minute is accounted for."[203]

The interior service regulations of the Soviet forces envisage that the men should have eight hours of sleep. The Soviet soldier is also entitled to one and a half to two hours a day "for his favorite pastime or simply for relaxing with his comrades."[204] Time is supposed to be allotted for individual study and mass political and cultural work, but it is precisely these activities and individual socialist obligations that rapidly overwhelm what little recreational or relaxation time the Soviet soldier and officer has. *Krasnaya zvezda* points out that the military can do much good by organizing free time. Organizing free time is, of course, a euphemism for extracting some military value from it. "Previously, plans for regular days off were compiled in units and on ships. Attempts are now being made to draw up longer plans as well—for a month or for a season. Such planning will help officers to utilize free time to maximum effect for intellectual and physical development."[205] Perhaps planning will forestall the need of ad hoc solutions to the problem of free time. On board one naval vessel on a long cruise, boredom had set in. "We understood that the personnel needed relaxation." And so, "on one of our free days," the ship sports committee decided to hold team contests in the assembly of the automatic rifle. "It would have been difficult to think of better relaxation."[206] During the Yug maneuvers, considerable attention was devoted by political officers to the resolutions of the Twenty-fourth Party Congress. It was not unusual for rest halts and pauses during marches and operations to be used to give the "resting" troops lectures on the Twenty-fourth Congress.[207] During the same maneuvers, one unit was rallied to a field by a loudspeaker that announced, "In a few minutes a lecture will begin on the topic 'The Soviet Electoral System —the World's Most Democratic.' We invite you to the propaganda center, dear comrades!"[208] Political officers are informed by their special journal that an effective way of preventing disciplinary infractions is holding "soirées" on various themes of importance to the military, such as "Serve the Motherland Faithfully" or "Drunkenness, Enemy of Combat Readiness and Source of Crime."[209] The pressure on a Soviet soldier to acquire a second military specialty or a higher rating in his present specialty is in large part a pressure to

---

[203] *KZ,* April 18, 1972, p. 4.
[204] *Soviet Military Review,* no. 7, 1970, p. 31.
[205] *KZ,* July 18, 1972, p. 4.
[206] Ibid., September 16, 1972, p. 4.
[207] Ibid., June 18, 1971.
[208] Ibid., June 12, 1971, p. 3.
[209] *KVS,* no. 13 July 1971, pp. 84–86.

get him to utilize his own limited free time for further study of military subjects.

Officers who must carry out certain troop training activities for which time is limited are almost inevitably forced to encroach on the soldier's free time. Indeed, *Krasnaya zvezda* frankly urges: "In order to make maximum use of available training time, the critique of the training operation is conducted, as a rule, during the period set aside for rest and nourishment."[210] Similarly, a medical sergeant points out that sometimes the military medical training of troops receives less attention than other activities of higher priority. As a result, training in this area sometimes has to be conducted in the soldier's spare time.[211] A particularly important political lesson devoted to miltary regulations provided for two hours of study time, and since this was deemed insufficient for so important a topic, political officers were urged that "self-study by the trainee should be organized in the evenings, just before the political class."[212] Thus, not only was the evening devoted to a political class but the free time of the student prior to the evening class meeting was also allocated to additional study activity. Soldiers and officers who act as consultants to the Young Pioneer and Komsomol military games, who help preinduction military training personnel in schools, plants, and summer camps, who assist preinduction youth in passing their physical training tests, and who assist civil defense teams in their exercises generally do so on their "day off."[213]

The Party has provided a sizable number of educational institutions devoted to political indoctrination that are attended by the soldier or worker on his "free time." Evening Party schools with both one-year and two-year curricula and Marxism-Leninism universities provide education and indoctrination on political matters to civilian and military personnel. The majority of the Party schools are of the one-year type and are attended mostly by soldiers and sailors serving their initial enlistments. During the five years 1966–71 the number of such Party schools doubled and the number of students attending them increased more than one and a half times.[214] Needless to say, these schools are attended at times that in most other military establishments would correspond with the soldier's leisure moments.

Senior officers in the Soviet military are not exempt from pressure to attend the evening universities of Marxism and Leninism. Indeed they are under special pressure to set a good example. "We took steps so that a wider group of senior officers studied in the departments of the higher schools of Marxism and Leninism. Now we have twice as many commanders of units and

---

[210] *KZ,* February 5, 1971, p. 4. Soviet training doctrine and practice emphasize the importance of critiques following a training exercise or training mission.

[211] *Starshina serzhant,* October, 1971, pp. 4–12.

[212] *KVS,* no. 19, October 1971, pp. 66–72.

[213] See, for example, *Sovetskiy voin,* September 1972, pp. 18–19; *KZ,* June 2, 1972, p. 4.

[214] *KVS,* no. 18, September 1971, pp. 47–51.

subunits and their deputies at night schools as was the case some two years ago. . . . Our generals and senior officers now penetrate more deeply into ideological study."[215]

Generals and senior officers are not only forcefully urged to be students in such evening classes, but also to act as instructors. "For over three years now Lenin readings have been conducted on the third Wednesday of each month with the officers and generals of the district directorate. . . . The participation of the senior commanders in the propaganda and agitation work is an important criterion for the effectiveness of their self-education and an effective means of indoctrinating their subordinates."[216] Nor is it sufficient for the senior officers to attend class or to teach class; they must devote additional time as well. "While improving the system of Marxist-Leninist training for leading personnel, senior officers, generals, and admirals must set a fine example in their study of Marxism-Leninism. . . . There are still some officers who are content to attend lectures and seminars and show no inclination for independently studying the primary sources and Party doctrines."[217] How the generals feel about this use of their time and what consequences it has for the effective performance of their military duties are not discussed by *Kommunist vooruzhennykh sil.*

The Soviet officer's need to spend a good deal of time in political activity and in various aspects of socialist competition tends to make particularly strenuous his assignment to the numerous special duties performed by officers in most military establishments. A naval captain, speaking of the training of young officers, points out that before a lieutenant is even able to get his bearings on a new ship he is burdened with a great number of responsibilities other than those for which he is mainly being trained. He immediately finds himself placed on a number of committees and required to conduct almost continual inspections. In general, he is badly overburdened. "There is not enough time in the day and he becomes confused."[218]

Officers have clubs where relaxation would seem to be possible, but officers' clubs are viewed by some political officers as "a place where ideological and indoctrinational work can be continued."[219] If officers try to escape indoctrination and other pressures on their free time through sports or other activities away from their garrison, they find themselves encouraged to leave in groups and to use these periods to improve their physical condition. A student who enters a military political school finds that his holiday periods and vacation leaves are to be used for mass indoctrination work. "Most of the students

[215] Ibid., no. 6, March 1970, pp. 17–23.
[216] Ibid.
[217] Ibid., no. 18, September 1971, pp. 3–8.
[218] *KZ,* January 28, 1971, p. 2.
[219] Ibid., November 27, 1970, p. 3.

strive to make speeches at enterprises and educational institutions in their home town during their holidays and leaves."[220]

The burden of work on higher officers seems to be no less than it is in the case of junior officers. A medical colonel who studied the working day of an air force commander found that the commander worked twelve to sixteen hours a day. *Krasnaya zvezda,* which reported the study, does not feel that the commander deserved any pity since he should have been able to shift some of his work onto the shoulders of a capable deputy.[221]

9. Incentives

The pressure in the Soviet armed forces for continual improvement of individual and unit performance and the use of socialist competition together with frequent inspections and grading of performance suggest the existence of an incentive system designed to motivate and support all this competitive training activity. And indeed such a system does exist. Soviet military and civilian authorities do not simply rely on exhortation, excessively fond as they are of this instrument of leadership. Material rewards and "moral incentives" give additional impulses to achievement, beyond those provided by the entire system of upbringing and indoctrination.

In most military establishments, excellence is usually viewed as being rewarded primarily through faster promotion, and this, of course, entails a material reward in the form of higher pay and greater privileges. Promotion, however, can occur only at relatively infrequent intervals. It is a principle of Soviet training doctrine that rewards have their greatest motivational effect when they are conferred as soon as possible after the performance that the reward is intended to recognize. This sound principle of animal training is more readily applicable to rewarding performances quite specific in time and place than it is to the reward of a general level of multidimensional performance over a span of time. But the Soviet practice of frequent exercises, surprise tests and inspections, and competitions and grading lend themselves perfectly to this desire to provide a reward "on the spot." The practice of withholding furloughs awarded for good performance until the end of the year is condemned precisely because it violates the principle of associating the reward with the performance that won it.[222] The principle is only partially based on the idea of reinforcing an individual's future progress by immediately rewarding his present achievement. The second rationale is the dramatic and more readily publicized character of immediate rewards, and the consequent impetus this provides to emulation by other soldiers and officers. Perhaps, too,

[220] *KVS,* no. 23, December 1970, pp. 33–38.
[221] *KZ,* August 5, 1971, p. 2.
[222] *KVS,* no. 9, March 1972, pp. 30–36.

immediate rewarding assures that the real winner, and not someone else, will receive the reward.

Dramatic and well-publicized rewards "on the spot" are frequently conferred by high inspecting officers who seem to make their rounds with their pockets well stocked with watches and other desirable objects. During the course of an exercise an amphibious tanker made an excellent river crossing, and an inspecting general from Moscow immediately came up to the tank commander, embraced him, and presented him with a gift.[223] Following another exercise, the inspecting officer presented a watch to one of the commanders whose success in training and indoctrinating his subordinates had been particularly evident.[224] A description of a flight crew refers to the fact that one member had a watch that carried the inscription "For a high level of flying skill, from an aviation commander."[225] Even as high-ranking a person as Minister of Defense A. A. Grechko observes this custom. Following the "combat" firing of a company that he was observing, Marshal Grechko presented the commander, a senior lieutenant, with a watch because of his excellent results. Soon thereafter the lieutenant was promoted to captain.[226] On another occasion, Marshal Grechko, together with a distinguished group of military leaders, inspected an airfield and its complement. The flight operations were highly successful, although, to be sure, the marshal did not fail to make some comments about raising combat readiness to further heights. Nonetheless, in conclusion, Marshal Grechko stated his pleasure: "I authorize a monetary award to be issued to the pilots."[227] Another senior officer, impressed by the speed with which a PVO unit got its missile into battle position, commended the crew and authorized each man to be given a brief leave.[228] A group of airmen who had distinguished themselves were awarded individual prizes during a ceremony before their unit. One was awarded a gun, another a camera, a third a nickel samovar, and a fourth a harmonica.[229] A rather different type of reward is the freedom granted graduating cadets who have achieved very high grades to choose the area in which they would like to be assigned on graduation.[230]

A new military order and medal introduced in October 1974, "For Service to the Homeland in the USSR Armed Forces," provides a series of material rewards: priority for living quarters, free use of local urban and rural transpor-

[223] KZ, June 23, 1971, p. 2.
[224] KVS, no 23, December 1968, pp. 53–57.
[225] Trud, August 18, 1971.
[226] KZ, June 27, 1971, p. 2.
[227] Aviatsiya i kosmonavtika, August 1971, pp. 4–5. See also KVS, no. 19, October 1973, pp. 66–71.
[228] Sovetskiy voin, November 1970, pp. 9–12.
[229] KZ, November 29, 1968, p. 2. The gift of a harmonica was viewed by KZ as being ill chosen, since it tended to incite laughter among the assembled air force personnel.
[230] Ibid., December 14, 1969, p. 2.

tation, free admission to rest homes once annually, 15 percent pension increase and free travel by rail, water, and intercity bus once annually.[231]

The use of material rewards has not diminished reliance by the military on moral incentives. In civil society, the economic reforms approved by the 1966 Party Congress led to greater use of material incentives, but not long thereafter a new emphasis was given to nonmaterial incentives for increasing productivity. *Kommunist vooruzhennykh sil* has told political officers to "take all possible measures to heighten the importance of moral stimuli and give due honor and praise to those who are rated excellent, giving wide publicity to their successes. This is in accordance with decisions of the Twenty-fourth Congress."[232] The emphasis on moral incentives is repeated by *Krasnaya zvezda:* "In particular, it is essential to rivet the attention of officers, ensigns, warrant officers, sergeants, and petty officers . . . on the use of moral incentives in encouraging the pacemakers of competition."[233]

In addition to ideological drawbacks and motives of thrift, the material rewards increase the already substantial incentives to cheat during socialist competitions and in other grading situations. A military writer notes the practice in some exercises of offering a leave to those who receive a grade of "excellent," while those who get only a "two" ("satisfactory") will have to look after the equipment. "Such a carrot-and-stick method had a negative effect on the men. . . . It caused nervousness and a desire to achieve results at any price. . . . And from here it was not far to deceit."[234]

In the strictest sense, moral incentives mean the willingness to undertake duties out of a devotion to the motherland and the Party and considerations of self-esteem. Nonetheless, moral incentives are generally viewed as involving some honorific recognition. Characteristic of this class of moral incentives are the pennants awarded by the minister of defense of the USSR to units and ships for military valor and for carrying out assigned tasks or turning in outstanding performances during exercises and cruises. The military councils of military districts and of groups of forces and fleets have also instituted "challenge red banners," and these are awarded both to outstanding military collectives and to leading army and navy personnel.

The regulations of the armed forces provide for a whole series of awards as incentives to individuals. These include expressions of gratitude to enlisted men and NCOs that are delivered before the serviceman's unit or in the form of orders, presentations of certificates, photographs of the serviceman unfurling the unit flag, entries made in the unit book of honor, the awarding of badges for outstanding work, and notification to the serviceman's former place of

---

[231] Ibid., October 29, 1974, pp. 1–2.
[232] *KVS,* no. 11, June 1971, pp. 3–8.
[233] *KZ,* February 20, 1972, p. 1.
[234] *KVS,* no. 14, July 1972, pp. 36–42.

work of his exemplary performance. In addition, there are, of course, the decorations and medals of the Soviet Union.[235] At an airfield of the naval command, pilots and crews of missile-carrying aircraft who have conducted practice firing with great success are often greeted with flowers upon their return.[236] Soldiers are presumed to be particularly aware of the high honor of being photographed in front of their unit banner. This should be done during solemn ceremonies, and copies of the photograph should be sent to the parents of the soldier accompanied by a letter of thanks.[237] Honors publicly conferred not only stimulate the emulation of others, but also commit the recipient to a defense of his newly won prestige. The more widespread the publicity, the greater is the recipient's incentive not to risk the loss of his honors.[238]

The importance attached to some of the titles that soldiers receive, such as that of "Outstanding Personnel," is indicated by the fact that the title can only be awarded and taken away by a regimental commander.[239] The air force has adopted a special title for combat airmen who have passed the requirements for flying under all weather conditions. These airmen receive the title of "Master of Combat Equipment."

The title of "Guards Unit" is awarded to units whose personnel have displayed unusual courage in the face of the enemy. A unit that has earned this honor is given guards colors, and each officer and soldier is given a guards badge.[240]

The procedure of conferring honors continues at the end of military service. Many soldiers after discharge receive honorary certificates from regional or other Communist and Komsomol committees in the union republic from which they come. The Central Committee of the All-Union Komsomol also sometimes awards the discharged soldier a military valor medal.[241]

Soviet military authorities are insistent that the awards given to soldiers and units, whether of symbolic or material value, be known to all the rest of the soldiers and to other units. Marshal Grechko has emphasized that the results of socialist competition must be fully disseminated among all individuals and units involved.[242] *Kommunist vooruzhennykh sil* accordingly recommends that after soldiers have received an award, Communist and Komsomol activists should immediately hold a discussion and acquaint all the soldiers with what was accomplished by their comrades. The principle of publicizing the news as soon as the award is conferred conforms with the principle,

[235] Ibid., no 6, March 1972, pp. 30–36, and no. 19, October 1973, pp. 66–71.
[236] *KZ,* June 23, 1972, p. 1.
[237] *KVS,* no. 6, March 1972, pp. 30–36.
[238] *Aviatisiya i kosmonavtika,* July 1972, pp. 1–2.
[239] *KZ,* September 11, 1971, p. 2.
[240] *Soviet Military Review,* no. 9, 1971, p. 44.
[241] *KZ,* September 25, 1971, p. 1.
[242] *Sovetskiy voin,* no. 1, 1972.

discussed earlier, that an award should be given right after the occurrence of the achievement it recognizes and not at some periodic ceremony several removes later. The conferring of symbolic awards on various holiday occasions is called "a seasonal approach" and is much condemned.

Some military units have been reproved for making awards too liberally, and particularly for giving awards for routine administrative work or "even for making one's own bed." *Kommunist vooruzhennykh sil* states that "we cannot view as normal . . . a situation in which . . . awards are issued on a frequent basis to clerks, warehouse workers, and the drivers of small vehicles, rather than to soldiers in leading military specialties—to those who decide the fate of combat and political training."[243] Rewards sometimes risk unfortunate results. A rear admiral points out that excessive praise of certain leading ships sometimes substitutes "sham sensationalism for efficiency and proficiency." As a result, a ship sometimes begins to show signs of complacency and the sailors begin to violate regulations.[244]

10. Military Training and Science

Soviet military training is not viewed as a process in which common sense suffices. Soviet writers claim considerable fondness for the application of cybernetics, cost effectiveness, and systems analysis to military problems. "The cybernetic approach makes it possible to solve the most urgent problems of scientific forecasting of the results of future combat, and to provide optimum troop control."[245] Systems analysis, it turns out, "is a concrete application of Marxist-Leninist dialectic to troop control."[246]

Marshal Grechko has emphasized that the training of cadres and recruits requires the application of scientific methods. He points out that scientists, particularly in the military academies, have made substantial contributions to Soviet military science, but that full use is not being made as yet of opportunities to apply science and to extend research in order to improve the training process.[247] The minister of defense emphasized that in order to improve the system of training cadres, it was necessary to renew the training and material base by strengthening the ties between higher educational institutions and the troops.

Officer cadet academies have been reproached for training students in particular skills without training them to teach these skills to those who will be under their care in the future. "Therefore, methodological training for the future officer must be of prime importance in his senior year at the

[243] *KVS,* no. 6, March 1972, pp. 30–36.
[244] *KZ,* December 22, 1970, p. 2.
[245] *KVS,* no. 17, September 1973, pp. 9–16.
[246] Ibid.
[247] *KZ,* March 24, 1972, pp. 1–3.

academy."[248] In order to facilitate the application of scientific findings and scientific methods to the training, testing, and selection of soldiers, the Soviet military forces have instituted "methodological councils" that operate in units as consultative bodies to work with commanders and their staffs and political organs, and to make it more feasible for them to acquire specialized knowledge of scientific teaching and training and also the results of experiences acquired in other units.[249] These councils are supposed to contain the most authoritative officers and experts and to operate under the control of commanders.[250] The methodological council is referred to frequently in Soviet training literature, and it seems that the commander who does not make adequate use of his methodological council is viewed as lax in the performance of his training responsibilities.

The high confidence placed in science tends to be transferred to a desire to exploit various types of instruments that have the earmark of modernity. Programmed teaching machines and information feedback systems are viewed not only as providing more efficient means of dealing with sizable numbers of students, but also as permitting the introduction of more refined methods of instruction and the reduction of instruction time.[251] Training in command has sometimes been pursued by taking officers out into an open area, where enemy positions and targets are visualized and certain tactical questions are posed. This requires a good deal of imagination concerning enemy dispositions. Automated and electronic training equipment has permitted the training field to be outfitted with instruments that generate light and sound signals simulating enemy forces engaged in various activities. This reduces the amount of visualization required and makes the posing of tactical questions more effective.[252] Similarly, division and regimental commanders and staff officers are able to exercise their command skill in laboratories, where extensive use of photographic procedures and tape recordings, together with radar display screens, permit a readier simulation of battle dynamics.[253]

The Soviet military, especially Soviet air force training personnel, are enthusiastic users of equipment that permits monitoring the trainee, particularly the pilot and his plane. This facilitates the much emphasized postsession training critiques.

The emphasis on scientific methodology in training is in part represented by an insistence on rationalization of the training process by means of advance planning. Each teacher must have a detailed outline of his lesson that not only

[248] Ibid., June 9, 1972, p. 4.
[249] Ibid., July 7, 1971, p. 2.
[250] Ibid., January 9, 1970, p. 1.
[251] *KVS,* no. 21, November 1970, pp. 73–78.
[252] *KZ,* July 9, 1972, p. 2.
[253] Ibid., July 12, 1972, p. 2.

makes it possible for him to make the most of each classroom minute and to lecture more effectively, but also permits his superiors to know what he is teaching. Similarly, a major activity of commanders is the preparation of detailed training plans for their units, often several months in advance, day by day and hour by hour. Since unforeseen events, for example, the nonavailability of a particular training terrain or an intervention by higher headquarters, may require alterations in these plans, it is sometimes desirable to have an alternative plan that is no less detailed. This is intended to forestall any waste of training time.

Soviet training and operational practice try to incorporate the results of research, particularly research on the reaction of personnel to problems arising in the performance of various types of military duties. We have already noted Soviet interest in the problems of maintaining alertness and habituating the soldiers to battle stresses, especially the very great stresses that the threat or actuality of nuclear war are presumed to impose on military personnel.

Most of the research in the area of personnel reactions deals with more readily studied phenomena than responses to nuclear weapons. Thus, temperamental differences among air force pilots are associated with differences in the handling of aircraft controls. Variations in response tendencies that are due to temperamental differences can be prevented only by a strict individual approach in training the cadet in the air, an approach based on a scientific awareness of human differences.[254]

Soviet students of military psychology emphasize the study of responses in emergency situations. In the case of flight personnel, emergency actions require a precise estimate of time. Thus, if the engine stops during flight, the pilot is supposed to delay five to seven seconds before pushing the restart button. However, many pilots delay only about one and a half to two seconds. The tendency to misjudge time is not only a function of psychological stress, but also of certain physical conditions, such as humidity and temperature changes.[255] Such studies tend to be cited with a certain nuance of pride that suggests the considerable satisfaction derived from the introduction of scientific procedures.

Soviet concern with training personnel in military specialties and developing technical skills in its officers and enlisted men creates a problem for personnel policy. The appointment of personnel to particular slots is often based on technical competence, but in fact many of these assignments require that the individual have the gift of military leadership and be capable of exercising a

---

[254] *Aviatsiya i kosmonavtika,* February 1972, pp. 46–47.
[255] Ibid., May 1972, p. 38.

command function. Frequently the tendency is to select in terms of skill and specialty and to ignore the leadership requirement. Because of this it has been proposed that before selecting personnel for various types of technical training, special efforts be made to determine whether they are capable of becoming commanders or "junior commanders," that is, NCOs. Decisions concerning the training of some inductees should not be made until it has been determined whether they have the potential of becoming military leaders as well as technical specialists.[256]

Krasnaya zvezda points out that scientific methods for the selection of persons with command capabilities have long been needed. The Party requires criteria that are scientifically rigorous and uncompromising. These Soviet discussions carry the implication that, although skills of a technical character can be trained into an individual and although he can be made to reach high levels of excellence in their performance, command capabilities are a function of personal traits that are of a more enduring, built-in nature. This requires that personnel specialists select individuals with a talent for command, rather than individuals who have to have this ability bestowed upon them by the appropriate training. Opinion, however, is not uniform on this matter. Indeed, some affirm that even the willingness or ability to perform deeds of great valor can be taught if only one has a proper understanding of these matters.[257] However, we find that although "it is true that necessary qualities can be developed . . . a decisive factor is a man's psychological attributes." This writer clearly implies that the mental agility and skill necessary for an officer are not things that can be instilled by training.[258] We even find that another writer is willing to affirm that the basis of the theory of selection and placement is the relation between inherited and acquired characteristics.[259]

The debate on whether selection should be done according to enduring characteristics of the individual or in terms of the current level of his learned skills leads to another problem in personnel policy. Assignment on the basis of an individual's current training status is acknowledged as simpler and cheaper, but it does not enable one to predict behavior very far in advance. Soviet writers claim that selection based on the immediate level of skill is particularly popular in capitalist countries, since capitalists are only interested in obtaining a quick profit from an individual and do not care about his future suitability. Besides, people who come from well-to-do families can get training more easily than others, and this prejudices capitalist countries in favor of the state-of-training criterion. Selection based on enduring talents is more suited to socialist society. It is acknowledged, however, that the armed forces still

[256] *KZ,* December 26, 1969, p. 2.
[257] *Aviatsiya i kosmonavtika,* December 1970, pp. 6–7.
[258] *KZ,* November 14, 1970, p. 2.
[259] Ibid., September 8, 1971, p. 2.

employ the state-of-training method because of its simplicity and immediate operational efficiency. However, selection based on talent should be used when lifetime vocations are involved, as at military institutions.[260]

[260] *KVS,* no. 9, May 1971, pp. 69–73.

Chapter V

Discipline

The potential effectiveness of military forces is generally assessed in terms of their manpower resources and the weapons at their disposal. These are clearly important determinants of success, both in the field and as a deterrent. Still, the almost exclusive role they play in estimates of military strength is due in large measure to the quantitative comparisons that they so readily, if not always validly, permit.

Discipline, morale, and military skills at both tactical and strategic levels are certainly acknowledged to contribute significantly to military success, but the difficulty of making even crude qualitative, not to mention quantitative, comparisons in these matters debars them from playing the role in military estimates that they deserve. This is particularly the case with respect to morale and discipline whose assessment is difficult enough for one's own forces let alone those of a foreign power, and whose wartime levels are in any case not readily deducible from their peacetime status.

Nonetheless, these difficulties hardly excuse the neglect often given to these features in the comparative study of military establishments. The present attempt to provide an account of them in the Soviet forces needs, then, no apology, despite the limitations of our knowledge and for that matter the limited knowledge of the Soviet authorities themselves. There are few topics that throw more light on Soviet conceptions of human management than do these.

A. "EXACTINGNESS"

Discipline is the "absolute observance of Soviet laws, military regulations, and the orders of command personnel."[1] Discipline, then, is obedience to externally imposed imperatives. No other sector of society, continues this Soviet statement, requires such detailed legal regulation as the armed forces.

For most military establishments, discipline in everyday matters is a training for the automatic obedience especially required in periods of great stress and danger. Individuality in behavior threatens the ability of members of a military team to respond without question to commands and to apply unhesitatingly learned routines. Individuality also complicates the administration of large numbers of men even in peacetime.

The military uniform reflects the desire for uniformity and the restraint of individuality. Detailed regulations covering all phases of military existence also produce a degree of uniformity hardly equaled in civilian life. Today there is a tendancy in western military forces, in response to the disinclination of the young to subordinate themselves to military regimes and to military discipline, to permit greater latitude in behavior. It is not so confidently assumed that individuality necessarily produces a deterioration of combat capabilities. In any case, military leaders of western armies have found it expedient to permit the recruits forms of behavior and modes of dress that the modern military had not hitherto tolerated. In the Soviet military establishment, there is great reluctance to make concessions similar to those made by some western armies. Nonetheless, as we shall shortly see, the Soviets recognize that they, too, have youth problems, and they have shown some willingness to adapt to them.

The importance of military discipline is, in the Soviet view, greatly increased under contemporary conditions. The threat of nuclear war demands a discipline "raised to the highest limit." "Even the slightest manifestation of carelessness or lack of discipline can lead to serious consequences. Deviations of any kind . . . are intolerable."[2] In an editorial, *Kommunist vooruzhennykh sil* points out that today when "the overwhelming majority of troops are armed with crew-served weapons . . . it is essential that they demonstrate exceptional precision in executing orders. . . . The smallest infraction of discipline by even

---

[1] *Voyenno-istoricheskiy zhurnal,* February 1971, pp. 13–21.
[2] *KVS,* no. 24, December 1969, pp. 3–8.

one soldier may lead to disastrous consequences in carrying out a combat mission."[3] The ability of a military organization to perform its task depends entirely on how precisely the requirements of military regulations are fulfilled.[4]

Soviet military authorities fear deviations from regulations, no matter how slight, not only because they might incite others to similar behavior, but also because of the subversive effect that tolerance for such deviations has on the individual's own behavior. In small, isolated units (for example, submarines and small PVO units separated from other military collectives), a relaxed attitude about regulations is no more tolerable than in situations where soldiers mingle with many other members of their own and other units. Precisely because there is a temptation in isolated units to take a more lenient attitude, deviations from regulations are especially intolerable in them.

Soviet military authorities rebuke young Soviet officers who, like their western counterparts, feel that many military regulations become pointless under battle conditions. Certain regulations may be necessary in peacetime, but in time of war they and many administrative procedures stemming from them no longer apply. Soviet authorities insist, however, that "this is a complete misconception. Regulations in the last war proved to be true companions of officers."[5] A regimental commander is approvingly cited who, during World War II, whenever there were no engagements, required his unit both to live according to regulations and to set aside time for studying them.[6]

Resistance to the study of regulations and to the regulations themselves is sometimes given a certain "theoretical" basis. "Supposedly, in our age, when the troops are saturated with electronics, the demand for shining buttons, for repeated parades . . . seems to be a hopeless anachronism. . . . Does a person who operates a complex automatic device have to be concerned, for example, with parading?" This question receives an unequivocal response: "I can state bluntly that this 'theory' is the purest obfuscation. One must be concerned with drilling, and not just parading. And the badges must be polished bright even more energetically than before. . . . An operator [of electronic equipment] who had been lazy in cleaning his boots . . . will scarcely show industry and patience in servicing the equipment."[7]

Soviet authorities, insisting on a precisionist attitude toward laws and regulations, reject the view that these can ever be treated in "too formal a manner." The Party and the government require that laws be observed strictly and be carried out just as written down, without any deviations.[8] Commanders, officers, and sergeants are sometimes reprimanded because they do not enforce

[3] Ibid., no. 19, October 1972, pp. 3–8.
[4] *Voyenno-istoricheskiy zhurnal*, February 1971, pp. 13–21.
[5] *KZ*, January 9, 1970, p. 2.
[6] Ibid.
[7] Ibid., March 3, 1973, p. 2.
[8] *Starshina serzhant*, August 1971, p. 36.

regulations "in the minute detail" that is demanded.[9] A term that runs through a good deal of Soviet military (and civilian) discussion, whether it deals with the training of soldiers or with conformity to military regulations, is "exactingness," or "demandingness." In military life, "an indispensable condition for the proper operational style of the regimental commander is exactingness, that is, avoiding all types of allowances and indulgences and demanding accurate fulfillment of all orders."[10]

An important consequence of this attitude is that everything becomes equally important. A military writer emphasizes that "everything influences success. At times a false impression is entertained by officers that some indulgences are allowable."[11] To Soviet disciplinarians "there are no trifles in discipline." Speaking of submarine duty, a writer emphasizes: "In the shipboard regulations there are no requirements of secondary importance. We must ensure that this fact is clearly understood by all of the sailors, particularly the younger ones."[12] The smallest failure of exactingness "leads to dissoluteness, slovenliness, and laziness."[13]

B. TYPES OF VIOLATIONS

Breaches of discipline involve nonconformity with either (1) Soviet military regulations, (2) Soviet criminal law, or (3) an order of the military commander.

Soviet military regulations that apply to both the army and the navy, that is, the combined arms regulations, include interior service regulations, disciplinary regulations, garrison and guard duty regulations, and drill regulations.[14] In addition to the combined arms regulations, there are special navy regulations for naval personnel aboard vessels.

Servicemen who commit crimes are dealt with, not under military disciplinary regulations, but under provisions of the criminal law governing criminal responsibility in military personnel.[15]

With respect to military commands, the armed forces demand an "undeviating subordination from the bottom to the top."[16] To execute an order unquestioningly means to execute it without any reservations or objections. It is impermissible to argue about an order or to doubt its accuracy. Such

---

[9] *KVS,* no 23, December 1969, pp. 45–50.
[10] *Voyennyy vestnik,* January 1971, pp. 2–12.
[11] *KZ,* April 20, 1972, p. 2.
[12] Ibid., December 18, 1969, p. 2.
[13] *Starshina serzhant,* October 1971, pp. 34–35. That "everything is equally important" is discussed at greater length in chapter IX.
[14] Brief articles on Soviet interior service, disciplinary, and garrison and guard duty regulations may be found in *Soviet Military Review* (English edition), May, July, and September 1973.
[15] *KVS,* no. 19, October 1971, pp. 66–72.
[16] Ibid.

arguments violate the most important disciplinary requirement—unquestioning obedience to the commander. Arguments with commanders are "decisively dealt with."[17] A lecture for military personnel carries the title "Obedience—the Highest Glory of the Soviet Fighting Man."[18]

Especially pernicious crimes are insubordination to the superior, failure to follow an order, absence without leave, desertion, misappropriation of weapons, intentional destruction or harm to military property, disclosing military or state secrets, and violation of the rules of guard duty, of charge of quarters, or of service at sea. The law on criminal responsibility for military crimes provides severe punitive measures for these crimes.[19]

1. Frequency

Our materials do not permit quantitative estimates of the frequency of violation of military discipline. That violations are not infrequent is certainly suggested by the emphasis in Soviet military literature on means of tightening conformity with regulations. Serious offenses, however, that is, offenses by military personnel that are criminally punishable, declined during the five-year plan, 1966–71, by almost 18 percent from the preceding five-year period. The number of such crimes in 1966–71 was the lowest during all postwar years. The number of units in which there were no incidents of criminal behavior among servicemen also increased.[20]

The decline in serious offenses is attributed to the Party's requirement that the army and navy intensify their struggle against violations. More likely, the decline resulted from the reduction in the age of inductees from nineteen to eighteen. In addition, the greater flow of persons out of Soviet educational institutions with secondary education has increased the average educational level of the military. The combination of the lower age of draftees and more education is more likely to have produced a reduction in criminal offenses than the intensified struggle against violations. This seems all the more plausible because a Soviet military study showed that those who violated discipline most frequently were the soldiers who did the least amount of reading of Russian classics.[21] Presumably, this reflects an inverse relationship between education and disciplinary violations.

The decline among military personnel of offenses that are dealt with under

---

[17] Ibid.

[18] Ibid., no. 8, April 1972, pp. 39–45.

[19] Ibid., no. 19, October 1973, pp. 66–71.

[20] Ibid., no. 15, August 1971, p. 26. Soviet military discussions of statistical data do not excel in sophistication, and it is not clear whether the reported reduction in criminal offenses was in absolute numbers or in rates. However, changes in the size of the military forces between 1966 and 1971 could scarcely have produced the 18 percent decline in criminal offenses.

[21] Ibid., no. 3, February 1971, pp. 65–69.

provisions of the criminal law does not necessarily mean that violations of military regulations have also declined. The rates for minor offenses are less likely to have been sensitive to the age reduction in Soviet conscripts.

2. Insubordination

Soviet military literature discusses the nature of offenses that concern Soviet disciplinarians more freely than the frequency with which they occur.

Insubordination, that is, outright refusal to execute an order, which is perhaps the most serious of disciplinary offenses, is rarely mentioned, although offenses marginal to it are not infrequently discussed. Thus, a naval aviator had to be "taken firmly in hand" because of a tendency "to be impertinent to seniors and to understand poorly the necessity of military subordination."[22]

A mild form of insubordination involves subjecting orders from higher officers to public criticism. Officers sometimes excuse themselves vis-à-vis their subordinates by saying that "the order is not mine, but that of a senior chief."[23] Such statements undermine authority. During a conference in his office, a commander received a telephone call from a superior officer. After he hung up, his tone of respect changed, and he said, "What are they thinking about! Don't I have enough to worry about? Now I have to take reports directly from my deputy as required by regulations."[24] Although this officer did not oppose execution of the order of his superior, his slighting remark concerning his superior's command was presumably reported by one of his subordinates who was present in the office and led to *Krasnaya zvezda's* discussion of the incident, not to mention possible disciplinary action.

Despite the sternness with which the requirement of instant and complete obedience is formulated, Soviet military literature provides numerous cases of soldiers and officers who resist orders in one degree or another. Thus, an inspecting officer from the general staff ordered a division commander, perhaps of higher rank, to take a certain action. The division commander resisted until the inspecting officer warned the "division commander officially that he was prepared to notify the general staff . . . and that he would take command himself if necessary. This worked."[25]

In some instances *Krasnaya zvezda* seems more concerned with the behavior of the superior issuing an order than with the insubordination or resistance of the junior. Military and Party authorities are particularly distressed by overt manifestations of anger, squabbling, and shouting between seniors and subordinates (see pp. 180–181), and incidents are cited where more attention seems

---

[22] *KZ,* August 18, 1971, p. 2.
[23] *Voyennyy vestnik,* January 1971, pp. 2–12.
[24] *KZ,* August 22, 1971, p. 2.
[25] *Voyenno-istoricheskiy zhurnal,* September 1971, pp. 54–59.

to be paid to the senior's loss of temper than to the subordinate's resistance. Thus, it is the emotional reaction of a lieutenant rather than the behavior of a sailor who refused to perform some work, saying that he was tired from his watch, that preoccupies *Krasnaya zvezda* in its account of the incident.[26] And it is a higher officer who screamed at a lieutenant for failing to carry out an order that is criticized in a similar account.[27]

The resistance of officers to what was virtually a command of a superior officer is clearly condoned in another case, where the commanding officer's action was viewed by *Krasnaya zvezda* as foolish. This commander required subordinate officers to sign a form acknowledging that they had been warned against alcoholism and against permitting it in subordinates, and stating that if they allowed instances of drunkenness, strict measures would be applied. Some of the officers refused to sign the form on the grounds that it was an insult to them. *Krasnaya zvezda* in effect approved their action and reprimanded the commander for his attempt to solve drunkenness and alcoholism by "paper work."[28]

The discrepancy between the persistent demand for unreserved and instant obedience to orders and the suprising tendency in some cases to ignore or gloss over a failure to obey orders is probably related to the existence of two sources of authority and power in the Soviet military forces—the commanders on one hand, and the political officers and Party activists on the other. Despite the principle of "one-man command," which is supposed to guarantee the sanctity of a commander's orders, it is clear that Party encroachments in matters of military training, discipline, morale, and indoctrination have in effect eroded the authority of the commander. In addition, the right of any Party member, no matter how humble his rank, to criticize his commander, no matter how high his rank, at Party meetings—provided he does not criticize direct orders—can hardly be indulged without some effect on the authority of the commander.[29] The patronizing tone adopted toward a Soviet major by a sergeant proposing improvements in political education in a letter to *Krasnaya zvezda* can only be understood in this context. "Major Gladkikh, the leader of our group, is intelligent and well trained as regards conducting political exercises. He could perform very successfully with us in a Marxist-Leninist training program. As students in his group, we are prepared to join him in this."[30] Since it is the duty of a Party member to oppose whatever he believes to be contrary to Party instructions and Party preferences, there is clearly a great deal of room for opposition to the commander, indeed for insubordina-

[26] *KZ,* February 3, 1973, p. 2.
[27] Ibid.
[28] Ibid., December 9, 1972, p. 3.
[29] On one-man command, tensions between political officers and commanders, and the role of Party activists, see chapter VIII.
[30] *KZ,* January 30, 1971, p. 2.

tion in a broad sense, even though no resistance to a direct command may be involved.

Violations of regulations concerning saluting are marginal instances of insubordination, at least insofar as they are interpreted by the authorities to be—as they sometimes are—a form of more or less intentional "rudeness," and insofar as they are motivated by a desire to avoid a gesture of subservience to a higher rank. According to the military commandant of Moscow, one-sixth of all the officers stopped by military police patrols for violations are detained for offenses involving saluting.[31]

Reluctance to salute is sometimes motivated by a sentiment of rivalry with other arms and services. "Unfortunately, it happens sometimes that a private for some reason considers it unbecoming to salute a PFC, a sailor 'doesn't notice' a tanker, or a flyer a military construction man."[32]

About two-thirds of all military personnel arrested by the Moscow military police patrols had violated uniform regulations. Many officers complain that some uniform items are not available. "Nobody can remove the guilt from the officers . . . or from their commanders, but . . . a certain amount of guilt rests with certain clothing supply organs."[33]

According to the Moscow commandant, a violation by a soldier or officer of "public order" (not otherwise specified) is viewed as an incident of particular importance and the commandant has to report it immediately to the commander in chief of the Moscow military district, who in turn informs the minister of defense.[34] This certainly seems like excessive attention at the top echelons and suggests a special sensitivity to irregular military behavior when it occurs close to the center of the country's political power and in a city where foreign observers are most likely to see it. "Fortunately," the commandant adds, "I cannot recall anything of this sort [happening]. The commandant's service is basically limited to reproofs."[35]

Among other regulations dealing with the relations between military

[31] Ibid., July 13, 1972, p. 4. Officers who live in Moscow fail to render salutes more frequently than do out-of-town officers. It is not only subordinates who fail to salute. The Moscow military commandant had to draw the attention of a lieutenant general to the fact that he had failed to return the salute of a sergeant.

[32] *Smena*, no. 6, 1972, pp. 3–5. The Moscow commandant was asked: When two members of the same rank but of different combat arms meet on the street, who is supposed to salute first? The commandant avoided a direct answer and observed that saluting does not simply include respect for a senior in rank. "Above all, it is a recognition of combat friendship, comradeship, mutual assistance." Ibid.

[33] *KZ*, July 13, 1972, p. 4. Shoulder-board insignia seem to be in particularly short supply, and officers are reprimanded for manufacturing their own.

[34] *Smena*, no. 6, 1972, pp. 3–5.

[35] Ibid. Nonetheless, the commandant does have a guardhouse that is used largely for military personnel who do not obey the order of a patrol or who are rude to a senior in rank. The commandant can detain military personnel for a maximum of fifteen days. Privates are kept separately from officers, but their cells are alike.

personnel, one that appears to be frequently violated stipulates that "on official service matters military personnel must address each other in the impersonal form ("you" = *vy*)."[36] It not infrequently happens that a sergeant and private who work together or officers who are closely associated use the familiar *ty* ("thou") and also address each other by their first names. According to Soviet military authorities this "would later lead to other familiarities,"[37] and, more seriously, to personal bonds that would facilitate "mutual protection" and other forms of collusion, not to mention a failure to report observed wrongdoing. Some sergeants in the missile forces, out of a fear that their relations with the men will be adversely affected, "permit this familiarity and sometimes tolerate violations and prefer 'not to wash their dirty linen in public.' "[38]

3. Violations of Technical Regulations

A major category of disciplinary violations consists of failures to conform with regulations specifying the manner in which various military duties are to be executed. Thus a commander is reproved for providing only forty minutes daily for soldiers to service their weapons, when regulations specify that they ought to spend at least one hour at this task.[39] An air force pilot violated regulations by not wearing the required flight suit.[40] Another pilot overflew a landing strip because he did not want to have to taxi so far to the parking area.[41] Still another pilot violated rules by taking his wife to a movie that ended at 11:00 P.M. when he had to be up at 4:00 A.M. for flight operations.[42]

Violations of technical regulations are generally treated, especially by Party activists in the military and by inspectors, as symptomatic of a more general disregard of discipline and as equivalent to a moral delinquency. It is characteristic of the Soviet outlook that accidents, too, presuppose a "guilty" party.

4. Offenses Against State Property

In a socialist society, crimes against property will in large measure be crimes against the state. This category of offenses is important not only in Soviet civil society but also in the armed forces.[43]

---

[36] *KZ*, February 10, 1973, p. 2.
[37] Ibid., April 12, 1972, p. 2.
[38] Ibid., April 14, 1972, p. 2.
[39] Ibid., August 22, 1971, p. 2.
[40] *KVS*, no. 11, June 1971, pp. 34–38.
[41] Ibid.
[42] *KZ*, March 30, 1972, p. 2.
[43] The Soviet Union has had for the last thirty-five years an organization called Service for Combating Embezzlement of Socialist Property and Speculation (BKHSS). According to Soviet research, almost one-third of all embezzlements result from unjustifiably high norms of raw material consumption and large tolerances in the packaging and weighing of the finished output. *Izvestia,* February 1, 1973, p. 5.

In September 1971 the military forces held a conference to strengthen legality in the military expenditure of state assets and to guarantee the safety of military property. This was in accordance with directives of the Twenty-fourth Party Congress.[44] As one would expect, both from the experiences of other military establishments and from a priori considerations, property offenses in the Soviet military revolve around the post-exchange system, the procurement and stocking of goods for military use, and the military finance offices.[45]

Lesser offenses in this general area include the transfer of military privileges, such as transportation vouchers, to unauthorized persons and, more especially, the use of military property, particularly vehicles, for private purposes.[46] The latter offense usually involves a series of other violations, such as making out spurious trip tickets.

5. Falsification of Records and Collusion

An offense that is widespread throughout the military forces is the falsification of unit and individual records with respect to the attainment of military training, disciplinary, and indoctrination goals. Socialist competition and the rewards and penalties involved in it are powerful incentives for the commission of these offenses. Soldiers are not immune to the temptation to wear badges and decorations—Outstanding Soviet Soldier, Military Sportsman, Specialist First Class, etc.—to which they are not entitled.[47] This is not surprising, since already in preinduction training, Soviet youth find that they can get physical training and specialist certificates that they have not earned.[48]

Collusion is usually the consequence of a prior or associated offense. Collusion may be passive, as when officers or enlisted personnel, including Party personnel, fail to report observed offenses either because of the principle of "mutual protection," or because of indifference or a desire not to make enemies. Some of these failures to report offenses are flagrant. Private travel of the wives and relatives of service personnel often occurs on the basis of service orders made out to persons with masculine names and specified military ranks.[49] Collusion is more active when military personnel join in the cover-up of an offense, a not infrequent occurrence, since some offenses such as the falsification of training, disciplinary, and other records often redound

---

[44] *KZ,* September 23, 1971, p. 2.
[45] See, for example, *KZ,* May 16, 1971, and February 18, 1973, p. 4. The careless use of military property may be more costly than conversion of state property to private use. See *KZ,* December 27, 1970.
[46] Ibid., June 19, 1971, and October 28, 1972.
[47] See, for example, *KZ,* July 26, 1973, p. 2.
[48] Ibid., July 27, 1973, p. 4.
[49] Ibid., June 19, 1971.

to the benefit not only of the soldier or officer whose record is involved, but of other personnel in the unit, and indeed often of the entire unit.[50] Political officers as well as unit commanders are likely to benefit from a spuriously good record, or the concealment of embarrassing unit events, and it is not unusual to find the complicity of political officers mentioned in connection with many different types of offenses.[51] Even finance inspectors, whose job it is to turn up evidence of the conversion of military funds to private use, sometimes connive at practices intended to conceal from their own superiors incidents of this character, provided, apparently, that the funds are in the meantime replaced.[52] Similarly, vehicle inspection personnel who stop and check vehicles on the road often accept trip tickets that are patently spurious as valid.[53]

6. Slander

An offense that concerns Soviet military authorities more than it does their counterparts in western military establishments is the use of slander and the malicious reporting of misdeeds in order to settle personal scores. Since the Soviet system places great emphasis on surveillance and reporting of violations, the temptation to settle personal scores by providing information, true or false, is great. The existence of "slander and anonymous accusations" is referred to as one of the more objectionable kinds of disciplinary violations.[54] Perhaps it is objectionable not simply on moral grounds, but because it weakens the surveillance value of other reports that may not be easily distinguishable from slander.

7. Exploitation

The propensity of second- and third-year and generally older soldiers to treat first-year and younger soldiers contemptuously and to "shove off their own duties onto them" may have increased with the reduction of the conscription age from nineteen to eighteen. "The morals of the bourgeois barracks are completely foreign to Soviet soldiers. . . . Vestiges of such vile morals cannot be tolerated in our friendly army and navy family."[55] Nonetheless, from frequent references in the Soviet military press it is evident that the exploitation of younger soldiers by older soldiers is worrisome to Soviet authorities and is

---

[50] See, for example, *KZ,* August 8, 1971, p. 4, and June 2, 1971, April 15, 1971, p. 2.

[51] Ibid., May 16, 1971, p. 2, and November 24, 1972, p. 1; *KVS,* no. 17, September 1972, pp. 24–29; *KZ,* May 23, 1972, p. 2, and March 12, 1971, p. 2.

[52] Ibid., February 18, 1973, p. 4.

[53] Ibid., October 28, 1972.

[54] *KVS,* no. 15, August 1971, pp. 25–32.

[55] Ibid., no. 19, October 1972, pp. 71–75.

a common occurrence in the Soviet forces, as it probably is in many other military establishments.

8. Drunkenness, Hooliganism, AWOL

Despite periodic campaigns to prevent drunkenness, offenses associated with alcohol both on and off duty still seem to be a major problem, perhaps in part because "some comrades [have] a flippant attitude toward this very important matter."[56] Hooliganism, uniform offenses, and being late in returning from leave seem to be associated with drinking, although Soviet military literature refers relatively infrequently to going AWOL as an offense.[57] Sometimes accounts of drunkenness, especially when associated with going AWOL, seem to suggest that the servicemen involved may be using this behavior to get themselves discharged.[58]

Only infrequently does one find mention, in Soviet discussions, of disciplinary problems involving what is usually termed "immorality," and only then gingerly and with great reserve. In one instance, reference is made to a commander fearing that soldiers were about to purchase "obscene materials."[59] In another discussion "instances of immoral conduct" are referred to without any further elaboration.[60]

C. ENFORCEMENT

1. Exhortation

Whether it is the parent and the child, the teacher and the student, the minister in the pulpit and the congregation, the doctor and his patient, the political leader and the citizen, or the manager and the worker—wherever the shaping of human behavior is attempted, exhortation is an almost inevitable way of trying to produce the desired effect. In communist societies, the existence of an official ideology and an extensive agitprop apparatus makes exhortation as

---

[56] *KZ,* November 23, 1972, p. 2. Over one-third of all law violations by military personnel are said to be committed in a state of drunkenness. Ibid., November 1, 1974, pp. 2–3.

[57] In March 1973 the western press reported the killing of two Russian MPs, a Russian deserter, and an East German soldier in a shoot-out with three deserters from the Soviet forces in East Germany. *Los Angeles Times,* March 29, 1973. Serious incidents of this type are never referred to in Soviet examples of disciplinary problems.

[58] *Starshina serzhant,* May 1971, p. 40. A book review describing a novel dealing with military life also seems to imply that the misbehavior of some soldiers occurs "so that in the end they will be discharged." *Literaturnaya Rossiya,* February 1971, p. 12.

[59] *KZ,* December 27, 1970, p. 2.

[60] *KVS,* no. 23, December 1969, pp. 5–8. In DOSAAF clubs where preinduction-age trainees are prepared for military service, "in one year alone, several instructors were made to answer for immoral actions." *Sovetskiy patriot,* March 21, 1971, p. 3.

a means of inspiring and controlling behavior a particularly widespread practice. Both in the form of concise May Day slogans or slogans celebrating a Party Congress or an anniversary of Lenin's birth, and in the form of speeches of several hours duration, exhortation is central to Party attempts to shape the behavior of elite groups and masses.

In the military, exhortation is not just a simple plea to be or do good in a particular way. Exhortation is often a rather extensive and complicated mode of address, such as when, following several incidents involving alcohol, a deputy commander for political affairs prepares an evening discussion entitled "Drunkenness, a Cause of Crime and Enemy of Health," accompanied by a film entitled "Wine Begets Guilt."[61]

In the Soviet Union at large and certainly in the Soviet military, greater use of psychological and sociological studies has increased sophistication and led to an awareness that exhortation is not enough. "Sometimes efforts to inculcate discipline in fighting men amount to appeals to be disciplined, and so on. Of course, there will be no progress without such appeals, but beyond this an officer must develop all aspects of a subordinate's personality."[62] It is no longer believed that by simply holding a meeting or doing a certain amount of lecturing, everything will be resolved. Problems are not solved by stereotypes.[63] Similarly, *Pravda,* speaking of the objectives of the Twenty-fourth Congress, points out that holding meetings and urging people to "improve" or "intensify" their efforts is not a very helpful way of making progress.[64] Referring to the tendency of second-year soldiers to exploit the new inductees, *Krasnaya zvezda* points out that a political officer, in order to combat this practice, gave a lecture on friendship and military comradeship. In addition, members of the Party bureau held discussions with the soldiers and called upon the old-timers to be more attentive to the youths arriving in the company. *Krasnaya zvezda* comments on this process of general exhortation: "The trouble is that the work of uniting the military collective is limited to such lectures and discussion. . . . The success of commanders and political organs lies in the fact that they not only arrange lectures and talks . . . but look further and attentively supervise the process of mutual relations among soldiers."[65] Although a distinction is increasingly made between relying on exhortation or "talks" and the use of incentives and various pressures to effect the changes desired, there is no great inclination, in actual practice, to diminish the time-honored procedure of issuing slogans, lecturing soldiers at every opportunity, and holding meetings.

[61] *KVS,* no. 2, January 1971, pp. 53–55.
[62] Ibid., no. 3, February 1971, pp. 65–69.
[63] Ibid., no. 5, March 1971, pp. 89–92.
[64] *Pravda,* September 18, 1971, p. 2.
[65] *KZ,* October 10, 1971, p. 2.

Exhortation in the Soviet context is not always as naïve as it may seem on the surface. Exhortation provides a crystal clear indication to those to whom the exhortations are addressed concerning the wishes of the authorities. Thus, part of its function is not by itself to change behavior, but rather to signal the direction of behavior that is desired. The actual motivation for then engaging in this behavior is the realization that the authorities have at their disposal rewards and punishments for those who do or do not conform to the exhortations. Still, not all exhortation can be rationalized in this way. In many areas of behavior the wishes of the authorities are only too well known, but this does not necessarily lead them to refrain from further exhortation.

2. Reward and Punishment

Most social systems struggle implicitly or explicitly to establish relative roles for punishment and rewards in encouraging conformity with the accepted norms. In the Soviet Union, just as there is tension between the use of exhortation and more constructive measures, so, too, there is some tension between the use of rewards and punishment.

Brezhnev noted at the Twenty-fourth Party Congress that discipline should not be based on fear or on methods of harsh administration "that . . . engender overcautiousness and dishonesty."[66] Nonetheless, although they are drawn to other means, Soviet military disciplinarians generally insist on making all undesired forms of behavior subject to detailed regulations that carry penalties if infringed. "The disciplinary code emphasizes that military discipline is based not on the fear of punishment and coercion, but rather on high political awareness. . . . But this does not prevent the use of constraint against servicemen who are remiss in the fulfillment of their military obligations."[67] A commendation "gladdens and encourages," but "punishment forces the guilty soldier and his comrades to a deeper appreciation of the impermissibility of violations of discipline."[68] Besides, in the Soviet socialist state, punishment has the aim not only of compelling individuals to observe the law but also of educating them.[69]

In addition to the military tribunals and disciplinary battalions for persons who have received court-martial sentences, the Soviet military authorities possess "officer comrade courts of honor." Similar courts have been introduced for ensigns, warrant officers, and extended-duty (enlisted) personnel. The officer comrade courts of honor are elected organs of the officer community. If the number of officers in a particular unit or garrison is too small, the officers

[66] Editorial, *Pravda,* October 12, 1972, p. 1.
[67] Editorial, *KZ,* January 11, 1973, p. 1.
[68] *KVS,* no. 24, December 1970, pp. 64–69.
[69] *Voyenno-istoricheskiy zhurnal,* February 1971, pp. 13–21.

participate in the election of the court of honor of one of the nearby military units. The courts of honor generally have seven to nine members elected by secret ballot for a period of two years. There are courts of honor for junior officers, in the election of which senior officers participate. One or two senior officers are generally elected to each junior officer court. The court for senior officers is, however, elected only by the senior officers themselves. "It is not recommended that a commander of a unit be selected to serve on it."[70] The prestige of the senior officer is preserved by the rule that junior officers cannot attend a court session involving senior officers.

Soviet military authorities have encouraged greater use of the court of honor. These courts deal with matters involving minor offenses that are viewed as unworthy of an officer, that is, offenses that violate military honor or are incompatible with communist ethics. They may also deal with property claims between officers, provided the amount does not exceed 100 rubles and the officers involved agree to have the matter considered by a court of honor. The punishments that a court of honor can hand down range from unofficial warnings and public admonitions to a reduction in rank of one grade or, in the case of a student officer, dismissal from a higher educational institution. The court of honor can also submit a petition for the exclusion of an officer from the armed forces, although it cannot directly impose this punishment. Reimbursement of property damage not exceeding 100 rubles can also be ordered.[71] The court of honor is an assembly where legal apparatus is supposed to be inappropriate; words like "defendant," "accused," and "sentence" are not allowed. Nonetheless, some discussions of the court of honor use much of the phraseology common to discussions of courts—"witnesses," "testimony," "the offense," and similar terms.[72]

The exercise of authority by military tribunals is said to be a function of command authority.[73] This seems to be used to justify the fact that misdemeanors by commanders who are Party members are dealt with not by military tribunals or by their superior officers but directly by the Party. Commanders of regiments and naval vessels, together with their deputies for political affairs, and commanders of political sections and of military educational institutions have their misdemeanors dealt with directly by Party commissions of the next higher political organ. Commanders and deputies for political affairs of battalions and equivalent units have their misdemeanors reviewed by Party bureaus or Party committees of regiments, warships, or equivalent units. All other Party, state, and military disciplinary violations by Party members are re-

---

[70] *KVS,* no. 4, February 1971, pp. 81–86.
[71] Ibid.
[72] Ibid.
[73] *Voyenno-istoricheskiy zhurnal,* February 1971, pp. 13–21.

viewed by the primary Party organization involved.[74] The extraordinary role played by the Party in the Soviet military disciplinary system is one among many indications of the close control that the Party exercises over the Soviet military forces (see chapter VIII). In effect, the Party role in discipline is equivalent to the affirmation that a commander or political officer who commits a misdemeanor is responsible first to the Party and only secondarily to his own commander, that is, to the armed forces.

Disciplinary action can, of course, be taken without the intervention of a tribunal or a Party commission. It is the command relation rather than the rank relation that often determines who can and cannot impose punishment. Thus a tank commander can impose punishment on a tank driver even though they are both of the same grade.[75] And a sergeant major cannot impose punishment on a lower-grade noncom if the latter is a platoon leader (that is, a "junior commander"), as is often the case.[76]

The relative desirability and severity of various types of Soviet commendations and disciplinary punishment are reflected in a Soviet list of rewards and penalties for ensigns and warrant officers. The commendations are: a statement of gratitude orally or in the form of a written order, removal of punishment imposed earlier, awarding of certificates, bestowing of valuable gifts or money, and awarding of the chest badge for an outstanding soldier. Disciplinary punishment includes admonition, reprimand, strict reprimand, arrest with detention in the guardhouse for a period of ten days, deprivation of the chest badge of outstanding soldier, removal from the post, discharge into the reserve until the expiration of the service period, and deprivation of military rank.[77]

Certain administrative measures may be used as a form of punishment or may accompany punishment. Disciplinary cases are sometimes transferred from other services to the infantry. A major complains with some bitterness in *Krasnaya zvezda* of a persistent violator of discipline and drinker who, after being sent to the stockade and reduced in rank, was then transferred "to the infantry." The major points out that there is no infantry in the forces. "The motorized rifle troops" also strive to maintain high levels, and it hardly helps to receive the misfits from other services.[78]

3. Leniency

In the struggle to secure conformity with regulations, Soviet military and Party

---

[74] *KVS,* no. 16, August 1971, pp. 25–31.
[75] *Starshina serzhant,* November 1970, p. 11.
[76] Ibid.
[77] *Bloknot agitatora,* May 1972, p. 27. On rewards see also chapter IV, section B,9.
[78] *KZ,* September 13, 1973, p. 2.

authorities sometimes feel that a certain moderation of the attitude of the strict disciplinarian is necessary. We have already noted a tendency for the military to be less severe sometimes than the emphasis on rigorous conformity to regulations would lead one to expect (see pp. 146–148 above). There are additional indications of a conflict between an insistence on "exactingness" and a desire to avoid an overly rigorous treatment that risks alienating personnel, thus negatively affecting morale, and reducing the attractions of the military as a career choice.

When the Soviets desire to moderate the rigor of military discipline, they tend to do so not by eliminating or modifying regulations, but by ameliorating the administration of the system and reducing in individual cases that seem to merit it the punishment specified by the regulations. A *Krasnaya zvezda* editorial points out that "every commander, irrespective of rank, must always remember that his subordinate is a Soviet citizen in military uniform, educated within a free society, and infused with the noble principles of the moral code of a builder of communism."[79] The moral of this is that "certain incidents of roughness employed in disciplinary actions" must be avoided.[80] Also to be avoided is the notion that a given type of offense must always receive the same punishment. The circumstances, prior record, and other factors may require that one soldier be given a reprimand and another a stricter form of punishment.[81]

Under the title "Be Exacting and Considerate," *Kommunist vooruzhennykh sil* emphasizes that "exactingness, no matter how categorical it may be, must not have anything in common with rudeness and with demeaning the personal dignity of subordinates. . . . Everyone has to keep well in mind that our Soviet soldier is a literate, cultured, and conscientious person."[82]

The persistent emphasis on the need to eliminate rudeness and foul language, together with numerous instances of these kinds of behavior that are cited not only among the old-style NCO but also among officers suggest a high frequency of such behavior. Part of the concern of the military and of Party authorities stems from the younger age of induction instituted in 1967. Soviet authorities are aware that at these early ages a year makes a considerable difference, and an eighteen-year-old is a sensitive creature. But the eighteen-year-old is also increasingly a well-educated youth. "A great cultural revolution has taken place in the Soviet Union and Soviet man has grown immeasurably. He has become accustomed to the achievements of science and

---

[79] Ibid., January 11, 1973, p. 1.

[80] Ibid.

[81] Ibid. Soviet civil practice sometimes makes use of the principle that higher levels of responsibility call for more severe punishment for the same offense. Thus, officials are fined two to five times more than citizens are for violations of fire safety rules in forests. *Sel'skaya zhizn'*, August 15, 1972, p. 4.

[82] *KVS*, no. 12, June 1971, pp. 48–55.

art. Any crudity lowers and insults him."[83] The new eighteen-year-old inductees require "warm, comradely treatment."[84] "Certain commanders are abso-
lutely wrong when they maintain that strong words do not offend subordinates,
but rather 'encourage' them."[85]

Soviet authorities have learned from studies undertaken in the military
that young recruits are far from adequately prepared for the strict discipline
of army life. "The high degree of subordination in the army was not customary
for young men brought up on the free, broadly democratic principles of
our way, and it was difficult to accept psychologically the necessity of immediate and flawless performance of the leader's command beginning with the
squad leader. At first it seemed to some that carrying out the order of a
sergeant who is their peer virtually means to submit to humiliation."[86] "The
mental restructuring from the civilian to the military way" has been easier for
draftees coming from production enterprises than for those entering the army
from educational institutions.[87] It is difficult to know whether this is due to the
discipline imposed by a production enterprise or whether it is due to the
selection factors that determine whether a youth goes to work early or continues in school. It is likely that the greater adaptability to the rigors of army life
noted by Soviet investigators among production inductees is the result of a
lower educational level, rather than the character of life in a production
enterprise.

Despite their interest in enforcing disciplinary "exactingness" and their
disapproval of commanders who "are anxious to be thought of as kind un-
cles,"[88] Soviet military authorities are sufficiently concerned with the effect of
very strict discipline, especially on young recruits, to impose restraints on
overly enthusiastic disciplinarians. "Soldiers are morally insulted by the implication that they are potential violators of military discipline."[89] A lieutenant
major was removed from his post for issuing punishments "in a reckless
manner."[90] Soviet military literature refers frequently to officers being reprimanded for imposing improper punishments. Officers have reduced sergeants
and petty offficers in rank by several grades, although reduction of only one
grade is permitted. Officers and extended-duty serviccmen have had their next
leave reduced in length, although this is not permitted by regulations as a form
of punishment.[91]

---

[83] *KZ,* November 21, 1970, p. 2.
[84] *KVS,* no. 23, December 1969, pp. 45–50.
[85] *Voyennyy vestnik,* January 1971, pp. 2–12.
[86] *KZ,* April 19, 1972, p. 4.
[87] Ibid.
[88] Ibid., January 14, 1970, p. 2.
[89] *Starshina serzhant,* August 1971, p. 36.
[90] *KZ,* February 21, 1973.
[91] Ibid., December 27, 1970, p. 2.

Actions permitted by regulations may be equally frowned upon. A major was investigated because of excessive disciplinary zeal. Having discovered candy under the pillows of several beds in the battery barracks, he summoned the platoon commander from his home where he was fast asleep. "Certainly, candy under pillows is an offense. But did this offense justify waking the platoon commander?" *Krasnaya zvezda* points out that the battalion commander did not care to recognize the morale losses resulting from his "exactingness."[92] The reprimand of the major is especially significant because this strict disciplinarian had succeeded in achieving for his battery the title of "outstanding unit," an award not lightly regarded in the Soviet forces.

Two administrative acts in 1972 also reflect a moderation of disciplinary rigor. A new 1972 list specifying those crimes classified as "grave" deleted from the list violations (presumably criminal violations) of regulations in the performance of military duties, provided there were no aggravating circumstances.[93] An amnesty decree in December 1972 in honor of the Fiftieth Anniversary of the USSR released from punishment (among others and with some exceptions) servicemen assigned to disciplinary battalions.[94]

Disciplinary action is mitigated by another device not intended by Soviet authorities. Military personnel, especially officers, who commit offenses that are not overly serious or who have been derelict in the performance of duties often escape punishment or, if punished, are reinstated rapidly into their former status or an equivalent status by their superior officers.[95] This seems to be, in part, due to the fact that much disciplinary action stems from the intervention of Party personnel and that those who are less dedicated to Party aims and discipline "close ranks." Given the stern requirements of Party morality, most officers who are not Party activists are likely to feel that they share, or might easily come to share, the same guilt as their disciplined fellow officer.

4. Family Pressures

A persistent aspect of the Soviet control mechanism is the use of the soldier's relations with his family to improve his performance and to restrain his behavior. Political officers, especially on naval vessels on long cruises, often arrange

[92] Ibid., January 4, 1972, p. 2.
[93] *Sotsialisticheskaya zakonnost'*, August 1972, pp. 16–22.
[94] *Pravda,* December 29, 1972, p. 1. Also given amnesty, with some exceptions (recidivists, cases with aggravating circumstances, etc.), were persons who had taken part in combat operations in defense of the Soviet homeland, those who committed crimes before the age of seventeen, men over sixty, women over fifty-five, women with children under seventeen years of age, pregnant women, and some others.
[95] See, for example, *KZ,* April 15, 1971, p. 2, June 2, 1971, January 19, 1972, p. 2, and May 20, 1972, p. 2.

to receive messages from family members to inspire the sons in the service to greater effort. A soldier's rewards and commendations are often communicated to his family and former work associates.[96] But, equally, inquiries about a soldier's past behavior in civil life and difficulties that officers currently are having with him are also communicated to the family in order to bring pressure to bear on him. It is characteristic of a more enlightened point of view that seems to be gaining ground in the Soviet forces that this form of pressure is sometimes viewed as objectionable. A Komsomol member who went AWOL was invited to a Komsomol meeting where threats were made to have his family informed of his bad behavior if he did not change. This incident was described in a book to illustrate how successful this procedure can be in improving the discipline of a soldier. But a reviewer of the book thought that this was not necessarily an acceptable practice and should not have been propagandized. "The commander and political officer have sufficient direct means for influencing men without alarming their relatives."[97]

The exploitation of family relations has not ceased. More than a year after *Kommunist vooruzhennykh sil* gave its opinion, a political officer, dissatisfied with the behavior of a private, required him to write a letter to his mother saying, "Mama, come visit our unit. My chief will tell you what kind of a son you have." The political officer took the precaution of mailing this letter himself. Upon receiving the letter, the mother, an elderly lady, hurriedly obtained a seat on the train and undertook a journey of several hundred kilometers. *Krasnaya zvezda's* comment on this incident is negative, but rather mild: "This action was prompted by good intentions, but it served to punish not only the soldier but his mother."[98]

Despite these indications of mild official disapproval, Soviet law itself is startlingly severe, in at least one respect, in its behavior toward the families of servicemen. The child allowances provided to the wife of a serviceman are stopped if the serviceman is sentenced by a military tribunal to serve punishment in a disciplinary battalion.[99] Given the age of most draftees, this would primarily affect extended-service NCOs, ensigns, warrant officers, and officers. Presumably this law is based on the expectation that forcing a serviceman's wife and children to share his punishment will reduce the likelihood that he will commit a serious breach of military regulations or of Soviet law.

5. Naming Names

Soviet political and military authorities emphasize the need to publicize as

---

[96] *KVS*, no. 19, October 1971, pp. 66–72.
[97] Ibid., no. 5, March 1971, pp. 86–88.
[98] *KZ*, October 6, 1972, p. 2.
[99] *Sovety deputatov trudyashchikhsya*, no. 5, 1971.

fully as possible punishments inflicted for misdeeds. "For those who violate the laws or ethical norms, publicity is sometimes more effective than administrative measures."[100] Lenin, whose authority is invoked on this matter, said that the deterrent value of an open court trial is "one thousand times greater than the Party cell-Central Committee idiotic quiet handling, without publicity, of a case of criminal procrastination."[101]

In order to give disciplinary measures maximum publicity, trials are often held in the manner of a spectacle. The trial of a soldier charged with violating regulations concerning sentry duty was attended by several hundred members of the garrison to which he was attached. The entrance to the trial room was "festooned" with slogans exhorting strict observance of military regulations.[102] Attendance at these trials is probably not voluntary in the case of enlisted men. Officer attendance at sessions of the officer courts of honor is apparently voluntary, since complaints are made that these court sessions are often conducted with a negligible number of officers present. Since the power of the court lies mainly in the use of "social restraints" (that is, setting an example), such trials are said to require the presence of all officers of the unit, since otherwise the sessions are of little benefit.[103]

One rather special way of giving an additional punitive and therefore deterrent character to discussions in the military press of persons who have committed violations, is to give the actual name of the person involved. This is consistent with a passage in the Soviet military oath: "If I should break this, my solemn oath, then let me be subject to the severe punishment of Soviet law and the general hatred and contempt of the workers."[104]

Soviet military journals and newspapers are full of accounts of various incidents in which soldiers and officers play good and bad roles. It is generally the practice to give the real names of the persons involved. Indeed if the name of a person who has behaved badly is not mentioned by the writer, the writer is likely to excuse himself and give a reason for not providing this additional punishment and thus adding to the deterrent effect of the narration. "I won't give his last name because he is not doing a bad job [now]."[105] "There is no point in citing the name of the commander. For the most part he was a diligent and erudite young man. During the inspection he clearly took note of his mistakes."[106] "One of the political officers (I will not give his name since the thing is in the past) had a one-sided approach."[107] A flight surgeon, speaking

[100] *KZ,* March 14, 1972, p. 3.
[101] *Voyenno-istoricheskiy zhurnal,* February 1971, pp. 13–21.
[102] Ibid.
[103] *KVS,* no. 4, February 1971, pp. 81–86.
[104] Ibid., no. 19, October 1972, pp. 71–75.
[105] *KZ,* December 24, 1969, p. 2.
[106] Ibid., January 30, 1971, p. 2.
[107] *KVS,* no. 10, May 1971, pp. 43–50.

of pilots who had been withdrawn from flying duty, states: "As a doctor I know my accounts could stir unpleasant memories. . . . Therefore, in some cases, the names of the actual individuals will be changed."[108]

Although, then, an individual's name may sometimes be withheld, the Soviet system does not approve of people escaping full public exposure of their sins of omission and commission. In most cases names are cited. Nonetheless, a writer in *Krasnaya zvezda,* discussing a breach of regulations by an officer, is led to the following reflection on the Soviet practice of naming names: "A pilot commits a mistake and is punished. This does not mean, however, that the name of this comrade must be publicized in all areas. It may happen that months following the violation this officer may distinguish himself and yet he may still be plagued by his old offense. It may never occur to those who publicize his name that they are doing a disservice to him." Oddly enough, the author of this statement had just mentioned *by name* a senior lieutenant who committed an infraction of the regulations.[109]

6. Criticism and Self-Criticism

Criticism and self-criticism sessions following instances of misbehavior have a punitive-educational function and, at the same time, provide desired publicity concerning the consequences of violating regulations. The Party is particularly strict on this matter. If the misdemeanors of Party members are not discussed by their comrades or if they are not made public, "it may result in their being repeated." Consequently the Party must conduct "an objective public evaluation of any particular incident, no matter whom it concerns."[110] A secretary of a Komsomol bureau knew that a second-year soldier was behaving offensively to first-year recruits. "But he did not bring up his behavior at a court of public opinion. Apparently the notorious opinion prevailed: 'What can you take from him? He will soon be released.' So they put up with his escapades and did not rebuff him."[111]

The value of criticism and self-criticism sessions was emphasized by Brezhnev at the Twenty-fourth Party Congress, and this is pointedly referred to by *Krasnaya zvezda.*[112] Such sessions permit a more informal approach to disciplinary action and are sometimes substituted for formal procedures in the case of violations of military discipline. It is, as one writer points out, sometimes advisable merely to discuss the soldier's action in the group or even

---

[108] *KZ,* September 19, 1971, p. 2.
[109] Ibid., March 30, 1972, p. 2.
[110] *KVS,* no. 16, August 1971, pp. 25–31.
[111] Ibid., no. 17, September 1972, pp. 24–29.
[112] *KZ,* May 23, 1971, p. 2.

merely to hold a conversation with him. "For every rule there is an exception."[113]

The criticism and self-criticism session is not confined to cases of a directly disciplinary character. Thus a pilot who, during a training session, flipped the wrong switch and therefore did not release his rockets was brought before a group of his comrades who analyzed his attitude toward military duty and discussed with him his sense of responsibility and how he might improve his behavior. "The lieutenant pilot accepted the advice of his commander, the communists, and his fellow servicemen and drew the required conclusion."[114] Failure to perform in a technically adequate fashion is not infrequently treated as moral delinquency requiring, in effect, disciplinary action. As noted earlier, the investigation of accidents often takes on a search for "the guilty party."

The willingness to admit guilt during criticism and self-criticism sessions is basic, but this does not in itself suffice, since the offending individual must not only acknowledge this "honestly" but also apologize for his offense.[115] A major who had offended a retired officer was compelled to admit his guilt. This did not end the discussion of the incident, since the major, after admitting his guilt, "forgot" (quotation marks in the original) to apologize to the officer whom he had offended.[116]

7. Studying the Regulations

Soviet military authorities believe that a continuous study of the regulations helps to produce conformity to them. This reveals itself both in the insistence on "legal education" (the study of regulations and laws) and in the conviction that violations are often the result of ignorance of the military regulations. In a discussion of violations of regulations on the wearing of the uniform, it is pointed out that "up to one-half of those arrested [for uniform violations] had no knowledge of the appropriate rules for wearing the military uniform."[117] In the Trans-Carpathian military district only three out of 100 officers were able to explain the conditions under which absence without leave was a punishable crime.[118]

[113] *KVS,* no. 13, July 1971, pp. 9–17. The substitution of a criticism and self-criticism session is likely to provide another opportunity for the Party to replace the commander in the field of discipline. Compare pp. 155–156 above.

[114] Ibid., no. 18, September 1971, pp. 42–46.

[115] Ibid., no. 4, February 1971, pp. 81–86.

[116] *KZ,* September 3, 1971, p. 2.

[117] Ibid., July 13, 1972, p. 4.

[118] Ibid., July 9, 1971, p. 2. There is a similar concern with ignorance of the law in the civil population. Thus, it appears that in Lvov only nine out of 500 students knew the age at which one becomes answerable for a crime. *Pravda,* March 15, 1972, p. 6.

Regulations require that one copy of Soviet military regulations be issued for every five to six soldiers. All commanders from the detachment commander up are required to have a copy of the regulations with them. However, complaints have been made that the regulations are difficult to find when one wants to get hold of them.[119]

Since "the more familiar all personnel are with the regulations the tighter discipline and order will be,"[120] the military authorities have, in addition to the usual slides and training films on regulations, provided some commanders with computerized question-and-answer programs for use in their units.[121]

It is evident from the Soviet military literature that neither officers nor soldiers take kindly to the constant pressure to study the regulations and especially to being examined on them. Sometimes officers, particularly the younger ones, complain: "You would think it's some kind of science. Each of us took exams on regulations and not just one time. How long can you study them?"[122] The answer of the political officer to this question is, of course, as long as you are in the army. Indeed, continuous study of the regulations is recommended by a Soviet army saying: "Old soldier, the service is your board and keep, read the regulations instead of going to sleep."[123]

8. Internalization

Exhortation, criticism and self-criticism, devotion to the Party, study of the regulations, and similar devices are intended to get Soviet servicemen and officers to incorporate or internalize the prescriptions that are supposed to direct their behavior. Having incorporated both the spirit and letter of the regulations, the serviceman will behave correctly without need of surveillance or the threat of punishment. Important in achieving this desirable state of affairs is "the power of the situation," that is, the general level of conformity with the regulations in the soldier's immediate environment. "The rapid metamorphosis in the behavior of one former violator of military discipline" is attributed to his transfer from a unit where discipline was lax (except in the presence of inspecting officers) to a unit where "the order of the day is observed without fail, each man is neat and smart in appearance, and every military ritual is carried out in precise accord with the given regulations."[124] Surrounded by an orderly environment, this violator's attitude changed. "The situation in the collective had a good effect on me. I became . . . ashamed of my misdeeds."[125]

[119] *KZ,* January 9, 1970, p. 2.
[120] Ibid.
[121] Ibid.
[122] Ibid.
[123] Ibid.
[124] Ibid., March 3, 1973, p. 2.
[125] Ibid.

9. Surveillance

Although the desirability of achieving internalized, automatic conformity with regulations is fully appreciated, the Soviet military system shows little tendency to forego the use of rewards and especially the threat of punishment. To these incentives is added an additional device of great importance in the Soviet System—surveillance. Surveillance and the awareness of its ubiquity depend in large part for their effectiveness on penalties (and rewards) associated with the behavior on which the surveillance system reports. The aim of continuous close surveillance is not just to uncover misdeeds and to punish them, but also to deter them. A conference of military prosecutors emphasized that "a great deal of attention must be concentrated on enhancing the role and effectiveness of general surveillance, particularly surveillance of the fulfillment of military regulations among the troops. . . . Preventing violations of the law is the main avenue of prosecution activity."[126]

Surveillance is an essential component of the Soviet control system. *Krasnaya zvezda,* defending the intervention of People's Control groups that check on military administration, especially for fiscal and property crimes, points out that Lenin often emphasized that controls should be universal and massive.[127] Lenin required good communists "to check people and to verify the actual fulfillment of their work—in this, still in this, and only in this lies the crux of all work, of all policy."[128]

Naturally, surveillance and control are easier to effect when the dispersal of personnel can be prevented. When soldiers go on an excursion or to the theater and number more than three, they must move to their destination in formation under the command of the senior man in the group.[129] Similarly, Soviet officers are encouraged to take their vacations in groups.

Although Soviet authorities are annoyed at the excessive expenditures incurred in both civilian and military life by various trips undertaken by personnel, and show a high regard for thrift, it is apparent that surveillance requirements have a higher priority. Thus, in warning military officers against unnecessarily sending personnel on detached trips, thereby wasting military funds, a writer points out that while economy is desirable, "the assignment of a group Party organizer to a collective of officer Communists departing on detached duty trips is also justified."[130]

The ubiquitous surveillance by political officers, Party activists, People's

---

[126] Ibid., March 30, 1972.

[127] Ibid., January 9, 1970, p. 2.

[128] Cited from volume 45, p. 16, of the *Complete Works of Lenin* (in the Soviet edition) by *KVS,* no. 4, February 1971, pp. 87–92.

[129] *Starshina serzhant,* June 1971, p. 36. During the Korean war many Chinese Communist troops, especially former Nationalist soldiers, could only go to the latrine if supervised by authorized Party personnel.

[130] *KZ,* January 13, 1970, p. 1. An additional motive for this statement may be the desire of Party activists to get in on these trips.

Control groups,[131] KGB agents and informers, and special inspecting officers representing various echelons and technical services extensively supplement the normal surveillance provided in military establishments by NCOs, officers, and commanders. These various forms of surveillance provide a great variety of checks. According to *Voyenno-istoricheskiy zhurnal,* "the following are the main checks in the army: on-the-spot checks, inspections, massive checks, selective checks, surprise checks, and others. All these forms of control presume the active participation of wide masses of servicemen."[132]

10. Letters to the Editor

The Soviet authorities have, in addition to more specialized agents of surveillance, sought to enlist the services of the entire personnel of the military forces to enforce conformity with regulations. Individuals are encouraged, as a duty to the state, the Party, and the people, to report all irregularities they note.

While other offices and channels are open to reporting or complaining military personnel, a particularly important Soviet control device, both in civil and military sectors, is the letter to the editor. This is an institutionalized, legalized form of initiating action against an irregularity that affects the writer or others. A decree of April 12, 1968, of the USSR Supreme Soviet that also applies to the armed forces provides that "suggestions, statements, and complaints by citizens coming from newspaper and magazine letters, as well as statements related to resolving them, and other materials published in the press, are to be reviewed in the manner and within the time envisaged by this decree."[133] The letters of military personnel and members of their families have some priority and must be dealt with in not more than fifteen days.

Letters to the editors of newspapers and journals are "one of the important forms for strengthening the ties of our Party with the people in the management of state affairs, a means for expressing public opinion, and a source of information about the life of the country. . . . In the army and navy, the letters are an objective source of information about the attitudes of the personnel and the channel over which suggestions arrive from the troops."[134]

Krasnaya zvezda especially, but also numerous other military newspapers and journals, become in many instances courts of appeal for servicemen and

[131] The People's Control groups now include about eight million activists. *Voyenno-istoricheskiy zhurnal,* April 1972, pp. 3–10. A People's Control group in the military cited by *Voyenno-istoricheskiy zhurnal* as an example consists of eleven officers, NCOs, and enlisted men.

[132] Ibid. The nature of these checks is not further specified.

[133] *KZ,* September 14, 1972, p. 1. *Pravda* provides an example of this form of surveillance in the civil sector. In connection with a series of thefts in Rostov province, *Pravda* received "no less than seventeen warning signals . . . in the form of letters." *Pravda,* February 12, 1972, p. 3.

[134] *KVS,* no. 15, August 1971, pp. 3–8. It should be noted that the information and suggestions arriving from the troops go not to the commanders of the armed forces but to editorial personnel who are in effect Party functionaries.

officers. In 1969, *Krasnaya zvezda* received an average of 400 letters per day,[135] and in 1973, 149,787 letters.[136] It is not possible to say what proportion of these represented complaints or reports of alleged irregular or improper behavior. On the other hand, it is perfectly clear from accounts in the military press that a substantial proportion of the instances of misbehavior cited by them was originally brought to their attention by letters.

Krasnaya zvezda investigates cases both by corresponding with local commanders and by sending inspecting officers. Since the editorial staff of *Krasnaya zvezda* and the inspecting officer sent by it are generally representatives of the Party organs in the military, they operate very much as agents of the Party.

The military papers generally have a special column reserved for letters of complaint and actions taken headed "Measures Adopted" or a similar phrase. The essence of the column is: "A signal has been heard and measures have been taken."[137] The editors of *Starshina serzhant* publish such material under the heading "Although the Letter Was Not Printed," indicating that the revelations involved and the actions taken stem originally from letters received in the editorial office.[138]

Criticisms made by the military press either as a result of letters addressed to them or as a result of independent investigations have to be taken seriously and responded to. This, of course, necessitates "naming names" (see pp. 160–162 above). In an editorial, *Krasnaya zvezda* pointed out that "the effectiveness of the press depends . . . on the correct reaction of officials and the appropriate organizations to the press articles. Not one critical article in the press must remain unanswered, and without the adoption of specific measures."[139] Thus, a letter published in *Krasnaya zvezda* on May 4, 1971, was given its follow-up on May 20, 1971, and involved the administrative punishment of a lieutenant colonel and two majors and very stern reprimands to several other persons. Even the USSR deputy minister of defense for construction and quartering of troops had to indicate compliance with various requirements.[140]

Despite the authority invested in them by the decree of the USSR Supreme Soviet, representatives of military newspapers sometimes have difficulty in eliciting responses from those who have been charged in letters with misbehavior. This explains in part the frequency with which inspecting officers are sent to investigate complaints that reach the press. Where distant units are involved, the intervention of the Party apparatus may be called upon. A master

---

[135] *KZ,* January 4, 1970, p. 2.
[136] Ibid., January 4, 1974, p. 3. On January 1, 1974, *KZ,* the central paper of the USSR Ministry of Defense, celebrated its fiftieth anniversary. *KVS,* no. 24, December 1973, pp. 84–85.
[137] Ibid., October 1971, p. 2.
[138] *Starshina serzhant,* May 1971, p. 40.
[139] Editorial, *KZ,* May 5, 1973, p. 1.
[140] Ibid., May 20, 1971, p. 2.

sergeant appealed to *Starshina serzhant,* and the journal wrote to his unit commander but received no reply. The journal then wrote again, pointing out that the period allowed by the Ministry of Defense for review of complaints had already expired. This second letter also went unanswered, and the editor of *Starshina serzhant* was forced to ask the political directorate of the Central Asian Military District to take action against the personnel responsible for ignoring the review of complaints by a serviceman.[141]

The encouragement given to individuals to report and to complain is not without cost. Slander and unjustified complaints reduce somewhat the effectiveness of the letter-to-the-editor system, and it has been necessary repeatedly "to rebuff those who try to convert criticism to malignity and slandering."[142] It is also necessary to give "a decisive rebuff . . . to scribblers who claim privileges to which they are not entitled."[143] Despite Soviet condemnations of these perversions of the system, it is apparent that the gains from encouraging individual reporting of irregularities are, in the Soviet view, too great to forego.

Disciplinary problems are often common in organizations, societies, and classes in which the deprivation of liberty or other punishments changes relatively little the general level of life of the persons punished. For the recruits, military life is a severe and punishing round of duties and neither the guardhouse nor the disciplinary work battalion may have quite the deterrent value that they have in a military establishment that provides for more indulgences.

The enforcement of discipline is almost always an ungrateful task, but it is especially so in the Soviet military where human weaknesses are generally treated as disloyalty to the Party, to the Soviet system, to national security, and to the Soviet people. The Soviets probably do not achieve a greater conformity to regulations by attaching to violations of them an ideological significance and then reacting with excessive emotion and severity. Indeed, it is likely that attaching a significance to violations of regulations that in many cases is not shared by officers and soldiers is negatively productive for Soviet disciplinary objectives. This is all the more likely because the very rigor and "demandingness" of Soviet military life are themselves responsible for numerous violations. They are responsible in two senses. First, by heightening the

---

[141] *Starshina serzhant,* April 1972, pp. 38–39. The civilian press also has problems in eliciting responses to criticisms. After publishing two articles on the need for staff reductions in small plants, *Izvestia* wrote, "Despite our having named specific enterprises," only one executive replied. "Naturally this [silence] is puzzling. . . . A few words about the practice of remaining silent. . . . " Not only individuals and enterprises, but government offices also, are required to respond to criticism. "The Russian Republic Ministry of Local Industry has not responded either." *Izvestia,* March 30, 1972, p. 3.
[142] *KVS,* no. 17, September 1971, pp. 3–12. See also ibid., no. 19, October 1971, pp. 27–33.
[143] Ibid., no. 15, August 1971, pp. 3–8.

requirements of behavior, violations are made more likely even given the best will in the world. Second, the "demandingness" of Soviet military life leads to violations by personnel who are thereby attempting to mitigate the rigors of their military existence.

The constant exhortation to conform, the persistent and forced study of the regulations, the blackmailing of soldiers vis-à-vis their families, the self-criticism and confession sessions imposed by the Party, and the public pillorying of officers in the national and regional military press are types of humiliating pressures that inspire as many efforts to evade surveillance as to conform.

Despite these handicaps or, in some instances, self-generated difficulties faced by Soviet military disciplinarians, the disciplinary problems of the Soviet forces are probably not too great. The limited free time available to troops and to officers, the tendency to impose, even in recreational periods, group movement under supervision of the senior person in the group, and the large amount of time spent on military exercises and under close observation lessen the occasions for committing many violations, except, of course, violations of technical regulations prescribing the performance of military duties.

Chapter VI

Solidarity and Morale

A. NATURE AND SOURCES OF SOLIDARITY AND MORALE

The welding of diverse individuals into effective units for the performance of military duties, especially in wartime, has long preoccupied military leaders and military analysts. This objective is treated, in part, as being equivalent to the development of solidarity, esprit de corps, and morale. Analysts have sometimes sought to give these terms more precise connotations than they usually carry in everyday discourse. When Soviet military writers discuss these matters, they usually content themselves with an elaboration in terms of the language of everyday life supplemented by some terms taken from the communist conceptual and terminological thesaurus. This has not excluded a developing interest among Soviet writers in western modes of analysis.

A political lesson on "military comradeship," prepared for the use of Soviet political officers and propagandists, equates military comradeship with the spirit of collectivism and defines "the essence of collectivism . . . [as] the relationship of comradely collaboration and mutual aid."[1] Collectivism involves having "collectivist feelings" and "experiencing collective will."[2] This is given a more vivid and "homely" meaning by writers who prefer to speak of a unit as "one great family . . . [living] according to the laws of military friendship," or simply as "a family."[3]

As in western writings, the concern for solidarity or cohesion is associated with "morale," and this in turn with a whole host of virtues: bravery, self-possession, the readiness to take a risk, friendship, mutual assistance, and indestructible comradeship.[4] All this "finds its highest expression in heroism and the heroic. . . . It personifies the main thing—the capacity to bear any hardships and an insurmountable will for victory."[5] The morale factor of an army is "the spiritual force of the fighting men in action." The most active component of this "is the readiness to withstand the severe stress of war without losing the will to win."[6]

The sources of solidarity and morale have been much discussed in western literature on the military, and although some attention is given to the role of patriotism and the objectives of national life and of war, it is apparent, following the experiences and studies of World War II, that emphasis has rested on the identifications that develop among small groups of soldiers in continuous face-to-face contact who have shared important experiences and who can each support the self-survival impulses of the individual members.[7] The Soviets find this consistent with the bourgeois outlook of western military establishments where morale and solidarity are the outcome of a purely "parochial" sentiment, or are only "a matter of regimental spirit." In the Soviet view, on the other hand, solidarity has a much broader base and involves political factors that produce in the soldier a "dedication and understanding of the people's role in history."[8] Solidarity in the military is closely related to solidarity in the society at large. Both forms of solidarity rest on "collectivism," which arises from the existence in socialist society of economic communal ownership.[9] As we shall see later, the Soviets are not indifferent to the value of cultivating a

[1] *KVS,* no. 24, December 1971, pp. 39–45, and no. 5, March 1973, pp. 69–75.

[2] *KZ,* January 26, 1973, pp. 2–3.

[3] Ibid., April 20, 1972, and September 30, 1972, p. 2. The "family" image seems more frequently to be evoked in the case of naval units or, more specifically, ship complements.

[4] *Aviatsiya i kosmonavtika,* July 1972, pp. 1–2; *KVS,* no. 17, September 1972, pp. 24–29.

[5] *Voyenno-istoricheskiy zhurnal,* June 1972, pp. 12–19.

[6] *KVS,* no. 24, December 1972, pp. 25–32.

[7] See, for example, Edward A. Shils and Morris Janowitz, "Cohesion and Disintegration in the Wehrmacht in World War II," *Public Opinion Quarterly* 12, 1948, pp. 280–315; Roger W. Little, "Buddy Relations and Combat Performance," in M. Janowitz (ed.), *The New Military* (New York, 1964); and Morris Janowitz and Roger W. Little, *Sociology and the Military Establishment* (New York, 1965).

[8] *Soviet Military Review,* 12, 1965, pp. 8–9.

[9] *KVS,* no. 21, November 1971, pp. 65–70.

"regimental spirit." In fact, Soviet views on solidarity and morale exhibit considerable diversity and at times contradictions.

A further Soviet view of American theories of solidarity and morale affirms that in the United States solidarity is believed to be the consequence of biological impulses. According to the field service regulations of the United States army, a Soviet journal tells officers, the behavior of the average man in combat depends more on instinct than on consciousness. Because of his herd instinct, man strives to fight as a member of a group.[10] This, of course, is a very different origin for group loyalty than the economic, class, and communal identifications that encourage the collectivist spirit in Soviet soldiers.

A Soviet analyst charges that bourgeois writers criticize the Soviet conception of a collective as an organization that "swallows the personality." Nonetheless, continues the Soviet analyst, official documents, including regulations of the US army, exhibit an increasing tendency in the United States to appeal to the cultivation of collectives and collectivism. This will not serve the US military very well, since the United States does not possess the "Party organizations [that] serve as the soul and core" of Soviet collectives.[11] Given this function of the Party in the collective, it is not surprising that in one Soviet view "the secret of turning a collective into a monolith lies in a source accessible to us all—military regulations. The most important lever in uniting a collective is strict and undeviating fulfillment of the regulations and maintenance of exemplary order in the unit and the subunit."[12]

Despite the sharp contrast that Soviet writers draw between their own and bourgeois conceptions of solidarity and morale, they have exhibited, when not preoccupied with these comparisons, views that have a distinct similarity to western ideas. Despite their disdain for a "parochial" morale based on regimental loyalty, Soviet writers are fully alert to the morale-building effects of unit tradition. The importance attached to the title of Guards Unit, given to Soviet units that fought with outstanding bravery in World War II, the iconic worship of unit mementos from celebrated combat actions, and the sedulously fostered combat reputation of various units are all very much in the vein of fostering a parochial regimental spirit. It is, however, true that in the Soviet case this is strongly supplemented by indoctrination that stresses much broader aspects of loyalty and attachment—the Party and the motherland. The increasing tendency to divide the solidarity and morale area into moral-political and psychological sectors permits Soviet writers to incorporate into their discussions both the older emphases deriving from collectivism and ideological loyalty (moral-political sector) and newer, more modern elements, especially relevant to battle situations, emphasizing habituation to and training

[10] Ibid., no. 3, February 1971, pp. 65–69.
[11] *KZ*, August 13, 1971, pp. 2–3.
[12] Ibid., August 15, 1971, p.2.

in facing physical dangers, and personal compatibility in small units (psychological sector).

Questions of personal compatibility among members of military teams are especially discussed as the work of Soviet sociologists and psychologists continues to penetrate more and more deeply into military literature.[13] Even ideological work in the Soviet air force exhibits an up-to-date, if not entirely clear, note in the proposal that the focus of political indoctrination should shift to the air crew or to the flight, that is, should have a small-group focus.[14]

Soviet readiness to adopt ideas, now old in the West, concerning the importance of small-group cohesion has been facilitated by an awareness that military weapons increasingly provide an "objective basis" for uniting people. Weapons are increasingly collective rather than individual weapons, and thus they create considerable small-group activity. The growing significance of military friendship derives from the use of group weapons and the need for **men to act together (as does the importance of discipline, see p. 142 above).** "There is also an extreme necessity for interchangeability. In battle, if one specialist is killed, his comrades must be able to perform his function. . . . Only strong military unity . . . can enable the work to be done."[15]

The existence of small teams or "microcollectives" based on a common weapon or a common specialty is viewed with some concern. Some Soviet writers are sufficiently modern to value the microcollective. On the other hand, such groups immediately present to the Party mind the possibility of dissent and conspiracy. Thus, one writer points out that while comradely mutual assistance in microcollectives is helpful, some microcollectives take "a negative direction."[16] Another analyst, referring to the fact that collective weapons combine people into small groups, warns that a "micropsychology" may develop and "in order to insure that this does not contain the seeds of opposition" Party and Komsomol activists are called upon to play a decisive role.[17] The ominous phrase, "the seeds of opposition," turns out in reality to refer most particularly and frequently to a tendency for members of a microcollective to develop such excellent esprit de corps that they get drunk together and engage in "mutual protection," that is, collusion to overlook and conceal each other's violations of various regulations.[18]

It is evident that in many social bodies an increase in social cohesion or esprit de corps at local points produces a decrease in the cohesion of the larger body. Cliques provide for greater solidarity within and lesser cohesion or loyalty without. Soviet authorities, like most authoritarian leadership groups,

---

[13] See, for example, *Sovetskiy voin.* November 1970, pp. 9–12.
[14] *Aviatsiya i kosmonavtika,* February 1971, pp. 11–12.
[15] *KVS,* no. 5, March 1973, pp. 69–75.
[16] *KZ,* October 10, 1971, p. 2.
[17] Ibid.
[18] See, for example, *KZ,* August 15, 1971, p. 2.

view with suspicion group loyalties that may detract from the single-minded loyalty of the members of the group to them, to the doctrines they espouse, and to the local leaders they impose. Western military commanders face a similar problem, but generally—and especially in combat—they have seemed to appreciate that the solidarity of the small military team far outweighs in value the possible desolidarizing effect of small-group loyalties on the larger unit. Soviet military and Party authorities, on the other hand, are more acutely conscious of the potential negative effects of a type of solidarity and morale that is "parochial" and divisive and may become "antisocial," that is, conspiratorial—if only for mundane, basically local objectives.

B. MORALE AND NUCLEAR WAR

From the official or Party standpoint, during war "there is only one decisive source determining the strength of the morale factor . . . the character of the economic and political order of the warring states, the dominant ideology in the countries, and the political goals of the war."[19] The importance of these factors ensures that the military heads of the imperialist states "cannot count on the conscientious attitudes of the military masses toward an armed struggle in the name of capitalist interests. Because of this they regard the training of a soldier robot to be of paramount importance, so that he will fill orders mechanically."[20] This Soviet view of the American outlook is corroborated by another writer who cites Anatol Rapoport's book, *Strategy and Conscience,* to the effect that the modern soldier sits at a control panel in comfort like a clerk behind a desk. He observes and obeys only signals. For him there is no call to bravery and self-sacrifice. "Death can overcome him at any moment, but the position of the hero does not differ from the position of the coward. There are no heroes, only victims."[21] This "widespread bourgeois view" is violently opposed—at least for the Soviet case—by the Soviet writer. Heroism and self-sacrifice, in all their infinitely rich manifestations, show themselves in just wars and are important components of morale.[22]

In nuclear war, problems of morale are affected by the "particularly big demands on the morale of the troops . . . made by nuclear weapons, whose destructive powers are unparalleled."[23] We have already stressed Soviet concern, one might say apprehension, concerning the possible effect of nuclear weapons on Soviet troops and civilians (see p. 109). This same concern also emerges in reference to the specialized and highly trained military civil defense

---

[19] *KVS,* no. 24, December 1972, pp. 25–32.
[20] Ibid.
[21] *Voyenno-istoricheskiy zhurnal,* June 1972, pp. 12–19. The cited passage is based on *Voyenno-istoricheskiy zhurnal's* version of Rapoport and not on the original English language text.
[22] Ibid.
[23] *KVS,* no. 24, December 1972, pp. 25–32.

units. "Fires and ruins can exert a strong psychological influence on the personnel. This makes it incumbent . . . to devote constant attention to moral-political and psychological training."[24]

Soviet military writers treat the possible reactions of troops and the civil population to a nuclear war as a grave problem, but they contend that the Soviet social order and Soviet collectivism (not to mention more specific measures taken to prepare the Soviet population for these contingencies) ensure that the Soviet people would survive, operate, and fight under nuclear conditions with greater devotion and courage than is possible for the populations of imperialist and capitalist nations.

C. CONSTRAINTS ON SOLIDARITY AND MORALE

1. Class Divisions

An army based on universal conscription will reproduce within itself the divisions of the civil society in addition to those specific to the military structure. Some Soviet writers, exaggerating the cohesion of Soviet society, affirm that "the social and national unity of society determine the monolithic nature of our soldiers' ranks. Distinct from the bourgeois armies, the USSR armed forces are staffed . . . from friendly classes, social groups, nations, and nationalities. . . . Their fundamental interests are common."[25] Nonetheless, even this writer concedes that some divisions exist. "Side by side with . . . the social and ideological unity of society, we have considerable differences between the city and the countryside, between physical and intellectual labor, and so forth. With all their communal spirit, friendly classes and social groups of the USSR have certain specific interests. . . . All this is also of great significance for military building."[26]

Soviet military writers seem increasingly disposed to recognize that the solidarity of the Soviet forces is fragmented by differences that are often sufficiently profound to induce "conflict situations." This recognition is made easier, no doubt, by Secretary Brezhnev's acknowledgement during the Lenin celebrations of 1970 of the diversity of interests of various Soviet classes and social groups and the Party's role in balancing and coordinating these often conflicting interests.[27] As for the military, "there are differences in the social and professional roles that different groups of servicemen play: a diversity of military work, age, cultural and aesthetic questions and tastes; different levels of political consciousness, and so on. Because of such differences the possibility of conflict situations arising in the mutual relations between individual service-

---

[24] Editorial, *KZ*, May 17, 1973, p. 1.
[25] *KZ*, February 2, 1972, pp. 2–3.
[26] Ibid.
[27] *Izvestia*, April 22, 1970.

men in army and navy collectives, particularly in the primary ones, cannot be excluded."[28] That, indeed, they cannot be excluded is illustrated by the case of a soldier who alleged that he was being mistreated by his sergeant who was giving him an excessive amount of KP and latrine duty. The sergeant defended himself on the grounds that it is useful to work the intelligentsia this way, the soldier involved having been a recipient of a higher education.[29]

Party policy is not entirely free of responsibility for the continuation of class frictions. Party suspicions of scientists, students, and intellectuals generally, and Party attempts to reduce the role of intellectuals and increase the representation of working-class and rural persons in various higher functions signal a "class war" waged by the Party itself (see chapter VIII).

2. Specialization

Specialization of function usually fosters a sense of common interests and mutual understanding among those who have a particular specialty, especially, of course, among those who work in continuous face-to-face contact. As we noted earlier, however, this solidarity may be gained at the expense of reducing the solidarity of the larger group.

In the Soviet air force, specialization in terms of flight personnel and ground personnel produces some conflict and loss of morale characterized by the sentiment of technicians and mechanics that flight personnel receive more recognition than they do.[30] These differences may be aggravated by a sense of superiority developed by one or another specialty. Thus, the tension between flight personnel and maintenance personnel in the air force is associated with the sense of superiority of flight personnel.[31] Similarly, some tension and rivalry exists between combat personnel and rear service personnel in other arms and services.[32] In the PVO (air defense forces), however, it is the "combat" personnel, that is, the launch personnel, who feel that they are not adequately appreciated and that the technical personnel concerned with the electronic spotting and tracking equipment have a higher status.[33]

The arms and services represent a more general level of specialization involving large aggregates, between whom rivalry is, in most armies, traditional. The "infantry," that is, the "motorized rifle troops," seem sensitive to their status in the military (see p. 156 above). These rivalries do not seem to represent an appreciable problem at the troop level, but this does not exclude a more intense interservice rivalry at higher command levels.

[28] *KVS,* no. 13, July 1972, pp. 9–15.
[29] *KZ,* June 19, 1971, p. 2.
[30] See, for example, *KZ,* August 29, 1972, p. 2.
[31] Ibid., April 20, 1971, p. 2.
[32] Ibid., May 12, 1972, p. 2.
[33] Ibid., October 10, 1971, p. 2.

Most forms of functional military specialization are common to the Soviet forces and western armies, and their effect on the social cohesion of the military is, very likely, much the same. There is, however, one type of functional specialization extremely important in the Soviet forces that has no real counterpart in western armies and that produces in the Soviet military strong desolidarizing effects. This is the specialization of the military professional officer and political officer, that is, the political professional in the military. This form of differentiation renewed its importance as the Party enlarged the political officer class (1967) and sought to increase its influence over all aspects of military administration (see chapter VIII).

The desolidarizing effect of the presence of political officers and Party activists in the forces stems from the following consequences of their activities: (1) The Party undermines the professional status of military men by attaching greater importance to the political than to the military qualifications of officers, by according great importance to political indoctrination and the functions of the political officer and the Party activists, by claiming Party supremacy in all military affairs, and by emphasizing that it is the Communists and especially the Communist activists in the military who are the best and the most advanced soldiers. (2) The political officers and Party activists interfere with and erode the command authority of the officers. (3) The new political officers do not graduate from the same officer cadet academies as the other officers, but from special political officer academies. (4) The political officers and Party activists act as Party surveillance agents and informers, and try to impose a strict Party morality on the officers and enlisted men of the Soviet forces. (5) The political officers and Party activists are responsible for imposing political education and other indoctrinational activities that reduce the leisure time of officers and troops and the time available for military training. In addition, the political personnel are largely responsible for organizing the socialist competitions that impose heavy burdens on all military personnel.[34]

It is not surprising, then, that the divisions created by these conditions are probably deeper and have a more negative effect on the cohesiveness of the forces than most other factors affecting the morale of the military. Since the 1930s, commanders have often avoided association with political officers, a form of exclusiveness probably not paralleled with respect to any other division within the forces except, of course, rank.[35] The cold reception often accorded the new company political officers expresses a state of mind among the military officers that probably applies to higher-ranking political officers as well. It reveals itself, however, more easily in relations with the company political officer because of his youthfulness and junior rank.

[34] For documentation of the foregoing points, see chapter VIII.
[35] R. L. Garthoff, *Soviet Military Policy: A Historical Analysis,* New York, 1966, p. 37.

3. Rank and Subordination

The existence of a hierarchy of clearly marked ranks characterized by strict subordination and associated with differences in privileges and status, and marked by restrictions on fraternization, has been viewed in modern western armies as a normal and indeed necessary structure for military forces. It is evident that this complicates the problem of achieving social cohesion or solidarity among all members of a military force, although of course it increases the solidarity within the individual rank or status levels.

In Russia, after the revolution, such divisions were viewed as inconsistent with the egalitarian aspirations of 1917. It was not until 1935 that ranks were partially restored, and not until 1940 that the various grades of general officer were reintroduced. The still higher Soviet rank of marshal did not exist in prerevolutionary Russia.[36] New salary scales increased the divergence between officers and enlisted men and between senior and junior officers. Marshals, generals, field grade officers, and junior officers have their own messes and recreational facilities. "A field grade officer and the company grade officer are not social equals."[37]

Soviet writers have reacted angrily to western observations of what seems (to western eyes) the excessive deference paid by lower to higher ranks. Nonetheless, it is a Soviet military officer who refers to officers yielding their seats in public conveyances, not only to women but also to senior officers.[38]

We have already noted the proscription of personal intimacy, such as the use of "thou" or of first names while performing military duties. This offense is exacerbated when differences in rank are involved. Thus a senior lieutenant, the immediate commanding officer of a lieutenant, is reprimanded for a breach of "strict subordination so essential in the service" when he addressed his subordinate: "Okay, Yura. . . . "[39]

Although intimacy and fraternization among ranks is frowned on and the status of the superior rank is jealously guarded, Soviet military authorities are equally insistent that higher ranks exhibit "correct" behavior toward their subordinates. One of the duties of military Party agencies is to develop in officers "a respectful attitude toward their subordinates."[40] Salutes must be returned and soldiers addressed correctly. The commander of a ship is certainly entitled to eat in his cabin, but he is encouraged to eat at least occasionally in the ward room with his subordinates.[41] According to *Kommunist vooruzhennykh sil,* "the true political officer will not keep his subordinates away or

---

[36] Ibid., p. 35.
[37] Ibid., p. 37.
[38] *KZ,* July 13, 1972, p. 4.
[39] Ibid., August 16, 1972, p. 2.
[40] *KVS,* no. 7, April 1973, pp. 16–26.
[41] *KZ,* September 30, 1970, p. 2.

openly emphasize his position of superiority. He will talk trustingly with his soldiers, sing with them, and take part in sporting competitions. There will be no loss in authority if he does this. There will be no crossing of the boundary that is based on the respect and trust experienced by the masses with respect to their leaders."[42] The offensive, patronizing tone of this passage ostensibly dedicated to fostering camaraderie is probably a reflection of the difficulty that many Soviet officers (or political officers) have in thinking of the enlisted man as a social, if not a military, equal.

The separation or barrier represented in the United States by the phrase "going through channels" protects top commanders from a variety of contacts, mostly unwelcome. Although detailed descriptions of administrative practices in the offices of Soviet commanders are not available in the sources studied, incidental accounts clearly suggest that lower ranks can directly approach a regimental commander more readily than is customary in western practice. Thus the commander of an air regiment has "walk-in" hours when visitors, including family members of military personnel, can talk to him. But accounts indicate that many visitors do not wait for such hours, that persons are constantly bursting into the commander's office with questions and forms, and that his telephone is constantly ringing. It does not seem uncommon for subordinates to go out of channels directly to the commander. When a regimental commander reproached an officer for sending one of his subordinate officers to him with a trivial matter, it turned out that the officer had not sent the visitor at all. When the officer asked his subordinate why he went directly to the regimental commander, he answered: "I thought that the regimental commander would immediately make a positive decision, but he then began to check it out with you."[43]

The picture of the Soviet commander harassed by his many visitors is not an uncommon one and makes understandable a plea by *Krasnaya zvezda* to its military readers to make sure that their questions are worth the commander's time before they pick up the telephone or knock at his door.[44] Although conformity with this might increase administrative efficiency, it would also reduce the pleasant sense of disorderliness and accessibility that may in some measure mitigate, for Soviet military personnel, the strict divisions and rigors of the military machine.

"Correct" behavior of higher toward lower ranks particularly involves avoidance of rude, insulting language and shouting. The frequency with which Soviet military authorities report and condemn this behavior indicates that it is a widespread and major problem. In this respect, some Soviet officers still seem to treat enlisted men as if they were illiterate peasants. But this is only

---

[42] *KVS,* no. 10, May 1971, pp. 43–50.
[43] *KZ,* April 1, 1972, p. 2.
[44] Ibid.

part of the problem, since many of the complaints of the rude treatment of subordinates refer to the treatment of a junior officer by a higher officer.

The negative effect of these displays of anger on the morale of the immediate recipient of the dressing down and on unit solidarity is more or less evident. Soviet military writers emphasize, however, an additional point: The officer or NCO who is treated in this rude, insulting, hectoring fashion frequently turns his resentment into precisely the same kind of coarse behavior toward his own subordinates. "Rudeness is passed from the top down as if along a chain."[45] The cohesion and mutual respect of unit members is dissolved. Thus, an executive officer on a submarine was so harsh in his treatment of various subordinates that each of them became "nervous," and their behavior progressively made others "nervous" too. "This destroys the unity of the collective."[46]

Rudeness, excessive shouting, and lack of self-control are sometimes accompanied by arrogance, haughtiness, and an offensive distrust of subordinates.[47] Arrogance is not always a function of rank relations and an impatience with subordinates: it emerges, too, from an excessive pride in certain skills. Soviet writers sometimes imply that air pilots are more self-satisfied than is desirable.

Leaving aside what may be a Russian propensity for excitability, the difficulty that Soviet commanders seem to have in controlling their anger toward subordinates is probably related in part to the fact that the performance of their juniors is important to their own position and rating. Commanders are not only responsible for their own behavior, but they are likely to be held responsible for the mistakes and errors of their subordinates, which lower their personal standing and that of their unit, especially in socialist competition.[48]

The severity and irascibility of some commanders is not the only problem. "Great harm is also caused by commanders who curry favor among their subordinates, lower their exactingness, tolerate various types of indulgences."[49] No doubt such commanders often represent a personality type different from one that is easily moved to anger. But it is also likely that the tendency to "curry favor among their subordinates" is sometimes due to the effect this is presumed to have in improving the commander's reputation.

4. Age Differences and Youth

The undesirability of rude behavior and coarse language in the performance of command functions is closely related to the increasing youthfulness of the

[45] Ibid., May 25, 1972, p. 2.
[46] Ibid., April 20, 1972, p. 2. See also ibid., December 28, 1973, p. 2.
[47] Ibid., August 22, 1972, p. 2.
[48] This is sometimes denied, but Soviet military literature is rich in illustrations of the contrary. See, for example, p. 102.
[49] *Voyennyy vestnik,* January 1971, pp. 2–12.

conscript ranks and of the junior officers, and the higher educational attainments that now distinguish them. Their younger age and higher educational level make them less tolerant of military subordination (see pp. 214–218) and some of the practices associated with it.

Military authorities are well aware of the problem created by the reduction of the age of induction from nineteen to eighteen. "It would seem, what does one year in age change in a person? But if the character of a young person has not yet been molded, one year means much."[50] The second-year men among the conscripts are only nineteen, but "they are still a year older and different from the eighteen-year-old inductees. Consequently, one must remind officers that they should take this age difference into account."[51] The difference in age is not all that is involved here, but also the ability of the more experienced second-year soldiers to exploit the younger first-year soldiers (see p. 151 above). Indeed, this tension between first- and second-year soldiers is a principal breach in the solidarity of the conscript ranks. Probably, at a time when the conscripts were divided into first-, second-, and third-year men in the ground forces, this breach was less pronounced. The division into two rather than three cohorts has probably polarized the conscript ranks.

The new recruits have "a broad cultural outlook and a highly developed feeling of personal worth."[52] It is precisely because of this that *Krasnaya zvezda* warns against a style of army relations that is no longer appropriate "with a lieutenant who graduated from high school . . . or with a soldier who has read many books,"[53] that is, a soldier who is no longer a muzhik. A soldier who wrote to *Krasnaya zvezda* complaining that an officer addressed him simply "Come here, Petrov," is supported by *Krasnaya zvezda,* which points out that the soldier should have been addressed "Come here, Comrade (or Private) Petrov." " 'Comrade' is not simply a matter of etiquette, but is the password of class unity. Thus, if one omits 'comrade,' one sets oneself apart instead of binding oneself to the other person."[54]

While the Soviet attempt to ameliorate the relations between superior and subordinate may have strengthened solidarity and improved morale, it is evident that for some officers "the password of class unity" represents not so much an opportunity to increase officer-soldier solidarity as an unacceptable surrendering to youths who have gone soft. Some officers find it intolerable that a soldier should feel insulted because he is addressed in the familiar form. *Krasnaya zvezda,* however, points out that such officers do not realize what is happening in Soviet society. "Why is this question becoming so acute now?

[50] *KZ,* October 19, 1971, p. 2.
[51] Ibid., December 20, 1969, p. 3.
[52] *KVS,* no. 10, May 1970, pp. 30–34.
[53] *KZ,* June 27, 1971, p. 2.
[54] Ibid., September 11, 1971, p. 2.

What has happened? Much indeed has happened. Our whole life and our society, to use a contemporary expression, have gone into a new and higher orbit and we have passed through not one but rather ten or twenty stages of development. We Soviet people . . . have gained a greater feeling of pride in individual worth."[55]

Although officers are slowly adapting to the requirement that youth be treated "correctly," that is, by past standards, gently, some still resent having to restrain their behavior toward them, partly because of the usual age and generation tensions between youth and their elders. A colonel general of the Soviet forces in East Germany, when questioned why he had said military work is "rather difficult at the present time," discreetly replied, "The men are different and have increased requirements and interests."[56]

The age or generation gap also shows itself in references to the failings of youth. It is not uncommon to attribute to young people an emotional instability related to their rapid physical development and various psychological changes. This instability often means that they are not reliable and one officer points out, in this connection, the excessive number of highway accidents attributed to drivers who are eighteen to twenty-four years of age.[57]

Young pilots, another officer points out, are in too much of a hurry and to older persons appear boastful and self-satisfied. "Young officers [are spoiled] by excessive kindness and lavish praise. If the pilot makes a good take-off you hear someone saying, 'good lad.' If he lands in accordance with the rules, again they pat him on the back, 'clever fellow.' "[58] A lieutenant colonel, after praising young officers, expresses what appeared to be his more sincere convictions. "But youth is youth. It is accompanied by inexperience, excessive fervor, and inability at times to orient oneself correctly in a situation."[59]

Associated with the lack of solidarity between older and younger personnel is the division between those who experienced combat in World War II and those whose military careers have been pursued during peacetime. The wisdom and experience of the older generation is essential for these younger persons.[60] Despite the fact that Party and military authorities have expressed great pride in the relatively young ages of officers at the regimental level, and have taken this as a mark of positive distinction for the Soviet forces, General Pavlovskiy, commander in chief of the ground forces, remarks: "Young, intelligent officers

[55] Ibid.
[56] *Sovetskiy voin*, January 1971, pp. 2–4.
[57] *KZ*, October 21, 1971, p. 2.
[58] Ibid., January 11, 1970, p. 2.
[59] *KVS*, no. 4, February 1971, pp. 70–74.
[60] *KZ*, January 21, 1970, p. 2.

have begun to take over the posts of regimental commanders. However, these individuals have not yet acquired the necessary experience and skills for controlling a unit. This is why, based on my own combat experience, I would like to share certain thoughts. . . . "[61] A major general of aviation also finds that there is an inadequate appreciation of the importance of the older generation's combat experience. "The study and introduction of [World War II] wartime experience is not simply a blind adherence to tradition as some might think, but rather an urgent requirement of our times. . . . Combat experience earned through blood . . . must serve as an inexhaustible arsenal for us."[62]

The internal solidarity of the older military generation and correlatively the reduction of solidarity with the younger generation finds frequent expression on ceremonial occasions. Speaking at the funeral of Marshal I. S. Konev, Marshal I. I. Yakubovskiy, first deputy minister of defense, characteristically refers to "we military people of the older generation and direct participants of the last war."[63]

Kommunist vooruzhennykh sil urges officers "to show constant care that all categories of officers . . . should be closely united among themselves, and united around the Party and the government."[64] It is evident, however, leaving aside other sources of division, that sheer age and generation differences, and the education and experiences associated with them, place strong constraints on the social cohesion of the officer corps.

5. Pressures

One of the chief characteristics of the Soviet forces is the enormous pressure brought to bear on all ranks, but especially on the new recruits and the young officers. The continuous pressure of a rigorous training process, the severity of discipline, incessant political indoctrination, the pressure to study for and acquire higher specialist ratings, the lack of genuine recreational facilities,[65] and the all-pervasive influence of socialist competition clearly have a depressing effect both on troop morale and on the morale of the officers who must

[61] *Voyennyy vestnik,* January 1971, pp. 2–12.

[62] *KZ,* February 4, 1971, p. 2.

[63] Ibid., May 24, 1973, p. 3. A year before his death Marshal Konev had also expressed his solidarity with those who fought in World War II. After pointing out that "the soldier who spent four years on the road of war remembers every day and every battle as if it were yesterday," Marshal Konev continued by charging that veterans are frequently bitter about their failure to receive the treatment and privileges to which they are entitled. *Literaturnaya gazeta,* February 2, 1972, p. 12.

[64] *KVS,* no. 13, July 1972, pp. 9–15.

[65] Even on vacation furloughs, the military authorities bring pressure on officers to engage in "joint tourism," in effect physical hardening exercises. *KZ* complains that officers prefer to go to vacation sanatoria, perhaps not so surprising since the "tourism" facilities consist of tents with holes and unsuitable sleeping bags. *KZ,* July 28, 1972, p. 4.

administer these programs and who have equally rigorous treatment imposed on them by their superiors and by the Party. Morale problems naturally affect solidarity as well. The military easily becomes divided into "they" (who are responsible for the pressure) and "we" (who have to bear it), where each "we" has its own particular "they" depending on the rank and Party level involved. This, of course, is not peculiar to the Soviet forces, but the intensity of the pressure very probably is.

Socialist competition, which provides much of the institutional framework through which individuals and units are driven to higher levels of activity and accomplishment, is of special interest in the contemplation of the effect of the Soviet high-pressure system on morale and solidarity. The Soviet desire to avoid "microcollectivism" or a parochial regimental loyalty has not prevented an unflagging insistence on the use of socialist competition, that is, of rivalry among individuals and units. This rivalry is attenuated in part by the ability, in principle, of all individuals and units to win the title of "outstanding" or "excellent." In principle, too, competitors are supposed to be willing to aid each other when it is relevant and feasible. But in many instances socialist competition clearly has a negative effect on solidarity. Thus, each platoon commander in the same company wants, naturally enough, to come out on top. "Otherwise, why compete? At times this aspiration out-grows the bounds of healthy competitiveness. There begin to be 'secrets' and certain reservations arise. And since the soldiers breathe the same air as the platoon commander, the same kind of guardedness toward 'rivals' appears in them as well."[66]

It is always possible, of course, to deny that socialist competition has negative effects on solidarity and morale by simply affirming the contrary. Thus, according to a Soviet general, "competition develops collectivism and teaches the men to approach one or another phenomenon from social, state-wide positions. It makes men . . . pure and more noble . . . "[67] Indeed, one way of increasing "exemplary friendship" among soldiers is to make this itself an object of socialist competition.[68]

The pressures under which Soviet military personnel labor can be exacerbated or mitigated by the physical conditions of military service. For recruits and junior officers these conditions are, on the whole, well below the standards of the US military and most other western military establishments. Nonetheless, Soviet authorities have in recent years paid increasing attention to creature comforts. The caloric content of food has increased and remains well above Soviet civilian consumption; new field kitchens have been developed to

[66] Ibid., August 15, 1971, p. 2.
[67] *Sovetskiy voin,* July 3, 1972, pp. 2–4.
[68] Ibid.

provide better food under field conditions. Clothing, both for dress and field use, has improved, and medical services during exercises in the field have been made more readily available.[69]

Whether these changes have been sufficient and widespread enough to have had a significant effect on morale is difficult to say. Articles in the military literature are not very likely to reflect the dissatisfactions of the recruits. However, complaints still abound with respect to the living conditions of junior officers, despite Soviet statements concerning efforts to improve them. One reason why these efforts have failed is suggested by the response to a group of officers who wrote to *Krasnaya zvezda* complaining about their quarters— no shower, no dayroom, the TV set broken, the ceiling leaking, the plaster peeling, cold in the winter, no mirror for shaving, and much more. The political officer of the unit provided *Krasnaya zvezda* with the following explanation for this state of affairs: the warehouse contained a complete set of new, modern furniture, the latest model TV set, a pool table, and other items. But these were intended for the new barracks building. Unfortunately, the new building, although started five years ago, was still not finished.[70] The *Krasnaya zvezda* commentator adds an interesting remark that throws some light on Soviet priorities in the military establishment: "If one were speaking about shortcomings in military studies or special training, I am sure that immediate and decisive measures would be taken."[71]

6. Nationality and Language

Nationality and language divisions within the Soviet population, and therefore within the military, are, of course, closely related.[72] Language differences stem from nationality differences, which in their turn are sometimes associated with religious differences, as in the case of some of the smaller republics with Moslem populations. In the Soviet Union another major religious difference is created not by attachments to one church rather than another, but rather by the difference between those who are nonbelievers (in any church) and those who silently or openly are still attached to a religious faith or to religious practices.

Although special considerations may produce other than a random mix-

---

[69] See chapter I, section D,3. See also an editorial in *KZ*, August 22, 1972, p. 1, and *Bloknot agitatora*, June 1971. The Soviet wheat and bread shortage in the fall of 1972 did not, however, spare the military forces, who were ordered to slice the bread thinner and serve less of it. *Los Angeles Times*, October 8, 1972.

[70] *KZ*, July 22, 1972, p. 2.

[71] Ibid.

[72] According to the Soviet census of 1970, the population of the USSR is distributed as follows, in percent: Russians 53, Ukrainians 17, Uzbeks 3.8, Belorussians 3.8, Tatars 2.4, Kazakhs 2.2, Azerbaijanis 1.8, Armenians 1.5, Georgians 1.3, and all others (28 nationalities) 12.6. Of these, approximately 35 million were, in 1970, of Moslem origin, an increase of 44 percent over the 1959 figure. The total population in 1970 was 242 million.

ture of nationalities among the inductees serving in some units, in principle Soviet military units are multinational and do not depend on recruits from the area in which the unit is located. References to the nationalities represented in Soviet company-size units indicate a high level of mixture. Thus, one battery is said to have twenty-four different nationalities among the new recruits.[73] An isolated air-defense unit is made up of "Russians and Ukrainians, Georgians and Armenians, Tatars and Kazakhs, Jews and Uzbeks, in all, seventeen different nationalities."[74] A submarine crew contains men from twenty-two republics and *oblasts* who represent eleven nationalities.[75] In the Red Banner Turkestan military district "companies where representatives of twelve to fifteen or more nationalities serve are a normal phenomenon."[76]

Writers interested in stressing the multinational character of military units may, of course, select for illustration units with a high mix of nationalities. However, assuming a unit of 100 men, the examples cited above are entirely reasonable on a probability basis, as the distribution in footnote 72, p. 186 indicates.

Soviet concern with nationalist feelings among its minorities, especially in the Ukraine, Armenia, and Georgia, has been too well publicized to require a review here. We may note, however, that in Georgia the Party attempt to root out nationalism and improper use of state property reportedly led to outbreaks that required the calling out of Soviet troops. Party concern is not likely to diminish. The Soviet census of 1970 indicates that the Russians will be a minority in about ten to fifteen years, and that even the Slav groups (mostly Russians and Ukrainians) may be a minority by the year 2000. The persistence with which various minorities have clung to their native languages is striking—indeed, in some cases an increase in the use of the native language was registered in 1970 over the corresponding 1959 figure.

That ethnic diversity does not negatively affect national security and on the contrary is a source of strength is a frequent Soviet theme. Hitler was badly mistaken when he thought that the USSR was "an ethnic conglomerate" whose lack of internal unity would make it easy to conquer.[77] Nevertheless, it still remains a major objective of Soviet mass patriotic activity "to solidify the people of all nationalities around the Party and the government."[78]

It is hardly to be expected that ethnic and linguistic divisions that create major problems for the Party in the civil society are without some effect on the military forces. Naturally enough, tensions among members of different nationalities are only occasionally and very discreetly referred to in Soviet military journals and newspapers, although the frequent contrary emphasis

[73] *KZ,* December 20, 1969, p. 3.
[74] *Pravda Ukrainy,* November 4, 1971, p. 4.
[75] *Kazakhstanskaya pravda,* October 28, 1971, p. 4.
[76] *KVS,* no. 17, September 1972, pp. 24–29.
[77] Ibid., no. 3, February 1971, pp. 70–77.
[78] Ibid., no. 21, November 1971, pp. 18–25.

that the Soviet nationalities serve together "in a friendly fashion"[79] may equally reflect an uneasy recognition of a problem.

In discussing the tasks of military indoctrination, an analyst gives as the two chief sources of division within the military age differences and "servicemen of different nationalities." These divisions compel "commanders and political workers to use the most effective measures to rally the military collectives."[80] Manifestations of nationalism are inimical to military effectiveness, since military collectives contain representatives of many nationalities. "It follows that the slightest hostility among the personnel of a squad, team, or crew can lead to disproportionate impairment in combat readiness."[81] Propagandists in the army are told that friendship among servicemen of different nationalities can be strengthened by implanting in them a "burning hatred" of the enemies of the motherland.[82] It is, of course, hardly likely that this will dissolve nationalist sentiments. That the latter are sometimes an aggravation is made clear by a major general of the Red Banner Turkestan Military District who points out that although "our commanders and political officers have a solicitous attitude toward national feelings . . . this does not mean that they are condescending toward manifestations of nationalism and conceit."[83]

Although their interpretation seems clear enough, references in the military press to nationalist tensions are relatively few. The Soviet military journals are, however, much more outspoken concerning the effect on both solidarity and military efficiency of Russian language deficiencies among the non-Russian nationalities serving in the forces. That these pose a significant problem in military and political training is suggested by the Soviet census of 1970. Sixty-two percent of the non-Russian population (29 percent of the Soviet population) do not speak Russian fluently.[84] Discussions in military journals reflect this situation. A political talk was well presented but "in fact it turned out that some of the soldiers . . . did not understand the leader's talk. They did not know Russian very well."[85] In a solidarity-building session recruits were introduced to a map of the Soviet Union. A corporal rose to describe his native Kazakhstan, but he had difficulties due to his limited Russian vocabu-

---

[79] *Pravda,* July 25, 1971, p. 6.
[80] *KVS,* no. 24, December 1972, pp. 25–32.
[81] Ibid., no. 3, February 1971, pp. 70–77.
[82] Ibid.
[83] Ibid., no. 17, September 1972, pp. 24–29.
[84] Unfortunately the census does not distinguish degrees of Russian knowledge in the non-fluent category. This includes, then, those who have no knowledge at all of Russian as well as those who speak with less than fluency. The percentage not speaking Russian fluently is highly variable among the individual nationalities. For example, it is 37.5 percent among Tatars, 51 percent among Belorussians, 64 percent among Ukrainians, 70 percent among Armenians, 79 percent among Georgians, and 85 percent among Tadzhiks and Turkmenians. Non-Russians constitute 47 percent of the USSR population.
[85] *KVS,* no. 23, December 1969, pp. 45–50.

lary.[86] A recruit from Central Asia who presented other problems also had "a poor command of the Russian language."[87] A company commander noticed that two privates were shunning their comrades. "The reason—poor knowledge of the Russian language—fear of saying something wrong and thereby causing the laughter of fellow servicemen. This feeling hampered them in asking questions of the sergeant."[88]

The difficulties stemming from deficient Russian language skills are increased by the exclusive role of Russian in the army and navy. Competitive entrance examinations to officer schools include examinations in the Russian language and sometimes in Russian literature.[89] Regulations and training manuals are written in Russian. Commands are issued in Russian and all combat and political training is conducted in Russian. "It could not be otherwise. Our army is a unified combat organism embodying the unity of will, action, and aspirations of the motherland's armed defenders. It is natural that Soviet soldiers use one language in all their duties and studies. This language is Russian—the most widespread language in our country and the language of international intercourse voluntarily chosen by all the USSR peoples."[90]

D. METHODS

We discussed earlier (pp. 171–175) Soviet views on the sources of solidarity and morale. Here we describe several steps taken by the authorities to act on these views and to overcome the constraints on solidarity and morale discussed above.

1. Psychology and Sociology

In dealing with problems of morale and solidarity, Soviet military authorities have made increasing use of techniques and theory developed by the new Soviet schools of psychology and sociology. In August 1967 the Central Committee of the Party passed a resolution "On Measures for Further Developing the Social Sciences and Heightening Their Role in Communist Construction." In October 1968 the Council of Ministers of the USSR instituted the scientific degrees of candidate and doctor of psychological sciences.[91] Special departments have been created in universities, and the teaching of psychology has been introduced in technical, medical, and legal higher educational institutions. The increased status of psychology was further evidenced in December

---

[86] *KZ*, April 15, 1971, p. 2.
[87] *KVS*, no. 10, May 1971, pp. 30–34.
[88] Ibid., no. 17, September 1972, pp. 24–29.
[89] *KZ*, March 7, 1972, p. 4.
[90] Editorial, ibid., January 20, 1973, p. 1.
[91] *KVS*, no. 15, August 1971, pp. 25–32.

1971, when a resolution of the presidium of the USSR Academy of Sciences created an Institute of Psychology in the academy's department of philosophy and law.[92]

Similar developments have occurred in sociology. In 1966 the Soviet Sociological Association (organized in 1958) had 580 individual members. Four years later, in 1970, individual membership had almost tripled to 1,469. At the 1956 meeting of the International Sociological Association in Amsterdam, only a few old-line Soviet theoreticians attended. Ten years later, in 1966, at Evian, eighty-three Soviet representatives were present. In 1970 at the seventh congress of the association at Varna (Bulgaria), the Soviets had the largest representation, 400 as compared with an American group of 300.[93]

Support for the development of social science beyond the confining limits of Marxism-Leninism has been provided by as high a Party personality as M. Suslov, secretary of the Central Committee. In an address entitled "The Social Sciences—The Party's Combat Weapon in Building Communism," Suslov viewed social science not simply as an instrument to improve economic management, but as one also providing direction in solving problems of domestic social-political development and in the rational analysis of foreign policy.[94]

The new prestige of psychology and sociology was felt almost immediately in the military establishment. The Central Committee of the Party in August 1967 had already dealt with the growing requirements of military cadres for psychological knowledge. As a result, the Main Political Administration of the Soviet forces set forth the basic directions for scientific research in military psychology. Both the Lenin Military Academy and the Novosibirsk Higher Military Political Combined Arms School in 1970 had departments of military psychology.[95] The Soviet Sociological Association has a military department.[96] Soviet writings on morale, solidarity, and discipline increasingly emphasize the importance of a knowledge of psychology and sociology for motivating and understanding soldiers. Company officers, particularly the company political officers, study the character, behavior, and attitudes of the men.[97] Students of morale are urged to discover the natural laws that determine the influence of "moral magnitudes" on the combat qualities of the armed forces and the population. It is equally important to discover the laws for undermining the morale of enemy forces.

There has been some resistance both among Party elements and among

[92] *Voprosy filosofii,* May 1972, pp. 135–159.
[93] Z. Katz, "Sociology in the Soviet Union," *Problems of Communism,* May-June 1971, p. 22.
[94] *Kommunist,* no. 1, January 1972, pp. 18–30.
[95] *KVS,* no. 15, August 1971, pp. 25–32.
[96] *KZ,* May 27, 1973, p. 2.
[97] See, for example, *KZ,* June 30, 1971, p. 2.

officers to the new claims of social science, but the authorities have continued to press for its further utilization. *Krasnaya zvezda,* in an editorial "In Step with Science and Technology," reprimands those "who speak well about new things and who fight for introducing scientific methods, but then really don't do anything about it."[98]

One outgrowth of the emphasis on social science generally and on psychology in particular has been the reinforcement of convictions concerning the importance of individual differences in handling people in the military forces. This, of course, has direct applications to problems of military training, but applies equally in dealing with questions of morale, discipline, and indoctrination. On long sea voyages, where boredom and restlessness may readily develop and morale may decline, it is important for the political worker to know thoroughly each person individually and be familiar with his state of mind.[99] The psychological preparation of flying cadets for their initial solo flight has to be based on an understanding of each individual.[100] General Gorchakov emphasizes that in the missile forces "individual work with all soldiers is essential."[101] The interest in the personal compatibility of members of a military team is also an offshoot of the psychological interest in individual variations.

It is easier to find references to the need to use scientific criteria in developing compatible military teams than it is to find any discussion of techniques for determining compatibility.[102] In general, one suspects that the enthusiasm for the use of psychology and sociology is greater than the specific knowledge and techniques for their application in specific circumstances. When a writer affirms that "interchangeability [of the members of a team] creates the necessary conditions for more complete mutual understanding and comradely mutual assistance,"[103] it is more likely that this statement is based on intuition or uncertain deductive reasoning than on empirically tested knowledge. Still, the introduction of scientific study and analysis of morale and other military problems on any substantial scale has been so recent that the infrequent reporting of empirical studies is hardly surprising. In sociological investigations the easy use of questionnaires has led to a greater amount of empirical work.

---

[98] Ibid., October 6, 1971, p. 1.
[99] Ibid., August 15, 1971. See also *KVS,* no. 2, January 1974, pp. 44–45 and 49–50.
[100] *Aviatsiya i kosmonavtika,* January 1973, pp. 16–17.
[101] *KZ,* April 14, 1972, p. 2.
[102] See *KZ,* January 26, 1973, pp. 2–3, and *Sovetskiy voin,* November 1970, pp. 9–12.
[103] *KVS,* no. 24, December 1971, pp. 39–45. The passage cited in the text continues: "Confidence of soldiers that their comrades will not let them down and will come to their aid in any situation increases manifold the solidarity of organized military groups and is the basis of collective feelings."

2. Ritual and Emotion

Partly as a consequence of the newly developed sophistication in psychology and sociology, the Soviet military has increased the use of rituals to inculcate a spirit of attachment to the military, to the Party, and to the duty expected of each serviceman. The use of ritual to enhance the solidarity of a collective, most of whose members have never seen each other before, contrasts with a similar development of ritual in Soviet civil society. In the civil society the motive for introducing special rituals is less for the purpose of creating new attachments than it is for loosening prior attachments to church ceremonies and nationalist sentiments. Characteristic of this development in the civil society are new and more elaborate rituals for marriages and funerals. In some areas eighteen-year-olds are given a ritual welcome together with coming-of-age certificates as a replacement for the religious ceremony of confirmation. "Last year more than 10,000 men and women in Latvia took part in coming-of-age holidays, while scarcely more than 100 were confirmed."[104] The Ministry of Culture in Latvia is the methodological center for the introduction of Soviet everyday traditions. "The introduction of the new civic ceremonies is a very subtle and delicate task. . . . We have set up special departments of Soviet traditions with a two-year training program under the people's universities."[105]

In the army, several rituals revolve around the introduction of servicemen and officers to their new units and colleagues. In the case of inductees, a ritual greeting occurs at the local military commissariat before they are sent off to their new units. The enlisted men are again greeted with special ceremonies when they arrive at their units. The ritual of introduction has become a tradition for young officers as well. "The ritual begins with a meeting with all the officers of the unit. In a solemn surrounding, the commander introduces the newly arrived officers and talks to them about the combat path and the traditions. Such meetings are organized in the Museum of Combat Glory."[106]

A ritual of considerable importance for new conscripts is held only after they have been in the unit long enough for the political officer to have been able to teach them the meaning and character of the military oath. The oath is then taken by the new recruits before all the personnel and the unit banner. Generally the ceremony is conducted at a historical site of revolutionary or combat glory. As each recruit's name is read out by the commander, the soldier or sailor leaves the ranks and reads the text of the oath aloud before his formation, after which he signs a special roster and returns to the ranks. After the oath has been taken, the band plays the national anthem and the unit then passes in review. The day on which the oath is taken is a holiday for that unit.[107]

---

[104] *Izvestia,* October 28, 1971, p. 5.
[105] Ibid.
[106] *Tekhnika i vooruzheniye,* no. 12, 1969, pp. 2–3.
[107] *KVS,* no. 19, October 1971, pp. 60–65.

In some services, where duty is particularly rigorous or difficult, special attention is given to ceremonies intended to mark the entrance of the inductee into this service. Thus, the ritual of "initiation of a submariner" is much emphasized in the navy. Similarly, in distant frontier posts where service is arduous, rituals are sometimes used to impress individuals with the importance of their incorporation into the unit. Thus, at one frontier post the lieutenant who assigns the guards to duty first reads the assignment for a soldier who in fact is dead and who died as a hero. The frontier guard who stands first in line answers "present" on behalf of the fallen man. In the barracks a bunk is still made up for him, with a photograph of the dead man above it.[108]

The interest in ritual, tradition, and ceremony is linked to the emotion generated by them and the conviction that through this emotion the individual is motivated in the desired direction and in some sense is made into a new individual. Speaking of the rituals of Soviet military units, *Krasnaya zvezda* remarks, "Who can remain indifferent after being dedicated as a commander in such a manner?"[109] Referring to meetings in the Museum of Combat Glory, a writer remarks, "Throughout their lives the young officers will keep in their memory that meeting with the glorious past of the division."[110] According to another writer, "Such measures [rituals] leave a deep trace in the minds of people."[111] Referring more specifically to the ceremony of initiating new submariners, *Krasnaya zvezda* states, "Naturally, this has a great emotional influence on the man, and engenders in him . . . the aspiration to endure the difficulties of life . . . steadfastly."[112]

Some Soviet writers, while acknowledging the desirability of "inventing traditions," emphasize the value of traditional ceremonial aspects of military life. According to *Krasnaya zvezda* there is a tendency to ignore older practices and various military ceremonies, such as retreat, carrying the flag, and singing. At a certain tank school the students no longer bother to sing, a regrettable state of affairs since singing is viewed by *Krasnaya zvezda* as having considerable virtue with respect to solidarity and morale.[113] Several Soviet writers view music as important, whether in the form of singing by the troops or as a type of entertainment. "In our view, it is the best means of reducing the tension of low morale, and it also has a positive emotional effect."[114] The use of music to stir military and patriotic sentiments begins in the Young Pioneer detachments, which end many of their assemblies with a song. "What an enormous charge of ideas and emotions a combat song has in itself."[115]

[108] *Bakinskiy rabochiy,* December 12, 1969, p. 4. This is a continuation of a practice of the Czarist army. See A. Lobanov-Rostovsky, *The Grinding Mill,* New York, 1935, p. 7.

[109] *KZ,* January 14, 1970, p. 2.

[110] *Tekhnika i vooruzheniye,* no. 12, 1969, pp. 2–3.

[111] *KVS,* no. 3, February 1971, pp. 45–50.

[112] *KZ,* February 5, 1971, p. 2.

[113] Ibid., June 18, 1970, p. 2.

[114] *Sovetskiy voin,* April 15, 1972, pp. 42–43.

[115] *KZ,* October 25, 1971, p. 4.

Song and music are not the only forms of "aesthetics" in the service of military units. In a book published in 1968 by the Ministry of Defense publishing house, the use of works of art of many types to stimulate profound feelings is treated at some length. "Their use . . . makes it possible to find those forms that evoke a vital interest in the men and influence not only their reason but also their feelings. . . . Aesthetics . . . [can] serve them and inspire them to feats in the name of the motherland. . . . Great causes require great words. For this reason it is difficult to overestimate the significance of aesthetics and art in military and patriotic indoctrination."[116]

A special objective of many ceremonies and "thematic sessions" is to develop hatred for the enemy. Thus a "thematic session" viewed as particularly successful was held on a Soviet cruiser in the Mediterranean whose captain had developed an evening session on the subject "Love your motherland and hate your enemies as V. I. Lenin directed." The session consisted of a compilation of accounts by eyewitnesses of fascist atrocities on Soviet soil during World War II, excerpts from films on the crimes of the American military in Vietnam, and various patriotic songs by the ship's chorus. "Such measures are intended to rally people on firm ground, influence their general attitudes, and strengthen the ideological foundation."[117]

Although the Soviets have considerable use for love when it is directed toward the Party or the country and hate when it is directed against the enemy, such strong emotions tend otherwise to be feared because they have a dissolving effect on large social collectives. To an authoritarian leadership, emotion is dangerous because it is not easily controlled. As we have seen, the emotions of loyalty or affection toward a small number of individuals rather than toward the Party, the country, or the entire military collective is viewed as "an incorrect interpretation of comradeship" that "tends toward . . . supporting a narrow circle of people." The decisive rooting out of this false understanding of comradeship "is an essential condition for binding collectives on a healthy basis."[118] Although fearing the development of friendships that may lead to a mutual toleration of disciplinary infractions, the Soviets have had to acknowledge the positive value of "military friendship and combat friendship" and have made available to the troops "the best example of military friendship and combat friendship."[119] From these remarks it appears that devotion to the army and the Party has not prevented Soviet soldiers from also engaging in heroic efforts to help each other. In the Soviet army the experience of numerous units even provides, we are told, "many examples where a soldier has

[116] Colonel E. M. Sapunov [*Aesthetics of Military Service*], Moscow, 1968.
[117] *KZ*, June 26, 1971. p. 2.
[118] Ibid., August 13, 1971, pp. 2–3.
[119] Ibid., April 5, 1972, p. 1.

rescued not only a friend, but also a comrade in arms with whom he was not personally acquainted."[120]

Although tolerating, with a measure of suspicion and reservation, "combat comradeship," the Soviets oppose cohesiveness based on the arms or services instead of the entire military collective. In order to prevent special skills and the different services from breaking down the unity of the military collective, *Krasnaya zvezda* has recommended that joint evenings and meetings between representatives of various specialties and combat arms be held so that personnel will realize that their military service is only a part of the military establishment.[121]

We have already noted the Soviet attempt to eradicate rude and angry shouting at subordinates. Quite apart from relations with subordinates, the Soviets prize "a calm and businesslike" officer who performs his duties with no "undue excitement." Examples of "clear and calm commands" and a "businesslike atmosphere" are provided to induce similar behavior throughout the officer force. Officers who appear calm and never raise their voices are praised. These same virtues of calmness, businesslike atmosphere, and nonexcitability are also much emphasized in the civilian sector and represent a strong distaste for anything that suggests nervousness and loss of self-control.[122]

3. Promoting the Russian Language

Soviet military authorities are making strenuous efforts to overcome deficiencies in the Russian language among the young conscripts. They have not simply relied on their own efforts to instruct minority recruits in Russian when they enter the army. They have also promoted, in conjunction with the civilian authorities who have similar interests, the instruction of Russian in the national (minority) schools and in special language classes.

The Central Committee of the Kirghiz Communist Party has brought pressure to bear on the appropriate parties to increase and improve the teaching of Russian in the schools where Kirghiz is the language of instruction. The Party has berated the Kirghiz Ministry of Public Education, the state univer-

[120] *KVS,* no. 21, November 1971, pp. 65–70.
[121] *KZ,* October 10, 1971, p. 2.
[122] In providing a photograph of Secretary Brezhnev in conversation with Prime Minister Willy Brandt of the Federal Republic of Germany, *Pravda* retouched the photograph in order to remove a cigarette in Brezhnev's hand. Since it was known that Brezhnev was trying to reduce his smoking, it is likely that the erasure of the cigarette was intended to prevent Brezhnev from seeming unable to maintain self-control. On the other hand, *Soviet Life* (July 1973, p. 1), prepared for foreign distribution, showed Brezhnev in a full-page portrait seated at his desk with a cigarette in his hand. For a discussion of the Bolshevik fear of excitement and emotional expression, see Nathan Leites, *A Study of Bolshevism,* Glencoe, Illinois, 1953, chapter V, especially pp. 203–208.

sity, and other institutes for their failure to do more in this regard.[123] Similarly, in Estonia the Party has pressed for more and better teaching of Russian in schools that use Estonian as the teaching language. Inadequate instruction "makes service in the ranks of the Soviet army more difficult for young men and constitutes an obstacle to their entry into military schools."[124] The military council of the Transcaucasus Red Banner military district recently urged that the district improve the teaching of Russian in its schools so that young men will be better prepared for military service.[125]

The teaching of Russian as a second language in schools where the language of instruction is not Russian has not satisfied the authorities. In some republics, special Russian language schools and classes have been formed. The Kirghiz Republic has 300 such classes with a total enrollment of 8,500.[126]

More substantial steps have been taken in the RSFSR (Russian Soviet Federated Socialist Republic), the largest of the fifteen union republics, which embraces fifteen autonomous Soviet socialist republics (ASSRS), six territories, and forty-nine *oblasts* and contains about three-fourths of all the Soviet territory and 54 percent of the population of the USSR. The RSFSR has almost eleven thousand national (i.e., minority) schools with close to five million students (1971). "Non-Russian schools in most autonomous republics and provinces [of the RSFSR]—with the exception of the Tatar and Bashkir republics—have shifted to the use of Russian *as the language of instruction in the ninth and tenth grades.* The study of Russian now begins in the first grade of all types of non-Russian schools."[127] (Emphasis added.) Because in the RSFSR 59 percent of the nonelementary national schools are eight-year schools and only 41 percent are nine- and ten-year schools, it is apparent that Russian as the language of instruction in the ninth and tenth grades will reach only some of the students. In principle the Soviets are moving toward a universal ten-year secondary education, but it is evident that this will not be attained for several years. For the national (minority) children who attend only the eight-year school, the entrance into Russian language study in the first grade is the major innovation. The earnestness and effectiveness of this instruction is an open question. It is apparent from Party interventions that in some national regions instruction in Russian is pursued far from enthusiastically.

If the use of Russian as a language of instruction in the senior secondary-

[123] *Sovetskaya Kirgiziya,* April 28, 1973, pp. 1–2.

[124] *Sovetskaya Estoniya,* July 5, 1972, p. 3.

[125] Domestic Service, in Armenian, March 4, 1973.

[126] *Pravda,* January 4, 1973, p. 2. In the Kirghiz Republic it is traditional to hold a schoolchildren's festival whose motto is "The Russian language—the language of peace and friendship."

[127] *Sovetskaya pedagogika,* November 1972, pp. 11–20. Evidently this will also affect the selection of teachers in the advanced grades and provide incentives for minority teachers to learn Russian well enough to teach science, history, and literature in it.

school grades continues in the RSFSR, it will represent an evasion of the *Draft Principles of Legislation of the USSR and the Union Republics on Public Education* submitted in April 1973 to the USSR Supreme Soviet by the USSR Council of Ministers. Article 18 of the draft reads: "Pupils in general-education schools are given the opportunity to receive instruction in their native language. . . . In addition to the language in which instruction is carried on, pupils may choose to study the language of another people of the USSR."[128] Article 20 of the draft reads: "With a view to preparing children for school who will be instructed in a language not native to them, and children who have not attended children's preschool institutions, schools are to organize preparatory classes if necessary."[129]

These articles of the draft appear to mean (1) that children in general education schools may choose to be instructed in their native language, presumably throughout *all* grades, and (2) that the children who choose to be instructed in a language not native to them (presumably Russian) are to have preparatory classes (if they have not already received some Russian instruction in preschool institutions).

It is likely, given current practices in the RSFSR, that the option to choose the language of instruction will not be honored in the senior grades. Or rather, that all students in these grades will find themselves "choosing" Russian. If, in fact, the use of Russian in the last two grades is not made compulsory, it would mean a significant retreat from the effort to impose Russian on the forty-seven nationalities of the RSFSR.

Since the measures in the civil society do not always prepare Soviet minority youth to speak Russian fluently, commanders, political workers, and the Party and Komsomol organizations in the military are compelled to deal with the problem after the recruits enter the service. "Societies for the study of the Russian language have been organized in the subunits and units. Measures are being undertaken to ensure that the study of the Russian language in these societies is being conducted in conformity with the uniform program for all of the armed forces. Extensive use is made of a system wherein Komsomol activists are assigned to furnish assistance to the soldiers who are weak in the Russian language. Usually by the time they complete their service they all possess a good knowledge of Russian. Russian language societies have been established in some areas for draft-age youth."[130] The statement that soldiers deficient in Russian generally possess a good knowledge of Russian by the time they complete their service suggests that during most of their service period difficulties continue to exist.

[128] *Izvestia,* April 5, 1973, pp. 3–4.
[129] Ibid.
[130] *KVS,* no. 21, November 1972, pp. 28–33.

E. CONCLUDING OBSERVATIONS

Soviet military authorities appreciate the value of solidarity and morale in the armed forces, but nonetheless they show a certain unease in dealing with these intangible, elusive qualities so different from the specificity of regulations and the judgments of guilt and innocence to which they give rise. Social cohesion and morale cannot be "ordered" and cannot be "enforced." Even the instilling of military skills lends itself to a certain degree of forceful imposition and to a precise testing of the degree to which learning has been achieved. But solidarity and morale are desired qualities not amenable to this type of treatment. This does not prevent one from trying. If *Kommunist vooruzhennykh sil* is to be believed, Soviet military regulations *require* that soldiers love their commanders.[131]

Uncertainty concerning the best means of developing cohesion and morale is common to most military authorities, but the inability to "demand" that individuals and units have these qualities is probably more distressing to Soviet authorities than to western ones. This distress or unease is especially concentrated among Party personnel in the military who have major responsibilities for political-moral (ideological) and psychological (morale) training.

Morale problems are almost certainly more damaging to the Soviet military than disciplinary problems. The major influences depressing morale at the troop and junior officer level are almost surely the enormous, unflagging pressure of military duties, of constant surveillance, and of political indoctrination. The special role of the Party in conducting socialist competition, in demanding ever more study of Marxism-Leninism and ever more attendance at political lectures and patriotic ceremonies, and in providing for surveillance must operate to focus a great deal of the developed resentment on the Party or the Party-in-the-army, rather than on those junior and middle-level officers who are not particularly identified as Party zealots.

The disregard for physical comforts—despite the improvement in the military living standards of recruits and junior officers—plays a role in depressing morale, a role that is moderated, on the one hand, by the relatively low standards of living of recruits from the countryside, and increased, on the other hand, by the accompanying pressures of Party-directed military life. The low military standard of living has a more depressing effect on morale than it would have without the reinforcing influence of the grim pace of military existence.

For the better educated and more advantaged urban youth, army life, with its strict subordination and endless political indoctrination, is more disagreeable than for the other recruits, although some of the urban youths may find compensations in the greater ease with which they can acquire various specialist ratings that provide personal satisfaction and, perhaps, more agree-

[131] Ibid., no. 18, September 1972, pp. 69–75. See p. 305 below for the quotation.

able duty hours. It is likely, too, that some personnel in the various arms and services have compensating rewards, such as opportunities in naval service to "see the world," or in the air force to be part of a "romantic" occupation. The Party and Komsomol activists, too, probably find military life less depressing than do others, partly because they are "dishing it out," partly because of career rewards that may come to Party activists, and partly because some of them are motivated by sincere Party fervor.

One very major group whose morale is subject to considerable pressure by army life is constituted by the recruits from the minority (non-Russian) nationalities, especially those whose knowledge of the Russian language is rudimentary. It is possible, of course, that such recruits develop a passive resistance to the system and an intentional noncomprehension that gives them a protective armor, somewhat similar to that which many Indians still exhibit toward their white or Spanish masters in some Central and South American societies. But possibilities, both of resistance and of advancement, that are open to the Soviet minority nationalities are far greater, and it is more likely that their response is much more variable and less passive.

Given the length and severity of compulsory military service—two years in the army, three years in the navy—it is evident that those who serve are, for the most part, greatly disadvantaged as compared to those who do not. Almost half of Soviet youths are not called up by "universal" military service. Persons in higher educational institutions are often exempted or, if they serve, serve only for one year. Whether these exemptions produce any special bitterness among those who do serve is hard to say. Although indications are not at all absent that youth do not want to be inducted, there are no indications that discrimination itself has especially depressing effects on the morale of those who do. It is likely that where such effects do exist, they are related to social discrimination associated with nationalities or classes whose members feel that their chance of escaping the draft is less, because of the social sector to which they belong.

A knowledge of the sources of malaise in the Soviet military forces does not permit confident interpretations of the depth or distribution of that malaise. Our materials give us every reason to believe that dissatisfaction with many aspects of life is widespread in the forces. On the other hand, they provide no ground for supposing that these dissatisfactions seriously affect the ability of the military to perform its primary missions. It seems clear, nonetheless, that Soviet insistence on pushing people to their limit is inefficient and negatively productive, especially because this pressure is associated with ideological and political justifications that are not accepted by many of the personnel.

If, as we suppose, despite some loss of efficiency, the Soviet forces in peacetime are not seriously affected by morale problems in the performance of their missions, then we clearly have even less reason to assume that peacetime "gripes" will be of decisive significance in time of war. Accumulated resentment or criticism of military or Party management would seriously affect the fighting abilities of the Soviet forces only if far more important questions, national and international, were to dominate the Soviet scene. One might imagine, for example, the development of several nationalist movements that claim the right of choosing independence from the USSR under Article 17 of the USSR constitution and vigorously strive to attain this objective. Were the military required to fight a war at a time when major nationalist campaigns were being waged in the Soviet Union, repercussions on military effectiveness, resulting from an intensification of the present nationality problems in the Soviet military forces, would be entirely possible. But short of such major developments of a national or international character, the present peacetime level of morale and solidarity is not likely to have a significant effect in either depressing or enhancing Soviet fighting capabilities.

Although the Soviet forces certainly face no crisis in the management of their recruits and junior officers, there is among some military and Party analysts an increasing awareness of some of the inefficiencies of Party "demandingness," close surveillance, socialist competition, and incessant political indoctrination. These high-pressure methods not only incite resentment, but they provoke protective countermeasures by those subject to them, and these countermeasures undo or forestall much of the good that the measures are intended to achieve. As in almost all armies, surveillance and discipline are never thorough enough to prevent individual and group ingenuity from devising means to escape some of the rigors of military life.

The increasing use of psychological and sociological research to guide military administration is an acknowledgment that the traditional Party and military recipes for dealing with men have deficiencies. It would not be easy for lower and middle Party personnel to forego their role of stern and demanding mentors for a more relaxed, and from a morale and solidarity standpoint, more productive mode of human management. But it is not impossible that at high Party levels the interest in cost-benefit analysis, the desire to exploit scientific sophistication, and the greater freedom to break out of old molds may lead to a reevaluation of present methods of human management. The political officers and their supporting administrative political sections throughout the armed forces are an expensive instrumentality, and all the more so since in addition to the cost of producing and maintaining them, they substantially lessen the amount of time available for the military training of the troops. If, in addition, their activity comes to be judged as inefficient or ineffective, a strong motive for an overall reform of Soviet political-moral and psychological (morale) training will exist. Whether high Party leaders are capable of initiating such drastic changes without fearing an erosion of their power is an open question. The Party leadership has shown on the international scene an ability to make radical changes in posture. Domestic policies are probably much more difficult to change. The Party leadership has exhibited in recent years a strong interest in strengthening the control of the Party over all spheres of life. It is likely that this is not just power-oriented, but is intended to provide a more effective instrument for a social administration that will overcome bureaucratic inefficiencies and individual and group depredations of state property. Even if the Party were interested, for the sake of military morale, in achieving a more human, relaxed mode of administration in the military, would it be possible for it to do so while at the same time striving to increase its capabilities for control? The first goal might require some relinquishment of the second.

Chapter VII

Political Indoctrination

At an international meeting of military historians, Soviet representatives presented four papers, all of which dealt with historical aspects of the training and indoctrination of Russian, Red Army, and Soviet soldiers.[1] This emphasis on the history of indoctrination, rather than, for example, the history of campaigns, reflects the great importance Soviet political and military leaders attach to the political indoctrination of the forces, an importance that makes it difficult to limit the boundaries of the subject. Political indoctrination in one form or another penetrates and affects just about every activity in the Soviet army. Chapters V and VI discussed at some length Soviet attempts to instill a high sense of discipline in the troops and to develop troop cohesion and morale. In some armies these subjects can be kept reasonably distinct from the study of political indoctrination. But this is hardly the case with the Soviet forces, and in reading the present chapter it will be useful to keep the content of these earlier chapters in mind. Similarly, it is hardly possible to understand

---

[1] *Voyenno-istoricheskiy zhurnal,* November 1970, pp. 94–99.

political indoctrination in the Soviet forces without some knowledge of the extensive Party apparatus in the military, which is largely responsible for indoctrination work. This will be reviewed in chapter VIII.

Earlier chapters also provide a substantial amount of material related to our present subject. Thus, the discussion of socialist competition in the military training process (chapter IV) is also a discussion of political indoctrination. Socialist competition is not only a way of organizing competitions to improve military skills; it is intended as well to instill definite political values. The present chapter gives principal attention to indoctrination in the more limited sense of instruction and persuasion with respect to the political, economic, national security, and ideological positions taken by the Soviet Communist Party.

A. THE IMPORTANCE OF POLITICAL INDOCTRINATION

Why does political indoctrination play the great role that it does in the Soviet armed forces?

1. The Past

The answer, in part, rests on the past experiences of the Soviet Communist Party and the Red Army and the role that propaganda played in the growth of Bolshevik power, in its maintenance against counter-attacks, and in the consolidation of power during the years of relative stability and safety. The necessity to persuade (as well as to coerce) various sectors of the Soviet population and, in the service of Soviet foreign policy, various sectors of foreign populations made propaganda activities a major responsibility of many of the principal figures of the Russian revolution, including Lenin. The pursuit of power in the apparent service of an ideology and of a social system radically different from those of established regimes, and authoritatively described in a series of more or less sacred texts written by more or less sacred figures (Marx, Engels, Lenin, Stalin), stimulated the Party to impose catechisms varying in complexity according to the political and educational status of the catechumens. The regime that imposed and preached these articles of faith was authoritarian, with little need to exercise restraint in the use of physical force and other forms of coercion, but this did not free it from the need to persuade. The ability to rule a modernizing, industrializing country with a mass army required a substantial measure of at least passive consent, especially given even minimum regard for the egalitarian aspirations of the revolution and its official ideology. But authoritarian and repressive regimes and the imposed character of their ideologies create suspicions in the minds of their leaders about the real beliefs of their subjects. This leads to more and more intensive efforts to ensure that indoctrination has been achieved, or at least to require recitation of the articles of faith as a sign of submission and obedience.

The economic and political vicissitudes of a new revolutionary regime almost inevitably led to more or less rapid alterations in the "political line," thus requiring changes in the corpus of sacred texts, in the prominence given to its components, and in the makeup of their guardians and interpreters. This magnified enormously the requirements for agitprop activities. Although this motive for the large role accorded to indoctrination was more important in the early decades of the Soviet Union, it still plays a substantial part in keeping a large army of Party propagandists and activists busy, especially whenever a Party congress or a Central Committee plenum occurs or a Party leader is dismissed. In the absence of a system of free political debate and tolerated divergences in belief and behavior, propaganda is required by the Party to inform and guide behavior in virtually all sectors of life.

All of this has required organizations and a large number of Party and Komsomol functionaries and activists devoted to indoctrination activities. These functionaries develop a strong interest in attaching importance to information and propaganda work. Writers and producers in the various media, trade union officials, mass patriotic societies such as DOSAAF and the Znaniye Society, and children's organizations, such as the Pioneers and the Red Pathfinders, also contribute to these activities.

Of course, past motives and circumstances combined with "inertia" do not by themselves account for the continued importance of indoctrination in Soviet society and in the military. Specific contemporary circumstances continue to reinforce the importance attached to it by Soviet authorities. *Kommunist vooruzhennykh sil* points out that changes in combat and technical equipment, the increased educational level of military personnel, the greater requirements for combat readiness, Soviet international obligations, the aggravation of the ideological struggle between imperialism and socialism, "and a number of other circumstances"—discreetly left unmentioned, but we will later find it easy to guess them—all give increased importance to Party political work.[2] Victories, after all, are achieved not by weapons but by men, and this requires that "we lay the main stress on their ideological and political education."[3] For Marshal A. A. Grechko, "it is obvious [that] political-ideological and military-patriotic indoctrination is an integral part" of military training.[4]

2. The Party First

That political indoctrination is an "integral part" of military training reflects, of course, the power of the Party in the military and its interest in using

[2] *KVS*, no. 7, April 1973, pp. 16–26.
[3] *Pravda Ukrainy*, March 19, 1972, p. 3.
[4] *Molodaya gvardiya*, February 1972, pp. 4–13.

political indoctrination to reinforce its power and the power of its leaders. The army is "a good school for ideological . . . development,"[5] and for the continuation of Party indoctrination begun in the years before induction into the service. Marshal Grechko does not hesitate to subordinate professional military skills to Party work. "The *first and foremost* requirement [of officers] is to be ideologically convinced . . . an active champion of Party policy."[6] (Emphasis added.) Colonel General M. Tankayev, commander of the northern group of forces, astonishingly affirms that "the Soviet officer is *above all* a political indoctrinator."[7] (Emphasis added.) And a *Krasnaya zvezda* editorial claims that "constant political work among servicemen is the *paramount* task of commanders."[8] (Emphasis added.) Marshal Grechko has warned graduating officer cadets that a Soviet officer "must appraise any matter and any step" of his own, his comrades or his subordinates "from the viewpoint of the interests of the Communist Party, the Soviet state, and the Soviet people," no doubt in that order.[9] Officers are for the most part Party members, and "Party members place overall Party and state interests above everything else."[10] This, of course, is more than justified since "Party political work is . . . [a] never-aging weapon that has always frightened and continues to frighten our enemies,"[11] and also because the armed forces are "indebted to the wise leadership of our Party for all their victories . . . and successes"[12] and the invincibility of the Soviet armed forces lies in the leadership of the Communist Party.[13]

It must not be supposed that motives of Party power and prestige appear only in explicit claims like those noted above. Since the Party initiates or authorizes almost all significant decisions in domestic and foreign policy, many indoctrination themes inevitably defend, directly or by implication, Party actions, past and present, and thus almost automatically become a defense of the Party.

3. Ideology and Military Effectiveness

Naturally, the Party does not justify the heavy expenditures of time and personnel on indoctrination in the military forces by indoctrination's enhancement of Party power. To be sure, the Party's conception of its central role in

[5] *KVS,* no. 14, July 1972, pp. 68–75.
[6] *KZ,* March 24, 1972, pp. 1–3. See also ibid., January 31, 1973, p. 1.
[7] *KVS,* no. 14, July 1972, pp. 36–42.
[8] *KZ,* March 27, 1973, p. 1.
[9] Ibid., July 3, 1973, p. 1.
[10] *KVS,* no. 16, August 1971, pp. 25–31.
[11] *Voyenno-istoricheskiy zhurnal,* September 1972, pp. 3–13.
[12] Editorial, *KZ,* March 27, 1973, p. 1.
[13] General Yepishev in *Pravda,* March 27, 1973, p. 2. That the Party leads the army in all spheres of military affairs is a very important theme of political indoctrination in the Soviet forces. We do not deal with it more fully in this chapter. A detailed discussion will be found in chapter VIII, E.

Soviet history could easily be made to justify this objective. The Party, however, finds it more expedient to defend political indoctrination in terms of its contribution to combat effectiveness, to troop morale and discipline, and, in later life, to civic responsibility, labor force productivity, and the development of the New Soviet Man.

As is usual, Lenin's authority is invoked, and *Kommunist vooruzhennykh sil* quotes him to the effect that "where the greatest care is taken with political work among the troops . . . [there] they have more victories."[14] To this the authority of Karl Marx is added. "Increasing the combat readiness of the men means first of all to mold their Communist world outlook. Ideological conviction, acquired on the basis of study of the theory of Marxist-Leninism, is one of the most powerful regulators of human behavior. Having penetrated the consciousness of an individual, ideas inspire him to act in a certain manner. They are transformed, as Karl Marx said, into a physical force."[15]

Competence in military skills and progress in military training are associated with effectiveness in indoctrination. Thus, the high level of combat effectiveness of an artillery regiment is imputed to the equally high level of political work.[16] The most important factor in promoting combat readiness is Party political work.[17] It is therefore not surprising that "the training process in our army is inseparably linked to the indoctrination process."[18] For the political departments, if not always the commanding officers, the association between teaching professional skills and ideological "conditioning" is close; the teaching of professional skills to flight crews is "inseparable" from their political conditioning.[19] Political officers affirm that the manner in which soldiers carry out their assigned tasks depends directly upon their degree of political consciousness.[20] Indeed, data are available to demonstrate that in both company-size units and larger formations grades in political training generally correlate with performance levels in tactical, gunnery, technical, and specialized training as revealed during inspections.[21]

Political indoctrination is equally important for the development of a fighting spirit. "One of the fundamental features of our armed forces and the basic source of their insuperable strength is the high political consciousness of Soviet fighting men."[22] Similarly, "ideological conviction constitutes the inner force inspiring Soviet officers and all Soviet fighting men."[23] "The profound

[14] *KVS*, no. 7, April 1973, pp. 16–26.
[15] *Aviatsiya i kosmonavtika*, no. 10, October 1973, pp. 12–13.
[16] *KVS*, no. 7, April 1973, pp. 16–26.
[17] Ibid., no. 6, March 1973, pp. 22–25.
[18] Ibid., no. 14, July 1972, pp. 36–42.
[19] *Aviatsiya i kosmonavtika*, February 1971, pp. 11–12.
[20] *KVS*, no. 1, January 1971, pp. 65–70.
[21] Ibid., pp. 18–26.
[22] Ibid., no. 23, December 1969, pp. 3–8.
[23] *Soviet Military Review*, no. 1, 1970, pp. 52–53.

ideological conviction of Soviet military personnel, their political awareness . . . have always been and remain the basis of high morale."[24] Persistence and self-sacrifice are the products of attitudes developed by ideological education.[25] These measures influence "the thought, feelings, will and character" of the soldiers and develop the qualities essential for combat activity."[26] Every victory in a war depends ultimately "on the moral fibre of the fighting masses,"[27] which is why "an ideological struggle . . . can have a very decisive influence on the outcome of a war."[28]

Political indoctrination is further justified because it carries over to the soldier's later return to civilian life, where the outlook inculcated in the army helps him "to overcome the difficulties along the paths and the goals set by life."[29] Party political work, by promoting combat readiness, provides favorable conditions for executing "our magnificent plans for building communism" and ensuring "the security of the creative labor of the Soviet people."[30] That Soviet youth return, after military service, to the national economy highly trained and brought up in the spirit of the best revolutionary combat and labor traditions is due to "the ideological-educational function of Soviet military science."[31]

Claims concerning the military efficacy of political indoctrination are intended to support the Party's authority and its extensive propaganda apparatus, but some Party propagandists probably are convinced that political indoctrination on imperialist threats, Chinese perfidy, "left" deviations, bourgeois ideology, the necessity for military expenditures, the gains and solidarity of the socialist block, the unity of Soviet peoples, and numerous other themes contribute not only to political awareness and Party loyalty but to the Soviet soldier's dedication to his military duties.

4. On the Defensive—For the First Time

The intensity of political indoctrination in the contemporary Soviet forces is above all related to the deterioration during the sixties of the Soviet position in "the struggle for men's minds." Soviet statements generally discuss this propaganda battle as an ideological struggle. Still, it is clear that what concerns the Soviets is not simply the "decline of ideology," or the development of

---

[24] General A. Yepishev in [*An Important Factor of Combat Readiness*] by Lieutenant Colonel B. T. Badmayev (Moscow, 1972).
[25] *KZ,* June 30, 1973, p. 2.
[26] Ibid., January 26, 1973, pp. 2–3.
[27] *Pravda,* March 27, 1973, p. 2.
[28] *KVS,* no. 10, May 1972, pp. 17–20.
[29] *Voyenno-istoricheskiy zhurnal,* September 1972, pp. 3–13.
[30] *KVS,* no. 6, March 1973, pp. 22–25.
[31] Ibid., no. 17, September 1972, pp. 9–16.

ideologies inconsistent with or hostile to official Soviet formulations of Marx-ism-Leninism, but rather the alienation of foreign (and domestic) groups from a sympathetic attitude toward the Soviet state, the Soviet Party, and Soviet political positions. This alienation is accompanied in many instances, espe-cially in the case of foreign groups, by an overtly friendly attitude toward political positions and political entities viewed as inimical to the Party and state.

The Soviets have, of course, long been accustomed to violent attacks by those whom they identify as defenders of imperialism and capitalist privileges. These attacks, coming from traditional enemies, legitimized Soviet claims to leadership of those in industrial and third-world countries who were disillu-sioned and repelled by the status quo, especially youth and the intellectuals. Although troubled from time to time by Trotskyist, socialist, anarchist, and other rival left political persuasions, the Soviet Union had until recent years maintained an aggressive, evangelizing posture against which both bourgeois and anti-Soviet left groups had to maintain a largely defensive political strug-gle. The Soviets generally could count on continuing accretions of influence among groups useful to them for foreign political operations, for espionage, or for enabling them to claim at home a high prestige abroad of the Soviet state. Major power considerations led to repressive measures in East Berlin, Hun-gary, and Poland, but ensuing Soviet losses among intellectuals and left groups were generally marginal or temporary.

This satisfactory state of affairs changed during the later sixties. The increasing alienation of youth from their "establishments," rather than rein-forcing Soviet influence abroad, was accompanied by a disillusionment with political ideology and with established political parties of both the right and the left, by a preference for "dropping out" from conventional activities, and by a more or less undisciplined "self-expression" that was at variance with the puritanical and disciplined character of Communist Party prescriptions. The growing power and influence of the Soviet Union deprived it of the appeal of the underdog and transformed it into another "establishment." Under these circumstances the Soviet invasion of Czechoslovakia in 1968 had a more enduring impact than earlier repressive acts.

In the United States, when antiestablishment attitudes did not dissolve political, ideological, or "philosophical" interests, political activity often took the form of civil rights movements, "women's lib," or the support of antiestab-lishment political candidates. These political movements were no longer as easily seized upon and influenced, as they often had been in earlier years, by Communist Party organizers. Among other sectors of politically active youth, an attachment to violence and to figures such as Che Guevara and Mao Tse-tung made them hostile to (and unacceptable to) the Soviet-controlled Communist Parties, which together with the Soviet Party itself tended to emphasize, both in the Third World and elsewhere, a cautious political and economic line that was little in accord with the romantic fervor of the new generation of revolutionaries. To this new generation it was Red China and not the Soviet Union that was the underdog and that mobilized sympathy and political adherence.[32] For the new generation, ideology was just as likely to mean Hermann Hesse, Herbert Marcuse, Mao Tse-tung, Franz Fanon, or Che Guevara as Marx, Engels, and Lenin.

These revisionist ideologies are just as dangerous as capitalist ideology and equally concern the commanders, political agencies, and Party organizations of the Soviet armed forces.[33] The resurgence of revisionist ideologies was, according to *Kommunist vooruzhennykh sil,* stimulated in the mid-sixties by the Maoists, who were able to use "ultrarevolutionary phraseology" and "leftist opportunism" to attack the Soviet Union. The unity of the Communist movement was then further undermined by various left-radical, anarchist, and Trotskyist groups.[34] According to the Soviets, the Moscow conference of 1969, in which seventy-five Communist and workers parties participated, halted "the hesitation and vacillation" in the Communist movement, and the election of Allende in Chile confirmed the correctness of Soviet interpretations of Marxism-Leninism. Nonetheless, the struggle against Maoism "continues to be an urgent problem for the Communist movement, as does the fight against right and left opportunism."[35] Discussions in Eastern Europe, the United States and other capitalist countries, and various third-world countries concerning different models of socialism, with their stress on democratic socialism, and discussions of convergence of socialism and capitalism are attacked by Soviet military-political writers for their mixture of both left and right anti-Soviet tendencies.

All these various developments help to explain the intensity of Soviet preoccupation with ideological and political training both in the general population and among the troops. Soviet statements clearly reflect concern about ideological deviation being imported from abroad and on occasion show a defensiveness that is quite new in the Soviet Union.

"We are living," said Secretary Brezhnev in the Twenty-fourth Congress report of the Central Committee, "under the conditions of an unceasing ideological war that is being waged against our country . . . by imperialist propa-

---

[32] Red China's rapprochement with the western world will no doubt disappoint and perhaps disillusion many of those who transferred their allegiance from the Soviet Union to Mao, but there are not too many choices open to them. Castro, Allende, and the Palestinian Liberation Organization mobilized some sympathies, but they did not possess or convey that sense of enormous power and potential that often plays an important role in attracting those who are hostile to their own authorities and seek a new political-spiritual home and leadership.

[33] *KZ,* March 22, 1973, pp. 2–3.

[34] *KVS,* no. 20, October 1972, pp. 24–32.

[35] Ibid.

ganda using refined methods and powerful technical media." "A battle for the minds of people has now unfolded in the international arena. It is a battle unprecedented in history. It intensifies and grows steadily."[36] The ideological struggle must be treated "with all seriousness," writes one Soviet commentator, who fears that some Soviet citizens do not pay enough attention to the apprehensions voiced by the directors of the Soviet side of the ideological struggle. "In recent years the strategists of anticommunism havebeen making desperate efforts to drive us back in the war of ideas from active offensive positions to defensive positions and to appropriate for themselves rights to historical initiatives that were irrevocably lost long ago."[37] What this writer really means is that the Soviets had assumed that the West had long ago lost its capacity for initiatives, but that now it is precisely the non-Soviet world that has passed to the ideological offensive. This is why, no doubt, a characteristic feature of the current ideological struggle is "its extremely acute nature."[38]

To justify their intensification of indoctrination, Soviet propagandists emphasize that because of the increasing strength of socialism "the monopolistic bourgeoisie . . . devote a greater effort to the ideological struggle."[39] Soviet military strength is too great for other forms of conflict resolution. "A narrowing of the military potential of imperialism tends to activate its efforts in the struggle against socialism in the more peaceful spheres of social development. . . . Particular importance is being attached to economic competition. . . . The conflict also occurs in the ideological battles."[40] "The turning of imperialism to psychological warfare is an indication of the increase in strength, including defensive strength, of world socialism."[41] Similarly, *Pravda,* under the title "The Subversive Strategy of 'Intellectual Warfare,' " points out that "the times have passed when our enemies could openly threaten socialism with an atomic holocaust. . . . However, despite the unfavorable change in the balance of power . . . imperialism has not renounced its major objectives. . . . We are living under conditions of incessant psychological war. . . . "[42] It is, then, not so much military attack as "the so-called quiet counterrevolution" that is to be feared.[43]

In their ideological campaigns "the imperialists . . . distort the prospects for further human development . . . present capitalism in a more attractive form . . . and defend it. . . . Theories of 'stages of economic growth,' 'one

[36] I. A. Seleznev [*The Philosophical Heritage of V. I. Lenin and the Problem of Modern Warfare*], 1972, pp. 275–297.
[37] *Sovetskaya Belorussiya,* February 4, 1972.
[38] *KVS,* no. 10, May 1972, pp. 10–17.
[39] Ibid.
[40] Ibid., no. 16, August 1972, pp. 9–16.
[41] A. N. Nikolayev [*Psychological Warfare*], Moscow, 1972.
[42] *Pravda,* January 13, 1972, p. 4.
[43] *Voyenno-istoricheskiy zhurnal,* September 1972, pp. 3–13.

industrial society,' 'convergence,' and 'post-industrial society' all portray the
old world as a worthy model of the future. At the same time they preach that
. . . capitalism and socialism will draw closer together."[44] The opponents of
socialism also preach the inevitability of political apathy and the inevitable
alienation of the individual under all socioeconomic conditions.[45]

Naturally, the imperialists also hope to stir up "nationalist moods" in the
Soviet Union, collaborate with the shameless chauvinism of Peking, spread
stories about imaginary Soviet threats, belittle and discredit Soviet reality,
distort the meaning of the 1968 events in Czechoslovakia, and infect the Soviet
Union with western music and other imports.[46]

Given the often oblique mode of Soviet discussion of these problems, it
is not surprising that it is *Wojsko ludowe (People's Army),* a Polish military
journal for army cadres, and not *Kommunist vooruzhennykh sil* that summarizes more effectively the dilemmas posed by current ideological confrontations. Addressing itself to issues raised by the East-West détente, *Wojsko
ludowe* points out the risks to the East inherent in cultural contact and ex-
changes with the West, particularly the risk of a weakened position in an
East-West ideological confrontation. The capitalist world has made an impressive, if temporary, technological advance and has also succeeded in reducing
its contradictions for the time being. The socialist countries, on the other hand,
have to adapt to the scientific revolution and deal with problems of a new
economic strategy. These difficulties are aggravated by additional complica-
tions—the lack of unity in the international Communist movement and in the
working-class world and the dilemma that would be created by an exchange
of tourists. If the socialist countries reject this exchange, the West will be able
to make capital of it and it may lead to increased tension and ferment at home,
especially among youth. *Wojsko ludowe* concludes that all of this requires a
major ideological-propaganda effort and points out that the socialist states
have some advantages too: an ideological confrontation with the West will
increase the chances of influencing the West, which at the moment is suffering
from "ideological erosion."[47]

5. The Ideological War Against the Soviet Armed Forces

The ideological war waged by the West does not simply have an undifferen-
tiated Soviet target—the Soviet army is one specific object of bourgeois ideological subversion. "Bourgeois ideologists are trying to weaken the combat

[44] *KVS,* no. 10, May 1972, pp. 10–17.
[45] *KZ,* April 12, 1973, pp. 2–3.
[46] *KVS,* no. 10, May 1972, pp. 10–17, and Nikolayev [*Psychological Warfare*].
[47] *Le Monde,* October 8–9, 1972, p. 6.

might of our armed forces [and] influence the political-moral state of the Soviet soldiers."[48] Indeed, "bourgeois propaganda has had a definite effect on individual servicemen. And although these are only solitary instances, we cannot underestimate them. Our armed forces are conducting active work to unmask bourgeois ideology . . . and measures are being taken to block off the channel of its penetration among military personnel."[49] According to *Kommunist vooruzhennykh sil,* a report of Radio Free Europe revealed that this station considers Soviet military personnel to be an important target of its ideological propaganda.[50]

These attacks on the Soviet army are, of course, at the same time attacks on the Party. The bourgeois propagandists direct "their primary efforts to falsify and distort . . . the guiding role of the CPSU in military building. . . . Knowing the colossal role our Party plays . . . the imperialist critics . . . would like to weaken the guiding role of the Communist Party in the military field."[51] They also portray the Soviet army as an army of "force and expansion" and compose "fables about contradictions . . . among our officer personnel, particularly between commanders, officers assigned to technical services, and political workers."[52] They strive to "build bridges" to Soviet soldiers,[53] and "force their noxious ideas into the socialist consciousness of the [Soviet] fighting men."[54]

6. Youth

Soviet propagandists like to attribute ideological deviations among Soviet youth, partly the result of an unplanned infiltration of ideas and partly the result of an independent development, as being due to "the imperialists [who] are in the process of organizing a broader and more insidious ideological sabotage . . . aimed first and foremost at our youth."[55] This ideological seduction of Soviet youth is, of course, equivalent to an attack on the Soviet armed forces. "The bosses of monopoly capitalism are betting particularly on the ideological degeneration of Soviet youth and are endeavoring to weaken its

[48] *KVS,* no. 17, September 1972, pp. 9–16.

[49] General Yepishev, Chief of the Main Political Directorate, in Badmayev [*An Important Factor of Combat Readiness*].

[50] *KVS,* no. 10, May 1972, pp. 10–17. This is probably one of a number of reasons why the Soviets have been especially sensitive to Radio Free Europe and Radio Liberty. See, for example, *Pravda,* September 8, 1973, p. 5. When, in the interests of their security conference objectives, the Soviets stopped jamming Voice of America, BBC, and West German broadcasts, Radio Liberty continued to be jammed. *New York Times,* September 13, 1973, p. 16.

[51] *Voyenno-istoricheskiy zhurnal,* September 1972, pp. 3–13.

[52] *KVS,* no. 10, May 1972, pp. 10–17.

[53] General A. Yepishev, in *Pravda,* March 27, 1973, p. 2.

[54] *Voyenno-istoricheskiy zhurnal,* September 1972, pp. 3–13.

[55] *Kommunistas,* Vilnius, no. 4, April 1972, pp. 31–38.

revolutionary enthusiasm and to dull class awareness. We cannot help but consider this, since the young people are the predominant majority among army and navy personnel; and in morale, political and psychological terms, we are preparing precisely the young people for skillful actions in modern war."[56] The imperialists seek to undermine the faith of Soviet youth in the justice of socialist ideology and the triumph of communism. The imperialists also hope "to turn youth against the older generation and eventually tear our younger generation apart morally."[57]

Not all of youth's negative reactions to army life can be attributed to bourgeois subversive propaganda. "The high degree of subordination in the army was not customary for young men brought up in the free, broadly democratic principles of our way, and it was difficult for them to accept psychologically."[58] The reputation or image of army life among Soviet teenagers must indeed be one of great rigor, since even before entry into the army 42 percent of a sample of draft-age youth anticipated that their most serious problem or difficulty when they entered service would be submission and adherence to military discipline.[59] Those who have recently been drafted find these predraft expectations confirmed: "Strict discipline [is] the most perceptible feature of army life."[60] A young recruit, whom *Krasnaya zvezda* takes the trouble to identify as a Lithuanian, when reproved for his poor work, replied that back at his kolkhoz he was not a private and therefore could not "crawl" the way privates do.[61] The chairman of the Moscow military commissariat, responsible for inductions in Moscow, speaking of the youths that appear before the commissariat, reports that "some appear embarrassed, others are beset by curiosity, and still others are defiant. The latter pose the greatest problem."[62] The recruits who come directly from schools are most likely to find army discipline hard to take. "We must remember that the majority of today's inductees are yesterday's schoolboys, who frequently do not yet have any work experience, who have never lived anywhere but in the bosom of their families. It is not easy for them to become accustomed to the difficulties and stresses of army life."[63]

Living "in the bosom of their families" suggests, and not unintentionally, a degree of physical and psychological comfort that may make youth unfit for

[56] General A. Yepishev, in Badmayev [*An Important Factor of Combat Readiness*].

[57] *Kommunistas,* Vilnius, no. 4, April 1972, pp. 31–38.

[58] *KZ,* April 19, 1972, p. 4.

[59] *Voyenno-istoricheskiy zhurnal,* no. 4, 1971, pp. 94–98. Another 21 percent thought the high physical work load would be their principal problem.

[60] *KZ,* April 19, 1972, p. 4.

[61] Ibid., December 20, 1969, p. 3.

[62] *Smena,* November 1973, pp. 16–19.

[63] *KZ,* May 21, 1972, p. 1.

the sterner realities of life. "The further the great days of October fade into history," said Secretary Brezhnev at the Fifteenth Komsomol Congress, "and the more boys and girls who have not endured hardships in life enter the ranks of the Party, the more important the role of ideological indoctrination becomes."[64] Brezhnev returned to the same theme a year later: "They [youth] know about the contrasts between the past and the present only from books and films, and it is difficult for them to imagine the misery and poverty that we witnessed. For this reason, it is important to educate our young people so that they will have a profound understanding and feeling for all that we older people saw and lived through."[65]

Others, however, who are not as understanding and indulgent as Secretary Brezhnev, complain about tendencies to pamper Soviet children and young people. Adults volunteer to repair furniture at the schools and to make a playground while the children stand around and criticize. "If the young people so much as lift a finger, then parents complain, 'Oh, the children are being forced to repair the school. . . . ' Then we wonder where the little lords and parasites come from."[66]

It appears that some disciplinary problems of youth develop well before military life begins. A Soviet teacher complains: "Lately a new breed of 'difficult student' has appeared. He often comes from a well-to-do family and has a doting papa and mama. Aware of his impunity, he behaves insolently. . . . Moreover, such adolescents . . . know their rights only too well: they know someone must teach and rear them . . . The term ['difficult student'] is now accepted in polite usage as though signifying an occupation or a kind of academic pursuit."[67] Such students are particularly susceptible, when they enter military life, to temptations that the Soviet military press rarely mentions. The deputy chief of the USSR MVD Internal Forces Political Directorate remarks: "One of the characteristics of our troop activity is the constant contact that the soldiers, sergeants, ensigns, and officers have with antisocial elements—people whose morals and conduct prevent the Soviet people from leading a normal life and cause them grief and trouble. Criminal elements often go to considerable lengths to try to win over young soldiers to their side. . . . Only people who are ideologically tempered, convinced of the correctness of our cause, and devoted to the Communist Party, the people, and their military duty can resist this cajoling and temptation."[68]

[64] *KVS,* no. 17, September 1972, pp. 55–62.
[65] *Pravda,* July 26, 1973, p. 1.
[66] *Uchitel'skaya gazeta,* July 15, 1972.
[67] *Izvestia,* September 5, 1972, p. 5. The importance attached to the military training of preinduction schoolchildren is reflected in the fact that "the seemingly reformed hooligan pledges to strengthen his moral fiber by making three parachute jumps." Ibid., June 13, 1973, p. 4.
[68] *KZ,* August 3, 1973, p. 2.

The hostility against "the little lords and parasites" becomes especially bitter when their behavior is associated with the external marks of the Soviet hippy. A military writer in *Krasnaya zvezda* is not pleased by an article in *Literaturnaya gazeta* entitled "Boys with Guitars" that stated, "Tomorrow they will go into the army, and the iron will of the solid collective, having torn them out of their environment for two years, will teach them to work and to see the target, and some will be taken in hand to such an extent that they will not dare to return to the old way." The military analyst does not want the army to be saddled with the indoctrination and reform of these types. "It is not desirable to waste valuable combat training time in the army reeducating these boys with guitars."[69]

The boys with the guitars and long hair are apparently sufficiently nonchalant and confident that they do not bother to disguise their outlook on life even when they are trying to evade military service as draftees. A military writer, discussing the selection of youths for officer cadet schools, reports: "Last year I happened to visit a number of [cadet] schools in the Leningrad area during the entrance examination period. In addition to those students who appeared to be industrious and loyal to their dream, I also noticed some who listlessly looked about the auditorium or strummed upon their guitars. They were slovenly dressed and many spoke as follows: 'Thank you, but I don't choose to enlist [be drafted]. A military school is the only answer for me.' "[70]

Krasnaya zvezda, which showed a remarkable preoccupation with guitars in the spring of 1972, revealed that in a certain construction unit a private was found to have a notebook filled with songs "that no respectable individual would read." This led to the discovery that another private who served as chief of the servicemen's club was a "purveyor of vulgar songs." Although his comrades said he was a good poet and played the guitar, the political officer of the unit "ought never to have allowed this person to be chief of the amateur art society." The officers of the unit promised to heed *Krasnaya zvezda's* advice. "However, they did not display any great enthusiasm."[71]

More constructive measures to deal with youth are sometimes proposed. *Komsomol'skaya pravda,* after noting that adolescents "are willing to pay fantastic prices for what they consider fashionable [foreign] items," asks: "Wouldn't it be easier to make a serious effort to satisfy this demand?"[72] *Krasnaya zvezda,* somewhat reluctantly it seems, reproved a deputy com-

[69] Ibid., April 19, 1972, p. 4.
[70] Ibid., May 14, 1972, p. 2.
[71] Ibid., June 20, 1972, p. 4.
[72] *Komsomol'skaya pravda,* March 18, 1973, p. 4. *Komsomol'skaya pravda* reports that blue jeans sell for 100 rubles at the Odessa secondhand market. *Komsomol'skaya pravda's* implied advice has apparently been taken. It has been reported in the western press that the Soviets have bought blue jeans from American-owned factories in Mexico.

mander of an air force garrison who grounded a young pilot who arrived from the cadet academy wearing a mustache and refused to follow his superior's advice to shave it off.[73]

Despite official unease about the hippy style, it appears that on Soviet TV "long hairs" are generally depicted as "good guys" and that in many TV programs and movies for schoolchildren loud shirts and "rivets" are practically a must. "How many times have we seen relatively big-name actors appearing before a TV audience of millions with clothes and hairdos that make one wonder if the kids are aping them or vice versa."[74] Parents whose girls wear eye makeup and whose boys have hair down to their shoulders and wear supermod trousers "do not stop to consider that youngsters sometimes go from trying on foreign fashions to trying on foreign ideas."[75]

Despite these indications that youth is developing a style of its own, "a distinguishing characteristic of the socialist society and its army is the fact that we have no so-called 'generation problem.' A socialist society and its armed forces develop on the basis of a revolutionary continuity of generations."[76] Nonetheless, the "tasks of training and indoctrinating youth grow more complex from year to year."[77]

It is not, of course, simply Soviet hippies that concern the political and military authorities. Much broader sectors of the youth population exhibit traits disagreeable to the molders and managers of the New Soviet Man. Indeed, all of youth are subject to unfortunate deficiencies inherent in the physical and psychological stage through which youth is passing, deficiencies that are compounded by their lack of experience. Even the young men who play a leading role in the Komsomol show in their committee and bureau work "a lack of coherence, the inability to determine the main points . . . a discrepancy between word and deed"[78] that has led to increased Party surveillance of the organization.[79]

Soviet youth do not generally show strong aspirations to pursue those high ideological and political goals urged upon them by Party and military leaders. Their interest in material well-being and luxury goods and in visiting

---

[73] *KZ*, May 26, 1973, p. 2. *KZ* was told that the young officer was "a difficult character" and apparently on the basis of the mustache was inclined to believe that "this is likely to be the case."

[74] *Uchitel'skaya gazeta*, July 29, 1972, p. 3. *Izvestia* has noted that many people were making amateurish wide ties by hand because Soviet tiemakers were two years behind current tie styles. *Izvestia*, August 27, 1972, p. 3.

[75] Ibid., June 13, 1972, p. 2.

[76] *KVS*, no. 13, July 1972, pp. 9–15.

[77] Ibid., no. 10, May 1971, pp. 43–50.

[78] *KZ*, April 5, 1972, p. 1.

[79] A study of labor discipline revealed that, contrary to the assumptions of the authorities, it was not young people but workers with considerable seniority who accounted for most of the transgressions of labor discipline. Zev Katz, "Sociology in the Soviet Union," *Problems of Communism*, May-June 1971, pp. 22–23.

foreign countries is too pronounced. They aspire to the more interesting and rewarding jobs and to a higher education.[80]

Those who graduate from higher educational institutes are likely to be particular about the jobs they accept and in many instances do not show up at their assigned places of work.[81] In the military they sometimes show disinterest and disdain for physical work.

The resistance of youth to Soviet indoctrination is reflected in warnings issued to propagandists. Military newspapers are criticized for pompous rhetorical phrases that alienate youth. The young reader "becomes increasingly exacting and *circumspect* about the growing flood of information."[82] (Emphasis added.) M. Suslov, secretary of the Central Committee of the Party, warned that "in educational work among the youth and students, the slightest degree of formalism, cliché, or quotation-mongering is inadmissible."[83] Such statements do not seem to have altered in any perceptible degree the frequency of the practices they condemn.

The statements of Soviet political and military leaders on the increasingly high educational and cultural level of youth reveal a curious compound of pride and apprehension. The apprehension derives from the frequent experience that intellectuals are less easily disciplined, directed, and controlled and may require kid-glove treatment, a form of human management not congenial to the Soviet system. Nevertheless, one must try, and Soviet officers sometimes find their servicemen attending an evening discussion on Pushkin. "Man is not satisfied with bread alone and he needs aesthetic education. . . . Many capable young people now enter military service. Some play musical instruments, others paint, still others write verse. . . . Access to the beautiful . . . raises their . . . conscientiousness for the assigned work,"[84] which no doubt makes access to the beautiful even more attractive. *Krasnaya zvezda,* however, after these far-sighted thoughts, seems to forget its own warnings about the dangers of rhetoric and clichés and adds: "However, it seems that in a certain unit the films that are being shown . . . have nearly pushed all historical revolutionary and military-patriotic content from the screen."[85]

7. Dissent

The concern of Soviet political and military leaders with youth is increased by dissent within the Soviet Union among groups other than youth itself. By

[80] Ibid., p. 36. It appears that many of these aspirants to a higher education receive medals and cum laude notations when they graduate from secondary school, but fail or show very mediocre ability in their entrance examinations to higher educational institutes. Such students often turn out to be the children of officials. *Bakinskiy rabochiy,* November 2, 1971, pp. 2–5.

[81] Ibid.

[82] *KZ,* December 19, 1971, p. 2.

[83] *Kommunist,* no. 1, January 1972, pp. 18–30.

[84] *KZ,* May 23, 1973, p. 4.

[85] Ibid.

"dissent" here we do not necessarily refer to the infrequent open challenges to the Party, but rather to passive resistance and the expression of views that do not deviate too sharply from Party and government prescriptions and ideology. The work, education, interests, and ability to communicate of many professionals sometimes enable them to express dissident views while skirting the dangers of open defiance. "We still run into cases in which attempts are made, under the guise of scientific debate . . . to question important proposition of Party documents."[86]

The rapid increase in the number of intellectuals magnifies the problem of dissent. The "intelligentsia" rose from a tiny fraction of the population in 1920 to one-fifth of the labor force in 1959 and to almost one-third today.[87] The number of scientific workers and the amount of expenditures on science have been doubling every five to seven years.[88] During the past ten years the number of employees of research organizations increased six times faster than the labor force.[89]

Although the Party has become increasingly severe in its treatment of dissidents, it has had difficulty in mustering the will to suppress manifestations of dissidence completely. In part, this seems to be due to the penetration within the bureaucracies, often at fairly high levels, of the attitudes to be suppressed.[90] An unauthorized exhibition by young painters in a Moscow suburb attracted many fine cars and people of obviously high rank who were not afraid to attend an exhibition that was closed by the militia two hours after it opened. Similarly, it was not just young people but also older persons who, at a club of journalists composed mostly of Party personnel, showed their determination to do the twist (1964) and exhibit their modernity.[91] These are not serious delinquencies compared to the behavior of a Sakharov or a Solzhenitsyn, but

[86] *Pravda,* June 4, 1973, p. 2.

[87] Zev Katz, "Sociology in the Soviet Union," *Problems of Communism,* May-June 1971, pp. 27–28. "Intelligentsia" is a broadly defined group almost equivalent to "white collar." But even the narrower group *spetsialisti,* that is, professionals and semiprofessionals, numbered over sixteen million in 1970, almost the size of the collective-farm peasantry. See L. A. Gordon and E. V. Kolpov, "The Social Development of the Working Class," in *Soviet Review,* Spring 1973, pp. 15, 30, reprinted from *Voprosy filosofii,* 1972, no. 2.

[88] *Neva,* January 1973, pp. 173–181.

[89] *Trud,* January 4, 1973, p. 2.

[90] "Speaking of the post-Stalin period, Stalin's daughter in her memoirs points out that in some families of the top Politburo elite the young people, the children, determine the mode of life in the homes. The elders 'lent an ear and adapted themselves to the views and tastes of the children.' Since the children represented an antiestablishment outlook, this aided the penetration of more liberal views and tastes into groups that otherwise might have been immune to their appeal. Similarly, Daniel Patrick Moynihan has pointed out the considerable hostility of top businessmen and bankers to the Nixon Administration because of an alleged reduction of civil liberties. 'As best as I can tell, they mostly get this belief from their children. . . . They believe their children and . . . detest the Administration.' " H. Goldhamer, *The Soviet Union in a Period of Strategic Parity* (The Rand Corporation, R–889–PR, 1971), p. 54.

[91] Nicole Chatel, *Carnets russes* (Paris, 1971), pp. 151 and 81 –82. An *Izvestia* writer, referring to the Italian movie *Mondo Cane* as sadistic and arousing repulsive emotions, is led to add, "Some

they reflect the attitude of a much larger number of persons, whose importance in the day-to-day administration of Soviet life is probably greater than that of a writer or a scientist.

Party personnel sometimes show an independence that indicates that Party discipline too is subject to erosion by democratic aspirations. *Krasnaya zvezda* was constrained, after a protest, to rebuke a company political officer who tried to upset the company election of its Party secretary in order to impose his own choice. And *Pravda* acknowledged in 1971 a tendency for primary Party organizations to ignore the recommendations of higher Party bodies in the election of Party secretaries.[92] It is little wonder, then, that the Party has imposed a review of Party membership.

Intellectuals who disagree with Party positions are not monolithic in their outlook. Some Soviet writers have little use for the advances in science and technology achieved by some of their fellow intellectuals. They fear the encroachment of the machine, its dehumanizing influence on man, and its ruination of an idyllic world of nature. This leads to a nostalgia for folk, agrarian, and patriarchical themes.[93]

Among the non-Russian nationalities, nationalist feelings, evidently still strong as manifested by the adherence to national languages, necessarily lead to conflict with Party positions on state or Soviet patriotism and on the importance of the Russian language. Despite the great pressure exercised by the Party, especially in Georgia, the defenders of nationalist positions did not lapse into silent opposition. "Those comrades who alleged that the interests of speaking the native language and the Russian language contradict one another are profoundly mistaken."[94] Nationalist feeling also leads to a sense of minority superiority over the Russian population and a disdain for the Party, which is viewed as being under Russian control. This in turn justifies taking advantage of the Party and the state.

Izvestia has noted that student dropouts from the eight-year schools are especially great in the Kazakh, Georgian, Azerbaijani, Moldavian, Armenian, and Estonian Republics.[95] With the exception of the Moldavian Republic, the non-Russian, that is native, populations of these republics have as high an

---

may dismiss it on the grounds that it is not art; the really terrible fact is that it is." *Izvestia,* March 11, 1972, p. 5. Surprising comments such as this are straws in the wind. A writer in *Literaturnaya gazeta,* speaking of profiteers and speculators in Georgia, says, "More than 2,300 years ago Plato wrote 'A citizen should be punished for his love of gain, which he has valued above all else.' " Perhaps only the reader of large amounts of Soviet material can appreciate the shock of finding Plato and not Lenin or Brezhnev quoted on such a matter. *Literaturnaya gazeta,* September 26, 1973, p. 10.

[92] *Pravda,* September 18, 1971, p. 2.

[93] See *Pravda,* February 1, 1972, p. 3, and *Literaturnaya gazeta,* June 21, 1972, p. 2.

[94] E. A. Shevardnaze, the new First Secretary of the Georgian Party Central Committee, in *Zarya vostoka,* July 31, 1973, pp. 1–2.

[95] *Izvestia,* July 19, 1973, p. 2.

educational level as the Russian population of the RSFSR.[96] Perhaps the high rate of school dropouts in these republics represents a dropout from or reaction to the "system" or the "establishment," rather than a depreciation of the value of education itself.

Religious beliefs accompanied by open avowal and by religious practices lead even more to open dissent from Party positions than do nationalist sentiments.

The Vinnitsa (Ukraine) Medical Institute distributed a questionnaire on religious beliefs that was answered by 350 students. Only one student said that he believed in God, but only 163 affirmed that they did not believe in God. Of the 350 families represented by these students, almost half had religious believers in the family and/or maintained religious traditions, celebrated religious festivals, and preserved beliefs in omens and magic.[97] Evidently, such findings represent a substantial amount of dissent from Party positions. Similarly, in Gorky a 1964–65 study of baptism revealed that the Party assumption that most fathers and mothers who baptized their infants are unskilled workers was wrong, and showed that skilled workers are well represented in this group.[98] A study of about 1,000 workers in Ukrainian industrial centers revealed that about 35 percent felt that religious convictions cannot be forced on others, and that if a person believes in God, that is his affair. About 40 percent, including Komsomol and Party members, felt that religion does not have a bad influence on man's spiritual outlook.[99]

That some religious believers more or less ignore Party condemnations of their behavior is not surprising. But one also finds in the military that nonbelievers and even Party officials show a tolerance for religious belief that is distressing to Party authorities. A *Krasnaya zvezda* investigator found in a certain unit that two of the young recruits were devout Moslems, one of whom boasted of his religious beliefs. *Krasnaya zvezda* confronted the secretary of the Komsomol bureau with this fact. "The secretary fell silent for a moment before answering: 'We have freedom of conscience in our country.' "[100] According to *Krasnaya zvezda* this Komsomol secretary did not seem to understand that "freedom of conscience in our country also implies an obligation on the part of each citizen to participate in antireligious propaganda work." *Krasnaya*

[96] *Istoria SSSR,* no. 5, September-October 1974, pp. 3–17.

[97] Ellen Mickiewicz, "Policy Applications of Public Opinion Research in the Soviet Union," *Public Opinion Quarterly,* Winter 1972/1973, XXVI, 4, p. 574.

[98] Ibid. *Le Monde's* Moscow correspondent, Jacques Amalric, writes: "One can affirm without much risk of error that there are more believers in the Soviet Union than members of the Communist Party." The 1974 Easter services were attended largely by older women, students, cadres, and white-collar workers, with very few industrial workers. *Le Monde,* April 16, 1974.

[99] *Nauka i religiya,* no. 2, 1974, pp. 6–7.

[100] *KZ,* August 22, 1972, p. 2.

zvezda also found that the wife of a warrant officer was a confirmed Baptist and could not be persuaded to drop her Baptist connections. A senior lieutenant had in fact notified the relevant political department worker about the presence of Baptists near the unit. The political department worker replied that "the sect was authorized and . . . was not to be interfered with," a response that also scandalized *Krasnaya zvezda*.[101]

Party pressure for corrective political indoctrination does not stem only from dissent among special groups such as scientists, youths, nationalists, and religious believers. Throughout the population, passive resistance to Party instructions is widespread, since a great deal of Party intervention in both the army and civil life takes the form of pressure to contribute one's scarce, and therefore precious, leisure time to numerous forms of "civic work" and to political training. According to Vladimir Yagodkin, Moscow Party secretary for ideology and propaganda, 3.3 million Muscovites (45 percent of Moscow's population) take political indoctrination courses.[102]

Resentment probably leads only rarely to antiregime behavior, but it is clear that Party authorities are, nonetheless, concerned about illegal behavior. *Kommunist vooruzhennykh sil* points out: "We have recently adopted laws that establish stricter responsibility for certain types of legal violations. In particular, we have intensified the responsibility for hooliganism, misappropriation of weapons, ammunition, and explosives."[103] *Kommunist vooruzhennykh sil* refers here, in part, to the addition in 1972 of the following crimes to those officially classified as "grave": smuggling, narcotic offenses, and theft of firearms, ammunitions, and explosives, whether or not with aggravating circumstances.[104]

Party concern with the theft of ammunition and weapons grew after 1967 when the military preinduction training program provided weapons for training purposes. Military training officers were reprimanded for carelessness in safeguarding these weapons. Hunting guns have also become a problem, not only because of accidents but also because young people get hold of their fathers' guns. Soviet Internal Affairs personnel think hunting guns should be more strictly controlled. Indeed, one proposal is "that hunting guns be kept in special storehouses—perhaps at hunters' societies or major enterprises—until the opening of the hunting season."[105]

[101] Ibid.
[102] *New York Times,* October 1, 1973.
[103] *KVS,* no. 21, November 1972, pp. 17–23.
[104] *Sotsialisticheskaya zakonnost',* August 1972, pp. 16–22.
[105] *Sovetskaya Rossiya,* January 17, 1973, p. 4. A few months after this suggestion four Soviet youths, the oldest of whom was twenty, were reported to have used sawed-off hunting rifles in an attempt to hijack a Soviet plane. Two of the hijackers were killed and two captured. *New York Times,* November 6, 1973.

Soviet action in 1972 to discourage and prevent the theft of explosives and weapons was, no doubt, seen as more than justified by the setting off of a bomb in September 1973 in Lenin's tomb that killed the bomber and two Soviet women tourists.[106]

B. THEMES

Kommunist vooruzhennykh sil conveniently summarizes the number and diversity of subjects that military-political agencies must teach to military personnel: the ideas of Marxism-Leninism; boundless devotion to the people, the homeland, the Communist Party, and the Soviet government; the invincible unity and fraternal friendship among the peoples of the USSR; proletarian internationalism and combat cooperation with the armies of the fraternal socialist countries; the moral code of the builder of communism; a spirit of high vigilance; class hatred for the imperialists and all enemies of communism; personal responsibility for defense of the Soviet homeland; readiness to give one's life itself if necessary to achieve full victory; the dometic and foreign policy of the Communist Party; the revolutionary, combat, and labor traditions of the Party, the Soviet people, and its armed forces; the successes of building communism in the USSR and the building of socialism in the fraternal countries; the advantages of socialism over capitalism; and pride in the homeland, its great achievements, and its noble history.[107]

When a briefer statement is desired, the foregoing objectives of indoctrination can be pared down to certain essentials. Thus, a Soviet air force journal emphasizes: the establishment of a Communist world view; boundless devotion to the homeland; hatred for the enemy; and faithfulness to military duty.[108] General A. A. Yepishev, head of the Main Political Administration of the Soviet forces, reduces the central task of ideological work to "the shaping . . . of a Marxist-Leninist world outlook, high ideological and political attributes, and Communist moral standards."[109]

It would be a mistake to suppose that even the lengthy list cited earlier exhausts or even adequately represents the content of Soviet political indoctrination. The Party's desire for all-inclusive control and its tendency to see a political implication in any deviation from preferred behavior or beliefs mean that virtually every subject has an ideological or political dimension and becomes a proper theme for political indoctrination. Drinking and dirty shoes

---

[106] *Le Monde,* September 5, 1973, p. 1. The action was presumably that of a single individual. The Soviets are especially sensitive to group crimes, even when they are without political significance, probably because group crimes spell conspiracy. *Sovetskaya yustitsia,* April 1973, pp. 9–10.

[107] *KVS,* no. 7, April 1973, pp. 16–26.

[108] *Aviatsiya i kosmonavtika,* October 1971, pp. 9–11.

[109] *KZ,* March 28, 1973, pp. 2–3.

have a moral and therefore political significance. So, too, does a low score on the firing range or addressing a fellow serviceman by his first name in the course of performing a military duty. Whatever else it may imply, anything that needs correction in individual or unit affairs also implies a need for further indoctrination.

The broad scope of indoctrination and propaganda does not, of course, preclude the omission of, or a restrained reference to, some topics. SALT I and II and MBFR (Mutual and Balanced Force Reduction) are not prominent subjects in the frequent indoctrination lectures, seminars, and readings thrust upon Soviet servicemen. References to Czechoslovakia 1968 are few and defensive, and, interestingly enough, the subject of China has not figured prominently in military indoctrination. We shall return to some of these reticences of Soviet military indoctrination shortly.

1. Hate the Enemy, Love the Motherland

These complementary injunctions of Soviet indoctrination were taught by Lenin himself, and it appears that one can scarcely have an adequate love for the motherland without having an equally intense hatred for her enemies.[110] Although love for the motherland is "a powerful source" from which Soviet fighting men draw their readiness to endure and take risks, hatred for the enemy "is the most important component part of the perseverence and heroism of the Soviet troops."[111] "The Communist Party educates the troops . . . to hate the enemies of the Soviet Union and always to be ready to destroy them."[112]

Soviet analysts of past military successes often attribute them to the two emotions of love and hate. Thus, the success of partisans and guerrillas in World War II was due to the fact that "they possessed the greatest of all things with which a war is won—passionate love for their country and burning hatred for the . . . invader."[113] Western writers have tended to note a decline since World War I in the intensity with which patriotic emotions motivate soldiers. Soviet propagandists, however, show no inclination to acknowledge a lesser role for emotion. A Soviet work on problems of political and psychological training contains chapters entitled "Instilling Love for the Motherland" and "Hate the Enemy."[114] Soviet instructions on indoctrination tend to emphasize hatred for the enemy somewhat more vigorously than they do love for the

[110] Ibid., June 26, 1971, p. 2.
[111] *Aviatsiya i kosmonavtika,* July 1972, pp. 1–2.
[112] *Voyenno-istoricheskiy zhurnal,* June 1972, pp. 12–19.
[113] *Soviet Military Review,* no. 4, 1965, p. 54.
[114] Colonel General A. F. Zheltov [*The Soldier and War: Problems in the Morale-Political and Psychological Training of Soviet Fighting Men*], Moscow, 1971.

motherland. Indoctrination must inculcate "a spirit of hatred toward the imperialists . . . [and] the enemies of communism."[115] Hatred of the imperialist aggressors must be persistently nurtured, and soldiers should be inspired by "a burning hatred" for them.[116]

The lesser emphasis on love for the motherland is due in considerable measure to the fact that love of the motherland tends to be compromised in many formulations by the precedence given to love of and loyalty to the Party. It is not uncommon for Soviet servicemen to be taught "to go through fire and water," not for the sake of their homeland, but "for the sake of the great ideals of the Communist Party."[117] Love of or loyalty to the motherland is diluted by its inclusion in a list (and not generally in the first place) of those whom the serviceman is to love or to whom he is to be loyal: "to the Party, the people, the homeland, and socialist internationalism."[118]

Much of Soviet indoctrination attempts to whip up hatred against rather abstract entities, such as "the imperialist aggressors," who hardly seem, depicted under this label, either ferocious enough or real enough to inspire a great deal of emotion. To be sure, the political officer in his lecture may translate such phrases into more concrete and hate-inspiring terms, but the popular military press often contents itself with these vague "imperialist" references. This, however, is not always the case. Thus, documentary movies are available that show "the cruelty of American imperialism in Vietnam and the heroic struggle of the freedom-loving Vietnamese people against the aggressors . . . [and] help to develop a correct understanding of the probable enemy in the soldiers and indoctrinate a feeling of hate for the enemy in them."[119] Anti-US propaganda is sometimes given a more immediately local context, as when personnel on a Soviet missile cruiser in the Mediterranean received a talk on "The US Sixth Fleet, A Weapon of Aggression and Plunder."[120]

Soviet propagandists are aware that references to the Nazis and to fascism are still capable of arousing deep emotion in the Soviet Union and the "hate the enemy" theme sometimes seems intended to revive World War II memories. This may in part be a propaganda attack against the Federal Republic of Germany, but generally it seems to be an attempt to use a concrete, emotionally charged target in order to arouse a hatred that the Party hopes can or will be transferred to all other entities specified by the Party now or in the future as "enemies."

[115] *Sovetskiy patriot,* May 26, 1971, p. 2.
[116] *KVS,* no. 21, November 1970, pp. 73–78, and no. 1, January 1971, pp. 18–26.
[117] *KZ,* June 10, 1971, p. 2.
[118] *KVS,* no. 1, January 1971, pp. 18–26.
[119] Lieutenant Colonel G. Suleymanyan in Badmayev [*An Important Factor of Combat Readiness*].
[120] *Starshina serzhant,* May 1972, pp. 10–12.

2. The Imperialist Threat

A major theme of the "political exercises" held by political officers for Soviet military personnel, a theme constantly reiterated in Soviet military publications, has been the threat of a war unleashed by the imperialist aggressors. The US-SU détente, the visits of President Nixon to the Soviet Union and Secretary Brezhnev to the United States, arms control talks, and commercial and industrial transactions on an increasing scale have all made this theme a difficult one for Soviet propagandists. These difficulties are faced in several ways: by a bland disregard of the changes in international relations, by an acknowledgment of surface changes accompanied by an emphasis on an underlying continuity, and by an attempt to reshape the propaganda line.

In 1971, despite its decreasing plausibility, Soviet military propagandists for the most part still emphasized that militarism was developing "on an unprecedented scale" in the capitalist world.[121] Militarization of the United States is described in terms that suggest an almost awesome development.[122] Although the Soviet Union has enjoyed peace for twenty-five years, "the danger of a military attack launched by the imperialists against the Soviet Union . . . has not been eliminated. Nor has there been any change in the aggressive nature of imperialism."[123] An embittered antagonism exists between the two social systems and imperialism's aggressiveness continues to grow.[124] The United States views Western Europe as the most important bridgehead for launching an aggressive war against the Soviet Union and other socialist countries.[125] It is clear that "the imperialists are betting on a sudden starting of a missile nuclear war."[126]

A subsidiary theme is that a new world war, should the imperialists unleash one, will differ considerably from previous wars. It will spill over into a decisive class struggle between socialism and imperialism on a global scale.[127]

In 1971 the Federal Republic of Germany shared with the United States the distinction of being "imperialism's most aggressive detachment," although the United States was distinctly *primus inter pares.*[128] Both Japan and the Federal Republic of Germany were becoming more insolent.[129] The attention

---

[121] *KVS,* no. 15, August 1971, pp. 65–73.

[122] *Bloknot agitatora,* May 22, 1971, pp. 1–5.

[123] *KVS,* no. 18, September 1971, pp. 20–28.

[124] *KZ,* September 14, 1971, pp. 2–3.

[125] *KVS,* no. 18, September 1971, pp. 57–62.

[126] Ibid., pp. 35–41.

[127] Ibid., no. 8, April, 1971, pp. 84–90. The vacillations in Soviet indoctrination themes are illustrated by the fact that just three months earlier *KVS* had criticized "serious oversimplifications when describing imperialist and aggressive wars generally as factors that favor the course of a revolutionary process." *KVS,* no. 1, January 1971, pp. 88–92. The theme that a new world war would take the form of a gigantic class confrontation between opposing social systems was repeated by *KVS* in no. 21, November 1972, pp. 9–16.

[128] *Partiynaya zhizn',* May 1971.

[129] *KVS,* no. 18, September 1971, pp. 57–62.

of political officers was called, in 1971, to the importance of pointing out to military personnel that the United States displays a preference for offensive weapons and for atomic blackmail as a principal means for achieving US foreign policy aims.[130]

Soviet propagandists were by no means entirely confident in 1971 or even in earlier years that these various contentions of Soviet indoctrination would be believed. Military personnel were warned that the United States hides behind a peace-loving ideology and gives misleading names (deterrence, finite deterrence, assured destruction) to aggressive military doctrines.[131]

Despite the diversity of propaganda voices and audiences, despite Soviet indecision and time lags in adopting new lines, the years 1972-73 saw, on the whole, a shift of themes and emphases. Propagandists acknowledged, with greater ease and frequency, a change in world affairs toward the relaxing of international tension. In one major indoctrination line, such statements are combined with affirmations of the continuing military threat of imperialism. Thus, a *Krasnaya zvezda* editorial points out that "appreciable changes for the better have been occurring in the international arena recently under the influence of the Leninist foreign policy of the Soviet Union and the other socialist countries. However, this must not give rise to any illusions with regard to the very essence of imperialism. It remains reactionary and aggressive."[132] Marshal Grechko himself concedes that "imperialists are not now deciding to make a direct military attack. They will understand that such a step would end in catastrophe for them. But they are still counting on achieving military supremacy . . . and at a favorable moment resolving the international dispute . . . by military means."[133] A little later, in a long article in *Kommunist,* the marshal emphasizes that despite the relaxation of tension, "we are realists and can well see that influential circles in the world of capitalism have not yet abandoned their attempt to pursue 'a position of strength' policy. The arms race . . . is still continuing."[134] In late 1972, *Kommunist vooruzhennykh sil* provided for political officers a set of political lessons lasting eight hours that dealt essentially with the point that although the Soviet Union has forced the imperialists to acknowledge the principle of peaceful coexistence, the latter cannot be trusted because war and aggression are inevitable companions of the capitalist system.[135] Thus, a basic point of Marxism-Leninism was maintained.

A second form of the 1972–73 revision emphasized that the change in the balance of military power led the imperialists to a new emphasis on ideological war and economic competition. We have already seen examples of this theme in discussing the increased importance that the Soviets attach to indoctrina-

---

[130] Ibid.
[131] Ibid., pp. 35–41.
[132] *KZ,* October 17, 1972, p. 1.
[133] Ibid., March 28, 1973, pp. 1–2.
[134] *Kommunist,* no. 7, May 1973, pp. 12–26.
[135] *KVS,* no. 21, November 1972, pp. 71–76.

tion. We need only note that this form of the theme of the imperialist threat does not necessarily imply that the imperialists have rejected the use of military means. The Soviet reader was, however, permitted to make this inference.

A third form of the 1972–73 shift frankly acknowledges gains in the easing of international tensions, without hastening to add the customary warning about the underlying hostility or aggressiveness of the capitalist states. The clearest examples of this nuance date from the spring of 1973. Thus, with regard to the struggle against the arms race, primarily the nuclear arms race, "one cannot now speak of stagnation here. . . . Businesslike talks on the limitation of strategic arms are being held. . . . A useful agreement has been concluded."[136] A month later, *Izvestia* notes that "the talks . . . confirm that the improvement of relations between the SU and the USA is possible. The development of businesslike cooperation is also possible."[137] In the meantime *Krasnaya zvezda,* referring to the April 1973 plenum of the Central Committe, had also noted with satisfaction that "the peace program is being implemented successfully. As a result . . . a noticeable easing of the international situation, and above all the situation in Europe, has been achieved. . . . A change away from 'cold war' is taking place. . . . The imperialist aggression in Vietnam has ended." Lenin is cited to justify "a readiness to develop newly beneficial relations with states of another social system."[138] It was natural, therefore, that in July 1973, *Krasnaya zvezda* should discuss Brezhnev's trip to the United States under the justifying title of "Leninist Principles of Foreign Policy in Action." The visit "was an event of tremendous importance and great fundamental significance."[139] No warning of imperialist deceit, no "but" dilutes the gains described in this article. On the contrary, a sense of optimism is conveyed by statements that the Soviet Union is striving to ensure that the positive changes in the international situation become "irreversible."[140] The socialist countries are seeking a realistic way to establish "universal and lasting peace on earth."[141] In the ideological sphere, however, "there is not and cannot be peaceful coexistence." But the struggle of the two ideologies must not be confused with cold war. Cold war is not inevitable, it is only due to provocative actions by the most reactionary imperialist forces. "Ideological struggle is another matter."[142] In any case, peaceful coexistence does not imply the "immutability of capitalism."[143]

These transformations of the indoctrination line did not take place in all

---

[136] *Izvestia,* March 30, 1972, p. 4.
[137] Ibid., May 30, 1973, p. 3.
[138] *KZ,* May 18, 1973, p. 1.
[139] Ibid., July 4, 1973, pp. 2–3.
[140] *Pravda,* August 22, 1973, pp. 3–4.
[141] *Kommunist,* no. 12, August 1973, pp. 3–11.
[142] Moscow Domestic Service, August 29, 1973.
[143] *Pravda,* August 22, 1973, pp. 3–4.

sectors with equal speed, or perhaps they were not unanimous. In the spring of 1973 *Kommunist vooruzhennykh sil* was also teaching that "modern imperialism continues to threaten the nations of the world with the possibility of a new world war," a position that in 1974 was more fully revived.[144]

3. The Crisis of Capitalism

Capitalism has been in a state of crisis for so many decades now that Marxist-Leninist interpretations of its fate are somewhat pressed to find formulations that carry some degree of conviction. A political lesson prepared for Soviet troops instructs propagandists to point out to the troops that modern capitalism "is adapting to the new situation in the world." However, capitalism is faced with growing resistance from workers, and the authorities have had to resort to more readily concealed forms of exploitation, and in some cases have even made partial concessions through reforms in order to hold the masses under ideological and political control. However, as the Twenty-fourth Party Congress pointed out, these adaptations do not mean the stabilization of capitalism as a system. On the contrary, the general crisis of capitalism continues to deepen.[145] Compared with the theme of capitalist and imperialist aggression or potential aggression, the crisis of capitalism receives rather limited attention in the military press, probably as a result of increasing East-West trade. Inflation and the energy crisis in the West, however, partially revived the interest of Soviet propagandists in this theme.

4. The Enemy in the East

Soviet military indoctrination, as we noted earlier, has paid more attention to enemies in the West than to the enemy in the East, that is, Communist China. This statement requires some qualification. When political lessons or materials in the military press refer to "capitalism" or to specific capitalist countries, the exclusion of China is clear enough. However, Soviet statements show a preference for the term "imperialist" that in most contexts certainly seems to include only the industrial and capitalist countries, but in some other contexts is intended not to exclude the enemy in the East, at least when read by people, probably officers, who can take a hint.[146]

One finds in many Soviet military articles vague references to "the times urgently demand . . . " or "the present situation requires . . . ," without any

---

[144] *KVS,* no. 8, April 1973, pp. 73–80.

[145] Ibid., no. 16, August 1971, pp. 73–80; *Znamenonosets,* no. 6, June, 1974, pp. 26–29. The last-mentioned journal replaced *Starshina serzhant* in January 1974. It is intended for ensigns and warrant officers as well as NCOs.

[146] Soviet military indoctrination has not found a convenient new term or a variant of "imperialism" to describe Red China, as the latter has to refer to the USSR ("social imperialism").

explanation of why the times urgently demand anything, or what it is about the present situation that requires this or that extra vigilance or increased combat readiness. References to "the complicated international situation" or "under present conditions" seem at times to take on the character of code terms to refer to the Chinese and a reader might infer that the complicated aspect of the recent world situation is that a principal enemy of the Soviet Union is another Communist state.[147]

Characteristic of the often allusive nature of Soviet references to China are statements in which the omission of the usual reference to the United States or the imperialists is clearly quite intentional. Thus Marshal Grechko assures the Soviet people that they "can be confident that at any time of the night or day the army and navy are ready to repel an enemy attack, *no matter from where it might come.*"[148] (Emphasis added.) Similarly, a political lesson instructs the military propagandist to point out "that in the face of a significant intensification of international tension, the CPSU [Communist Party of the Soviet Union] and Soviet government are doing everything necessary in order that *no one* catches us unaware, in order that the world politics of the Soviet Union are strengthened . . . by the readiness of the armed forces to destroy *any* aggressor."[149] (Emphasis added.) The "intensification of international tension" must, in 1970, have been more plausibly interpreted by Soviet military readers as a reference to Soviet-Chinese clashes in 1969 on the Ussuri than to events in the West.

Somewhat more explicit hints are provided in articles that have a Far Eastern setting. Thus the description of a naval antisubmarine exercise ends as follows: "This event took place in the Far East. The vigilant eyes of our brothers . . . are reliably protecting the peaceful silence and the eternal beauty of our distant territory."[150]

Articles or references of a historical character may equally have an anti-Chinese flavor. Thus *Voyenno-istoricheskiy zhurnal* gives an account of Chinese aggression against the Soviet Far Eastern borders in 1929 entitled "Provocations by Chinese Militarists Along the Soviet Far Eastern Border in 1929 and Their Suppression."[151] The same events inspired in 1972 in Khabarovsk a commemorative plaque to honor a Soviet platoon commander who fell in fighting against the Chinese.[152] When Army General B. F. Tolubko, former commander of the Far Eastern Military District, now commander of the

[147] See, for example, *KZ*, February 9, 1971, and *Sovetskiy voin*, October 1971, p. 37.
[148] *Sovetskiy patriot*, March 29, 1972, p. 1.
[149] *KVS*, no. 21, November 1970, pp. 73–78.
[150] *Sovetskiy voin*, October 1971, pp. 34–35.
[151] *Voyenno-istoricheskiy zhurnal*, August 1972, pp. 70–75.
[152] Khabarovsk Domestic Service, October 1972. In January 1973 an obelisk was erected in the center of Khabarovsk to perpetuate the memory of border guards who died defending the state frontiers in the Far East. Moscow Domestic Service, January 5, 1973.

strategic missile forces, was interviewed on the Far East, he avoided all references to Red China and spoke only of Japanese militarism and the war in
Indochina. But after the interviewer referred specifically to the border troops
on the Amur and the Ussuri, the general launched into a detailed account of
the combat operations of 1929.[153]

Statements that refer to the "aggravation of the ideological struggle"
without further specification are frequently references to the western ideological offensives, but when they are accompanied by refences to "left wing infan-
tilism" or "revisionist ideology," Red China and the Maoists often are the
targets.

These reticences of Soviet military propaganda on China do not mean, of
course, that explicit attacks on the Chinese leadership do not occur, but they
occur less commonly than in the nonmilitary press. In September 1971, *Kommunist vooruzhennykh sil* began a series of major articles on vital indoctrination themes. In the first of these, China is attacked for its "great power
chauvinism and double-dealing anti-Soviet policies."[154] In the same issue of
Kommunist vooruzhennykh sil a political exercise in the Far Eastern Military
District is described dealing with "the military-political situation in the Far
East, and the tasks of soldiers in improving vigilance and combat readiness."
It appears that "the ideology and policies of Maoism [are] a source of aggravation of the military-political situation in the Far East."[155] No doubt the treatment of the military-political situation in the Far East and the improvement
of combat readiness as a single subject is intentional.

The following month *Kommunist vooruzhennykh sil* discussed a new
political exercise whose "importance and complexity" is underlined by the
requirement that the lectures be delivered by senior officers of units, ships, and
formations. Quoting Secretary Brezhnev's Twenty-fourth Party Congress
statement, "Everything that the people have created must be reliably defended," *Kommunist vooruzhennykh sil* deals with "the intensified nature of
imperialist aggression, the threat of a new war, and the need to strengthen the
defensive might of the Soviet state." But after a long and violent explanation
of imperialist aggression, *Kommunist vooruzhennykh sil* concludes the discussion of the first point of the political lesson with the following statement: "The
anti-Soviet and schismatic policy being pursued by Mao Tse-tung and his
group in China is serving to further stimulate the aggressive policies of the
imperialists. It has submitted territorial claims against the Soviet Union, and
it even provoked armed incidents along the border during the spring and
summer of 1969. . . . The anti-Soviet line in Chinese policy and propaganda
is continuing. Under these conditions, the Communist Party was forced to take

[153] *Sovetskiy voin,* June 1972, pp. 1–3.
[154] *KVS,* no. 18, September 1971, pp. 9–19.
[155] Ibid., pp. 70–74.

the required defensive measures and to reinforce its peaceful policies by strengthening its defensive capabilities and improving the combat potential and combat readiness of its armed forces."[156]

The real point of the message, then, is the attack on China and the consequent Soviet need to strengthen its armed forces. In the same lesson, military propagandists are instructed to stress "the importance of heavy industry being developed at a rapid rate of speed."[157] Thus, the sacrifice of consumer interests to the expansion of heavy industry is associated with the machinations of the Maoists,[158] and the entire message is underlined by being delivered by senior officers.

In early 1972, *Krasnaya zvezda* attacked China far more sharply than it had in the past, accusing it of whipping up an "atmosphere of war psychosis . . . based on unrestrained anti-Soviet propaganda." China's foreign trade has been devoted to building up her strategic weapons and her population is being prepared for war. "It is being impressed on the people that war is inevitable and that . . . China will certainly win. . . . Peking propaganda identifies the 'inevitability of war' with the inevitability of a war against the USSR."[159] The same theme of increasing militarization of China is stressed by *Voyenno-istoricheskiy zhurnal* in an article for officers. This article gives special attention to China's 300,000 border troops "educated in a fanatical hatred for the peoples of the USSR" and to her "nuclear missile elite."[160]

In a 1973 article for political officers called "Modern Political Map of the World," *Kommunist vooruzhennykh sil,* speaking of China, affirmed: "Obviously nothing will force us into abandoning our basic Marxist-Leninist policies. Nor will we fail to defend the state interest of our Soviet people or the inviolability of the territory of the USSR."[161] In another article in the same issue *Kommunist vooruzkennykh sil* charged that "aggressive NATO circles are not overlooking the possibility of creating a partnership with the present leaders of China. . . . The NATO journal . . . has said that 'this is the chance of a lifetime . . . we cannot ignore it.' The NATO propaganda organ issued an appeal for an alliance to be drawn up with the Chinese leadership on an anti-Soviet basis."[162]

Krasnaya zvezda continued its attack in 1973 with an article ("Maoist Objectives and the Real Facts") that begins with the statement that it is being

[156] Ibid., no. 20, October 1971, pp. 68–74.
[157] Ibid.
[158] In a Mandarin broadcast to China, November 20, 1972, the Soviet propaganda service, answering Chinese charges that the Soviet military budget is increasing year by year, attributes Soviet military expenditures to "certain countries" that fan anti-Soviet sentiments among their people.
[159] *KZ,* February 25, 1972, p. 3.
[160] *Voyenno-istoricheskiy zhurnal,* September 1972, pp. 93–97.
[161] *KVS,* no. 8, April 1973, pp. 73–80.
[162] Ibid., pp. 81–85.

published in response to readers' requests for an article on the situation in China.[163] This almost apologetic statement to introduce an article on China is characteristic of the hesitations of Soviet military propaganda on Communist China.

The relative, although clearly declining, restraint of Soviet military indoctrination on Red China, accompanied by occasional outbursts, raises obvious questions. Several explanations seem relevant, although their overall weighting in the Party mind is not easy to guess.

A continual stream of anti-Chinese or anti-Mao propaganda in the Soviet military indoctrination material would be especially likely to feed both foreign and Chinese beliefs of an impending (if not imminent) Soviet attack on Red China. Besides, Soviet officers and soldiers are substantial consumers of the civilian press and radio, which bring anti-Chinese news and propaganda to them without the disadvantage of seeming to be directed to a military audience.[164]

Second, the Soviets are surely not abandoning all hope that a future Chinese change of leadership may permit some sort of rapprochement with Red China. Soviet anti-Mao statements in both the civilian and military press are often softened by invitations for China to join the Soviet Union against the capitalist nations.

Third, Soviet propagandists hardly have to carry on as intensive a campaign against the Chinese as they do against the West. The West is esteemed and respected by many Soviet citizens, but according to western observers, the Soviets have generally a deep and widespread animus against and suspicion of the Chinese. Even members of the dissident intellectual-scientist class clearly share this anti-Chinese sentiment, which seems to be based on ethnic and racial dislike and to be by no means simply an opposition to Maoism. In this situation a great propaganda effort to promote hostility toward the present Red Chinese regime is unnecessary.

Fourth, excessive attention to China might detract from the value of Soviet political indoctrination on the threat of the imperialist powers, a threat needed for ideological reasons and to justify military expenditures.

Finally, changes in Soviet military dispositions in the Far East speak more eloquently to military personnel than any "political lesson." A little more than

---

[163] *KZ,* February 3, 1973, p. 3.

[164] The reluctance of the Soviets to make anti-Chinese propaganda in the military too explicit or public is implied by a Soviet letter of uncertain authenticity "smuggled" to the West alleging that for the last twelve months Soviet political officers in all military units have had "secret" instructions to do all they can to encourage hostility among the men against China, the Chinese way of life, and the Chinese. *Daily Telegraph* (London), August 9, 1973, p. 4. Given the large number of political officers and the public character of what they are required to do, the secrecy of such instructions could hardly be much more than that required of most internal Party documents.

ten years ago the Soviets had about fifteen divisions in the Far East and Outer Mongolia.[165] In 1972 they were reported to have forty-four divisions in the Sino-Soviet border area, including two divisions in Mongolia.[166] The Far Eastern buildup of both troops and matériel, including missiles, together with the reassignment of top military figures to the area, probably contributed to the widespread rumors in the Soviet Union in February and early March of 1967 of an impending war between the Soviet Union and China. In at least one region of Central Russia (Lipetsk), peasants began to stock everyday essentials.[167] Apparently, then, the Party might certainly feel that it has to tread a delicate path between responding vigorously to Chinese acts, and not so vigorously as to alarm domestic and foreign opinion or to cut off possibilities of rapprochement in the future.[168]

5. Military Expenditures—The Cost of Security

Soviet indoctrination is sensitive to possible domestic criticism of the amounts spent on the military forces. Soviet commanders and propagandists are told that "it is important to explain to the soldiers that the Soviet Union is obliged to spend significant amounts in the defense of the country because imperialism, being a source of military danger, has undertaken an armaments race."[169] US military expenditures, the war in Vietnam, and NATO are described at some length with a view to justifying Soviet military expenditures and force sizes.[170] These expenditures are deemed necessary despite the victories of the socialist bloc.[171]

Soviet indoctrination materials acknowledge an increase in Soviet military expenditures from a defense budget of 13.4 billion rubles in 1966 to 16.7 billion rubles in 1968 and 17.9 billion rubles in 1970. These increases are

[165] John Erickson, *Soviet Military Power* (London: Royal United Services Institute for Defense Studies, 1971), pp. 91–100.

[166] The International Institute for Strategic Studies, *The Military Balance, 1972-1973* (London, 1972), p. 7. This number compares with thirty-one divisions in Central and Eastern Europe, sixty in European USSR, eight in Central USSR, and twenty-one in southern USSR. In September 1972 the Soviet Union was reported to have added three mechanized divisions to its borders on China. This report attributes forty-nine divisions to the border, or nearly one-third of the entire Soviet army. *New York Times,* September 10, 1972. In the meantime, additions to the European front have also been reported.

[167] Chatel, *Carnets russes,* pp. 173–174.

[168] This does not preclude hints to the Chinese forces concerning Soviet military strength. In a broadcast in Mandarin (November 9, 1972) to the "dear Chinese soldiers" of the PLA, the Soviets describe the enormous firepower of their rockets and the superb accuracy of their strategic missiles, their missile-bearing tanks that can go 500 kilometers without refueling, and their soldiers steeled by political as well as military training. The broadcast then blandly adds that the Soviet Union is equipped with everything necessary to defend its borders against invasion by the "imperialist aggressors."

[169] *KZ,* December 24, 1969.

[170] *KVS,* no. 1 and no. 2, January 1971.

[171] *Bloknot agitatora,* May 22, 1971, pp. 1–5.

"taking place in conformity with the degree of military threat" and are justified by dangerous new US doctrines such as "assured destruction" and "counterforce."[172] Presumably the US threat did not increase in 1971, since it is claimed that the Soviet defense budget for that year remained at the 1970 level. Despite the alleged leveling off of Soviet military expenditures, it was not uncommon in 1972 for statements to be made defending "a further strengthening of our country's defenses."[173] Marshal Grechko himself stated: "Naturally in a complicated international situation . . . the Soviet people do not have the right to forget for a minute the necessity of further strengthening our armed forces."[174] Indeed, it appears that following decisions of the Central Committee of the CPSU important steps have been taken "in recent years to improve further the system of bringing troops up to strength."[175] These various admissions, taken in conjunction with charges made in the West, may have prompted a *Krasnaya zvezda* statement denying western claims that the Soviet forces and Soviet military expenditures were increasing.[176]

Although the United States and imperialism have generally been made to bear most of the responsibility for Soviet military expenditures, both in Soviet military indoctrination and in some broadcasts to China the Maoists are increasingly blamed for the Soviet need to strengthen their military capabilities. "At the Tenth Congress of the Communist Party of China in August 1973, held in strictest secrecy, the Soviet Union was declared Enemy No. 1. As a result, our Party is constantly concerned with strengthening further the defense capabilities of the country."[177] It is likely that the greatly increased Soviet military activity in the Far East reinforces this claim in the minds of Soviet soldiers, as does Soviet propaganda on Chinese preparations for war and Mao's instructions to "dig tunnels deeply."[178]

Soviet military expenditures receive a rather different justification in the claim that "together with their main assignment . . . our armed forces play an important social role and carry out large-scale educational tasks."[179] This social-economic service has been heavily emphasized since Secretary Brezhnev pointed out at the Twenty-fourth Party Congress that the military forces are "a good school of ideological and physical tempering, discipline, and organization." Thus, it appears that the army enables the Soviet male population to "graduate, so to speak, from a unique nationwide university."[180]

---

[172] *KVS,* no. 18, September 1971, pp. 20–28.
[173] Ibid., no. 15, August 1972, pp. 73–80.
[174] *Pravda,* February 3, 1972, p. 2.
[175] *KVS,* no. 7, April 1973, pp. 16–26.
[176] *KZ,* July 10, 1973, p. 3.
[177] *KVS,* no. 20, October 1973, pp. 67–73.
[178] *KZ,* February 3, 1973, p. 3.
[179] *Pravda,* July 22, 1973.
[180] Ibid.

6. Who Is Winning?

Behind Soviet self-congratulatory behavior lurks another and more realistic strain, one that recognizes the difficulties facing Soviet ideology and the dissension in the communist world and in the ranks of the workers. In 1971, Soviet military propagandists were told to emphasize that "today's socialist world is still a young and growing organism. It has not yet completely settled down and it still bears the imprint of the past."[181]

The need to express high esteem for oneself often stems from a lack of confidence. Given the defensive posture of the Soviet Union in the war for men's minds (see pp. 210–212 above), it is not surprising that Soviet political officers have been given the task of teaching a six-hour political exercise called "The USSR as a Great Socialist Power." The purpose of this exercise is to enable personnel to gain an idea "of our remarkable motherland," and to understand "the gigantic significance of the achievement of the USSR." The lesson should deepen the love of Soviet military personnel for the motherland and develop in them the patriotic desire to strengthen its might.[182]

Soviet propagandists are instructed to emphasize the prestige of the Soviet Union and its importance in the world by pointing out that the USSR is represented by 144 embassies and consulates (1971). It participates in 400 international organizations, and the seal of the Soviet Union is attached to more than 7,000 active international agreements and conventions.[183] This theme reflects the continuation, in some Soviet minds, of a sense of isolation from the main stream of the world and an attempt to assure oneself and others that the Soviet Union has, in fact, arrived in the "big leagues."

A particular mark of recent Soviet success is the achievement of its foreign policy. "The principles of peaceful coexistence [have] received widespread acknowledgement."[184] Propagandists are instructed to emphasize that the success of Soviet foreign policy indicates a change in the ratio of forces in favor of socialism. The resulting prestige of the Soviet Union was expressed in Brezhnev's visit to the United States—"an event of tremendous importance and of fundamental significance"[185]—and, at lower levels, in the warm reception accorded Soviet sailors in far-off corners of the world. In this connection, Marshal Grechko blandly observes that "one of the characteristics of modern fleets consists of the fact that . . . their former attachment to coastal areas is a thing of the past," thereby endowing not only the Soviet fleet, but all the fleets of the world, with a newly won mobility and a release from the security of coastal waters.[186]

[181] KVS, no. 11, June 1971, pp. 65–71.
[182] Ibid., no. 9, May 1973, pp. 70–78.
[183] Ibid., no. 11, June 1971, pp. 65–71.
[184] KZ, May 18, 1973, p. 1.
[185] Ibid., July 4, 1973, pp. 2–3.
[186] KVS, no. 12, June 1971, pp. 36–41.

It is clear who is winning. In 1969, one and a half billion people, or 35 percent of the world population, were living in socialist systems.[187] People in developing countries are 46 percent of the world's population, and only 639 million, or 19 percent of the world's population, live in developed capitalist countries. Socialist countries occupy 26 percent of the earth's territory, developing countries 51 percent, and developed capitalist countries only 23 percent. In 1937 socialist countries controlled only 10 percent of all industrial output; this figure rose to 20 percent in 1950 and 38 percent in 1967.[188] The economically developed capitalist countries trebled their industrial production from 1950 to 1972, but CEMA (Central European Market) countries increased their production eight-fold. Between 1950 and 1970 the CEMA share in world industrial production rose from 18 to 33 percent, and their share in world national income rose from 15 to 25 percent.[189] In addition, the growth of influence of the Communist Party, particularly in France and Italy, is emphasized.

That socialism is the wave of the future is evident to Soviet propagandists when they view the economic-political development of the third world. Many of these countries are developing along socialist lines. "Failures and defeats may be encountered; nevertheless the forces of national and socialist inspiration will continue their attack."[190]

7. The Soviet Union and the Fraternal Republics

Soviet political indoctrination makes frequent reference to the Soviet bloc, to Soviet leadership of it, and to the excellent political and military relations between the Soviet Union and the fraternal socialist countries. However, a considerable part of this indoctrination is defensive in spirit and is intended to deal with criticism of its interventions in Eastern Europe. The Soviet army, it is insisted, has an international mission because of its responsibilities to the Soviet bloc. "Today the falsifiers of history in the West are trying to convince credulous people that in entering other countries the Soviet armed forces allegedly pursued their self-interests. . . . The facts of history play havoc with such allegations."[191] The Central Committee of the Czechoslovakian Communist Party has affirmed that "the entry into Czechoslovakia of allied troops from five socialist countries was an act of international solidarity."[192] The publication of a Soviet book called *The Soviet Armed Forces' Liberation Mission in World War II,* under the general editorship of Marshal Grechko, provided

---

[187] The Soviets refrain from drawing attention to the fact that the majority of these are Chinese living under a regime that the Soviets seem interested in expelling from the socialist world.

[188] B. G. Grigor'yev [*Economic and Moral Potentials in a Modern War*], Moscow, 1969.

[189] *Izvestia,* September 29, 1973, p. 5.

[190] Ibid., no. 8, April 1973, pp. 73–80.

[191] *Soviet Military Review,* no. 6. 1971, p. 3.

[192] *KVS,* no. 20, October 1971, pp. 18–24.

Pravda with an opportunity to emphasize that the book demonstrates, contrary to the claims of anti-Soviet propaganda, the disinterested assistance of the Soviet Union to the peoples of Europe and Asia.[193] Indeed, according to the commanding general of the Central Group of Forces, "Our troops in Czechoslovakia often take on the role of Party political instructors and explain its [the Party's] Leninist policy."[194]

Whether to excuse the past or to prepare opinion for similar undertakings that may be required in the future, Soviet propaganda in the armed forces sets out to show that "the majority of difficulties that have occurred in certain areas of socialist building [can be traced] to a deviation from internationalism in an effort to please narrow national tendencies."[195] While affirming "an attentive regard for national interests," the Soviet propagandist continues by pointing out that "realizing a unity of working-class national and international tasks means establishing a priority of international and long-lasting interests over the temporary national interests of the present."[196] This position is necessary even though "imperialist propaganda and the left and right revisionists have created the myth of the so-called theory of limited sovereignty, as well as the fable of the two superpowers deciding the fate of the world behind the backs of the people."[197]

The political cooperation of brotherly countries requires not only unity of action on the basic problems of foreign policy but also unity of internal policy.[198] Divergences among socialist countries are engendered by differences in economic development, in social structure, and in international position, or they may be connected with special national features. In any case, these phenomena can and should be resolved on the basis of "proletarian internationalism by comradely discussion and voluntary brotherly cooperation."[199] Soviet propagandists emphasize the importance of the Warsaw Pact and the common military effort of the socialist bloc, especially as exemplified by the joint military exercise, Brotherhood of Arms, conducted in the fall of 1970 in the territory of the German Democratic Republic. Such military collaboration provides a sense of common purpose and feeling.[200]

The Soviets are sensitive to events in Eastern Europe that might suggest a breach in Soviet relationships with its fraternal socialist republics. After it

---

[193] *Pravda,* February 18, 1972, p. 3.
[194] *Sovetskiy voin,* no. 16, August 1973, pp. 2–3.
[195] *KVS,* no. 20, October 1971, pp. 18–24.
[196] Ibid.
[197] Ibid.
[198] Ibid., no. 3, February 1971, pp. 3–8.
[199] Ibid.
[200] *KZ,* July 6, 1971, p. 1; *KVS,* no. 2, January 1971, pp. 23–29, and no. 6, March 1971, pp. 3–8.

was rumored that the Rumanians had executed a Rumanian general for passing secrets to the Russians, a Soviet paper commented: "The combat fraternity of Soviet and Rumanian soldiers continues to strengthen. The USSR gave much aid to the young Rumanian army to train cadres. . . . The alliance and friendship between the peoples and armies of our countries were set forth in the Soviet-Rumanian Treaty of Friendship."[201]

Despite the brave show of innocence in Soviet statements, the limited attention given to Czechoslovakia and to western charges against the Soviet Union is striking. Clearly, the Party and Soviet propagandists decided that, on the whole, discretion was the better part of valor, and for the most part refrained from an active defense of the invasion, which would have necessitated referring to it. The muted discussion of a major act that was fully known to the Soviet public is an acknowledgment that not all the efforts of the Soviet military propaganda apparatus were capable of making the invasion of Czechoslovakia palatable.

8. The Nationality Problem

In the context of Soviet indoctrination the terms "international" and "internationalism" refer both to relations within the socialist bloc countries and to relations among the nationalities of the Soviet Union. Internationalism in the latter sense has become a major theme of Soviet military as well as civilian indoctrination, and was greatly stimulated by the propaganda opportunities afforded in 1973 by the celebration of the Fiftieth Anniversary of the USSR. But propaganda on this theme was primarily motivated by the existence of nationalist sentiments in the non-Russian republics. Associated with these sentiments were tendencies to openly resist Party discipline, to preserve minority languages, and to ignore the claims of the Russian language. In 1971, well before the Fiftieth Anniversary celebration, a major political exercise was introduced in the Soviet forces on the theme: "Friendship and Fraternity of the Peoples of the USSR—A Source of Might for the Soviet Union and its Armed Forces."[202] This exercise was allotted ten hours of political training

[201] *Sovetskaya Kirgiziya,* February 16, 1972.

[202] *KVS,* no. 3, February 1971, pp. 70–77. This 1971 exercise was perhaps prompted not only by continuing nationalist sentiment in resistance to "Russification," evidenced in minority literature, and in incidents like the disorders that accompanied the Russian-Uzbek soccer matches in Tashkent in the spring of 1969, but especially by data pouring in from the Soviet census of 1970. These revealed that Central Asian nationalities and Azerbaijanis had increased in population by 50 percent over the 1959 census figure. Their annual increase of 4 percent is one of the highest in the world today. The Central Asian nationalities constituted 6 percent of the population of the Soviet Union in 1959 and 8 percent in 1970. *Literaturnaya gazeta,* April 28, 1971, p. 10. Approximately one Soviet citizen in eight is of Moslem origin.

time, well in excess of the six hours that many other themes receive. In this exercise the propagandist was instructed to stress that 100 nationalities and ethnic groups live in the Soviet Union, that they are all involved in building the country, and that Hitler thought that this "ethnic conglomerate" would be easy to conquer. Soviet emphasis on the 100 nationalities (although nine of them account for 74 percent of the 1970 non-Russian population) seems to be intended to reduce the claims of any one minority nationality, make national aspirations for independence seem ridiculous, and legitimize Soviet claims that its experience in solving the national question in the USSR is of "world historical importance."[203]

Soviet indoctrination, without denying the domestic sources of nationalism among minority groups, accuses bourgeois propaganda of whipping up nationalism as part of its ideological struggle against socialism.[204] It appears that "the national question is one of the acute sectors of the struggle between socialism and capitalism. Bourgeois propaganda is striving . . . to use nationalism to undermine the socialist system."[205] That difficulties exist is obliquely acknowledged: "Anti-Communists pass off the fortuitous as the law-governed, and the partial as the general."[206]

The principal strategy of Soviet indoctrination in the nationality area is to combat minority particularism—"national self-awareness cannot be nour-

[203] *Izvestia,* February 23, 1972. What may in the long run help to alleviate the national question is not the promotion of the Russian language and a Soviet-wide patriotism, but rather intermarriages resulting from the Soviet practice of sending large numbers of Russian cadres to the minority republics. In 1968–70 there were 13.9 million interregional migrations in the USSR. The highest rate of migration was among Russians. *Zhurnalist,* no. 2, February 1974, pp. 73–75. In discussing possible projections from the 1970 census data, which showed a surprising tenacity of national identification along with the rapid growth of Moslem populations and some other non-Russian groups, writers sometimes fail to take intermarriage into account. In 1959, 102 of every 1,000 marriages involved members of two nationalities. It is said that the rate of intermarriage is rapidly increasing and that about 35 percent of the marriages at the Kiev Wedding Palace in 1963 were mixed marriages and that 20 percent of the marriages in Tashkent and Samarkand are mixed. In Frunze, Russian-Kirghiz marriages are said to be frequent, a fact that should not be at all surprising, since 30.2 percent of the population of the Kirghiz SSR is Russian and 40.5 percent is Kirghiz. Most mixed marriages are said to be between young people in new cities. Seven hundred of 1,690 marriages registered in Temir Tau were mixed. In families of mixed nationalities the children and parents are bilingual, as a rule. The 1973 article from which these figures are taken persists in citing data from 1960, 1963, and 1965, and one naturally wonders why more recent statistics are not given. *Literaturnaya gazeta,* January 24, 1973, p. 13. One also wonders about the 1970 census data on the growth of minority nationalities if these marriage data for the sixties are correct. Does the intermarriage of Russians with minority nationalities represent a loss of Russians to the minority nationalities rather than the reverse?

Literaturnaya gazeta printed another discussion of mixed marriages a few months later. From this it is evident that when a child of a mixed marriage is asked, "What nationality are you?" a desirable answer is "I am a Soviet." But Soviet administrative practice still requires the specification of a nationality. Ibid., August 15, 1973, p. 13.

[204] *Sovetskaya Litva,* April 5, 1972, pp. 1, 3.
[205] *Komsomol'skaya pravda,* December 5, 1972, p. 3.
[206] Ibid.

ished by pride in the cultural heritage of the past alone"[207]—and to foster a "pan-national Soviet pride."[208] *Krasnaya zvezda* assures the troops that "a feeling of nationwide pride is a great feeling. It grows and strengthens in Soviet soldiers."[209] And Marshal Grechko affirms that "friendship of the [Soviet] peoples is an important factor in the might of our multinational state."[210] Although it still recognizes that the USSR is a multinational state, Soviet propaganda has introduced the notion of "a new historical community of people—the Soviet people."[211]

9. Projection and Imitation in Soviet Indoctrination

A characteristic device of Soviet propaganda and indoctrination is to accuse other nations of practices that play a prominent role in Soviet behavior. This tendency to project onto enemies actions that are especially notable in the Soviet Union is sometimes supplemented by a tendency to imitate what enemies of the Soviet Union do in their propaganda.

Anyone familiar with Soviet indoctrination devices should not have been surprised by Soviet charges that the Israelis were locking their dissidents in mental hospitals.[212] Similarly, it was hardly surprising that the Soviets should charge West Germany with inviting military officers into their schools, arranging excursions for students to military garrisons, and providing informational material on various branches of the German armed forces.[213] This is, of course, precisely what the Soviets do on a far more intensive scale. As the Soviet nuclear missile program brought the USSR nuclear parity with the United States, Soviet military propaganda accused the United States of triggering an unprecedented arms race and using nuclear weapons for nuclear blackmail.[214] Similarly, the Soviets accuse the capitalist countries of broadcasting more than 1,400 hours weekly in twenty-two languages spoken in the Soviet Union, uninhibited by the fact that the Soviet Union leads all other countries in the

---

[207] *Sovetskaya kul'tura,* July 6, 1973, p. 2. "The idea of the superiority of some people over others, especially wild ideas about national exclusiveness, are alien to the very nature of our society." Ibid. Such statements usually refer to minority sentiments of superiority, but the Soviets also attempt to discourage Russian sentiments of superiority and some Russian or Slav tendencies to idealize old Russian and Slav culture.

[208] General A. Yepishev in *KZ,* March 28, 1973, pp. 2–3. "No matter to which nationality a Soviet man may belong," states General Yepishev, "he is primarily proud that he is a citizen of the USSR." Thus he is stating as an accomplished fact what is actually the primary objective of Soviet military indoctrination on nationalism. *Pravda,* March 27, 1973, p. 2.

[209] *KZ,* July 26, 1973, pp. 3, 4.

[210] *Kommunist,* no. 7, May 1973, pp. 12–26.

[211] Ibid.

[212] *Los Angeles Times,* May 9, 1972.

[213] *TASS,* April 21, 1972.

[214] *KVS,* no. 18, September 1971, pp. 57–62.

number of hours of foreign broadasting.[215] The United States, *Kommunist vooruzhennykh sil* alleges, spends tremendous amounts for the ideological training of its military personnel in a spirit of loyalty to the bourgeois system and hatred for communism.[216] This lengthy article, "Ideological Conditioning of Military Personnel in Imperialist Armies," is perhaps intended to moderate any resentment that Soviet military officers may have over the large expenditures on propaganda provided by the Soviet military budget.

In the last several years China has become a special target for Soviet projections of its own practices. The Soviets have imperturbably accused the Chinese radio and press of providing economic data only in percentage form and with having kept absolute statistical data about their economy secret since 1960.[217] Similarly, the Soviets accused the Chinese of alloting time in elementary and secondary schools to military drills and to the militarization of the children, for which purpose soldiers have been assigned to the schools—a charge that can be made with equal justice about the Soviet Union.[218] The Soviets also accuse the Chinese of taking up most of the free time of the students and controlling their extramural activity, another charge that Soviet secondary school students could equally well make of their own political, military, and educational authorities.[219]

In another manifestation of unease, a Soviet propagandist, no doubt sensitive to the accusations of antirevolutionary gradualism made against the Soviet Union by the Chinese, accused the Chinese of exerting pressure on revolutionary movements to curtail their struggles.[220]

So persistently is Soviet behavior (and perhaps thought) reflected in charges that the Soviet Union makes against others, that one is naturally led to examine some of these charges from the standpoint of what they might reflect concerning the Soviet Union itself. Thus, when Soviet propagandists charge in a broadcast to China that the Chinese leadership understands that its system is unstable and has no confidence in its own future and is striving to set up a more solid foundation through intensive control of the young people, one wonders whether this does not accurately reflect the feelings in the Soviet elite concerning their own system and Soviet youth.[221] We have seen, as a matter of fact (pp. 213–218), indications that this question greatly concerns the Soviets.

Moscow's interest in curbing the influence and independence of its intellectual class (and not simply the few who are openly dissident) also finds an echo in Soviet charges that in Red China intellectuals are confronted with

---

[215] Ibid., no. 10, May 1972, pp. 10–17.
[216] Ibid., no. 14, July 1973, pp. 16–23.
[217] Moscow Domestic Broadcast, February 19, 1972.
[218] *KZ,* February 25, 1972, p. 3.
[219] Ibid., p. 4.
[220] Ibid., July 13, 1973.
[221] In Mandarin, April 1, 1972.

difficulties. "The Peking authorities need them, but trust none of them. Therefore the Peking authorities try to ruin the prestige of the intellectuals in society. . . . The intellectuals thus have to cover up what is really on their minds and demonstrate their loyalty and trustworthiness all the time. As a result, they lack self-confidence and dare not act boldly."[222] This would be a reasonably accurate summary of the situation in the Soviet Union.

The Soviets sometimes seem to imitate what their enemies do. Probably what an enemy does is viewed as dangerous, and therefore it is useful to turn the weapon against him. The One Hundredth Anniversary of the Birth of Lenin in 1970 certainly called for a very special celebration in the Soviet Union, but the extremes to which Lenin-worship went at this time raise a question about its motivation. Even *Komsomol'skaya pravda* was moved to denounce the excesses of the cult of Lenin and to ask that various celebrations that were in bad taste be ended.[223] It seems not implausible that the cult of Mao Tse-tung in China and the increased appeal of Mao, the Great Helmsman, to radicals and radical nationalists in other countries may have provoked Soviet propaganda into a desperate attempt to exploit the opportunity provided by the anniversary of Lenin's birth.

C. METHODS, PROBLEMS, AND RESULTS

1. Methods

Imperialist propaganda uses, according to Secretary Brezhnev, "refined methods and powerful technical media."[224] Perhaps Soviet propaganda is less refined, but it compensates for this by its massiveness. Following the Twenty-fourth Party Congress, *Pravda* proclaimed that propaganda work in the Soviet Union was being carried on by 1,100,000 theoretically trained and politically mature Communists, that is, by one propagandist for every 150 persons in the Soviet Union sixteen years of age and over. The documents of the Party Congress were printed in various languages of the USSR in twenty million copies.[225] When the 1973–74 academic year opened in October 1973, the Moscow city Party secretary for ideology and propaganda announced that 100,000 Party propagandists were active in Moscow.[226]

Since a substantial proportion of the newspapers and journals published in the Soviet Union contribute in varying degrees to spreading Party messages,

[222] Moscow broadcast in Mandarin to China, March 7, 1973.
[223] *Komsomol'skaya pravda,* February 26, 1970. A Soviet joke from this period tells of a couple who go to a furniture store and order a bed large enough for three persons. "Why for three persons?" "Because Lenin is always with us." Chatel, *Carnets russes,* pp. 245–246.
[224] Report of the Central Committee, Twenty-fourth Party Congress.
[225] *Pravda,* September 18, 1971, pp. 2–3.
[226] *New York Times,* October 1, 1973.

the 140 million copies of newspapers per issue and 150 million copies of journals per issue published in the USSR provide impressive indoctrination facilities for the Party, not to mention, of course, the Party's control over TV, radio, and movies.[227] DOSAAF publishes newspapers and journals with a total circulation of 3.5 million copies; that is, well over one out of every 100 copies of newspapers and magazines issued in the Soviet Union is a DOSAAF military-patriotic publication.[228] In 1972, DOSAAF had 3,000 propagandists operating out of its various groups in Volgograd Oblast.[229] This *oblast* had, in 1970, a population of 2,345,000. Thus, DOSAAF alone provided one propagandist for every 500 persons in the *oblast* sixteen years of age and older.

Military personnel, being a captive audience, receive more intensive indoctrination than probably any other major sector of the Soviet population. Commanders, political organs, and Party organizations in the military are called upon to arrange matters "so that not a single serviceman is outside continuous political influence."[230] Patriotic printed matter, radio, movies, and TV[231] are supplemented by political lessons (lectures, seminars, individual study), special "thematic evenings" on propaganda subjects, attendance at evening universities of Marxism-Leninism,[232] patriotic and political ceremonies and gatherings, "cultural" evenings at officers' and servicemen's clubs that turn out to be additional indoctrination ("the work of these officer clubs . . . must be distinguished by high ideological content"),[233] Party and Komsomol meetings, political meetings with civilian groups, individual discussions with political officers, and conferences on fundamental questions of Marxism-Leninism.

An article describing political work on a submarine about to set sail on a training voyage points out that fuel and food requirements can be calculated exactly, and it is also possible to calculate approximately "the demand for spiritual 'fuel.' " Some of the measures for just one day taken by the submarine's political officer are listed as follows: a political information session

---

[227] *KZ,* August 10, 1972. About thirteen to fourteen million persons attend movies every day in the Soviet Union. Soviet TV reaches 70 percent of the country's population. Ibid. On the other hand, the secretary of the Communist Party of Georgia has reported that there are 2,000 populated centers in the republic without radio, "and this means that a considerable portion of the rural population is left without effective ideological influence." *Sovetskaya kul'tura,* July 6, 1973, p. 2.

[228] *Sovetskiy patriot,* November 29, 1972, p. 2.

[229] Ibid.

[230] *KVS,* no. 4, February 1973, pp. 3–9.

[231] In the last five years the provision of TV sets to troops has trebled and the supply of radio sets has increased tenfold. *KZ,* November 1, 1972, p. 2.

[232] Attendance at these institutions has increased approximately 20 percent in the past two to three years.

[233] *KZ,* June 17, 1972, p. 2. The Leningrad district officers' club has a lecture bureau that provided approximately 2,000 lectures just on the subject of the Twenty-fourth Party Congress. "All the work of these officers' clubs . . . represents an indispensable part of Party political work in the forces." Ibid.

on the theme "Sailor, protect and add to the heroic traditions of the Baltic submariners"; radio newscasts on "Talks by advanced production workers in the socialist competition in honor of the Fiftieth Anniversary of the USSR"; a seminar with warrant officers on "Help subordinates to fulfill socialist pledges"; a radio meeting on "Roll call of outstanding combat posts"; an evening meeting on "Unabating hatred for the enemies of the socialist motherland"; and at the evening's end, verses and songs about the motherland.[234]

Political indoctrination is not the responsibility only of the political officers, the political organs, the Party organizations, and the Komsomol and Party activists. "The foremost duty of every officer is to carry the ideas of the Party to the masses of soldiers and to conduct political work."[235] Officer cadets at the Leningrad Higher Combined Arms Command School are, in addition to their military studies, instructed in the art of propaganda and political lecturing and practice their new skills on local garrison troops.[236] Requiring nonpolitical officers and commanders to do political work not only provides for a larger personnel devoted to indoctrination; it is viewed as a way of indoctrinating the commanders themselves.

The Party organs responsible for military indoctrination are no less insistent than other military and civilian administrations on the need to employ scientific methods. General Yepishev urges that in Party political work, fuller consideration must be given to scientific recommendations.[237] This eagerness to associate oneself with the prestige of science is sometimes, even in the field of military training, largely a mere slogan, involving in fact only a modest exploitation of scientific knowledge and methods. This is especially so in political indoctrination and propaganda work. Scientific knowledge or insight here sometimes confines itself to an awareness of the emotional impact of music and the value of ritual and tradition, accompanied by the belief that traditions can be invented and established overnight.[238]

2. Problems

Soviet propagandists in the military forces experience a number of difficulties

[234] Ibid., June 10, 1972, p. 2.

[235] Ibid., April 15, 1972, p. 2.

[236] *KZ*, July 25, 1973, p. 2. *KZ* criticizes officers who, in reporting on the probationary period of officer cadets, make little mention of their propaganda work. During the probationary period, the cadet officer should do his lecturing before his unit commander and political worker as well as the leader of the probationary training.

[237] Ibid., March 28, 1973, pp. 2–3.

[238] Speaking of a new ceremony introduced in Zaporozhye province, a writer in *Pravda* proclaims, "This is the first time our province has had one of these celebrations on such a scale. Henceforth it will become a tradition." *Pravda*, April 18, 1973, p. 3. In the article "Traditions Are Born," *Pravda* points out the value of television in Central Asia in weaning people away from "outmoded traditions" and presenting "attractive and democratic alternatives" to the "backwardness of the old customs." *Pravda*, March 23, 1973, p.3.

in the pursuit of their indoctrination objectives, some more or less beyond their control, others of their own making.

1. The 1967 reduction in the term of service for draftees by one year deprived the political organs and activists of the longer period of influence to which they were able to subject earlier draftees. This is probably not a very serious handicap. Given the intensity of Soviet indoctrination, it is unlikely that what has not been achieved in two years (army) or three years (navy) could be achieved by an additional year of indoctrination.

2. A more serious problem for the propagandists is the introduction of two periods of call-up each year, requiring them to deal with large numbers of fresh draftees twice annually.[239] Since units are often composed of draftees with no service record and those with six months, one year, and one and one-half years service, the older recruits often find themselves listening several times to some of the standard indoctrination subjects.

3. The recruits and younger officers are now, compared with Soviet military personnel of even a few short years ago, substantially better educated, more independent, more critical, and consequently more resistant to persuasion. This situation has not only created new objectives for Soviet propagandists, but has at the same time made their realization much more difficult.

4. Soviet propaganda and indoctrination contents and procedures seem to be designed to maximize not conviction, but boredom. Party authorities in the military are not unaware of the often "dry and unexpressive"[240] "primitive superficial exposition"[241] and repetitive content of lectures, seminars, movies, and written indoctrination materials. Even officers show "at times an incomprehensible preference . . . for foreign films."[242] It is unlikely that this preference is quite as incomprehensible to the *Kommunist vooruzhennykh sil* writer as he pretends. *Krasnaya zvezda* recommends that "each day of rest should be used to restore a soldier's cheerfulness and strength, sufficient to last him throughout the [next] training period."[243] But recreation uncontaminated by ideological, political, and volunteer work is hardly available for the performance of this function.

5. Soviet indoctrination in military and civil life is often called upon to perform almost impossible tasks, given the access of substantial sectors of the population to competing sources of information, and given also the direct experience that contradicts Party claims and that leads to an inevitable discounting of Party-controlled sources. Soviet attacks on and rebuttals of non-Soviet statements not only indicate that non-Soviet sources penetrate the

---

[239] *KZ,* January 26, 1973, pp. 2–3.
[240] Ibid., April 14, 1973, p. 3.
[241] *KVS,* no. 3, February 1973, pp. 9–17.
[242] Ibid., no. 9, May 1972, pp. 18–27.
[243] *KZ,* June 17, 1972, p. 2.

Soviet Union too deeply to be ignored, but adds to their circulation. The reimposition of jamming following the Soviet invasion of Czechoslovakia and the fact that several years later Soviet propaganda still tried occasionally to persuade the population that the Soviet troops entered not as "interventionists" or "occupiers," but as "friends," is typical of the difficulty Soviet propaganda faces in its attempts to achieve credibility.[244]

6. Soviet propaganda and indoctrination is not notable for its measured, let alone subtle, approach to problems of persuasion. Occasions such as the Twenty-fourth Party Congress, the Fiftieth Anniversary of the USSR, the Fifty-fifth Anniversary of the Armed Forces, and the One Hundredth Anniversary of the Birth of Lenin produce a massive outpouring of propaganda whose intemperate extremes in the case of the Lenin anniversary were, as we noted earlier, severely criticized by *Komsomol'skaya pravda.*[245] The heavy-handed excesses of Soviet progaganda are in part nurtured by a more or less total monopoly of domestic media and by the inertia of propaganda practices that were more suitable to the period of the Iron Curtain and to a population less educated and less open to western contacts than is today's. An increasing Party respect for and interest in the guidance of contemporary social science does not seem to have reduced the crudity of Soviet propaganda practices.

7. Neither the political officers appointed at the company level nor the Party activists in the company or battalion units strike one as having a genuine fervor capable of moving their audiences. Even given some of the personal qualities of a Savonarola, it is doubtful that lessons and lectures whose detailed outlines are provided by the indoctrination authorities could provide a substance or scope that would permit such personal qualities to make an impression on the troops. The professional military propagandist is often more interested in addressing "an imposing audience" at the regimental level than talking to troop details in the subunits.[246] In addition, a substantial amount of propaganda is carried on by persons not trained in the academies for political officers. "In some places political information lectures are literally assigned to everybody in succession. . . . It is hardly possible to agree with this practice."[247] This statement is significant not only for what it suggests concerning the adequacy of the lectures and their effect on the auditors, but also for what it implies about the attitude toward propaganda work as a *corvée* that everybody ought to share. Despite *Krasnaya zvezda's* criticism of "nonprofessional" indoctrination work, *Kommunist vooruzhennykh sil,* the principal Party authority on indoctrination in the armed forces, recommends that sergeants and

---

[244] See, for example, *Sovetskaya Moldaviya,* February 21, 1970, pp. 2–3.

[245] It was also *Komsomol'skaya pravda* that wryly remarked that according to the Soviet press there are no items in "shortage," only items in "high demand." *Komsomol'skaya pravda,* August 4, 1971, p. 2.

[246] *KVS,* no. 4, February 1971, pp. 35–39.

[247] *KZ,* May 6, 1972, p. 2.

petty officers be called on to do indoctrination work. "First of all, the NCOs should explain to the fighting men Lenin's ideas on patriotism, and they should explain the decisions of the Twenty-fourth Congress and propagandize the achievements of the Soviet people."[248] *Kommunist vooruzhennykh sil* also recommends that the NCOs first be given some lectures by the political officer, but this handing down successively of a political message already sterile in its first stage from *Kommunist vooruzhennykh sil* to the political officers to the NCOs to the troops does not seem calculated to stimulate either interest or belief.

8. The large number of persons engaged in propaganda work and the enormous amount of propaganda material in written or oral form that they produce almost inevitably mean that, quite apart from dullness and "formalism," the wrong line is sometimes taken, or a line that detracts from the desired image of the military. Two tales of army life published by none other than the Military Publishing House itself in Moscow portrayed two young men who had been drafted into the missile troops after being expelled from Moscow University for low grades. The anti-intellectual bias of some Party and military authorities was too clearly revealed for Party comfort in the comment of an officer: "It won't be easy making men out of you pen-pushers." Nor did the Soviet critic of these tales care for the humor in a cynical statement by one of the draftees concerning propaganda on the unity of Soviet peoples.[249] Soviet propagandists often have a hard time treading judiciously between pitfalls— military newspapers should provide material on the heroic exploits of Soviet soldiers, but they should not "concentrate only on exploits that end with heroes dying. . . . Many war veterans currently reminiscing about the past tell only of hard sacrifices and the death of their friends."[250] Similarly, propagandists must stimulate people to take civil defense seriously, but they must not exaggerate the power and dangers of nuclear weapons.

9. Soviet propagandists in the military are handicapped by the frequent need to carry on their activity during evening and other hours deemed part of free time. The reception of material that for the most part is not intrinsically entertaining, interesting, or educational can hardly be enhanced by being imposed on leisure time. This imposition is even greater because free time is whittled away by numerous other demands.[251] Political officers, eager to use "free time" for political work, find it difficult to refrain from organization and formality, which destroy the myth of voluntary participation. "Discussions in the wardroom have many possibilities. Of course, there are people who keep

---

[248] *KVS,* no. 8, April 1973, pp. 73–80.

[249] *Oktyabr',* February 1973, p. 219.

[250] *Sovetskaya Litva,* August 7, 1973, p. 2.

[251] At an air force garrison, Komsomol activists issued a challenge for "a garrison of immaculate order." As a result, "Each soldier will plant five or six trees and work for fifty hours of his free time toward the enhancement of the garrison." *KZ,* September 28, 1972, p. 1.

track of the attendance at these discussions, those who will draw up plans that will have everything but vitality."[252]

The concern in Soviet political and military circles with Soviet youth has led to several steps to improve and intensify Soviet indoctrination of the youth population, both in and out of the military. The prestige of scientific analysis is invoked here, too. "The Military Council of the air force, political organs, and Party organizations have made a penetrating, in-depth analysis of the processes that are taking place in contemporary youth circles."[253] Even the private who refused "to crawl" (see p. 214) is treated in the spirit of modern progressive education. "The commander did not wound this man's pride, but showed him by concrete examples that the unit is a single organism and here everything must fit and operate harmoniously. Finally, the recruit understood that he was wrong." Another recruit, well educated and well read, who apparently felt that he knew more than most people, was treated patiently and "shown that it was knowledge of political literature and of the Leninist political line that was the important thing."[254] Though political literature outranks poetry, a modernizing trend has led, despite some criticism from conservative quarters, to the occasional substitution of literary topics in place of conventional political-military subjects in "thematic evenings."[255]

Party concern with youth does not simply rely on political indoctrination in the restricted sense of a propaganda barrage. It includes a continuing program of control over youth life and youth activity that sees "service in the armed forces as an important stage in the formation of the individual—a stage that begins in the family, in school, and in production."[256]

3. Results

How effective is Soviet indoctrination?

The persistent and costly indoctrination and propaganda programs of the Party in the military forces suggest that the Party views them as productive, at least in the sense that the state of mind and the behavior of those subjected to them are made less undesirable than they otherwise would be and sufficiently so to justify the material and political costs of the effort. One cannot be entirely confident that such convictions are in fact widespread in the Party. Indoctrination and propaganda have been such basic elements in Soviet political style and political weaponry for so long and they employ such a large

[252] Ibid., September 30, 1972, p. 2.
[253] *Kryl'ya rodiny,* January 1971, pp. 18–19.
[254] *KZ,* December 20, 1969, p. 3.
[255] Ibid., May 23, 1973, p. 4.
[256] General Yepishev, *Pravda,* November 28, 1972, pp. 2–3.

number of specialists, that their continuation and even intensification need hardly imply considered Party views of their effectiveness. Besides, "cost effectiveness" estimates, if any, are likely to be weighted in favor of indoctrination campaigns by a Soviet tendency to view much of the propaganda effort as being cost-free. The Party does not seem to understand very well the nature of opportunity costs in this area. It is easy to suppose that some Party spokesmen and propagandists are convinced that large-scale political indoctrination is quite essential and certainly as valuable as its intensity and ubiquity would imply.

Nonetheless, clear, confident claims for the proven value of the military indoctrination program as a whole are surprisingly difficult to find, and Soviet propagandists themselves are more inclined to stress the importance of their objectives than the success of their programs. Confidence is often expressed in the value of certain special techniques or limited programs—singing, telling "stirring" tales of World War II, taking mass hiking tours to the sites of military victories—but these are, on the whole, minor accompaniments of the major indoctrination effort, and hardly any evidence is ever cited that the confidence in them is justified. Current Soviet indoctrination efforts are much easier to understand as a response to felt problems than as a response to past indoctrination successes.

The success of some programs is presumably easily measured—for example, the recruiting programs to draw students into officer cadet schools. "The improvement in military patriotic education can be gauged from the . . . growing interest displayed by the young in being an officer."[257] But these programs, even if successful, are not so much a tribute to indoctrination in the conventional sense as they are a tribute to the introduction of preinduction military training in secondary schools and to the use of the military instructors in the schools to encourage enrollment in officer cadet academies.[258]

Occasionally *Kommunist vooruzhennykh sil* reacts against the common tendency to measure indoctrination success in terms of the amount of propaganda material issued, the number of lectures given, the number of movies shown, the number of persons participating in tours of patriotic sites, or the number of persons making pledges in socialist competition. "At times an attempt was made to measure directly the results of propaganda in . . . tons [of materials]. Such an oversimplified approach has been criticized. . . . The effectiveness of ideological work is determined primarily by the degree to which it influences the solution to problems of developing a new man. . . . Effectiveness is expressed in high labor enthusiasm and in the sociopolitical activity of the Soviet man."[259]

---

[257] *KZ,* November 29, 1972, p. 3.
[258] Ibid., September 14, 1971, p. 1, and *Kazakhstanskaya pravda,* February 18, 1971, pp. 2–3.
[259] *KVS,* no. 3, February 1973, pp. 9–17. The dangers of equating the issuing of materials with their consumption is illustrated in an inquiry by DOSAAF into its own propaganda activities.

Unfortunately, we have no means of assessing Soviet indoctrination in terms of its creation of "high labor enthusiasm" or participation "in the sociopolitical activity of the Soviet man."[260] But we have every reason to believe that the application of these criteria of effectiveness would hardly benefit the reputation of Soviet propagandists.

Purely "formal" results frequently conceal a high level of ineffectiveness. Even the department of Marxism-Leninism of the Kharkov Guards Higher Tank Command School concedes that the students in the department "get a three instead of a failure or a five instead of a three."[261]

An instructor at one of the evening universities of Marxism-Leninism for field grade officers complains that the students do well as long as they are reciting from their study folders, but when the study folders are put aside and they have to answer a question without them, they falter. "Imaginary activity on the part of the students is passed off as actual achievement."[262] Both in military training and in indoctrination it is clear that a great deal of " 'prettying up,' conceit, carelessness, indifference, simplification, and indulgences" occurs.[263] The meaninglessness of many Soviet measures of performance is neatly revealed in the statement that the struggle for high performance "is not just a struggle for good indicators. Above all it is a struggle for effectiveness."[264]

Given the pressures on soldiers and officers and the dull content of what they have to absorb from indoctrination and study, it is little wonder that "some comrades" restrict their studies to "listening to lectures . . . making no particular effort to study primary sources independently. . . . They spend their leisure time on useless, sometimes dubious pursuits."[265] Such people, *Krasnaya zvezda* continues, "who have an irresponsible attitude to their ideological and moral growth frequently suffer from maladies such as political apathy, passiveness in work and social life, and indifference." There seems to be little doubt that political apathy is widespread, but despite such acknowledgments, *Krasnaya zvezda* is far from ready to concede that Soviet political

---

Of 100 copies of a book distributed to the Lithuanian warehouse of DOSAAF, only six were ever distributed. Of 260 copies of a political exercise, only twelve were sold to local DOSAAF committees. *Sovetskiy patriot,* April 11, 1973, p. 2. Of course, even had all copies been distributed or sold, this would not have guaranteed that they would be read, or even if read, that they would have been propagandistically effective.

[260] Such participation appears in fact to have increased in 1973, certainly not as a result of Soviet indoctrination, but as a result of the 1973–74 "exchange of Party cards," that is, as the result of a threat of expulsion or disciplinary action by the Party.

[261] The same allegation is made with respect to training in technical military subjects. An engineer with high grades who turned out to know no engineering "that could be relied on" was referred to as "a fairly typical" case. *KZ,* November 15, 1972, p. 2. The title of the cited article is "We write 'five' when we know it is 'three.' "

[262] Ibid., May 16, 1973, p. 2.

[263] *KVS,* no. 7, April 1973, pp. 16–26

[264] Ibid., pp. 27–33.

[265] *KZ,* October 22, 1972, p. 1.

indoctrination itself contributes to the political apathy it is supposed to over-come.

If we reexamine the themes and objectives of Soviet propaganda that were discussed earlier, it is evident in a number of instances that success was hardly to be anticipated. Thus, minority nationalist sentiments, developed from child-hood in family and community and reinforced by the observation of Russian dominance, are not likely to be dissipated in the army (or in civil life) by repeated affirmations that "state pride," "Soviet patriotism," or "multina-tional pride" should replace them. Career advantages accruing to those who master the Russian language may in the long run lead to changes favorable to "state pride," but there is little evidence as yet that "Soviet patriotism" is undermining the identification of minority individuals with their respective national groups. In any event, whatever changes may eventually occur in this respect, they will be the result of political and social development inside and outside the society and probably will have little to do with Soviet indoctrina-tion efforts to hasten them.

Similar conclusions seem justified with respect to indoctrination efforts directed toward youth. Efforts to lessen the shock of military service, to impose restraints on a "tough" attitude toward recruits, and to take account of mod-ern youth's cultural interests have no doubt softened, if only very modestly, the rigors of military service. But it is not very likely that Marxism-Leninism as interpreted by the Party and political information as provided by Party propagandists have any great effect in modifying those youth attitudes and aspirations that most concern the political authorities in a direction favorable to the Party. Party and military authorities are not entirely unaware of the limited value of exhortation and other propaganda activities in such circum-stances. Many political groups use such methods in an attempt to control tendencies that are deeply embedded in the society, but they can only very partially, with very great difficulty and at great cost, be subjected to control.

Ineffective as superficial methods may be in changing attitudes and behav-ior, they nonetheless are not without usefulness to the regime that uses them. Their energetic employment masks to some extent, both from the authorities themselves and from the subject population, the uncertain and limited control that the authorities are able to exercise, at least by these means. The Party's ability to force indoctrination on the population very probably contributes to the leadership's sense of domination and control and helps to convince those subjected to this enforced indoctrination that the Party is indeed powerful. Perhaps, too, propaganda and indoctrination reduce conflicts among the au-thorities, some of whom might otherwise be inclined to emphasize harsher methods of persuasion.

When Soviet military indoctrination deals with Soviet enemies and poten-tial enemies, it does not face the type of deep-rooted obstacles that affect indoctrination on nationalism and youth behavior. This suggests a greater likelihood of propaganda successes in these areas. In addition, many of these themes concern events outside the country and are not so easily subject to the check of direct experience. Further, they revolve very largely around the United States as the leader of western capitalism, a country for which earlier cold-war conflicts and more recently the Vietnam war have long provided favorable circumstances for Soviet propaganda. Finally, with respect to another enemy, Communist China, Soviet indoctrination has even more favorable conditions. Mass anti-Chinese sentiments probably have a strong racial component, but this serves Soviet propaganda objectives as well as, if not better than, one largely based on political beliefs that are generally subject to more rapid change.

Despite the relatively favorable circumstances under which anti-imperialist and national security propaganda themes are pursued as compared with themes that revolve around domestic issues, the former also pose substantial problems for the propagandist. The embarrassed, hesitant, changeable and contradictory content of Soviet indoctrination indicates that current Soviet audiences—as well as Soviet propagandists—find some difficulty in believing in "the crisis of capitalism" in a period in which capitalism has provided food, machinery, and industrial organization to the Soviet Union; or believing in the "imperialist (military) threat" in a period in which the symbolic and practical manifestations of détente have been paraded before the Soviet people.

One cannot, of course, conclude with confidence that Soviet military indoctrination serves Party and military objectives only minimally, or in fact negatively, although it would be difficult to provide evidence that would justify rejecting this hypothesis. Even direct studies of the Soviet population might not provide conclusions of high confidence, and it is doubtful that Party leaders and propaganda specialists really know how effective or ineffective Soviet military indoctrination has been, or what the consequences of a large-scale reduction of indoctrination time and effort would be. Perhaps in the future the Soviets will be better able to evaluate their indoctrination efforts. *Pravda,* in discussing the tasks of social science, pays particular attention to the need for centers to do public opinion studies and to evaluate the effectiveness of press, radio, television, and propaganda.[266] The Academy of Social Sciences attached to the CPSU Central Committee has been asked to devise and organize, in conjunction with the CP republic Central Committees, studies of the effectiveness of the massive new program of "economic education of the working people."[267]

[266] *Pravda,* September 14, 1973, p. 3.
[267] *Ekonomicheskaya gazeta,* no. 39, 1973, p. 2. It is characteristic of Soviet mass programs that this program, reported to involve thirty-one million persons in 1972–73, will receive its evaluation only after a large-scale, massive all-union effort has been made. Small-scale, experimental pilot projects in the mass indoctrination area rarely seem to appeal to Soviet administrators or Party leaders.

Soviet political indoctrination is only one part of a social system and control apparatus that is attempting to create the New Soviet Man. The latter, in the sense understood by the Party—an industrious, sober, conscientious, well-disciplined, literate, cultured, hardworking, and self-sacrificing person devoted to the Party and to the state—has hardly emerged as a dominant social type, but on the other hand, it would be equally incorrect to suppose that Soviet society produces the same distribution of human political and social types as do western nations.[268] But as far as the more immediate objectives of Soviet propaganda are concerned, our materials strongly suggest that certainly not the military, and probably not even the Party, receives adequate benefits from the immense effort devoted to it.

[268] Valid and reliable data for the empirical study of these matters are as yet much too limited to permit conclusions. Interesting glimpses into one or another dimension of these problems is occasionally provided by Soviet or other observers. Thus a Soviet investigator writes, "When I ask schoolchildren what qualities they want to develop in themselves, they usually answer 'a strong will' or 'self-control.' " "What about feelings?" They reply, "Of course! Feelings, too! But you have to know how to control them." *Izvestia,* June 15, 1973, p. 5. This suggests at least one Party success in molding personality. See Nathan Leites, *A Study of Bolshevism* (Glencoe, Illinois, 1953) pp. 186–208; and chapter VIII below on the emphasis by the Party and the military on the importance of self-control.

The Party and the Army

The armed forces in the Soviet Union do not have a monopoly on capabilities for the exercise of physical force. The Committee of State Security (KGB) controls the border troops, and the Ministry of Internal Affairs (MVD) the security troops. In addition, of course, the USSR has its police forces, generally referred to as militia.[1] Nonetheless, it is evident that the Ministry of Defense, with its more than three million ground, naval, air defense, and rocket forces, has a far greater potential for the exercise of physical force than any other element in the Soviet state.

Except where military regimes are in power, that is, where the leaders of government are also leaders or controllers of the military, the military's large potential for physical force often poses difficult problems regarding their subordination to the authority of government.[2] In the USSR, where political

[1] The Soviet militia (police) is not a paramilitary force in the sense in which the term "militia" is customarily employed in western countries.

[2] Of course, even where military regimes are in power, generals may find themselves threatened by colonels, or colonels by captains and sergeants.

power is concentrated in a party—or rather at the top levels of a party—that has pursued with great energy total control and total obedience and loyalty to itself, it is to be expected that Party concern with and involvement in the armed forces will be correspondingly pronounced. And indeed, this is the case. This involvement does not simply appear at the top levels of the Ministry of Defense, or at the top commands of the military districts, the services and arms, and the force groups, but penetrates to every sector and level of the military establishment down to the lowest echelon. Party surveillance and Party direction and control of the military forces are implemented through political organs that operate throughout the armed forces.

The Party does not rely solely on its political organs in the military or on individual officers and servicemen. The KGB plays, no doubt, an important surveillance role, but the unclassified Soviet materials used in this study maintain a total silence on this instrument of control, and we shall, perforce, do the same. The Komsomol, the People's Control groups, and DOSAAF are additional instruments under close Party direction. The Party leaders have, of course, instruments other than the groups and individuals who report to them or who implement their preferences. As controllers of the state, the economy, and the society, the Party leaders, in addition to exercising budgetary leverage, can provide or deny individuals and groups access to an enormous range of services and opportunities and can impose severe sanctions.

Many discussions of civil-military relations focus, understandably enough, on actual or potential conflicts between professional military interests and constraints imposed by political authorities. Conflicts of this nature can broaden into a struggle for supreme power, in which the motive on the military side may not be a desire to run the state and society, but rather a concern for the prerogatives of the military and the pursuit of national and foreign objectives related to the development and uses of military power. In many contemporary societies the military desire to displace civilians as controllers of national destiny has also precipitated military takeovers. In the Soviet case the strength of the civil power centers, principally the Party, and the latter's by no means indifferent attitude to the claims of the military have prevented tensions from reaching such a stage of acuteness.[3] This, however, does not mean that conflicts have been reduced to the point where they no longer affect military or Party behavior. We shall examine some current manifestations of tension below.

[3] On tensions and conflicts in Soviet army-Party relations, the reader will find Roman Kolkowicz, *The Soviet Military and the Communist Party* (Princeton, 1967) an indispensable guide. The reader may also wish to consult Ellis Joffe, *Party and Army: Professionalism and Political Control in the Chinese Officer Corps, 1949–1964* (East Asian Research Center, Harvard University, 1965).

Despite the importance of tensions in army-Party relations, there are other aspects of the relationship that deserve study. The Party makes—or attempts to make—a contribution to the effectiveness of military training and of operational activities. It imposes procedures (for example, socialist competition) on the military that are intended to achieve objectives at the least cost. Its policies on manpower requirements, recruitment, personnel selection and promotion, military training, indoctrination, discipline, and morale building affect the military in many ways other than their possible role as sources of Party-army tension and conflict. The nature of these interventions and their importance for Soviet military organization were dealt with in the preceding chapters. In the present chapter we shall only refer on occasion to this Party role.

A. ORGANIZATION

The supreme organ of the Party is the Party Congress, which is supposed to be convened at least once every four years. The Twenty-third Party Congress met in March 1966, and the Twenty-fourth Party Congress in April 1971, one year late. The congress elects a Central Committee, which is required to meet at least once every six months and which guides the Party in between meetings of the congress. The Central Committee, in its turn, has a political bureau (Politburo) that directs the work of the Central Committee in between meetings of the latter. The Central Committee also has a secretariat and a Commission of Party Control that deals with Party disciplinary matters. A parallel organizational structure exists in the regional, territorial, and republic Party organizations. At the base of the Party there are 365,000 (1971) primary Party organizations or units. These Party units exist in industrial and agricultural enterprises, in offices, in villages, and in units of the Soviet army and navy wherever there are at least three Party members.

The highest political organ of the Soviet armed forces is the Main Political Administration of the Soviet army and navy, currently headed by Army General A. Yepishev. It operates with the rights of a department of the Central Committee of the CPSU. The Main Political Administration guides lesser political administrations of the army and navy, as well as the Party and Komsomol organizations. In accordance with Party decisions, it directs ideological work, selects political worker personnel, and controls and monitors the carrying out of decisions of the CPSU and directives of the Ministry of Defense by political organs and Party organizations.[4] The phrase "political organs and Party organizations" draws attention to two types of Party elements in the

[4] N. A. Petrovichev et al. [*Party Structure: A Study Aid*], Moscow, 1971, pp. 215–217.

armed forces: (1) political sections functionally similar to the Main Political Administration (but of course subordinate to it) attached to the various commands of the Soviet forces at all echelons; and (2) the Party organizations proper, the primary organizations that contain the actual membership of the Party. A member of a political administration or a political section is also, and necessarily, a member of a primary Party organization, and it is this latter membership that constitutes his Party membership.

Subordinate to the Main Political Administration are the political administrations of the services of the armed forces and of the military districts, groups of forces, and air defense districts. The status of these political administrations underwent an important change in 1973. In March 1973, General Yepishev, in a lengthy statement that appeared in *Krasnaya zvezda*, revealed the existence of two new "documents of great political importance."[5] The Regulation on Political Organs applies to the various echelons of political administrations, and the Instruction to Party Organizations applies to the primary Party organizations. These documents replaced similar documents that had been in effect since 1963. General Yepishev pointed out that "in particular . . . the political administrations of military districts, PVO districts, groups of forces and fleets, and the political sections of armies and flotillas exercise leadership over Party political work. . . . The political administrations of military districts and groups of forces are the senior political organs in relation to the political sections located in the district territory. These political sections are obliged to report to the political administrations of military districts and groups of forces on Party political work and the state of military discipline."[6]

The raising of the political administrations of the military districts and groups of forces to the status of "senior political organs" seems consistent with, and may be related to, an emphasis that coincided with it on strengthening the relations between civilian Party organizations and the Party organizations in the military. The civilian Party is organized along territorial lines, and the desire to enforce coordination and cooperation between elements of the civil

[5] *KZ,* March 2, 1973, pp. 2–3.

[6] Ibid. See also *KVS,* no. 7, April 1973, pp. 16–26. "Due to the fact that units and large units of various branches of the armed forces and airborne and railroad groups are located in the territories of military districts and groups of forces, the statute establishes the principle of their relationships. The political administrations of military districts are senior political agencies in relation to the political branches of those . . . units. These political branches report to the political administrations of military districts and groups of forces on Party political work and the state of military discipline." Note also that the formation of Party committees and units where there are less than 100 Communists is authorized by the political administrations of the military districts or groups of forces in which they are located and not by the political administrations of the arms and services to which they belong. Ibid. See also *KZ,* August 14, 1973, p. 2, for a further indication that an air force political branch in a military district is subordinate to the political administration of that district.

Party and the military Party would probably be facilitated by the heightened role of the political administrations of the military districts. This may represent increased surveillance and supervision by the civilian Party of the Party-in-the-military, although, of course, such a conclusion is not explicitly confirmed in the various statements dealing with civil-military Party relations.[7]

Party commissions preserve Communist morality and purity, examine decisions of the primary Party organizations concerning admissions and expulsions, supervise similar decisions of the Komsomol, and deal with questions connected with the removal of Party punishment.

The "key link" in the political apparatus of the armed forces is the political department of the regiment (army) and the ship (navy). This follows from the fact that the regiment and the ship are "the basic units" of the armed forces.[8] From an administrative viewpoint, the justification for viewing the political department of the regiment as the "key link" is probably its ready access to company units and to the primary Party organizations at the base of the pyramid. The primary Party organizations do not routinely come under the direction and supervision of the political apparatus of divisional, and especially higher, headquarters, although, of course, this happens in individual instances where some special difficulty or scandal lends particular importance to a primary organization.

The political organ of the regiment includes the regimental deputy commander for political affairs, a trained propagandist, and the club officer, all of whom are appointed and not elected.[9] The regimental deputy commander for political affairs is responsible for Party political work and shares responsibility for the state of military discipline and preparedness with the commander. The regimental propagandist is trained in theory and methods at special officer schools. With the assistance of the deputy political commander and Party secretaries in the primary Party organizations, the propagandist selects the agitators who do much of the day-to-day work of getting information sheets and inspirational materials to the troops. The officer in charge of the regimental club also has political functions, in addition to being concerned with sports activities, the club library, and other cultural facilities.[10]

The basic political work with the troops is carried out at the company level, although battalions, too, have their own deputy commander for political affairs. The institution of a deputy commander for political affairs at the company level is a recent (1967) and important development. We will deal

---

[7] On civil-military Party relations see *KVS*, no. 6, March 1973, pp. 40–49; ibid., no. 7, April 1973, pp. 16–26; *KZ*, March 22, 1973, pp. 2–3; *KVS*, no. 3, February 1973, pp. 3–9; *Pravda*, March 27, 1973, p. 2; editorial, *KZ*, April 10, 1973.

[8] Petrovichev et al. [*Party Structure: A Study Aid*], pp. 220–226.

[9] Ibid., pp. 226–228.

[10] Ibid.

more fully with him below. Here we note only that he is appointed and performs his functions with the assistance of an elected company Party secretary and the Party personnel that are elected to the company Party bureau. They, together with the Party agitators, generally constitute the unit "Party activists."

The number of officers attached to the political department of a division is substantial. It is not uncommon to read that a group of such officers has been detached in order to work for a week or two in a battalion where training and disciplinary problems had arisen. Presumably, such an assignment of a group of officers must be made without entirely depleting the political department of the division. Thus, a group of officers detached from a political department "studied the status and effectiveness of Party political work [in a battalion], attending many exercises and held many discussions with the personnel in all the companies. . . . They participated in preparing and conducting Party and Komsomol meetings and general meetings for the military personnel. They were to be found in the vehicle pool, at morning inspection, and at the evening roll call, and also at the mounting of the guard. With the assistance of these officers, the commander and deputy for political matters and the Party organization were able to carry out a great amount of work toward eliminating deficiencies."[11]

Of the numerous subsidiary organizations directly controlled by the Party, the Komsomol (Young Communist League) is the most important for the military, given the youthfulness of most of the armed forces personnel. With approximately thirty-two million members (1974), the Komsomol is twice the size of the Communist Party. In many units almost all of the draftees and the younger junior officers are Komsomol members. The Komsomol has functions parallel to those of the Communist Party, but with special reference to youth. Its organizational structure is similar to that of the Party, and thus it has a Central Committee at the top and at the company level, a Komsomol bureau, and a unit secretary. As we shall see later, the Party maintains close control over the Komsomol apparatus.

Subsidiary organizations of some importance are the People's Control groups that operate under Party supervision. The committees, groups, and posts of People's Control act as watchdogs over the use of funds and material, and are particularly dedicated to the prevention of waste and corruption. In the military, the People's Control groups direct their basic efforts toward economy in the use of military matériel: they check on the accounting of property, money, and equipment and promote improvement in living conditions and medical and trade services for military personnel. The control groups do not just bring shortcomings to light; they strive to eliminate them. In order

[11] *KVS,* no. 8, April 1972, pp. 39–45.

to improve the quality and increase the objectivity of checks made by People's Control groups, more engineering and other technical workers, who are not themselves responsible for matériel and military property, are now being appointed.[12]

The People's Control groups, according to the Party, "do not replace commanders, but operating with modes and methods peculiar to them, contribute in every possible way to an increase in discipline and effectiveness."[13] The members of the control groups in the military are "as a rule, the most disciplined, principled, authoritative soldiers and manual and office workers," that is, Party activists.[14] The Party affirms that People's Control acts "under the immediate supervision of the commanders, political bodies, and Party organizations,"[15] but in fact divisions and higher units of the People's Control groups are headed by the deputy of the directors of political sections; and in regiments and separate battalions by a member of their primary Party organizations.[16] People's Control is primarily a surveillance organization, but "the creation of military organs of People's Control is based on the high trust of the Party and government in Soviet military personnel."[17]

B. MEMBERSHIP[18]

In 1971 the Communist Party of the Soviet Union had close to 14.4 million members, of whom .6 million were candidate members.[19] In 1972, 22 percent of the army and navy were members of the Party (see table 3, line 33). Taking the army and navy in 1972 at 3.375 million,[20] it follows (1) that there were about 742,000 members of the Party in these forces, and (2) that about 5.2 percent of the Party, that is, about one out of every twenty Party members, was in the army and navy. If we take into account the fact that 22.2 percent

---

[12] *KZ,* April 18, 1972, p. 2.
[13] *KVS,* no. 22, November 1969, pp. 55–59.
[14] Ibid.
[15] Ibid.; no. 17, September 1973, pp. 82–86.
[16] Ibid., no. 22, November 1969, pp. 55–59.
[17] Colonel General I. Shikin, in preface to F. K. Bolovich and N. I. Kuznetsov [*People's Control in the Armed Forces of the USSR*], Moscow, 1973.
[18] In our initial discussion in this section on Party membership, the calculations and the estimates derived from them refer to 1971 and 1972. The 1974 data on the percentages of all officers and all military personnel who are Party members have become available and will be taken into account and discussed below (p. 265). Interesting changes that seem to have taken place between 1972 and 1974 make it desirable to deal with the former year first.
[19] Petrovichev et al. [*Party Structure: A Study Aid*], p. 60. In October 1974, *Pravda* announced that Party membership was over 15 million. *Pravda,* October 13, 1974, pp. 2–4.
[20] The International Institute for Strategic Studies, *The Military Balance for 1971-1972* (London, 1971), p. 5. The cited figure does not include security and border troops. The latter are excluded from our calculations, since Soviet data on Party membership refer only to the army and navy and not to the armed forces.

Table 3
Percent of Different Classes of Soviet Military Personnel Having Membership in the Communist Party or the Komsomol

Line		Year[a]	CP[b]	Komsomol	CP and Komsomol
	OFFICERS				
1.	All officers[1]	1920			20
2.	All officers[5]	1924	32		
3.	All officers[5]	1928	65		
4.	All officers[7]	1940			"about 80"
5.	All officers[1]	1941			79.9
6.	All officers[8]	1969			93
7.	Navy lieutenants[c, 4]	1969	"half"	"almost half"	"almost 100"
8.	"Young" officers[f, 19]	1970			"more than 85"
9.	"Young" officers[3]	1971	66.2	28.8	95.0
10.	Entering cadets[d, 6]	1971		97.5	
11.	"Outstanding company commanders"[9, 13]	1971	"more than 80"		
12.	All officers[10]	1971			90
13.	Navy officers[11]	1972			90
14.	Navy officers[12]	1972			"more than 90"
15.	All officers[9]	1972	"more than 80"		
16.	All officers[1]	1972	71	17	88
17.	All officers[21]	1972			"about 90"
18.	Navy officers[23]	1973			"about 90"
18a.	All officers[28]	1974	75		
	ENSIGNS, WARRANT OFFICERS				
19.	Ensigns, W/O[24]	1973	40	20	60
	ENLISTED MEN				
20.	"Soldiers"[8]	1969			"somewhat more than 80"
21.	Draftees[14]	1970		"somewhat more than 60"	
22.	Draftees[1]	1972		"three-quarters"	
23.	Moscow draftees[20]	1972		"three-quarters"	
24.	Draftees[23]	1973		"three-quarters"	
	OFFICERS AND ENLISTED MEN				
25.	All personnel[5]	1931			50[e]
26.	All personnel[5]	1933			60[e]
27.	All personnel[5]	1939			50[e]
28.	All personnel[2]	1939	11.5	41	52.5

Table 3 (Continued)

Line		Year[a]	CP[b]	Komsomol	CP and Komsomol
	OFFICERS AND ENLISTED MEN (Con't)				
29.	All personnel[17]	1971	"every fifth person"		
30.	All missile and artillery personnel[15]	1971			"in absolute majority"
31.	"Young" pilots[h, 18]	1971			"more than half"
32.	Air force personnel[16]	1972			"more than 80"
33.	All personnel[2]	1972	22	"more than 60"	"more than 82"
34.	All personnel[22]	1972			"more than 80"
35.	Strategic missile troops[25]	1972			"about 90"
36.	Air force[26]	1973			"more than 80"
37.	Moscow Military District[27]	1972			"about 90"
38.	All personnel[28]	1974	20		
39.	All personnel[29]	1974			80

NOTES

a. The year cited in this column is in some cases the year to which the statistics are specifically attributed by the source, but in many instances it is simply the year of publication of the source (when the latter presents the statistics as current).

b. The column CP should be assumed to include not only full Party members but also candidate members. Soviet military journals rarely bother to distinguish these two categories from one another.

c. A sample of 230 navy lieutenants and senior lieutenants chosen for a navy questionnaire study.

d. Officer cadets entering the combined arms and naval cadet academies in Leningrad.

e. These figures are cited by Garthoff as Party membership figures, but given the 1939 data in line 28, it is likely that they really represent Party plus Komsomol membership and should be in the last column.

f. Young officers "in units and subunits where combat readiness, combat and political training are . . . determined," that is, presumably in operational units, probably at regimental and lower echelons.

g. In the ground forces.

h. "In an outstanding unit."

SOURCES

1. *KVS,* no. 15, August 1972, pp. 9–16.
2. Ibid., no. 13, July 1972, pp. 9–15.
3. *Bloknot agitatora,* June 1971, pp. 1–5.
4. *KZ,* November 25, 1969, p. 2.
5. R. L. Garthoff, *Soviet Military Policy: A Historical Analysis* (New York, 1966), p. 35.
6. *KZ,* January 29, 1971, p. 2.
(Sources continued on following page)

SOURCES (Continued)

7. Ibid., January 20, 1970, p. 2.
8. *Soviet Military Review,* no. 1, 1969, pp. 59–60.
9. *Voyennyye znaniya,* no. 7, 1972, pp. 3–5.
10. *KVS,* no. 14, July 1971, pp. 3–12.
11. *Sel'skaya zhizn',* July 30, 1972; *Moskovskaya pravda,* July 30, 1972, p. 1.
12. *Zarya vostoka,* July 25, 1971, pp. 1–3.
13. *KZ,* September 12, 1971, p. 2.
14. *Sovetskaya Latviya,* May 5, 1971, p. 1.
15. *KVS,* no. 20, October 1971, pp. 25–29.
16. *Aviatsiya i kosmonavtika,* January 1972, pp. 1–3.
17. *KVS,* no. 17, May 1971, pp. 66–71.
18. *Agitator,* July 1971, pp. 45–46.
19. *KZ,* January 20, 1970, p. 2.
20. Moscow Domestic Service, December 7, 1972.
21. *KVS,* no. 18, September 1972, pp. 69–75.
22. *Partiynaya zhizn',* no. 24, 1972, pp. 39–44.
23. Moscow Domestic Service, February 24, 1973.
24. *KZ,* January 31, 1973, p. 3.
25. *Sel'skaya zhizn',* February 23, 1973, p. 2.
26. *Sovetskaya Litva,* August 19, 1973, p. 2.
27. *Leninskoye znamya,* February 23, 1973, p. 2.
28. *KVS,* no. 4, February 1974, p. 73
29. Ibid., no. 19, October 1974, pp. 47–54.

of Party members in 1971 were women,[21] and if we assume that virtually all armed forces Party members were men, then approximately 7 percent of all male Party members, or one in fourteen, were in the army or navy.

A majority of the 742,000 military Party members were officers. In 1972, 71 percent of officers were Party members (see table 3, line 16). Assuming that one out of every five members of the army and navy is an officer (see p. 4), there were 675,000 officers. If 71 percent of these were Party members, we have a figure of 479,000 officers who were also Party members.

It follows, then, that there are about 263,000 Party members who are not officers and therefore must be either extended servicemen, warrant officers and ensigns, or compulsory service (draftee) personnel. The draftee population probably provided relatively few Party members, given the youthful age of the draftees who enter the service in their eighteenth year. To be sure, membership in the Party is open to persons from the age of eighteen on, provided they are members of the Komsomol,[22] which about three-fourths of the draftees are (table 3, lines 22 and 24). From both Soviet statistics of Komsomol membership in the military and discussions in the military press, it appears that the Soviet political and military authorities have, at least until the last several years (see p. 266), encouraged Komsomol rather than Party membership among compulsory service (draftee) personnel. Only about 5 percent of Communist

---

[21] Petrovichev et al. [*Party Structure: A Study Aid*], p. 83.

[22] Persons who are not members of the Komsomol cannot enter the Party until they are twenty-three years old. Komsomol membership can begin at the age of fourteen and can continue to the twenty-eighth year. The foregoing rule suggests that Soviet authorities may view twenty-three as the "age of reason" for acquiring Party membership.

Party members are twenty-five years of age or under.[23] Even if we were to assume that these are distributed evenly among the ages eighteen to twenty-five, this would mean that only 1.4 percent of Party members are in the eighteen- and nineteen-year-old age groups. In fact, the probability of membership almost certainly increases with age, and it is doubtful that the Party members of age eighteen and nineteen constitute more than about one-tenth of the age eighteen to twenty-five Party membership, or more than about 0.5 or 0.6 of the total Party membership. Taking into account that a little more than one-fifth of the Party membership is made up of women, it is likely that the eighteen- and nineteen-year-old male group in the Party numbers about 60,000–70,000. This estimate would be close to the maximum number of draftees in the Party.[24] Probably 30,000–40,000 would be a reasonable estimate of the true number.

It appears, then, that the great majority of the nonofficer Party members were extended-service personnel. If the various estimates given above are at all reasonable, this group must constitute about 230,000 of the approximately 742,000 military Party members.

Figures for 1973–74 Party membership in the army and navy show some interesting changes from 1971–72. Membership among officers rose from 71 to 75 percent (table 3, lines 16 and 18a) and membership among all military personnel fell from 22 to 20 percent (table 3, lines 33 and 38). The decline from 22 to 20 percent can hardly be interpreted as a result of the exchange of Party cards (see pp. 269–270), given the increase in officer membership.

If we repeat the calculations of p. 264 and use these new 1973–74 Party membership figures,[25] we arrive at an estimate of 685,000 members of the Party in the army and navy, of whom 514,000 are officers and only 171,000 are noncommissioned personnel. This represents a gain of 35,000 officer members and a loss of 92,000 noncommissioned members. How is the latter to be accounted for?

A plausible explanation is that the phasing out of the extended-service personnel in 1973, prior to the reinstatement of this category (see pp. 13–14), led to the release of large numbers of older, poorly educated, extended-service NCOs who, as long-time cadres, must have been, in the majority of cases, Party members. We have seen that following the reinstatement of the extended-service category, it was described for the first time as "youngish" (see p. 14), which tends to confirm the release of the older men and the retention or recruitment of younger extended-service personnel. The announced intention of the military in 1972 was to transform the entire extended-service category

---

[23] "KPSS v tsifrakh," *Kommunist,* no. 15, October 1967, p. 98.

[24] The addition of some older draftees who were originally deferred might increase this estimate, but probably not by very much.

[25] And use an estimate of 3.425 million for the Soviet armed forces. The International Institute for Strategic Studies, *The Military Balance for 1973–74* (London, 1973), pp. 5–7. This figure does not include security and border troops.

into the ensign and warrant-officer grades (see p. 11). We assume that the 1974 extended-service category plus the new ensign and warrant-officer ranks must number roughly the same as the old extended-service group, that is, about 400,000 (see p. 6). If only 171,000 of this combined noncommissioned group are now Party members, as we have estimated, then 43 percent of the group are Party members. Given the uncertainties of some of the figures that are used in these calculations, 43 percent is in accordance with the known percent (40 percent) of ensigns and warrant officers in the Party (table 3, line 19). This, in turn, suggests that our inference above, concerning the reduction in the number of noncommissioned Party members, may be correct. It also would provide an explanation for the decline in Party membership among soldiers and sergeants, as noted by *Kommunist vooruzhennykh sil,* and makes more understandable the insistence that Party membership in the enlisted ranks be reinforced.[26]

Some changes have occurred in membership policy. The reduction of the age of draftees in 1968 and the "rejuvenation" of the officer corps with substantial numbers of very young officers coming out of the cadet schools "have led to a reduction in the number of Party organizations and Party groups operating directly in the subunits."[27] To compensate for the decline of Party groups, primary emphasis was placed on strengthening Komsomol groups in subunits and having greater reliance on them.[28] However, a later writer, referring to the decline in the number of Party members among the soldiers and sergeants, concludes that Party units should be encouraged to "select [for Party membership] soldiers who are serving under compulsory [drafted]service."[29] *Kommunist vooruzhennykh sil* returned to this subject two months later in an editorial. "Some Party committees and bureaus desiring to ensure themselves against mistakes have generally ceased to concern themselves with reinforcing the Party organization with new blood from among the outstanding servicemen."[30] In 1973, General Yepishev found that "we still have many companies that do not have Party organizations and Party groups. In this connection . . . the battalion Party organ . . . can and must insure Party influence at the lowest link."[31]

[26] The reader should be warned that the foregoing estimates have involved an earlier assumption that he may not have noted, namely, that officers constitute 20 percent of the Soviet forces (see p. 4). If this estimate is off by much, the entire edifice of calculations and inferences dissolves.

[27] *KVS,* no. 8, April 1972, pp. 39–45.

[28] *Sovetskiy voin,* January 1971, pp. 2–4.

[29] *KVS,* no. 16, August 1972.

[30] Ibid., no. 19, October 1972, pp. 3–8.

[31] *KZ,* March 28, 1973, p. 2.

Just as the majority of officers are members of the Communist Party, so most Soviet enlisted men are members of the Komsomol. As we noted above, three-quarters of the draftees are already members of Komsomol at the time they enter the armed forces (table 3, lines 22 and 24). During the two years of army service a number of the remaining draftees become Komsomol members. Given the small number of conscript Party members, it is apparent that the great majority of draftees retain their Komsomol membership during their military service.

The young officers now come mostly from officer cadet schools, and almost 100 percent of these cadets belong to the Komsomol before they even enter the officer cadet school (table 3, line 10). Indeed, it is likely to be exceptional for a young Soviet man who has not had the foresight to join the Komsomol to be accepted in an officer cadet school. Once the young cadet has graduated into military service proper, he is unlikely to remain a Komsomol member very long, especially given the pressure to recruit young officers into the Party. Speaking of the small number of Party members at the company level, *Kommunist vooruzhennykh sil* points out: "A large detachment of young officers has now gone to the companies from the schools. This is an important replacement for the Party ranks."[32] Nonetheless, progress is sometimes slow, and a year later *Krasnaya zvezda* was still reprimanding units that had not replenished Party ranks. *Krasnaya zvezda* conceded that in many instances platoon leaders are very young and that preparations for the exchange of Party cards (see pp. 269–270) also created difficulties. Nonetheless, these obstacles should not prevent the recruitment of worthy personnel.[33]

Among "young officers" less than 30 percent are still members of the Komsomol, and almost two-thirds are already members of the Communist Party (table 3, line 9). It is apparent, then, that the rate of transfer from the Komsomol to the Communist Party must be relatively rapid after the young officers enter service.

The importance of Party membership in staff positions is reflected by the fact that 40 percent of all army and navy Communist Party members work in military staff and military administrative bodies. "These comrades, as a rule, have high training as well as great service and Party experience."[34] If line officers far outnumber staff and administrative officers, this would imply a lower proportion of Party members in line units, a situation that the Party seems to be attempting to correct. In the past year, the proportion of new Party memberships made up of line officers and graduates of cadet schools increased. Indeed it appears, in the language of Soviet statistical reporting, that "up to

[32] *KVS,* no. 17, September 1971, pp. 3–12.
[33] *KZ,* November 23, 1972, p. 2.
[34] *KVS,* no. 17, September 1973, pp. 48–57. Forty percent = 274,000 (1972).

80 percent" of all persons admitted to the Communist Party in the first half of 1973 were serving in line subunits and ships.[35]

Approximately 80 percent of noncommissioned personnel are in either the Party or the Komsomol (table 3, line 20). This estimate accords well with the fact that approximately 75 percent of Soviet inductees are Komsomol members.

The Party maintains strict control in sensitive areas. Somewhat more than 80 percent of all army and navy personnel are Party and Komsomol members, but 90 percent of the personnel of the Moscow military district and 90 percent of the strategic missile troops hold Party and Komsomol memberships (table 3, lines 35 and 37).

Almost all the younger officers are members of either the Party or the Komsomol (table 3, lines 8 and 9). From line 16 of Table 3, it appears that about 12 percent of all officers are neither members of the Party nor of Komsomol. Given the almost universal Komsomol membership among the newly graduated officer cadets, most of the officers who make up the 12 percent without Party or Komsomol membership must be at least senior lieutenants or of higher rank, and for this group those who are not Party members must consequently constitute more than 12 percent. This may seem surprising, especially in view of a tendency to treat Party membership in the army as virtually equivalent to the number of officers.[36] However, the Party does not accept all officers as members of the Party. Some candidates are rejected, others whose records are not encouraging do not find sponsors or do not bother to seek admission, and still others are expelled from the Party but remain officers. Perhaps the 12 percent of officers without Party membership contain a substantial number of engineer-officers called up from the reserve who are waiting out their period of service before returning to civil life.

The applicant for Communist Party membership must make out an application form, answer a questionnaire, write an autobiography, be interviewed, and provide with his application a statement concerning his inner convictions and the goals he seeks in joining the Party. He must have recommendations from three Party members who have been members for at least five years. Members making recommendations have to have known the applicant for at least one year, both in his work and in his civic or general life. If the applicant is a member of the Komsomol, a recommendation by his primary Komsomol organization is taken as equivalent to one recommendation of a Party member.

Party papers severely criticize members who recommend officers not worthy of membership. Party organizations, we are told, are beginning to deal

[35] Ibid.

[36] See, for instance, John Erickson, *Soviet Military Power* (London: Royal United Services Institute for Defense Studies, 1971), p. 14.

more strictly with members who vouch for such individuals. *Krasnaya zvezda* has particularly criticized recommendations for Party membership that praise the applicant's military virtues but say nothing about his ideological level or his characteristics as a dedicated Communist.[37]

The pressure of the Party to recruit commanders of platoons and companies, that is, to build up Party personnel in company primary Party organizations, has aggravated the problem of maintaining proper standards for the admission of personnel to Party candidacy. According to *Krasnaya zvezda,* candidates who have drunk on duty or exhibited other deficiencies are being admitted to membership. Some comrades, "to put it mildly," adopt "a flippant attitude toward this very important matter."[38] In view of an "approach to selection for the Party that has led to errors," a number of Party candidates have been excluded from the Party.[39] *Krasnaya zvezda* notes that the hasty acceptance of candidates by the Party often leads to a later rejection, sometimes almost immediately after their acceptance into the Party.[40]

Explusion from the Party is a two-stage process. "If a member fails to carry out regulations, violates discipline, drinks, plunders state property, or commits other mistakes incompatible with the title of Communist, he may be dropped from the rolls of the Party. . . . The decision of the primary organization will be considered adopted if no less than two-thirds of the members present at the Party meeting vote in favor of it."[41] Expulsions from the Party or cases of nonincorporation into it do not mean that the remaining Party members satisfy the high requirements of Party leaders. Both in the country at large and in the army, Party members have come under severe criticism for their failure to show the fervor and self-sacrifice that are required to give the Party the high instrumental value desired by the Party élite.

Dissatisfaction with the quality of Party membership and the failure of Party members to live up to the expectations of their leaders is particularly evidenced by the "exchange of Party cards" that began on March 1, 1973, and continued into 1974. The exchange of Party cards meant that all Party members had to reregister and release their old Party cards. If, after being interrogated and investigated and having their dossiers reviewed, they were deemed sufficiently good members, they received new Party membership cards. Secretary Brezhnev took pains to reassure Party members that this was not a purge,

---

[37] *KZ,* September 18, 1971, p. 2. It should be noted that the pressure to require people making recommendations to vouch for the ideological level and dedicated Communist fervor of an applicant is one way of bringing pressure to bear not only on those who make recommendations but also on the young officers who plan, as most of them certainly do, to become Party members. Recommendations that are contingent on a substantial level of political activity force young officers into greater political activity even prior to becoming members of the Party.

[38] Ibid., November 23, 1972, p. 2.

[39] *KVS,* no. 17, September 1971, pp. 3–12.

[40] *KZ,* January 27, 1972, p. 2.

[41] *KVS,* no. 22, November 1972, pp. 45–48.

but clearly it was intended to put pressure on them. General Yepishev, chief of the Main Political Administration of the army and navy, emphasized that the exchange of Party cards provided "a strict and exacting check" on members.[42]

The exchange of Party cards was announced two years in advance. The Party thus provided an incentive for members and prospective members to use the intervening time to improve their political attitudes, their political responsibilities, and their daily work. This strategy clearly succeeded, at least at a formal level. "Practice shows that the majority of Communists with whom conversations have been held draw the necessary conclusions. Many of them have begun to take a more active part in sociopolitical life. Thus, in the Kazakh Republic Party organization, more than sixteen thousand Communists joined in additional social work [i.e., uncompensated volunteer work] in the last month."[43] A similar process occurred in the armed forces. According to an article that dealt especially with the Moscow Military District, "the nearer we get to the time for exchanging Party documents, the deeper and more thoroughly Communists realize its huge political significance. Everywhere we see an increase in their activity. . . . The increased interest and attention of commanders at all levels to Party work is extremely significant. This is showing up literally everywhere and in everything."[44] What also shows up is that the Party can be very persuasive—at any rate, while the new Party cards are being issued. But after "the members received their new Party cards, the comrades decided that business was finished and that they could take a rest."[45]

C. RESPONSIBILITIES AND PROCEDURES

A Communist, even if he is serving in a unit where Party membership has declined and where he is the only Party member in the unit, must assume responsibility for "rallying the military collective" and maintaining high discipline. The Communists must be the very first to speak up against any disorganization, against "any manifestations of mutual protection or abnormal relations between the older servicemen and the new soldiers."[46]

The Communist Party member must above all set an example of Communist morality and zeal. It is of particular importance that he show no moral deficiencies and that his family life and daily work be beyond criticism. Since a major responsibility is to correct the failings of other people, it is essential that his own actions be beyond reproach.[47]

[42] *KZ,* December 10, 1972.
[43] Moscow Domestic Service, February 19, 1973.
[44] *KVS,* no. 18, September 1972, pp. 53–58.
[45] Ibid., no. 13, July 1974, pp. 9–16. For a similar complaint of backsliding see *KZ,* March 26, 1974, p. 2.
[46] Ibid., September 21, 1972, p. 2.
[47] Ibid., February 2, 1971, and September 21, 1971, p. 2.

Members of the Komsomol have similar responsibilities, although, of course, the object of their attention is youth in particular. The Twenty-fourth Congress of the Communist Party defined the central task of the Komsomol as the education of youth in the spirit of Communist ideals and devotion to the Soviet motherland.[48] But in the army the Komsomol also has quite specific tasks, such as getting out wall newspapers, issuing operational news sheets, and engaging in criticism that will keep young soldiers in line with military regulations and with the requirements of their studies and their military work.[49]

The rights and privileges of a Communist as recorded in the regulations are "inseparable from his obligations, and their purpose is to ensure that the Communist is able to carry out his obligations in the best possible manner."[50] In effect, then, Communists do not have privileges, and when a candidate is interviewed at a Party meeting he is sometimes asked what privileges are enjoyed by Party members. The astute candidate will not be able to think of any privileges, but only obligations.[51]

A Party member does indeed have one possibility open to him that might be viewed by some as a privilege, but which in the Soviet Union and in the Party is viewed rather as an obligation or duty (sometimes a rather dangerous one). This is the right to criticize, at Party meetings, any Communist regardless of his position. "A Party member may never and nowhere have the right indifferently to ignore any negative facts whatsoever. . . . The CPSU rules lay down his right at Party meetings to criticize any Communist regardless of his position. Persons guilty of suppressing criticism and persecuting criticism should be brought strictly to Party account, and may even be excluded from CPSU ranks. All this applies to the Communists of the Soviet armed forces. For understandable reasons, only criticisms of commanders' orders and commands are not permitted under army and navy conditions."[52]

Despite continued urging by Party leaders, many military members do not participate actively in Party discussions or in criticism of Party personnel. Members are often indifferent to or fearful of the exercise of Party duties. Members who do not have officer status, for example sergeants, often sit quietly at the meetings and say to themselves, "We are unimportant people,

---

[48] Ibid., April 20, 1972, p. 2.

[49] The Komsomol has had a special relationship with the Soviet navy and has helped to provide training for young people in naval colleges. In the postwar years the link between the Komsomol and the fleet gained in strength. Many Komsomol groups composed of youths who have not yet been drafted are active in conducting young sailor circles and running a variety of naval training and inspirational activities. *Pravda,* October 16, 1972.

[50] *KZ,* February 2, 1971, p. 2.

[51] One candidate was able to think of a privilege: "A Party member goes into battle only in the front ranks!" *Sovetskiy voin,* April 15, 1972, pp. 8–10. There is at least one other privilege that some Party members acquire. Party membership often provides opportunities to get into full-time Party jobs or jobs controlled by the Party. These jobs often have favorable pay rates and provide Party members with a substantial interest in following the Party line.

[52] *KZ,* November 29, 1972, p. 1.

is it of any use for us to get involved?"[53] This attitude is strengthened by a tendency for young members who make criticisms to be criticized in turn and asked whether they are any better than the people whom they criticize. As a result, many of the young Party members say to themselves, "It is better if I just sit quietly at the meeting."[54]

In 1969 the Central Committee of the Party issued a directive intended to encourage participation in Party meetings and to overcome the tendency for Party meetings to "become a convenient place for one and the same person to speak," generally the secretary.[55] Some improvement may have resulted. One writer notes that subsequently, in meetings of Party groups in the military, more than 90 percent attendance was recorded and "almost half of all the Communists spoke."[56] *Kommunist vooruzhennykh sil* put the matter more firmly. "The Party teaches us that it is wrong to have anything to do with passive members, such as those Communists who work well and behave themselves correctly, but—for whatever reasons—do not have assignments and rarely speak out at meetings."[57]

As it often happens, Party pressure and zeal in one direction produce excesses that result in a countermovement, often very timid, in the opposite direction. A writer defends a Communist officer in these terms: "I know that he is a person who speaks very rarely at Party meetings. And thus, tacitly, the opinion was formed that this Communist was inactive. . . . Recently I met the secretary of the Party organization, and he told me 'we do not consider X to be unenterprising. . . . If we give him a Party job, he carries it out wholeheartedly. . . .' I thought to myself, well, the secretary is correct. It is impossible to judge a Communist merely from ardent speeches. Unfortunately, we do have comrades who are all too willing to take the floor. But when it is a matter of deeds, you won't find any people around."[58]

Even more serious is the fact that Party members break not only Party rules but also the rules and obligations of military behavior. Thus, "even Party personnel tend to put up with violations [of flight regulations] as long as they do not have undesirable consequences."[59] Many Communists do not struggle to ensure that their unit gets the rating of "outstanding" or "excellent." "They are quite content to be average. As long as they are not being reprimanded,

---

[53] Ibid., June 24, 1971, p. 1.
[54] Ibid.
[55] Ibid., September 21, 1971.
[56] *Partiynaya zhizn'*, no. 3, 1971, pp. 8–15.
[57] *KVS*, no. 18, September 1972, pp. 53–58. The desire to have persons "speak out" seems to be not only a desire to get the benefit of their views, but also a desire to commit the individual who speaks to a position and to force him unwittingly to make revelations about himself or others that may require correction.
[58] *KZ*, October 10, 1972, p. 2.
[59] *KVS*, no. 11, June 1971, pp. 34–38.

everything is fine."[60] Nor are Communists beyond the temptation to help out their units or themselves individually by cheating in socialist competition. Two Communists who conspired to evade military rules in order to achieve high marks in firing practice suffered no penalties. This is, pernaps, not surprising since the captain of the unit was himself the secretary of the Party Bureau.[61]

At the company level, Party administration is often in the hands of one person, the elected secretary of the Party Bureau. "It is from this, frankly, that many of our troubles flow: the decisions at Party meetings are not always put fully into effect, the level of activity of certain members and candidate members of the CPSU is low, and certain comrades do not set a good example."[62] At the company level the position of Party secretary may be held by junior personnel. But in the Party units of regimental and equivalent headquarters, the military rank of Party secretaries may be substantial. A major, a lieutenant colonel, and a naval captain third rank are some of the ranks mentioned in the case of such Party secretaries.[63]

Older personnel who have been in the Party longer are generally overloaded with duties, while many of the younger Communists have never been assigned to Party tasks. A study carried out for the political administration of the Siberian Military District revealed that persons who have been in the Party fifteen to twenty years are generally overworked.[64] Unit commanders are, of course, greatly encouraged to take an active role in Party affairs, but sometimes they use Party meetings simply "as a convenient place to give out regular instructions."[65]

The Communist Party maintains tight control over organizations under its supervision, especially the Komsomol. We shall discuss this more fully later. Here we only note the continuous line of supervision. Just as the Party maintains control over the Komsomol, so the Komsomol in its turn has a responsibility for supervising the Young Pioneers in the ten- to fifteen-year-old range.

The Party shows proper concern "for furnishing commanders, political workers, and Party and Komsomol organizations with the decisions, directives, and orders of higher organs."[66] However, Party emphasis seems to be placed primarily on strengthening the transfer of information from lower to higher levels, that is, strengthening surveillance. "Here we are speaking of reports and accounts on combat and political training, the status of military

[60] *KZ*, September 30, 1971, p. 1.
[61] Ibid., May 23, 1972, p. 2.
[62] Ibid.
[63] Ibid., January 27, 1972, p. 2; *Sovetskiy voin,* April 15, 1972, pp. 8–40.
[64] *KZ*, February 2, 1971.
[65] Ibid., January 15, 1970.
[66] *KVS,* no. 6, March 1972, pp. 48–54.

discipline, statistical data, and also letters and complaints from the military personnel. A careful study of this information furnishes the political department with a better understanding of life in the units."[67]

The great amount of reporting, especially the reports moving upward from below, provides considerable information that the Party seems anxious should not fall into the hands of unauthorized persons. "The loss of Party documents in some organizations is increasing. Communists display clear negligence and carelessness and often keep Party documents in overcoat pockets or leave them in suitcases. And this leads to unpleasantness."[68] Considerable concern is expressed over the care and loss of blank membership cards and other forms. "There is no need to prove how important it is to organize the irreproachable accounting for and storage of unused blanks . . . and to assure timely reporting on them. Unused blanks . . . should be stored in fireproof safes. But at times, simple iron cabinets are used. . . . New cards issued for Party cards alleged to be lost are often issued too freely, without proper investigation."[69]

Four months after the above admonition, *Kommunist vooruzhennykh sil* returned to the same subject. Work in connection with the exchange of Party cards revealed that 5 percent of the Party cards in the Leningrad military district contained inaccuracies, outright errors, and omissions. Some of these turned out to be intentional and resulted from a falsification of the member's status. Party documents were revealed to contain serious deficiencies. Some had erasures and strikeovers. Documents with poor-quality photographs had been issued. Membership cards were found with slovenly impressions of Party seals, blots, and other defects.[70] Presumably, *Kommunist vooruzhennykh sil* was not so much concerned with neatness and good appearance as with a fear of altered and counterfeit documents.

D. THE COMPANY POLITICAL OFFICER

The key figure in ensuring Party influence at the troop level is the company political officer, the former "commissar." The commissar system was not simply a practice of the early postrevolutionary years. During the first months of World War II about 60,000 members of the Communist Party and 40,000 members of the Komsomol were sent into the army as "political fighters."[71] However, after the death of Stalin and the purge of Beria in 1953, the influence

---

[67] Ibid.
[68] Ibid., no. 13, July 1972, pp. 49–54.
[69] Ibid.
[70] Ibid., no. 21, November 1972, pp. 51–56.
[71] Ibid., no. 13, July 1971, pp. 84–86.

of political officers gradually declined, and in late 1955 the political officer position was abolished at the company level.[72]

More than a decade was to pass before this measure was rescinded and the Party decided to supplement its political officers at higher echelons with deputy commanders for political affairs at the company, battery, squadron, and analogous small-unit level. This was accompanied by repeated emphasis on the company as the center of political (as well as combat) training. Both Lieutenant General Gorchakov, chief of the Political Directorate of the Strategic Rocket Forces, and General of the Army V. Tolubko emphasized in articles that appeared simultaneously in April 1972 the need to convert the company (battery) into the primary locus for political training.[73] It is, after all, only at the company level that a political officer can be in contact with, exert influence and control over, and report to his political superiors on the behavior of each individual soldier—one objective in the Party's mind of reinstituting the company political officer.

To implement the new measure, higher political military schools were established in 1967 by a decision of the Central Committee of the Party. These schools replaced the two-year military political schools that had ceased to operate in 1959.[74]

The establishment of the new political military schools reveal a clear decision to provide maximum prestige and capabilities for the company political officers. The schools have a four-year curriculum, during which students receive their higher education. In addition to work in "the social sciences," that is, in Marxism-Leninism, together with some modern elements of psychology and sociology required for training the New Soviet Man, the political worker receives a substantial military training. Students study tactics, weapons, gunnery, the handling of combat matériel, topography, and communications, in addition to physical training and military drill. They are introduced to higher mathematics, physics, electronics, applied mechanics, and engineering drawing. The study of a foreign language is mandatory.[75] In some political schools the officer cadets practice political and agitational work among the workers in the *oblast* in which the school is located. On the eve of graduation they spend a period of probationary service in line units and acquire practical skills in conducting Party political work.[76]

The military political schools are now specialized according to different types of arms or services. A listing of openings in these institutes mentions eight different schools—higher military political schools for combined arms, tanks, artillery, air defense, construction troops, aviation, engineering and

---

[72] R. L. Garthoff, *Soviet Military Policy: A Historical Analysis* (New York: 1966), pp. 47, 51.
[73] *KZ*, April 4, 1972, p. 2; *KVS*, no. 8, April 1972, pp. 39–45.
[74] *KVS*, no. 14, July 1971, pp. 3–12.
[75] Ibid.
[76] *Aviatsiya i kosmonavtika*, August 1971, pp. 26–27.

communications, and naval service.[77] Since the new schools for company political officers were opened only in 1967 and provide a four-year course, it was not until 1971 and 1972 that a regular flow of deputy commanders for political affairs began to be provided to the companies and similar units of the armed forces.

Entrance into the military political academies has been determined by competitive examination. However, military educational institutions are following in the footsteps of civilian and higher schools in de-emphasizing competitive examinations and giving more prominence to the applicant's secondary school results and his record in "civic work." This gives the authorities more flexibility in selecting candidates whom they consider politically suitable. Candidates from these schools come in considerable numbers from among the enlisted men and noncommissioned officers who are serving an initial term in the armed forces or who have re-enlisted. Others come from industrial and agricultural enterprises and civilian educational institutions. Most of the candidates have had experience in Party, Komsomol, or other political work.[78] Most are said to come from worker and peasant families.[79] But in connection with one school, apparently an air force school, we learn that "many sons of political workers are being taught at the military political institutes, thus testifying to the continuity of generations."[80] This is a generational continuity that has been noted among regular as well as political officers.

The Soviet authorities like to have their junior political officers begin training at an early age. A higher institute for military political training announced that it will accept servicemen who are either on regular or extended service and who are not more than twenty-three years of age. Graduates of the Suvorov (army) and Nakhimov (navy) military schools for the sons of officers, and civilians from seventeen to twenty-three years of age who are members or candidate members of the Communist Party or Komsomol and have shown an inclination for political work are accepted.[81] The L'vov Higher Military Political School trains not only political officers but also personnel for the editorial boards of military newspapers. This clearly places military newspapers under Party rather than military control. All applicants for the L'vov school must be recommended by a Party organ or by their Komsomol district committee. They must have displayed an aptitude for club or newspaper work.[82] The Ministry of Internal Affairs has not only its own military schools for the security forces but also its own higher political school.[83]

[77] *KZ,* January 29, 1971.
[78] *KVS,* no. 14, July 1971 pp. 3–12.
[79] *KZ,* July 28, 1971, p. 2.
[80] *Aviatsiya i kosmonavtika,* August 1971, pp. 26–27.
[81] *KZ,* January 14, 1970, p. 4.
[82] Ibid., March 7, 1972, p. 4.
[83] Ibid., March 22, 1972, p. 4.

Graduate military-political courses are also available for older officers. The Lenin Military Political Academy accepts officers for full-time graduate study who are members of the Party and who are not more than thirty-five years of age.[84]

The company deputy commander for political affairs has immediate responsibility for the organization and conduct of Party political work in the subunit to which he is attached. His principal objective is "to secure effective Party influence on the personnel, to achieve the development in the men of a solid moral fibre and political consciousness."[85] To this end, his training in the military academy emphasizes an ability to lecture well, to speak with conviction and clarity, and to exercise an emotional influence on the men in his unit.[86] He is largely responsible not only for political indoctrination, but also for stimulating and managing socialist competition and other activities intended to promote greater zeal and effectiveness in military training and operations. He also has some of the functions of an information and education officer in the US army, and of a chaplain who gives attention to family problems and personal affairs. The company political officer also guides the company officers. "He heads their preparation for conducting political training. He advises them how to use literature, graphic aids, and propaganda equipment. The political worker persistently teaches officers the art of educating men."[87]

Although the Party is anxious for political officers to gain the affection and respect of the men, it is opposed to political officers becoming nursemaids or being drawn into work that is the responsibility of others. A deputy commander for political affairs whose apparent concern for the comfort of the men led him, in preparation for a field exercise, to look after the billeting of the personnel and to work with axe, hammer, and nails to ensure that tents were properly set up, was not commended for his zeal, but on the contrary was reprimanded. Even above the company level the same problems occurs. A major, deputy for political affairs of a battalion or regiment, personally went to a warehouse to get potatoes for the soldiers. *Krasnaya zvezda* views this as a neglect of the organizational work proper to a political officer. "The political officer should be ensuring that the personnel are in the proper combat, moral, political, and psychological mood for carrying out the combat tasks assigned to them, and not be bringing potatoes and hammering tents. A political worker works best when he is organizing people. The work carried out by a political worker can be described as human management. The most important tool of a political worker is the spoken word."[88] Perhaps, too, the political administra-

[84] Ibid., December 3, 1969, p. 4, and November 25, 1970, p. 4.
[85] Ibid., January 16, 1970, p. 1.
[86] *KVS,* no. 23, December 1970, pp. 33–38.
[87] *KZ,* April 14, 1972, p. 2.
[88] Ibid., October 6, 1972, p. 2. The miscellaneous duties sometimes performed by political

tions in the military do not want the status of their personnel lowered by the performance of physical work.

The various duties of the political officer do not absolve him from the need to be a competent soldier. On the firing range the company commander fires first to set an example of good performance. "Then it is the turn of the political officer. He fires and there is anxious expectation of victory. And so it is. It cannot be otherwise."[89] But the Party is also impatient with political officers who sacrifice their political work to achieve satisfaction and distinction in the exercise of purely military skills. Two months after reprimanding political officers for raising tents and fetching potatoes, *Krasnaya zvezda* took to task a deputy commander for political affairs, a major in an air force squadron, for neglecting his political duties in favor of being a squadron instructor and maintaining his skills as a first class pilot. He is reminded that his primary duty "is to carry the Party word to the troops."[90]

E. THE PARTY LEADS THE ARMY

Party-army relations are not independent of Party policy and Party experience in Soviet civil society. We shall, therefore, briefly examine some developments in general Party policy before turning to Party-army relations.

1. The Party and the Civil Society

a. The Right to Supervise Management.   The Twenty-fourth Party Congress of April 1971 extended Party control over a large number of Soviet establishments by increasing the number of primary Party organizations having the right to supervise the administration of the establishments in which the primary Party groups are located. Thus, Party groups, through special commissions made up of a number of their members, acquired the right, indeed the duty, to supervise the administrators of the organization for which the members work. The Twenty-fourth Party Congress decision more especially granted primary Party organizations of scientific research institutes, educational institutions, cultural-educational, and medical establishments the right of supervision.[91] In the Ukraine in 1971 approximately eighteen thousand Party primary organizations had the right to supervise management activity.[92]

Some Party activists found these new powers rather heady wine, espe-

---

officers are not always the result of zeal, but are imposed on them by commanders who do not view their political duties as having a high priority.

   [89] *KVS,* no. 5, March 1971, pp. 86–88.
   [90] *KZ,* December 16, 1972, p. 2.
   [91] *Pravda,* July 31, 1971, p. 2, and February 9, 1972, p. 2.
   [92] Ibid., August 20, 1971, p. 2.

cially, it seems, when they provided an opportunity to supervise intellectuals whose respect for the Party may not have been all that some Party members desired. Some Communists took the attitude: "Now, the sky's the limit."[93] A Party member, discussing problems arising from the Twenty-fourth Party Congress decision, writes, "Is sugary 'tact' appropriate here? It seems to me we must pose the question of suppression of criticism more sharply."[94] Another Party member, referring to problems in educational institutions, writes, "No fundamental question of the higher educational institutes' work should remain outside the Party organization's field of vision. Not one! Let us remember this."[95]

The attitude "Now we'll show management a thing or two" did not become universal. Some skeptical Party members asserted that nothing would change.[96] Indeed, some primary Party organizations were less than enthusiastic about increasing their responsibilities. Describing the situation at a medical station, a Party member points out that the organization had seventeen Communists already busy serving on the Party bureau, the People's Control group, a local trade-union committee, the editorial committee for the wall newspaper, and several other committees.

The Party advised its members "to avoid giving peremptory orders or administrative fiats in exercising supervision."[97] Some Party members were not disposed to do so in any case. One secretary of a Party group asked, "How can I, the assistant to a department head, supervise the work of my chief?" *Pravda* acknowledged that the right of supervision over management activity is something new for scientific, secondary school, higher school, and certain other establishments, and "therefore it requires a break with some deeply ingrained concepts, perhaps even some psychological readjustments."[98] The Party suggested that to avoid excessive conflicts of authority, the Party commission might well include a broad set of the leading professors and department heads, as well as the Party activists. "In this atmosphere the question of . . . violation of 'subordination' will gradually lose urgency."[99] If the opinions of the Party commission and the director of the institute do not coincide, one Party member recommended that "one should not . . . create a 'scene.' We should improve our work . . . and not stir up trouble, which could be the height of folly."

Some leaders and staff members of scientific institutes found that the new directive interfered with and contradicted the principle of "one-man manage-

[93] Ibid., February 11, 1972, p. 2.
[94] Ibid.
[95] Ibid.
[96] Ibid., May 22, 1972, p. 2.
[97] Ibid., February 11, 1972, p. 2.
[98] Ibid., March 3, 1972, p. 2.
[99] Ibid.

ment" in effect in scientific institutions.[100] One-man management is, as we shall see, a particularly important principle in the military structure, where it is called one-man command.

b. The Party and the State. Party authorities, both through the Twenty-fourth Party Congress and in subsequent pronouncements, have shown a concern to convince the Soviet public that the strengthening of state institutions is an objective of Party policy. "In recent years, a conclusion was drawn concerning the entry of the socialist state into a new period of its development. The regular law of the growth of the role of and the significance of the state in Communist construction was disclosed. . . . Ways for the development of the socialist state system and democracy were worked out."[101] *Pravda* began an editorial with the words: "The interests of society and the state above everything."[102] The summary report of the Twenty-fourth Party Congress by the Central Committee of the Party had also emphasized the increasing participation of the public in the administration of the country and thereby the broadening of socialist democracy. "We see the meaning and content of socialist democracy in the participation of ever-broader masses in . . . public affairs."

Since the Twenty-third Party Congress, the Party has increasingly made efforts to persuade the Soviet public not only that they do participate in the direction of Soviet affairs, but also that the "attempts of our ideological opponents to find a contradiction between the lines of development of socialist democracy and the strengthening of the Soviet state are groundless."[103] Despite this concern with ideological opponents, the Party does not hesitate to associate the development of socialist democracy with aspects of the Soviet order that to most people would hardly indicate either an increase in personal freedom or a lessening of Party control. After emphasizing "the interests of society and the state above everything," the *Pravda* editorial cited above continues by showing that "constant Party control is an effective method of strengthening state discipline. . . . A major role belongs to the organs of People's Control."[104] The importance of the state seems, then, to reside not so much in its ability to fulfill the needs of citizens, as in its utility to the Party for maintaining state discipline. "The CPSU considers the most important condition for the development of socialist democracy to be the strengthening of lawfulness and law. . . . Especially great in this matter is the role of the procurator's office, the police, and the organs of state security." Some may

---

[100] Ibid.
[101] *KVS,* no. 19, October 1972, pp. 17–20.
[102] *Pravda,* October 12, 1972, p. 1.
[103] *KVS,* no. 19, October 1972, pp. 9–16.
[104] *Pravda,* October 12, 1972, p. 1.

question the contribution that the police, the prosecutor, and the organs of state security make to democracy. Nonetheless, it is these contributions that show that "the Party displays tireless concern for the strengthening of the Soviet state and the development of socialist democracy."[105] Given the role of the police, the prosecutor, and the organs of state security in strengthening democracy, it is not surprising that Secretary Brezhnev found it useful to affirm that the discipline desired by the Party ought not to "deprive people of confidence and initiative."[106]

Despite Party affirmations about the importance of the state, representation of members of the state apparatus in the Central Committee recently declined. In 1971, just prior to the Twenty-fourth Congress, 32.7 percent of the Central Committee members worked for the state apparatus. Among the eighty-two new members added in 1971, however, only 14.6 percent were members of state organs.[107] On the other hand, perhaps this fact is outweighed by the election in April 1973 of the ministers of defense and foreign affairs and of the head of the KGB to the Politburo.

c. The Party and the Working Class. In an address to the Fifteenth Congress of Soviet Trade Unions, Secretary Brezhnev said: "Contrary to the fashionable anti-Marxist theories that the scientific and technical revolution is, allegedly, leading to a shrinking of the working class and even to its liquidation, the real facts of life point to just the opposite: scientific and technical progress is everywhere leading to a growth of the working class. . . . At the present stage of Communist construction, the alliance of the working class with the collective-farm peasantry and the intelligentsia of our country acquires an even deeper meaning. The working class, which plays and will play the leading role in Communist construction, remains the cementing force of this great alliance."[108]

This affirmation of the increasing role of the working class seems more a revelation of Party policy than a reflection of a spontaneous development. In fact, the striking changes of the last decades have been not the relative growth of those categories of workers usually called the working class, but rather the great increase in the categories called the intelligentsia. This has been accompanied by the more or less stationary status of the workers and a sharp decline in the relative proportion of farm workers. In 1920 only a negligible percentage of the employed population could be classed as intelligentsia. By 1959 this category had risen to 20.5 percent of the labor force, as

---

[105] *KVS*, no. 19, October 1972, pp. 9–16.
[106] *Pravda*, October 12, 1972, p. 1.
[107] Robert H. Donaldson, "The 1971 Soviet Central Committee: An Assessment of the New Elite," *World Politics*, vol. 21, no. 3, April 1972, p. 394.
[108] *TASS*, March 20, 1972.

compared with 48 percent for workers and 31.5 percent for farm workers. By 1968 the intelligentsia had risen to 29.5 percent, with the workers stationary at 48 percent and collective-farm workers falling to 22 percent. In 1971 the intellingentsia was estimated at thirty million, as compared with eighteen million collective-farm workers.[109]

There is, of course, one sense in which it is perfectly true, as *Krasnaya zvezda* affirms, that the "social homogeneity of Soviet society is increasing and raising the role of the working class in Communist building."[110] The spread of secondary and higher education has made it easier for persons from worker and farmer families to attain more rewarding positions, although they probably have difficulty competing with the children of the intelligentsia for access to the highest ranks of the educational process.

Soviet leaders seem intent on diluting the present intelligentsia by introducing into the occupations that it occupies the sons and daughters of working-class and rural families. The Party established in 1969 a large number of preparatory divisions in higher educational institutions in order to permit young workers and collective farmers to acquire the knowledge that would enable them to study at higher educational institutions. By the spring of 1972 some 524 institutions of higher learning had preparatory sections or centers at which more than sixty-eight thousand industrial and agricultural workers and servicemen released from the Soviet army were studying.[111] This new type of educational institution is "intended to play a big role in regulating the social composition of the student body."[112]

On September 1, 1972, in accordance with decisions of the Twenty-fourth Party Congress, student stipends in higher schools were increased.[113] *Izvestia* pointed out that previously the awarding of student stipends depended on student achievements and financial situations. Now stipends are to depend on achievement and on participation in public life,[114] that is, on conformity with Party and Komsomol requirements.

Another indication of Party interest in diminishing the influence of the intelligentsia and increasing that of the workers is found in the changes in the social composition of the Communist Party and of its Central Committee. Between 1966 and 1971, the category "workers" was the only one that increased its representation in the Party. Both the categories "peasant" and "employees-others" declined. In terms of total membership, these changes

---

[109] Zev Katz, "Sociology in the Soviet Union," *Problems of Communism,* May-June 1971, pp. 27–28.

[110] *KZ,* January 26, 1973, pp. 2–3.

[111] *Trud,* March 23, 1972, p. 2.

[112] *Bakinskiy rabochiy,* November 2, 1971, pp. 2–5.

[113] *Pravda,* October 25, 1972, p. 1.

[114] *Izvestia,* September 30, 1972, p. 5.

were not very great.[115] However, if we look at recent admissions to Party candidacy, the changes are more striking. Of those admitted to Party candidacy, 44 percent were workers in 1962–65, 52 percent in 1966–70, and 57 percent in 1972.[116] Peasants declined from 15 percent to 13.4 percent, and employees, students, and technicians declined from 40.3 percent to 34.6 percent.[117]

Changes in the composition of the Central Committee of the Party also indicate an intent to favor workers and peasants to the disadvantage of the scientific-academic-intellectual class. In 1971, less than 1 percent of the Central Committee incumbents were classified as workers and peasants, whereas 12.2 percent of the new members elected in that year fell into that category. The scientific-academic-intellectual category was 3.3 percent among incumbents and 1.2 percent among new full members.[118] Ten of the eleven persons currently described as workers or collective farmers were newly elected at the Twenty-fourth Party Congress.[119] These changes are probably more indicative of a Party fear of intellectuals than they are of an interest in increasing the power of workers and collective farmers.

d. The Party and the Komsomol. The Party's concern to tighten its control over sectors of the population that are viewed as likely to make trouble is also reflected in its increased direction of the Komsomol. Like the intellectuals and the scientists, Soviet youth are a major concern of Party leaders. The thirty-two million members[120] of the Komsomol constitute, according to Party leaders, an increasingly important population requiring Party attention. In 1966 approximately 20 percent of the secretaries of Komsomol organizations were Party members. By 1971 this figure had risen to 40 percent.[121] In some regions of Party concern the increase is much greater. In Azerbaijan, 80 percent of Komsomol activists in 1971 were Party members.[122] "The Party attaches exceptional significance to the management of the Komsomol. . . . It is essential to strengthen further the Party nucleus in Komsomol organizations."[123] The combination of youth and intellectual is, no doubt, especially dangerous. A 1972 discussion of reforms by the Economic Institute of the

[115] N. A. Petrovichev et al. [*Party Structure: A Study Aid*], p. 63.
[116] Ibid., p. 77.
[117] Editorial, *Pravda,* February 19, 1973, p. 1.
[118] R. H. Donaldson, "The 1971 Soviet Central Committee: An Assessment of the New Elite," *World Politics,* vol. 21, no. 3, p. 394.
[119] Ibid., p. 386. In 1974, over 40 percent of the members of district and city Party committees were workers and collective farmers. *Pravda,* October 13, 1974, pp. 2–4.
[120] *KVS,* no. 6, March 1974, pp. 36–44.
[121] *Pravda,* October 16, 1971, p. 2.
[122] *Bakinskiy rabochiy,* November 2, 1971, pp. 2–5.
[123] *KVS,* no. 7, April 1973, pp. 16–26.

USSR Academy of Sciences recommended that the Communist Party bureau give more attention to increasing Communist Party leadership of the institute's Komsomol group.[124]

e. The Exchange of Party Cards. This important measure (see pp. 269–270 above) to purify the Party and to bring pressure on present and prospective members is clearly intended to make the Party a more serviceable instrument.

The Party has grown much more rapidly than the population:

	Soviet Population[125] (in millions)	Party Membership[126] (in millions)
1939	191	2.3
1959	209	8.2
1970	242	14.2

Today one out of every five Soviet males between the ages of twenty-five and seventy and one out of every three between the ages of thirty and sixty is a member of the Party. For a party that attempts to act as a vanguard, an elite, and an instrument of control over the society, this represents a dangerous dilution of its membership by "ordinary," nondedicated individuals. The Party faces a dilemma. It seeks to accomplish two tasks: (1) by incorporating people into the Party, to subject them to Party training, discipline, and use; (2) to make the Party an elite group to drive and control the non-Party masses. The first objective leads to membership expansion, expansion to "dilution," and dilution to failures in the second objective.

The Party's dilemma is mitigated in part by having, in effect, two classes of membership—the ordinary members and the activists. The activists constitute the real elite, the real spearhead, and the controllers. However, dilution of the membership at large by nondedicated members leads to some dilution of its leaders or activists. This is increased by the fact that Party offices are elective and that Party recommendations are increasingly ignored in the voting for officers. The need to co-opt ordinary members who are far from being true activists for the multifarious Party activities reduces further the effectiveness of Party work, as do careerist motives among the activists. The Party's dilemma is magnified in the Komsomol, to which the great majority of young people belong.

---

[124] *Kommunist,* no. 1, January 1972, pp. 3–5. More than two-thirds of all new members of the Party are recruited from the ranks of the Komsomol. *Pravda,* October 13, 1974, pp. 2–4.
[125] Soviet Census of 1970.
[126] N. A. Petrovichev et al. [*Party Structure: A Study Aid*], pp. 59–60.

The exchange of Party cards reflected the need for a more disciplined and dedicated instrument (1) to deal with groups actually or potentially alienated from the Party—intellectuals, youth, non-Russian nationalities, and the military; (2) to implement the drive for labor discipline and the protection of state property; and (3) to combat the erosion of the Party-defined Marxist-Leninist ideology.

2. The Party and the Armed Forces

a. The Party Leads.

The Party loses no opportunity to instruct officers and troops that it, and not the military commanders, is the leader and controller of the military. A political lesson provided for political officers to be taught to the troops allots eight hours to ensuring that military personnel understand the full scope of Party dominance. The points that the lesson was to cover included: (1) the Party is the leader and indoctrinator of the armed forces; (2) leadership of the armed forces by the Party constitutes the foundation of military construction; (3) the Party "indicates and implements" military policy and "develops" military doctrine; (4) the Party determines the general direction of the life and combat activity of the armed forces; and (5) the Party develops basic measures with respect to the maintenance of combat readiness and determines the content of the moral, political, and psychological training of the troops.[127]

A few months later, *Kommunist vooruzhennykh sil* returned to these questions in language that displays little in the way of restraint: "Party leadership over the armed forces is carried out in all areas . . . determining the main direction for the development of types of armed forces, their organizational structure and equipping with modern technology and weapons, the training and indoctrination of military personnel, [and] the taking of specific measures related to further raising the level of Party political work. . . . In essence, there is no area of military affairs in which the leading role of the Communist Party, its Central Committee, and the Politburo of the CPSU Central Committee would not be manifested."[128] In another statement, *Kommunist vooruzhennykh sil* points out, "In the field of military construction and as regards the country's defense, there is not one question that does not fall under the watchful eye of our Party and its combat staff, the Leninist Central Committee."[129] Defense Minister Grechko assured the assembled secretaries of Party primary organizations in the military that "there is no question of greater or lesser importance concerning the building of the armed forces with which the Party Central Committee and the Politburo itself, led by Comrade L. I. Brezhnev,

---

[127] *KVS,* no. 10, May 1971, pp. 66–71.
[128] Ibid., no. 21, November 1971, pp. 59–64.
[129] Ibid., no. 18, September 1971, pp. 63–69.

would not deal."[130] And General Yepishev assured the same assembly of the special role played "particularly by meetings between Comrade L. I. Brezhnev, CPSU Central Committee general secretary, and Comrades N. V. Podgorny and A. N. Kosygin and leading armed forces personnel, as well as by their visits to troops and fleets."[131] The emphasis on the Politburo implies that Party direction of the military is not exercised by Party elements who are in the military, but by Party civilians.

The role attributed to the Party in regulating military affairs applies not only to the present and the future but equally to the past. The acute problems following World War II concerning the structure of the armed forces were solved, not by military leaders, but by the Central Committee of the Communist Party and the Soviet government.[132] It is not surprising then that Marshal Grechko found it expedient in issuing his order of the day on Tank Day (1972) to end his order with "Glory to the CPSU—the inspirer and organizer of all our victories."[133]

Not only is the Communist Party the leader of the military forces at large, but the individual Communists within the forces are represented as the most valuable members of the military collective. "The Communists are the nucleus and soul of the collective, its honor and conscience, and certainly its most active principle."[134] General Yepishev points out that "Communists comprise more than 80 percent of those receiving awards for exemplary fulfillment of service tasks."[135] M. A. Suslov, member of the Politburo and secretary of the CPSU Central Committee, affirms that "the Communists in the army and navy have always been an example . . . to members of the Soviet armed forces."[136] And in the air force, "The Communists are the first to master the latest equipment, the first to become experts and marksmen."[137]

Since the Party claims to be "the inspirer and organizer of all our victories," it is little wonder that its demands on the military are more in the direction of loyalty to it than to its commanders. As we noted earlier, when Marshal Grechko spoke of the six demands made upon officer personnel, he pointed out that "the first and chief demand is . . . that the Soviet officer must be an active champion of Party policy."[138] Addressing a meeting of Soviet warrant officers and ensigns, the marshal again affirms that the first requirement for such personnel "is for boundless devotion to the cause of the Commu-

[130] *KZ,* March 28, 1973, pp. 1–2.
[131] Ibid., pp. 2–3.
[132] *Voyenno-istoricheskiy zhurnal,* August 8, 1971, pp. 29–38.
[133] *KZ,* September 10, 1972, p. 1. *KZ* announced a new book whose title is *The CPSU is the Organizer of the Socialist Motherland's Military Defense.* Ibid., January 3, 1973, p. 2.
[134] Ibid., January 26, 1973, pp. 2–3.
[135] Ibid., March 2, 1973, pp. 2–3.
[136] Moscow Domestic Service, March 27, 1973.
[137] *KZ,* March 28, 1973, p. 3.
[138] Ibid., March 24, 1972, pp. 1–3.

nist Party."[139] *Kommunist vooruzhennykh sil* states that Party members "place overall Party and state interests above everything else."[140] *Krasnaya zvezda* reminds the new graduates of military academies that one of their major tasks is "to develop soldiers in a spirit of infinite loyalty to Party ideals." The young officers must be "active Party warriors and conductors of Party policy."[141] Another *Krasnaya zvezda* editorial, in naming the most important command qualities, lists ideological conviction first. The military skills of an officer come last in this, as it did in Marshal Grechko's list.[142]

In light of the foregoing, it is not surprising that in discussing promotion policy *Krasnaya zvezda* makes it perfectly clear that the most important point for a commander to learn about his subordinates in considering their promotion is the strength of their ideological conviction. If the subordinate officer does not have "Party passion and firmness," he will not make a good commander, no matter how brilliant his knowledge of military technology and military affairs.[143]

b. Instruments of Control.   The Party's claim to exercise total leadership of the army is not left as a simple matter of affirmation. The Party has taken steps, as it has in the civil society, to implement its control. The right extended by the Twenty-fourth Party Congress to many primary Party organizations to supervise the management of establishments for which they work is not supposed to apply to the administration, that is, to the command, of military units. The right of Party primary organizations to control administration was, however, accorded the primary Party organizations of the cost-accounting, production, and trade enterprises of the Ministry of Defense.[144] The Twenty-fourth Party Congress extended the number of these Ministry of Defense organizations in which primary Party groups have the right of supervising management. "In accordance with the changes in the CPSU regulations introduced at the Twenty-fourth Party Congress, the primary Party organizations of financially autonomous production enterprises, construction organizations, cultural and educational establishments, and trade enterprises of the Ministry of Defense are accorded the right of control over the activity of the administration."[145]

The Party campaign to persuade the Soviet public of its increased participation in the affairs of state (see pp. 280–281) has its counterpart in Party indoctrina-

[139] Ibid., January 31, 1973, p. 1.
[140] *KVS,* no. 16, August 1971, pp. 25–31.
[141] Editorial, *KZ,* July 13, 1972, p. 1.
[142] Ibid., June 8, 1972, p. 1.
[143] Ibid., November 23, 1969, p. 2.
[144] *KVS,* no. 4, February 1971, pp. 87–92.
[145] General Yepishev in *KZ,* March 2, 1973, pp. 2–3.

tion in the military, where emphasis is also placed on the growth of socialist democracy in the military forces. Here, however, "it has a number of special features . . . here it is necessary to disclose the role of Party and Komsomol organizations as well as of general meetings of servicemen, gatherings and conferences of the leaders, and the activity of various councils and permanent commissions in the upbringing of the servicemen and in the accomplishment of other important tasks in army and navy life."[146] That is, democracy in the military is achieved largely through participation in the Party and in Party-inspired meetings.

There are hints that military Party organizations will be more closely integrated with civilian Party organs. In discussing the exchange of Party cards in the military, *Kommunist vooruzhennykh sil* points out that arrangements for issuing new Party cards are "being carried out jointly with the territorial Party organizations."[147] This suggests a cooperation of civil and military Party organizations that does not normally seem to occur. Another indication of the Party's interest in bringing military Party groups into a closer relationship with civilian activity is provided in a statement by General Yepishev. He urged military Party secretaries to "strive to extend creative links between commanders, political organizers, and Party and Komsomol organizations [of the armed forces] and local Party, soviet, and Komsomol organs; between army and navy collectives and the collectives of enterprises, construction sites, kolkhozes and sovkhozes, and scientific, educational, and cultural centers."[148] This and similar statements suggest that Party leaders seek to integrate the military forces more fully into a civilian framework and to prevent Party units of the military from being isolated from the Party at large. General Yepishev's reference to "creative links" with civilian enterprises could, of course, involve anything from casual get-togethers to military contributions to civilian labor tasks.[149] The subordination of the political administrations of the arms and services to those of the military districts, that is, to the territorial organizations (p. 258), and the large-scale use of the military forces in getting in the harvests of 1972 and 1973 (p. 325) both seem related to this emphasis on "creative links."

The Fifth All-Army Conference of Party Organization Secretaries in 1973 was the first such conference to be held since May 1960. Like the 1973–74 Party

---

[146] *KVS*, no. 19, October 1972, pp. 17–20.
[147] Ibid., September 1972, pp. 53–58.
[148] *Pravda*, March 27, 1973, p. 2.
[149] On the use of the military for civilian labor, see Kolkowicz, *The Soviet Military and the Communist Party*, pp. 155–156, 264.

card exchange revived after a lapse of almost twenty years, the conference of Party organization secretaries occurring some thirteen years after the preceding assembly, was a further attempt of the Party to call on old Party institutions to strengthen the Party and put it more firmly in control. According to General Yepishev, an assembly of Party secretaries in the military forces must increase Party influence in all aspects of military life.[150] Two months before the conference took place, *Krasnaya zvezda* expressed its expectation that the meeting would have a "positive effect on increasing the influence of Party organizations" throughout the military forces.[151]

Party concern with exercising greater control over Soviet youth through a tighter grip on the Komsomol (see p. 283) is also reflected in the military forces. Since the overwhelming majority of military personnel are Komsomol members, "Komsomol leadership is the most important obligation of the primary Party organization."[152] Marshal Grechko also "laid particular emphasis on the need to improve the leadership of the Komsomol. . . . The main source of increasing the activity and militancy of the Komsomol organizations lies in improving Party leadership of the Komsomol."[153] Somewhat earlier, a *Kommunist vooruzhennykh sil* editorial had already emphasized that the task of military Party organizations "is to improve on a daily basis supervision of the Komsomol, and to strengthen its Party nucleus."[154] And, in fact, "secretaries of Komsomol primary organizations have increasingly come from the Party itself. In addition, the majority of young officers who acquire Party membership continue to work in Komsomol organizations."[155] Although by 1974 the Party nucleus in Komsomol had been "markedly" strengthened, "great efforts" were still being made to improve Party guidance of the organization.[156] In the air defense forces the Party stratum represented 3.4 percent of the Komsomol membership.[157]

An earlier step taken by the Party to increase its control over the military forces is now beginning to reach maturity. Only in the last three years have graduating classes of the new four-year officers' schools for company political officers been sent to the forces. Young political officers brought up to be loyal to the Party rather than to their commanders will increasingly provide the

[150] *Pravda,* March 27, 1973, p. 2.
[151] *KZ,* January 23, 1973, p. 1.
[152] Ibid., March 2, 1973, pp. 2–3.
[153] Ibid., March 28, 1973, pp. 1–2.
[154] *KVS,* no. 19, October 1972, pp. 3–8.
[155] Ibid., no. 17, September 1973, pp. 48–57.
[156] *KZ,* March 14, 1974, p. 3.
[157] *KVS,* no. 6, March 1974, pp. 36–44.

Party in the coming years with representatives in the lower echelons of the forces. Many of these Party representatives are likely to think of themselves as professional Party workers rather than professional military men.

Party control over admission to the schools for company political officers will provide a class composition more consistent with the Party's policy of increasing the representation of industrial and farm workers in positions important for social control (see pp. 281–283). Less emphasis on competitive examinations and more emphasis on "points" acquired by "civic work" in selecting candidates for the cadet academies will facilitate this. The warrant officers' and ensigns' schools have provided another opportunity for the Party to select students in such a way as to achieve a class structure agreeable to it.

In 1926, 77.5 percent of the military forces were peasants and only 14.3 percent were workers. By the end of the sixties the military had the following composition, which probably reflects Party preferences as well as the great change that had taken place in the occupational structure: 56.7 percent from industry, transportation, and construction; 29.9 percent from agriculture; and 13.4 percent from office workers and students.[158]

Until Marshal Zhukov became both minister of defense (1955) and a candidate member of the Politburo (1956) and full member for three months in 1957, no full-time professional military officer had been a member of the Politburo. After the marshal was dismissed from these posts in 1957, fifteen years were to elapse before the military was once more represented in the Politburo.[159] Marshal Grechko became a full member in April 1973.

Military representation in the Central Committee of the Party shows little or no gain. In 1952, at the time of the Nineteenth Party Congress, nineteen officers were full and candidate members of the Central Committee.[160] At the Twentieth Party Congress in 1956 the military were represented in the Central Committee by eight full members and twelve candidate members.[161] In 1966 and 1971 military representation remained more or less static.[162]

In writing of the participation of military men in state (nonmilitary) affairs, *Kommunist vooruzhennykh sil* points to the fact that 197 officers, generals, and marshals have been elected as deputies of the USSR Supreme Council and the Supreme Council of the Union Republics, and that thousands

---

[158] Ibid., no. 4, February 1974, pp. 9–17.

[159] For an account of the conflict between Marshal Zhukov and the Party, see Kolkowicz, *The Soviet Military and the Communist Party*, pp. 398–418.

[160] Ibid., p. 391.

[161] Ibid., p. 402.

[162] Donaldson, "The 1971 Soviet Central Committee: An Assessment of the New Elite," *World Politics*, vol. 21, no. 3, p. 394. The Central Committee had 360 full and candidate members in 1966, and 390 in 1971.

of servicemen are deputies of local councils. As for the Central Committee of the CPSU, *Kommunist vooruzhennykh sil* avoids giving a separate figure that might seem small, and it cites only the combined military membership of the Central Committee of the CPSU and the Central Committees of the union republic Communist Parties: a total of 132.[163]

The representation of military men on nonmilitary Party organs raises questions concerning the role they play in performing these functions. Are the military members on the various republic Central Committees of the Party representatives of military interests or are they rather a form of liaison between Party and army, transmitting Party preferences to the military rather than military claims to the Party? Our sources hardly permit us to speak on these matters. Where the Central Committee of the Party is concerned, most of the leading military figures show, in their speeches and articles, a decided humility. Who is master and who is servant is perhaps expressed by Marshal Grechko's closing remark to the All-Army Conference of Party Organization Secretaries: "Allow me, on your behalf, to convey to the Politburo of the Central Committee that we will fulfill the tasks that have been placed before us."[164]

c. Justifications and Motivations.   Party statements stress that over the last several years the Party has not only aimed at, but has in fact achieved, increased control. Although such claims are conventional in Party statements, they have taken on a special insistence, justified no doubt by the concrete measures that the Party has taken. *Kommunist vooruzhennykh sil,* in acknowledging "the increased leading role played by the Party in military organizational development," finds it desirable, in an almost apologetic tone, to explain why this increased role has become necessary not only in the military, but also throughout Soviet society: (1) There has been a growth of the creative activity of the masses and an inclusion of millions of new workers in directing government affairs and production. Presumably it is their participation that enables the Party to assume increased responsibilities and increased authority. (2) The theory of scientific communism and the need to overcome vestiges of the past has become increasingly important. Here the leading role of the Party is essential. (3) It has become increasingly important to foresee the future and to select a true political course free from errors and subjective decisions. This is particularly important in a period marked by a "complex international situation." (4) As for the armed forces, the increased role of the Party in Soviet military affairs is particularly required because of the "broadening international missions of our armed forces."[165] Marshal Grechko has also explained the increased role of the Party in the military "by the complexity of the

---

[163] *KVS,* no. 18, September 1972, pp. 69–75.
[164] Moscow Domestic Service, March 23, 1973.
[165] *KVS,* no. 11, June 1971, pp. 3–8.

international situation, the intensification of the struggle on the ideological front, and the new demands made on the armed forces."[166]

Other writings have spelled out related and additional justifications. Particularly significant is the emergence of nuclear weapons and the threat of nuclear war. "The enhanced role and importance of CPSU leadership in military building is also conditioned by military-technical factors. The unprecedented military-technical revolution that has taken place in the past few years exerts tremendous influence on military building. During this revolution it was important to determine correctly the correlation of all elements in the structure of the complex military organism and to take into account the potential of the latest achievements of science and technology."[167] According to General Yepishev, it was the leadership of the Party and its mastery of Marxism-Leninism and of the Soviet art of war that enabled the problems of nuclear warfare to be solved and the army to be properly equipped.

However, nuclear weapons impose more than problems of equipment on the political leaders. A work issued by the Ministry of Defense publishing house asks, "What has caused an increase in the role of political leadership [in military affairs]?" Colonel Skirdo, the author of this work, first calls attention to "the increased complexity of many problems," which presumably the Party can solve better than the military. Second, he continues, it "depends on the political leadership whether or not there will be a world thermonuclear war." At this point, the author shows an interesting hesitation. It is, he adds, *mainly* the political leadership and not the military command that determines the need to use strategic means of mass destruction and plans the main objectives and moments for the launching of strikes. The necessity of a *single* political leadership is particularly important because the war will be a coalition war, and a single political leadership of the coalition will be needed, one that is authoritative, possesses great power, and is extremely flexible. "The ability to expose in timely fashion the aggressor's immediate preparations for attack, to penetrate his intention, and to adopt necessary measures" also depend on the political leadership *to a considerable degree*. The political leadership is also responsible for the correct determination of the goals of the war and works out military doctrine. Having just stated that "to a considerable degree" exposing the aggressor's immediate preparation for attack is a political responsibility, Colonel Skirdo continues: "One of the most important tasks of *military* leadership is the timely determination of the onset of the threat that directly precedes the unleashing of war and the enemy's nuclear missile attack." (Emphasis added.) The distinction is far from clear, perhaps intentionally so. Apparently, however, the penetration of enemy intentions is the job of the political leadership. The determination of the precise moment at which the enemy is about

---

[166] *KZ*, March 28, 1973, pp. 1–2.
[167] General Yepishev in *Pravda*, March 27, 1973, p. 2.

to launch his missiles is the job of the military leaders. The role of the military is not, however, reduced to this function. Colonel Skirdo in the last chapter of his book deals with the role of the general as the organizer and leader of armed conflict.[168]

The claim of the Party heads to be military leaders able to diagnose the strategic situation is supported by references to past experience. "Scientific prediction of the future is an urgent problem in military . . . science. Lenin, by a clear-sighted analysis of class forces, was able not only to predict scientifically the course of military actions on the front but also to anticipate the plans of the enemies."[169] However, in speaking of World War II, *Voyenno-istoricheskiy zhurnal* distributes credit for predicting the course of military events among the Party, the GKO (State Defense Committee), and the Supreme Headquarters.

In an earlier article dealing with World War II *Voyenno-istoricheskiy zhurnal* pointed out that the Party converted the country into a single military camp, directed the efforts of the Soviet people both at the front and in the interior zone, and "raised Soviet military science—the science of victory—to a new level."[170] Indeed, the Party armed the country with Marxism-Leninism —the world's most powerful weapon, a method for resolving all problems of military building and troop education and training. The increased significance of Party activity in the armed forces is further explained by the need for the moral, political, and psychological training of the troops "for possible stern testing in a war."[171]

After discussing military-technical factors requiring an enhanced role for CPSU leadership in the military, General Yepishev continues, "The enhancement of the Party's role in leading the armed forces is determined [also] by spiritual and ideological factors."[172] Indeed, given the Party's concern to intensify political indoctrination and disciplinary training, it sometimes appears that the Party is very much concerned with using the army as an institution for preserving the loyalty of Soviet youth to the Party. According to the chief of the political administration of the Baltic military district, "The imperialists' ideological diversions are aimed, first and foremost, at our youth, for the express purpose of undermining their faith in the justice of socialist ideology and the triumph of communism." He seems to come closer to a confession of concern for the power of the Party when he adds, "The imperialists also hope to turn youth against the older generation [the Party leaders?]."[173]

The Party is also motivated by a desire to develop the New Soviet Man,

[168] Colonel M. P. Skirdo [*People, Army, General*], Moscow, 1970.
[169] *Voyenno-istoricheskiy zhurnal,* January 1973, pp. 71–75.
[170] Ibid., September 1972, pp. 3–13.
[171] Ibid.
[172] *Pravda,* March 27, 1973, p. 2.
[173] *Kommunistas,* Vilnius, no. 4, April 1972, pp. 31–38.

that is, a Soviet citizen who is disciplined, hardworking, and capable of productive economic activity: "During the process of military service, a world outlook is formed in the young people, their international tempering is consolidated, their patriotic feelings are strengthened, positive character traits are developed, moral qualities are polished, and capabilities are educated into them to overcome difficulties along the path to the goals set by life."[174]

Soviet studies have determined that "up to 95 percent" of soldiers and NCOs believe that army service has played a major role in the formation of their characters. Perhaps more relevant to Party officials is the finding that about 52 percent of soldiers learned trades or professions in the army that were useful in civilian life.[175] The Twenty-fourth Party Congress had stressed that Communist education in the army and navy enables the forces "to play the role of a unique 'university.' " [176]

The Party has, finally, still another argument in favor of its leadership. Just as the "necessity for strengthening centralized leadership of the socialist economy becomes more and more obvious"[177] and just as the Party arbitrates disputes in the economy between management and specialist, so also the Party acts in the military to settle all issues and take into account the diverse claims of different groups.[178] Brezhnev, during the Lenin celebrations in 1970, expressed this role of the Party very clearly. "We neither have nor can have any other political force that would be capable of taking into account, combining, and coordinating the interests and requirements of all classes and social groups. . . . The Party acts as the organizing nucleus of the entire social system."[179]

Despite its success in increasing its control, the Party is sensitive to allegations that it has failed to achieve a guiding role or that its guiding role is being eroded. Some Party analysts have apparently been upset by western discussions of the conflict between, on the one hand, the military man with his professional skills and desire for professional autonomy, and on the other hand, the political authorities who attempt to limit his freedom for fear he will become politically independent. According to General Yepishev, "Particular efforts are concentrated on falsifying and distorting the role of the CPSU in military building."[180] His cryptic reference is spelled out more clearly by *Voyenno-istoricheskiy zhurnal.* "In recent years bourgeois theoreticians and propagandists have given special attention to the armed forces of socialist states. They are directing their primary efforts to falsify and distort . . . the guiding

---

[174] *Voyenno-istoricheskiy zhurnal,* September 1972, pp. 3–13.
[175] *Sputnik,* February 1973, p. 46.
[176] General Yepishev in *Pravda,* March 27, 1973, p. 2.
[177] *KVS,* no. 17, October 1972, pp. 9–16.
[178] *Pravda,* February 9, 1972, p. 2.
[179] *Izvestia,* April 22, 1970.
[180] *Pravda,* March 27, 1973, p. 2.

role of the CPSU in military building. . . . Knowing the colossal role our Party plays . . . the imperialist critics would like to weaken the guiding role of the Communist Party in the military field. In a number of bourgeois military journals the masters of falsification hinted that allegedly 'there is a weakening of the Party's role' in the Soviet armed forces." *Voyenno-istoricheskiy zhurnal* accuses these bourgeois writers of treating as reality what they would like to see happen.[181]

3. Conflicts and Tensions

a. The General Staff and the Party. There appears to have been in recent years no publicly visible Party-army conflict involving action against a major military figure similar to the dismissal in 1957 of Marshal Zhukov as minister of defense and a member of the Politburo. However, one prominent military personality may have attempted to resist Party encroachments in the area of strategic planning. In 1970 the late Marshal M. V. Zakharov, then chief of the general staff and a first deputy minister of defense, published an article in the September-October 1970 issue of *Novaya i noveyshaya istoriya.* In this lengthy article Marshal Zakharov examined the events leading up to World War II. In the midst of this paper the marshal interrupted his chronological account and introduced what seems, in the context of the paper, an aside:

> In speaking about planning in the military field, I should like to stress the following points. I am deeply convinced that the general staff is not only a directing organ for the control and leadership of the armed forces. . . . It also represents "a watchful eye" which is constantly looking ahead into the future and which does not let out of its field of view the trends and general development of military affairs. . . . In this connection I recall that . . . B. M. Shaposhnikov told me that in the course of a report he hinted to J. V. Stalin concerning the load of current matters. In reply Stalin, smiling slightly, noted that the chief of general staff is required to plan his activity in such a way that [he should be able to] lie on a couch and think persistently about the future. Of course, he had scientific forecasting in mind. All . . . planning . . . may turn out to be pointless and may not reflect the actual requirements . . . if they are not supported by thoroughly thought through calculations and considerations of the general staff on the strategic deployment of the Soviet armed forces in case a real threat of an attack on our country by the imperialist aggressors arises. Unquestionably, considerations of such a type are the fruit of a profound analysis of the foreign policy and military-strategic situation of the Soviet state. . . . This field of activity represents an intellectual competition between opposing general staffs and the ability to forecast correctly and represent dependably the course of impending events. Many components form the total of that scientific knowledge which permits delving deeply into the holiest of holies

[181] *Voyenno-istoricheskiy zhurnal,* September 1972, pp. 3–13.

—the sphere of probable strategic planning of the supreme leadership of an enemy state. The timely disclosure of enemy intentions and the adoption of precautionary measures or sufficiently convincing and weighty responsive actions can prevent much.[182]

In the course of the article Marshal Zakharov complimented the general staff on the excellence of its forecasts in 1938–39. He gave credit to the Party for its military preparations, but in attributing useful actions to the Party he generally linked them with the contribution of the government. He emphasized the importance of scientific forecasting without a single reference to Marxism-Leninism.

Marshal Zakharov's remarks on the role of the general staff stand in sharp contrast with, indeed one might say, in contradiction to, the claims of Party leadership in the area of strategic planning. The above passage should be compared to the discussion on pp. 285–286 and especially pp. 291–293.

Coincident with the publication of his article, Marshal Zakharov went into semiretirement in October 1970 and disappeared from the military scene for some six months.[183] His age at the time (seventy-two) lent plausibility to the supposition that this semiretirement in 1970 and his total retirement in 1971 were due to illness and age. In any event, what is of interest here is not whether the marshal was relieved of his post for having attempted to challenge Party authority in military affairs, a speculative matter, but rather that this leading military personality implicitly opposed Party claims.

b. One-Man Command. Party desire to control all sectors of the society runs into a special difficulty in the military establishment, whose hierarchical organization and strict subordination to the commander raise questions concerning the role of Party authority. These have presumably been resolved by the principle of one-man command whose origin is attributed to Lenin.

One-man command faces difficulties on two accounts. First, the commander as a member of the Party is subject to the criticism of even the lowliest member of the Party in his primary Party organization (see p. 271). However, the principle of one-man command is maintained, since orders or commands of a commander are not themselves subject to criticism or questioning. A second difficulty facing one-man command is the Party's desire to give political officers and political organs a strong voice in military matters. The political administrations, the political officers, and the Party committees and bureaus are almost necessarily involved in military command functions by virtue of the

---

[182] *Novaya i noveyshaya istoriya,* September-October 1970, pp. 3–27. This journal is published by the Institute of General History of the Academy of Sciences.
[183] Radio Liberty Dispatch, no. 23, 1971, p. 1.

tasks imposed upon them by the Party. However, in principle, "one-man leadership signifies that the Communist Party and the Soviet government have vested a commander with full rights and placed in him all responsibility for training and educating the personnel of the military collective entrusted to him and for maintaining strict discipline and constant combat readiness."[184]

Although affirming the integrity of one-man command, Party-oriented writers generally hasten to add qualifications. "In all his activities the commander relies on the active support of Party organizations."[185] "The principle of one-man command is strictly observed in the army and navy. But as a rule, commanders and chiefs at all levels actively rely for support on Party organizations . . . consult with their deputies [for political affairs] and assistants and with political workers and other Communists."[186]

General Yepishev makes it clear that the principle of one-man command has limits and is contingent on the commander's cooperation with the Party. "This principle [one-man command] . . . presupposes high ideals and Party-mindedness on the part of the commander, invariable and active personal participation by him in educational work [that is, in Party work] . . . the ability to rely constantly on the Party organizations in his activity. . . . We can note with satisfaction that the education of people [Party work] is occupying an ever increasing place in the activity of our command cadres. This is of tremendous significance. 'Though a leader is invested with the powers of one-man leadership,' Comrade L. I. Brezhnev said at the Twenty-fourth Congress, 'nevertheless he cannot rely solely on the power of command.' The guarantee of success is to be found in an organic combination of organizational [command] and educational [Party] work."[187]

More explicit and threatening statements are not lacking. One-man command "does not mean that he [the commander] is free to act as he wishes. . . . One-man leadership in the USSR armed forces is organized on a Party basis. . . . [The commander] always and in every matter strictly follows the requirements of the Party. . . . In all his activities he relies actively on the Party. . . ."[188] The Party "strengthens" one-man command by ensuring that the Party actively indoctrinates the officers, the generals, and the admirals in Party attitudes, by providing them with "kindly guidance on urgent questions," and by supervising and checking the execution of their work.[189]

That such qualifications lend a peculiar air to one-man command is recognized by *Kommunist vooruzhennykh sil.* "The peculiarity of the Soviet single command consists in the fact that it is particularly combined with an

---

[184] *KVS,* no. 23, December 1969, pp. 45–50.
[185] Ibid.
[186] Ibid., no. 12, June 1971, pp. 26–35.
[187] *KZ,* March 28, 1973, pp. 2–3.
[188] *KVS,* no. 17, September 1973, pp. 3–8.
[189] Ibid.

increase in the role of political organs and Party organizations, upon which the single commander depends. The Communist Party steadfastly strengthens the single commander on the Party foundation. . . . "[190] What is even more peculiar is the singular amount of double-talk in this passage. Some writers do not hesitate to associate the political officers with the military leadership on a more or less 50/50 basis. Thus a rear admiral refers to military units as being "under the leadership of the commanders and political workers."[191]

The uncomfortable juxtaposition of statements affirming both one-man leadership and the commander's dependence on the Party is sometimes glossed over by pointing out that the commander is after all a representative not only of the military but of the Party and the government. This resolution of the conflict of responsibility was foreshadowed by an attempt to integrate the functions of commander and Party leader. Such an integration was encouraged in the October 1958 decree on political organs of the armed forces in which commanders at lower echelons were urged to assume leadership of Party units.[192] In the same spirit writers today emphasize that "command cadres are widely represented in the Party organs."[193] Credit for a highly successful air regiment that has been flying for twenty-five years without any accidents is attributed to the fact that the military commander himself directs the work of the Party organization.[194] That this dual function is not assumed too often is suggested by frequent statements to the effect that commanders do not participate in Party and Komsomol meetings to the extent desired. They often avoid invitations to make information speeches despite the fact that such speeches would increase their prestige and permit them to learn more about their subordinates.[195]

c. The Right to Criticize.   The right of Party workers in military units to advise and to criticize inevitably leads to infringements on the principle of one-man command. Supervision of the management of civil establishments by the Party group is, in effect, transferred to the military structure. As in the civil society, "supervision is supervision. . . . Awkward moments are possible."[196] The political officers are, after all, subordinated to the political administrations and they to nonmilitary Party organs. The loyalty of political officers to military commanders can at best be a divided loyalty.

The Soviet military literature is rich in examples of actions in which Party activists intervene in areas of command responsibility. When the failure of an

---

[190] Ibid., no. 7, April 1971, pp. 86–88.
[191] *KZ,* January 26, 1973, pp. 2–3.
[192] R. L. Garthoff, *Soviet Military Policy: A Historical Analysis* (New York, 1966), p. 57.
[193] *KVS,* no. 17, September 1971, pp. 3–12.
[194] *KZ,* February 9, 1971, p. 1.
[195] Ibid., January 10, 1970, p. 2.
[196] *Pravda,* March 3, 1972, p. 2.

airplane motor during flight led to an investigation, the guilty individual "had to answer to the Party."[197] Similarly, when a sailor received a bad score on a firing examination, it was taken up at a Komsomol activists meeting and the sailor was required "to answer to his comrades." *Kommunist vooruzhennykh sil* comments, "To some it might seem that it is hardly the business of a Komsomol bureau to discuss the weak knowledge displayed by a sailor. However, the activists had acted properly."[198]

Party organs have the right to recommend, but when a lieutenant colonel did not follow a recommendation of a Party organ, he was reprimanded by the political administration of the military district.[199] It is the privilege of a political officer "to caution the commander against making certain mistakes or rash decisions," especially in areas that might affect the morale of the unit. Failure to respond to the cautionary statements of political officers can result in reports being sent by the latter to the political department above them. In one case a commander forbade the political officer to write such reports, whereupon the latter responded by appealing to *Krasnaya zvezda.*[200] The commanders are not only subject to criticism from political officers and Party activists but also from the Party-controlled military press.

The manner in which Party recommendations turn out in fact to be orders is further illustrated by the case of a secretary of a Party committee, a major, who made a number of recommendations to a senior lieutenant in order to correct the training process in the latter's unit. He hoped that the company commander would take his remarks into account. In fact, the company commander did not implement his recommendations. Higher political authorities, however, now reprimanded the secretary of the Party committee because he had not checked on whether his recommendations had been carried out. In short, in the eyes of the higher political section, recommendations were commands.[201]

Although company political officers cannot give orders to their company commanders, political officers above the company level are indeed able to issue orders to unit commanders in echelons below them.[202]

Party spokesmen continually urge military commanders not to try to do everything by themselves. *Kommunist vooruzhennykh sil* points out that lead-

---

[197] *KVS,* no. 20, October 1971, pp. 37–42.
[198] Ibid., no. 2, January 1972, pp. 52–56.
[199] Ibid., no. 22, November 1969, pp. 55–59.
[200] *KZ,* January 4, 1972, p. 2.
[201] Ibid., November 24, 1972, p. 1. According to the Instructions to CPSU Organizations in the Soviet army and navy, the commander must base himself on the policy of the Party in all his activity and rely on the strength and influence of Party organizations. Relying on the Party organization means "to maintain constant, close contact with the communists, . . . to consult with them, to listen to their views and suggestions carefully." *KVS,* no. 19, October 1974, pp. 47–54.
[202] *KZ,* July 20, 1971, p. 4.

ing Soviet officers, generals, and admirals experience an urgent need to confer constantly with their deputies for political work and with their Party organizations. A major general who confers with the chief of the political division before he makes his decisions is cited approvingly.[203] The commander is urged to take the advice not only of political officers, but also of the "communists" in his unit. Since most officers are members of the Party or the Komsomol, the injunction to pay attention to the "communists" clearly refers to the Party activists.

There are, as we shall see shortly, some areas in which conflict with the commander is likely to be more limited. However, the "soldier-communists" have also been given responsibility by the Party for areas central to the responsibility of the military commander. At the recent conference of military Party secretaries "the soldier-communists stress that questions of the forces' constant combat readiness should always be at the center of attention of Party political work."[204]

d. The Military Professional and the Political Professional. Party-military tensions arise also from the Party's undermining of the status of Soviet military officers. Marshal Grechko's list of the six requirements of a Soviet officer put political duties "first and foremost" and high general military and technical efficiency in sixth place (see p. 286). This hardly promotes professional pride.

The professional military officer is probably not led to esteem his political colleagues more highly by statements to the effect that at the political-military academies political officers are trained to be "totally dedicated to the cause of the Communist Party. . . . "[205] The statement "Party members [Party activists] are warriors who think and act in unison" certainly suggests, as so many other Party-oriented statements do, that the political officers and the Party activists are an army within the army.[206] The preeminent importance of ideology and Party loyalty induces further tension since it affects promotion, that is, the career rewards of professional military skills (see p. 287).

Not all officers are enthusiastic about the use of political criteria. General Pavlovskiy, chief of the ground forces, in the course of a rather lengthy article on the qualities required of a regimental commander, lists a number of skills and qualities from which political leadership and Party conviction are notably absent until the last two or three paragraphs, where the regimental commander as a leader of Marxist-Leninist training groups is given rather perfunctory

[203] *KVS,* no. 12, June 1971, pp. 26–35.
[204] Moscow Domestic Service, March 28, 1973.
[205] *Voyenno-istoricheskiy zhurnal,* December 1969, pp. 36–39.
[206] KVS, no. 16, August 1971, pp. 25–31.

treatment.[207] Two months later General Pavlovskiy acknowledged that the quality of a senior commander's own self-education in political matters can be measured by his willingness to participate in and lead propaganda and agitation work.[208]

Given their high professional military status, many regimental commanders and generals probably have good reasons to resent the incursion of political criteria and political objectives into their work. These tensions lead some commanders to a jealous defense of their prerogatives. Thus a regimental commander countermanded an order of his deputy for political affairs given during his absence and reproved him in public for another order because it had not been coordinated with him.[209]

Some aspects of the conflict between political officers and commanders are more acute at the company level. The youthfulness of the company political officer, his recent graduation from the political academy, and his occasional brashness and political zeal all provide opportunities for daily tension and conflict in the limited confines of a company. Indeed it appears that when the company political officer gets into difficulties and appeals to the political officers of higher echelons, they sometimes side with the unit commander.[210]

It is, no doubt, the Party zealots among the new company officers who probably occasion the most friction with their colleagues. A young political officer, in an article in *Krasnaya zvezda,* points out that it is now the young Communists who must fill the ranks of the "commissars." His use of this term, even in the jocular manner indicated by the quotation marks in the original, does not lessen the vague threat that the term conveys, nor moderate the impression that indeed the political officer still performs many of the functions of the old commissar. This same young political officer stresses that the political officer in the army represents the Communist Party. Of course, he adds, commanders are Communists, too, but anyone can be a member of the Communist Party, whereas political work is a profession.[211] Such brash attitudes, surprising even in *Krasnaya zvezda,* can hardly ingratiate young political officers with their colleagues, who would probably prefer them to have a little more the attitude of a military professional and a little less that of a political professional.

One source of conflict is virtually ineradicable, and this is competition for the time of the soldiers. Commanders can hardly find adequate time for their training responsibilities and operational exercises, and this produces a conflict

---

[207] *Voyennyy vestnik,* January 1971, pp. 2–12.
[208] *KVS,* no. 5, March 1971, pp. 17–23.
[209] *KZ,* March 4, 1973, p. 2.
[210] See, for example, *KZ,* January 4, 1972, p. 2, and February 13, 1971, p. 2.
[211] Ibid., June 19, 1971, p. 2.

with the political officers, who also have large demands for the time of the soldiers in order to fulfill their obligations with respect to political indoctrination, socialist competition, disciplinary reviews, and Party and Komsomol tasks.

A delicate issue is whether the deputy for political affairs can take command of a unit in the event that the military commander is incapacitated. *Kommunist vooruzhennykh sil* does not directly discuss this matter. However, in reviewing a book of reminiscences by a political officer, *Kommunist vooruzhennykh sil* emphasizes that one particular idea permeates the book. "In battle it was frequently necessary to replace command personnel. The experience of World War II showed that political workers did an excellent job."[212] Thus *Kommunist vooruzhennykh sil* seems to establish the capacity and perhaps the right of a political officer to take military command. General Yepishev is more direct: "Deputy commanders must always be ready to take over all the duties of commanders."[213] This seems even more justified because the deputy for political affairs at the company level is increasingly an officer with intensive military training (see p. 275 above). At the regimental and battalion level the Interior Service Regulations of the USSR Armed Forces (1973) list the commander, the deputy commander, and then the political deputy to the regimental or battalion commander, in that order. But at the company level the deputy commander for political affairs is listed second before the deputy commander for technical matters (equipment). It is likely that the training in military skills in the four-year academies for political officers was intended by the Party to make it more feasible for the political officer to take over command, if this becomes necessary, without a major loss of military effectiveness.

Some officers have a certain amount of contempt for the political officer, his duties, and his career. An officer who transferred to political work reports that he was advised against this change by one of his colleagues, who told him, "You are looking for worries for yourself. I have gone into equipment. At least you do not have to be responsible for your subordinates." The political officer then continues, "It has to be confessed that there are still people among our officers, and above all, among our young ones, who underestimate the importance of political work and who doubt that one can become a political worker by vocation in the same way as, say, one becomes a commander or military engineer."[214] Officers who are being pressed into political instruction express similar attitudes. "Once I witnessed a lieutenant who refused to lead political instruction, saying, I have no talent for propaganda. I am a technician."[215] Another officer is criticized by *Krasnaya zvezda* because he requested that he be excused from educational work. "Let the political officer educate them.

[212] *KVS*, no. 14, July 1971, pp. 88–89.
[213] *KZ*, April 28, 1973, p. 2.
[214] Ibid., July 7, 1971, p. 2.
[215] Ibid., April 28, 1971, p. 2.

. . . He wanted to be involved only with technical concerns."[216] *Krasnaya zvezda* reports cases where by silent agreement of the commander or with his encouragement the political officer primarily does military instruction and neglects his political work. An air force political officer asserts, "I am not simply a political officer. I am also a pilot."[217] This indicates to *Krasnaya zvezda* "the necessity for constant concern to instill professional pride in the political officer. The army political officer has an excellent, captivating, and romantic profession. But do we speak of this often. . . . It also happens that a graduate of the military political school is not innoculated with professional pride."[218]

A prejudice against political officers also seems to exist in the preinduction military courses in schools and factories. *Krasnaya zvezda* complains that a candidate for the job of teaching a preinduction military course was rejected because he had been a political officer in the army.[219]

The defensive attitude of *Krasnaya zvezda* is clearly revealed when it finds it necessary to urge military officers to remember that the "duties of the company political worker . . . are honorable."[220] It is not uncommon to read that new company political officers and their commanders have not yet "really begun to understand each other."[221]

The position of the political officer seems to be sufficiently difficult when he joins his unit after graduation from the political academy to require *Krasnaya zvezda* to urge units "to surround the young political officers with concern and attention, to greet them warmly, and joyfully admit them to the regiment or ship's family of officers. It is important that they should feel at home immediately and realize that they are an integral part of a harmonious military collective."[222] One seems entitled to infer that it is not easy to persuade their military colleagues to give political officers as warm a welcome as might be desired.

The reserve felt for political officers also expresses itself in their assignment by their commanders to duties that prevent them from carrying on fully their political work. It is a common complaint of both political officers and the political administrations that support them that political officers are frequently assigned such duties. Thus a company political officer complains that he had to serve as firing instructor on the range and then as duty officer, and later had to engage in gunnery training demonstrations. *Krasnaya zvezda,* condemning this common situation, asks, "Who will be sent out on a temporary duty assignment? A political worker. Who will be placed in charge of administrative duties? The political worker. At the present moment he has been assigned as

[216] Ibid., June 24, 1971, p. 2.
[217] Ibid., December 16, 1972, p. 2.
[218] Ibid.
[219] Ibid., July 14, 1971.
[220] Ibid., September 14, 1971, pp. 2–3.
[221] *KVS,* no. 5, March 1971, pp. 86–88.
[222] *KZ,* September 14, 1971, pp. 2 –3.

chief of a club. Someone must surely travel on temporary duty assignments and serve as chief of the club and direct the administrative work. But why is the political worker always chosen . . . ? But if an unpleasant incident occurs, then they look for the political worker and they want to know what he did to prevent the incident from occurring."[223] On another occasion, *Krasnaya zvezda* complains that "it is becoming almost a rule to give company political workers jobs that are very far from their direct duties. They are sent off on long assignments."[224] Clearly they are thus gotten out of the way or made use of in a way that, for the commander, is more productive. The inexperience and immaturity of the company political officers facilitate this behavior by the commanders. These young officers "become confused," "do not find their place when the subunit carries out combat training assignments," and frequently are not adept in planning their workdays.[225]

Commanders often transfer company political officers from one subunit to another with a frequency that makes it impossible for them to get a grasp on the subunit to which they are attached. This presumably renders them more innocuous. *Krasnaya zvezda* reprimands commanders for this practice and urges that every graduate of the new political academies should be allowed to work for at least two or three years as a deputy commander for political affairs in the same subunit. "Unjustified transfers from one subunit to another must not be allowed. . . . This will enable the young political workers to acquire confidence . . . feel themselves to be real political fighters . . . in a calm and familiar atmosphere."[226] It is apparent from such practices that the relation between the political officer and the commander has not developed with the degree of "sincerity and trust in each other" that the Party desires.[227] *Krasnaya zvezda's* reminder to the forces that Major General L. I. Brezhnev was head of the political administration of the Fourth Ukrainian Front is perhaps intended to lend greater prestige to the political officer.[228]

e. Alleviations. There are some countervailing factors that tend to reduce Party-army friction. The army, after all, is treated with some care, both in terms of the pay and prerogatives of the officer class and of the new ensign-warrant officer ranks, and in terms of the generous share of Soviet GNP allocated to national security. Strategic parity, the restoration of roles and missions to conventional forces after Khrushchev, and the growth of the Chinese threat have certainly lent new status, importance, and satisfaction to the military. Nor can the Party afford to alienate in any radical fashion an

[223] Ibid., May 20, 1971, p. 2.
[224] Ibid., July 8, 1971, p. 1.
[225] Ibid., December 2, 1973, p. 2.
[226] Ibid., September 14, 1971, pp. 2–3.
[227] *KVS,* no. 10, May 1971, pp. 43–50.
[228] *KZ,* May 9, 1973, p. 3.

officer class that may be needed for its own protection. In addition, of course, the Party's foreign interests require an army free from gross manifestations of discontent.

Second, the army can take some comfort from the fact that Brezhnev, unlike Khrushchev, has not, at least publicly, had himself named commander in chief.

Conflict and tension are also controlled and to some extent reduced by virtue of the fact that at the highest levels of command there is a good deal of overlap between what might be viewed as politically oriented and militarily oriented officers. Marshal Grechko is no doubt a professional military man, yet at the same time it is difficult to think of him other than as a Party personality. No Party leader speaks more strictly in a Party vein than does Marshal Grechko, whose statements often verge on the servile and humiliating. The articles that appear under the names of many top generals have a similar Party ring and represent an intimate mingling of Party discipline and professional military status. To be sure, some leading military figures seem on occasion capable of emphasizing their loyalty to professional military interests rather than to the Party. This perhaps is the case with Marshal Zakharov (see pp. 295–296 above) and General Pavlovskiy (see p. 301 above).

Tension and conflict are somewhat mitigated too by virtue of the fact that the Party, if only hypocritically, pays tribute to the principle of one-man command and extols the commander to his subordinates. "The commands of the Soviet one-man commander emanate from the lips of the fatherland itself. In implicitly obeying their officers, noncommissioned officers, and petty officers, Soviet soldiers and sailors are carrying out the will of the Party and serving their people."[229] Even more touching is the Party's requirement that the subordinates of a commander love him. "Love for the commander—the demanding mentor and solicitous superior—is not only a requirement of regulations but also one of the glorious traditions of the Soviet armed forces. Soviet military regulations require servicemen to protect their commanders in battle."[230]

On rare occasions *Krasnaya zvezda* takes political section leaders and young Party zealots to task for interference with command functions. "Officers of one of the political sections repeatedly pointed out to a young secretary of a Party organization . . . that he was giving jobs to Communists that forced them to act in the place of the commander, and that constituted, thus, an interference in the latter's service function."[231] Although it was comforting, no doubt, to commanders to know that the young secretary was reprimanded,

---

[229] *KVS*, no. 18, September 1972, pp. 69–75. In emphasizing the authority of the commander, *KVS* is careful to derive that authority from the Party.

[230] Ibid.

[231] *KZ*, May 23, 1972, p. 2.

gratification was probably diminished on reading that the "young" Party secretary was an engineer captain, a rank that suggests that this sort of interference was hardly the result of youthful inexperience.

The commanders of units have a common interest with the political officer in achieving success in political training, in socialist competition, and in maintaining discipline and order. The commander's future promotion may depend on how well the political officer can mobilize the members of the unit into a zealous pursuit of socialist competition, an interested study of their political lessons, and a firm adherence to regulations. Besides, the commanding officer will generally be only too happy to have the chores of stimulating socialist competition and providing political training handled by the political officer. The political officer, too, relieves him of types of duties associated in western armies with the chaplain. The commanding officer is, then, as *Kommunist vooruzhennykh sil* perhaps maliciously points out, "completely aware of how important it is for him to receive support from the Communists and members of the Komsomol."[232]

The common interests of commanders and political officers are strengthened by the fact that some political officers are not very zealous in the pursuit of Party objectives, and indeed are willing to connive, together with their commanders, at falsifying figures on the achievement of disciplinary and military and political training goals.[233] The growth of a large new class of company political officers may increase the number of political officer careerists who do not have a strong Party morality and whose trustworthiness and close obedience to Party orders and discipline may be less than the Party desires. In any case, some political officers are clearly capable of being "friendly" and of not imposing Party morality on the commanders of the units in which they serve.

Tension between political officers and commanders is reduced in some instances by virtue of the fact that some commanders are not strongly dedicated professional military men with a high sense of military honor and the prestige of the military profession. Consequently their attitude toward the political officer is pragmatic and influenced by career considerations rather than by professional sentiments.

Finally, the sharpness of Party-army tensions is blunted by virtue of the fact that neither side is monolithic. Party leaders like to present a seamless Party facade, but divergences in views on issues important to both the Party and the military (budget allocations for heavy industry and for defense, détente, and disarmament) are sufficient to prevent Party-army differences from having the character of two solid blocks with internally homogeneous and externally opposed views.

[232] *KVS,* no. 24, December 1970, pp. 40–45.
[233] *KZ,* November 24, 1972, p. 1.

F. CONCLUDING OBSERVATIONS

The Party's claims to military leadership, its increased control over the armed forces, and Party-army tensions are, of course, by no means unique to the last several years. Party-army tensions have existed throughout most of Soviet history. The army has had its periods of relative independence and political influence and the Party, more frequently, has had its periods of reasserted authority and tightened control over the armed forces.[234]

Following the ouster of Khrushchev in late 1964, the military, whose interests had been so severely manhandled under the Khrushchev regime, appeared to regain some of the ground lost in the preceding years. Marshal Zakharov, dismissed as chief of the general staff by Khrushchev after the Cuban missile crisis, resumed this position and gave expression to the military's interest in protecting the claims of professional military expertise and the need for a high level of investment in heavy industry.[235] The continued Soviet strategic buildup, accompanied by a restored importance for conventional forces, and the increased prominence of Soviet naval forces on the seven seas were no doubt satisfying to different sectors of Soviet military leadership. Granted these important sources of satisfaction to the military, it remains nonetheless true that beginning in 1967 the Party dealt several important setbacks to military interests, although as we have seen these were not necessarily motivated by an antimilitary animus. These setbacks affected especially the day-to-day training and operational activities of the forces. Clearly, Party priorities and Party controls were far from coinciding with military preferences.

The infusion of a large number of political officers at the company level will have consequences that the Party probably is only now beginning to face (see p. 302 above). These young officers cannot be kept indefinitely at the company level. If the political officer is not to be condemned to a low status and if recruitment into the four-year political officer academies is to be maintained, the young political officers will have to receive promotion at a speed normal for young officers. General Yepishev has stated: "Care must be taken to insure that deputies [for political affairs] do not remain too long in their posts and to promote them in good time."[236] In fact, since the political officers start as deputy commanders, they may become commanders more rapidly than other junior officers. The political sections of the battalions, regiments, divisions, and military districts will hardly be able to absorb this large number of upward-moving political officers. It is likely that there will be some increase

---

[234] The vicissitudes of Party-army relations up to 1966 are traced in Kolkowicz, *The Soviet Military and the Communist Party.*

[235] Ibid., pp. 301–302.

[236] *KZ,* April 28, 1973, p. 2.

in the number of Party functionaries in the higher echelons of the military, but many of the deputies will presumably be promoted to company commanders, a development that may, at least temporarily, lessen the military effectiveness of their units.

Do Party inroads in matters affecting major military interests and the intensification of Party controls signify a deep conflict between the Party and the armed forces or a deep sense of Party distrust, or even fear, of the military? The answer to this question is almost certainly "no."

Much of Party action in the military is an extension to the military of measures that the Party has taken in the civil society (pp. 278–285). Were Party actions vis-à-vis the military viewed in isolation from Party policy in the civil society, one would get a highly exaggerated sense of Party-army conflict. No doubt the military is not happy to be subjected to the degree of scrutiny and intervention that marks its relations with the Party, but it makes a difference that the army has not been the only target of intensified Party influence.

The institution of the political officer at the company level, the hated "commissar," is, however, a likely candidate as a specific antimilitary measure, that is, a measure based on apprehensions concerning the military. Still, the "youth problem" and the use of the military as a strategic locus for indoctrinating youth in their duties to Party, state, and society and for inoculating them against revisionist ideologies and blue-jean aspirations probably also had a good deal to do with the decision to reintroduce the company political officer.

There is one respect in which the Party seems to have had a special concern about the military. We have noted (pp. 284–285 above) the dilemma of the Party in trying to make a vanguard and elite out of a Party in which one out of every three men thirty to sixty years of age are members. This "dilution" of the Party is far more extreme in the military, where over 70 percent of the officers are members of the Party and 90 percent are members of the Party or Komsomol. Clearly, under such conditions there is a danger that rather than being a vanguard, the Party *in* the army may become the Party *of* the army and represent military rather than Party interests. Party measures, such as the exchange of Party cards, may serve to counteract Party dilution in the civil society, but it is unlikely to be very effective in the military unless the criteria for membership are far more vigorously applied. The Party will therefore continue to have a special concern for the purity of the Party in the army, a concern obviously fortified by the importance of the military as a locus of physical and political power. The interest in military-Party and civilian-Party cooperative relations and the concern with intensifying relations between military and civilian collectives (see p. 288 above) point to this continuing concern.

There is another point on which Party concern with the military has a character specific to the military. Experts, technicians, and managers may view themselves as far more competent than their Party bosses, but the Party is hardly likely to feel that its right to direct the economy or other civilian sectors is seriously challenged. With the military, the situation is different. Military doctrine, planning, and strategy are generally viewed as requiring military experience and a continuing exercise of professional military skills. Party claims in recent years to leadership in all military matters, high and low, has a certain stridency stemming, no doubt, precisely from the realization that Party authority in these matters is less easily established and defended than in matters of the national economy. No doubt there are also substantive differences over doctrine and military planning, although these probably stem in part from the Party's overall concern with national economic planning.

That Party treatment of the armed forces does not preclude relatively tranquil Party-army relations is indicated by the election in April 1973 of Marshal A. A. Grechko, minister of defense, to the Politburo. This is not, we believe, a sign of increased military influence over the Party. It is, very likely, a sign that the Party has the military well under control and is rewarding it for its acquiescence in matters disagreeable to it. It is also a personal reward to Marshal Grechko, whose subservience to Party policy, to the Politburo, and to Brezhnev specifically has made him indistinguishable from the most zealous Party spokesman (see p. 305 above). It seems related to the interest in increasing the status of the state apparatus (see pp. 280–281). Perhaps it is also inspired by the Party's realization that in a period in which a great new military and world power hostile to it is rapidly developing on its eastern border, it is appropriate to add a military figure to its inner circle.

Chapter IX

Some Peculiarities of Soviet Military Administration

A. AVOIDING DECISIONS

The Soviets have a pronounced tendency to provide regulations for almost all aspects and contingencies of military life in order thereby to constrain behavior within narrow, authorized limits. It is consequently a striking feature of Soviet military management that it sometimes tolerates ambiguities in important matters that one would expect to be subject to very clear regulation or definition. An examination of these lapses suggests that they are by no means due to administrative oversight, but that they represent, in fact, a deliberate avoidance—at least for a time—of a clear-cut decision. These evasions seem intended to sidestep issues the consequences of whose resolution, whether in one or another direction, are feared to be undesirable. In some instances the authorities have a preferred choice but are unwilling, for the moment, to face anticipated negative reactions or confrontations between interested parties. In some cases the motive is to permit or to encourage administrators to insinuate the leaders' preferred solution into the system without the authorities having to take responsibility for it or make the specific acknowledgment that a clearly defined regulation or definition would provide. By allowing administrators and subjects in the system to struggle to arrive at their own preferred and often conflicting resolutions of the ambiguity, the leaders are able to judge both the state of opinion and sensitivity on the matter and some of the consequences that one or another resolution is likely to produce.

Where the resolution that will be ultimately imposed is known in advance to the leaders, the period of indecision permits a gradual acclimatization of the subjects to that resolution and avoids the shock of a definite choice made without a buffer period. In some instances the leaders do not seem to know how far they can go or want to go, and the conscious cultivation of ambiguity permits a gradual clarification of these matters. The leaders may themselves have no strong preferences and may be trying to avoid a too openly partisan position with respect to contending interest groups in the military. They therefore avoid decisions and permit each of the contending interests to interpret the situation in a fashion advantageous to it. This permits considerable variability in the de facto regulations, a situation that in general is not welcome to Soviet leaders, but in these particular cases seems more desirable, at least for an initial period, than a clear resolution that would sharpen antagonisms or dissatisfaction. In a very broad sense, the evasiveness and ambiguity of regulations serve to thrust upon the administrative system itself the requirements of adjusting on an ad hoc basis to the ambiguity and thereby producing at least local solutions, which may later be reduced to uniformity by a clear regulation.

Some specific cases will illustrate these interpretations of Soviet administrative behavior.

In 1971 a Soviet major wrote to *Krasnaya zvezda* asking for an authoritative ruling on whether a deputy commander for political affairs of a battalion or regiment had disciplinary authority over company commanders directly subordinate to the battalion or regimental commander. *Krasnaya zvezda* gave a direct and unqualified positive answer to this question.[1] That clarification was required (and given) at this late date (1971) on such a major point concerning the line of authority can only have been due to an earlier attempt to avoid strict definition or regulation of the relative authority of political officers and military commanders. Party-army tensions were probably reduced by avoiding a clear decision or by permitting specific cases to be resolved on an ad hoc basis by the parties involved. The introduction of the company political officer in 1967 no doubt increased the sensitivity of both the political administrations in the military and the military commanders to questions of authority and

---

[1] *KZ*, July 20, 1971, p. 4.

placed a premium on avoiding sharp confrontations between these two lines of authority. The reestablishment of the company political officer had shown that the Party was able to impose its views and its priorities on the military in this area, and the blunt 1971 declaration by *Krasnaya zvezda* probably reflected a Party decision that habituation to the increased role of the political officers had gone far enough to permit an open clarification and resolution of the political-military lines of authority.

A further example of the Soviet preference for hedging is the 1963 Regulation on Political Organs (see pp. 258–259). This failed to specify in a clear and explicit fashion the duties and relationships of the political administrations of the arms and services. The Party and military authorities hesitated in particular to define the relations of the political administrations of the arms and services to those of the military districts, and it was only in 1973 that a new Regulation subordinated the former to the latter. What is of interest in the present context is the Party's admission that in the earlier (1963) Regulation the relations of these political agencies had not been explicitly stated and were "completely formulated *for the first time*" (emphasis added) in the 1973 Regulation.[2]

The Soviets have a fondness for assigning responsibility and leadership for a program or activity to a number of different agencies, partly motivated, it would seem, by a desire to increase the number of parties who can be required to contribute to a program and perhaps also to prevent any one agency from acquiring too much power. Although some areas of action may receive more or less emphasis in the work of one or another agency, the general tendency is to blur lines in the division of labor and of authority. Thus in the preinduction military training program the Party and the press assigned responsibility, with little or no differentiation of function, to school directors, factory managers, DOSAAF, and the military commissariats. Even when the commissariats were assigned an increased role (see pp. 40–41), no clear-cut distribution of administrative functions appeared in the press. The tendency is for all agencies to be made responsible in some measure for everything. This permits the authorities to bring pressure on whomever they wish and to assign, in any particular locality or situation, increased responsibility (or blame) to one or another agency as circumstances may dictate.

These practices make it possible for the authorities in other instances to *seem* to be assigning a leadership function to a group when in fact they are really seeking to confine these functions to certain selected and trusted agencies. Thus, the People's Control groups are repeatedly said to be under the "immediate supervision of commanders, political bodies and party organiza-

---

[2] *KVS,* no. 7, April 1973, pp. 16–26.

tions." In fact, in a division or higher unit the People's Control group is headed by the deputy chief of the political administration, and at lower echelons by a member of the primary Party organization (see p. 261). Thus, while commanders are said to share "immediate supervision" of People's Control groups, this supervision is in fact in the hands of the Party. Such formulations permit the Party to provide for control over the commanders while blandly affirming that increased surveillance of the military by People's Control "is based on the high trust of the Party . . . in Soviet military personnel" (see p. 261).

The reader will perhaps have noted that all the examples cited above involve questions of authority and seniority. This is not accidental. It seems that the avoidance, in fact or publicly, of clear administrative regulations or definitions is particularly employed to prevent, at a given moment, conflicts over authority and precedence that might have more disagreeable consequences than those resulting from a (temporary) failure to resolve issues or clarify responsibilities.

B. HAVING THE BEST OF BOTH WORLDS

It is generally taken to be a sign of maturity to recognize that having more of X may require having less of Y. When both X and Y are highly desirable, the need to give up one for the sake of the other or to make trade-offs between them often imposes a difficult decision. It is not congenial to the Communist temperament to forego one advantage or good in order to achieve another. The Soviet Communist is often unwilling to acknowledge to himself, much less publicly, that any desirable objective or desired form of behavior need be pursued with less than the fullest effort. Rather than making a compromise, Soviet leaders and administrators may insist on pursuing two conflicting goals with equal fervor. When they do seem to recognize the need for compromise and trade-offs, Soviet authorities act as if a public acknowledgement by them would lead to disaster by providing encouragement to the masses to ignore one or another duty or responsibility. The desire to avoid compromises and trade-offs is heightened by the fact that strict rules or instructions for making such trade-offs often cannot be formulated. Consequently the path of compromise, if followed, may also become a path of greater freedom of action for the subordinated individual or agency, a development generally not desired by Soviet leaders. Although Soviet military and political leaders like to talk about the importance of employing cost-benefit analysis, they do not at all seem to be at ease with some of the fundamental notions required in such analyses.

Trying to have the best of both worlds exhibits itself in striking form in connection with the drive to develop greater initiative and independence among military officers. We have already examined at some length (see chapter IV, section A,5) the Soviet practice of insisting on "bold decisions," "creativity," and initiative, while at the same time requiring, with equal or greater emphasis, an undeviating adherence to regulations and instructions. We also reviewed Soviet attempts to resolve this conflict and the evident failure of these efforts. This case is particularly interesting because both of the required directions of behavior are, from a Soviet standpoint, of great importance. On the one hand, it is clear to Soviet political and military leaders that the conditions of nuclear warfare demand a greatly increased freedom of action for military commanders. Probably this view is also reinforced by Soviet World War II experience. On the other hand, no disposition is more deeply ingrained in Soviet political leaders than that which demands total control and total conformity of personnel to prior instructions and regulations. Any attempt to increase the freedom of action of those who are the subjects of the system tends, in the Soviet mind, to undermine the very foundations of Party power and the authority of military leadership.

There seems little doubt that both military and political leaders would, in some sense probably not entirely clear to themselves, really like to see both junior and senior officers exhibit greater "creativity" and initiative. But they would like to achieve this objective without in any way eroding "undeviating adherence to regulations and instructions." That these two demands cannot be simultaneously maximized does not seem to prevent the Soviet authorities from attempting to do so. In part the conflict is waged in the minds of individual leaders, and partly it is a conflict whose opposing sides are supported variously by different elements of the military. The Soviet air force journal *Aviatsiya i kosmonavtika* is willing on occasion to weigh the balance a little more heavily in the direction of pilot freedom, whereas *Krasnaya zvezda*, a more strictly Party-line newspaper, emphasizes the importance of total conformity with all "the laws of flight duty." The conflicting demands for initiative and conformity are, however, far from being related to a simple opposition of the military and the Party mind.

It is not surprising, then, that the important issues at stake here have hardly been resolved or even substantially advanced. Since the full penalties imposed by limiting the ability of officers to make independent judgments will only be revealed in time of war, it is relatively easy for the authorities to content themselves with this irresolute treatment of the problem.

The same desire to have the best of both worlds exhibits itself in the civil defense program. The managers of industrial establishments are instructed to engage in elaborate civil defense exercises, but at the same time are told not to allow this to affect production. In fact, the Soviets have had to accept some costs in the form of interruptions of production schedules, but in general they attempt to persuade industrial managers that they can fulfill both their civil defense obligations and their production schedules. Indeed, managers have been told that civil defense training can be so organized that it not only does not interfere with production, but aids it. Similarly, in military training, combat realism must be rigorously enforced, but military matériel must be economized and severe penalties are imposed if accidents happen. Practical training must be emphasized more, but naturally theoretical training must not be emphasized less.

C. EVERYTHING IS EQUALLY IMPORTANT

The refusal in many instances to sacrifice some of X in order to have more of Y is reinforced by the Soviet Communist sentiment that everything is equally important and therefore one cannot afford to relinquish some of X for the sake of Y. "A Communist does not have secondary responsibilities. They are all important."[3] A military writer points out that there is nothing more erroneous than the breakdown of disciplinary requirements into different parts according to their supposed importance. "There are no trifles in discipline" (p. 144).

A major general, commandant of the city of Leningrad, pointed out that when he questioned a serviceman concerning a violation of discipline, the soldier conceded that he was guilty but added that it was just with respect to a minor detail. The general then lashes out, "Such a reply always makes me mad. In our army life there are no details; here everything has been thought out, everything is necessary, everything is essential and important."[4] Everything is equally important because from little things great consequences grow. Ignoring the first symptoms of disciplinary violations is fraught with the most dangerous consequences. "Moreover, as is known, everything begins with a minor detail. Today a button was not fastened, tomorrow a glove will be forgotten, then a salute is not given, and the commander is disobeyed."[5] Thus, from the failure to button a button may grow a revolution.[6] From the Soviet standpoint, this insistence on attending to all details with equal fervor is supposed to provide effective and foolproof administration, but in fact the treatment of all aspects of military life on the same level of importance hinders effective administration and reduces attention to the more important requirements of military training, discipline, and indoctrination.

The tendency to act as if "everything is essential and important" is related to the inability to discard ineffective procedures when more effective substitutes have been found. The realization that a certain training or disciplinary

<hr />

[3] *KZ,* February 2, 1971.

[4] *Starshina serzhant,* October 1971, pp. 34–35. The general's admission that the behavior of the serviceman made him angry is an admission of an emotion strongly disapproved of by Soviet military authorities. See pp. 180–181 and p. 195.

[5] Ibid.

[6] Ibid. The principle that unfavorable developments must be nipped in the bud (*principiis obstat*) before they grow out of control is an important rule of Bolshevik political behavior. See Leites, *A Study of Bolshevism,* pp. 449–461.

strategy is not effective often leads not to its elimination but to the addition of other means. Criticisms of the tendency to issue sterile slogans, to lecture soldiers, and to hold meetings instead of employing incentives and other constructive measures did not lessen reliance on these self-defeating procedures (see pp. 152–154). In this instance important organizations and personnel —the political sections, the Party groups, and the political officers—would have found themselves at some loss had they had to abandon or sharply reduce exhortation and "talk." It is understandable, therefore, that even a Party writer who emphasized the need to take positive actions and not just to exhort the troops nonetheless carefully prefaced this critical remark with the phrase, "Of course, there will be no progress without such appeals."[7] (See p. 153.)

D. THRIFT

The Soviet tendency to find that everything is equally important and that a good Communist must have the best of both worlds does not mean that the system authorizes exorbitant expenditures in order to achieve these exorbitant goals. On the contrary, Soviet writers dealing with troop management and with similar problems in civil life insist on thriftiness as a major virtue. Intensive practice in firing is desired in order to assure the highest development of firing skills. At the same time, however, the increased use of ammunition for firing practice is objected to by the authorities, who insist that firing skills be developed as much as possible by techniques that do not depend on the use of live ammunition. Similarly in the case of pilot training, drill and frequent repetition of basic routines in the air are emphasized together with the importance of training in situations simulating all of the risks and dangers of actual combat. However, when the costs have to be faced, Soviet authorities discover that a great many pilot skills can just as well be inculcated by work in ground trainers. When pilots and their instructors emphasize the obsolescence of many of the stationary trainers, they are told that even though they do not correspond to current models, many useful skills can still be learned in them. This, of course, does not mean that training in the air is largely avoided. The Soviets claim that pilots spend much more time in the air now than they did ten years ago. Nonetheless, despite the unrelenting demands for realism made by the authorities, motives of thrift clearly interfere with air force training programs. Here again the Soviets want to have the best of both worlds: since thrift and high performance are equally important, one is not to be sacrificed for the other.

The insistence on thrift is facilitated, especially in an authoritarian system, by transferring the sacrifices and costs involved in thrift onto the in-

[7] *KVS,* no. 3, February 1971, pp. 65–69.

dividual, who is required to contribute more and more of his free time or to sacrifice more and more of the privileges to which he is entitled. It is characteristic that when faced with the expansion of DOSAAF local and regional activities following the introduction of the complusory preinduction military training program, DOSAAF headquarters (that is, the Party) warned that problems are not solved by increasing staffs and making new capital investments but rather by strengthening discipline and involving more political activists in the work (p. 44).[8]

E. ADMINISTRATION OF MASS MILITARY PROGRAMS

It is characteristic of a number of Soviet mass programs that they manifest what appear to be extensive fumbling and disorganization and slow and erratic progress. Given the authoritarian and centralized nature of the system, this could easily suggest an indifference to the programs by the top leadership. The Soviet preinduction military training program and the civil defense program exhibit these characteristics in striking form. Ambitious goals are established; rules, regulations, and laws are enunciated and universal adherence and conformity on a national scale are immediately demanded even though funding, adequate personnel, nationwide communications, relevant experience and skills, and administrative control systems are almost completely lacking for the execution of the programs as formally announced. This seems very much the result of a deliberate, conscious administrative strategy. The Soviets do not hesitate (as we would) to initiate important mass programs by what in reality is a piecemeal ad hoc development with extremely modest commitments of resources. The programs, if actually carried out as formally announced, would generally involve an immediate consumption of massive resources and would be totally disruptive of other ongoing activities. To set the program going on a full and proper scale would risk its total collapse. On the other hand, the Soviets want to avoid acknowledging publicly that the program, which in principle must apply to all parts of the Soviet Union, will in fact operate only in some localities or with a lesser range of content or application than is indicated in its formal announcement. They prefer to start the program off as if it were full-scale but allow it to adjust to the realities of the lack of funds and the lack of administrative and other inputs. The Law of Universal Military Training specified in 1967 that the preinduction training program was to be introduced *everywhere* in *all* secondary schools, but this goal has not yet (1974) been attained. Programs therefore stumble along for some time in a way that bears no resemblance to what they are ultimately intended to be. The Soviets are thus able to get something moving that gradually acquires momentum,

---

[8] For additional remarks on Soviet thriftiness, see pp. 327–328.

whereas any attempt to insist on a really serious and effective program right from the start would simply paralyze all efforts.

The Soviets realize that ambitious programs such as civil defense and preinduction military training can only be built up over a number of years. Effective programs in such areas require enormous investments and a long indoctrination and training of the population. The longer time perspective of most Communist leaders, in conjunction with the high level of political control, makes them less likely than us to be paralyzed by the inability to achieve useful results immediately or even in the first few years. Besides, Communist morality insists on the necessity of facing problems and doing something about them, no matter how difficult. A passive attitude is a major vice. This outlook facilitates the initiation of difficult, expensive, long-term programs such as civil defense.

The Soviet preference for getting as much as possible done by voluntary efforts necessitates in mass programs a large measure of flexibility and a prolonged period of accelerating pressure and indoctrination. In 1968, when the preinduction military training program started, there were in the Ukrainian SSR only 320 indoor firing ranges available in the republic's schools. By late 1973, however, there were more than 2,000, many of them constructed with the help of student labor.[9] Resistance to mass programs, to the discipline that they impose, and to the contributions of precious personal time create problems for the Party. But the Soviet ad hoc, haphazard, and slowly developing program is an excellent salami-slicing tactic for wearing down opposition and gradually extending habituation and conformity to wider and wider areas and sectors.

Since a great deal of the required leadership and funds are based on voluntary effort, it is predictable that the program will start off in a highly uneven manner. Despite the fulminations of the higher and intermediate leadership, they clearly view this as a period during which they can train the population and modify goals and administrative measures. The sharp criticisms of local failures to conform to the full program are not so much signs of unanticipated failure as they are a routine means of indoctrination and pressure whose need was fully appreciated in advance. The difficulties, failures, and shifts in these programs should not, then, be interpreted as either high-level indifference nor as predictive of an indefinite ineffectiveness. A study of these programs shows that the Soviet ad hoc, chaotic and underfunded approach can, if one maintains a longer time perspective, produce impressive results. Gradually problems are straightened out, gradually funds accumulate, gradually skills and personnel are acquired, gradually the population submits to the required effort and discipline, and a program that was a travesty of what was intended eventually shapes up in an extremely useful fashion.

[9] *Sovetskiy patriot,* November 12, 1973, p. 1.

Chapter X

Some Constraints on Soviet Military Effectiveness

Soviet military training is marked by the extraordinary attention and effort that military leaders devote to it. It manifests an uncompromising dedication to announced objectives and an unwillingness at times to sacrifice, even in part, one objective in order to facilitate the pursuit of another. The demands made on personnel, both enlisted and commissioned, are relentless. Soviet military training is all the more onerous, all the more demanding, because it embraces not only the development of military skills in the conventional sense, but also a wide range of ideological, political, moral, and character traits and attitudes. Training so permeates the hour-to-hour and day-to-day activities of the Soviet forces that the distinction between operational and training activity becomes blurred.

The application of various means toward the achievement of training objectives equally manifests the intemperance and zeal characteristic of a political or religious fellowship. This fever pitch, the attempt to avoid the loss of a single minute, the abhorrence of any sign of laxness, and the imposition of the very highest standards as goals in the achievement of military skills, discipline, physical fitness, and political and moral behavior might well suggest both a high level of training effectiveness and a correspondingly high level of operational efficiency.

On the other hand, the frenetic spirit that surrounds the Soviet training system might in itself make its efficiency and an imputation of excellent results highly suspect. Socialist competition and the associated grading and inspecting system sometimes give the impression of mechanisms out of control and running wild. Soviet military writers are themselves the harshest critics of the "formalism," slackness, evasions, and cheating that mark much of socialist competition—"that mighty weapon" of Soviet military training.[1] Acknowledgments of difficulties and criticisms of the results of training and indoctrination are sufficiently severe and frequent to make one question the value of Soviet efforts in the military training field.

Which of these two interpretations comes closer to the truth? In the absence of readily applicable standards for evaluating the training and operational efficiency of the various arms and branches of the Soviet forces, and in the absence, in any case, of adequate data from the sources here reviewed that would permit valid comparisons with other armies, what considerations can nonetheless be brought to bear to aid in an overall assessment of the immense Soviet training effort?

Soviet training objectives are set high—perhaps higher, in many instances, than military leaders realistically aspire to. That these goals are not attained does not in itself spell failure. Considerably lower levels of attainment could, relative to the standards of most military establishments, represent a good degree of training success and operational efficiency. This, for example, would seem to be the case in the training of first-, second-, and third-class specialists and in the production of multiple specialists, even though Soviet quotas and objectives in these areas clearly are not met. Nonetheless, an appreciable number of recruits and, of course, a larger proportion of cadre are induced or coerced into using their free time as well as duty hours to acquire important technical skills. In addition, compared with western military establishments, the Soviet military benefits from the increasingly elaborate preinduction training program, which facilitates the acquisition of military specialties. This, together with the negligible pay and spartan conditions of life, makes Soviet training costs per man far less than in the West.

Although it certainly seems incorrect to say that Soviet training and operational procedures are *ineffective,* it is probably fair to say that they are, in many respects, *inefficient.* Certainly training results do not seem at all proportionate to the extraordinary intensity of the effort involved. From the

---

[1] *KZ,* August 22, 1971, p. 2.

means employed and the intensity of their application one might indeed infer that Soviet soldiers are all 10 feet tall, but the preceding chapters and some considerations provided below clearly suggest that they have a number of the limitations of the servicemen of other nations, and some that are peculiar to, or at least especially prominent in, the Soviet system. The armed forces hardly seem to have achieved the degree of excellence vaunted by high Soviet military leaders on ceremonial occasions when, for the time being, the irascible or ironic criticisms of Soviet military writers are forgotten.

Although we cannot compare the effectiveness of Soviet training and operations with that of other military establishments, it is possible to establish the existence of circumstances that, according to both common experience and Soviet comment, produce serious deficiencies and limit military effectiveness. We shall review a number of these factors that almost certainly have important consequences for individual, team, and unit effectiveness.

1. There are some training areas—especially those involving a certain amount of enforced mechanical repetition—where Soviet training procedures are able to produce results that come close to desired norms. Thus, for example, conscripts who "finish off" their strenuous morning exercises with a two-mile run will develop stamina irrespective of their attitude toward military service and of the overall sophistication of the training system. On the other hand— to take an equally elementary example—Soviet military drivers in East Germany who have passed DOSAAF preinduction driving standards and in addition have absorbed army driving discipline and training are, nonetheless, easily unsettled by the "high speed," narrow streets, and other demanding circumstances of East German urban and rural traffic and motorways.[2] This is not a trivial illustration. Where a certain finesse and ease born of protracted familiarity with the everyday life and problems of a society are required, high-pressure Soviet training does not necessarily suffice as a substitute. The technological backwardness of some sectors of Soviet society probably also accounts for the fact that some young soldiers are afraid to fire the submachine gun, the machine gun, and the grenade launcher. "No one of course made fun of them. . . . It was explained to them . . . that there was no danger involved in firing these weapons."[3] Excessive reserve when faced with an unfamiliar technology is not confined to rural Soviet youths. *Krasnaya zvezda* has complained of air defense commanders who resist the use of automatic control systems that have been provided for them and argue that even the most perfect

[2] *Starshina serzhant,* June 1972, pp. 26–27.
[3] *Bloknot agitatora,* no. 22, November 1973, pp. 6–8.

piece of equipment can never substitute for experience and intuition.[4] Prescriptions to encourage the independence, initiative, and "creativity" of officers do not suffice to produce them in a society where precisely these attributes are often penalized. In short, the Soviets certainly get some worthwhile results from their high-pressure training system, but it would be a great error to overlook the flaws in, and limitations of, a military system embedded in a society that not only fails to produce certain important skills and habits, but creates others that are seriously detrimental to military objectives.

2. The heavy investment in political indoctrination has negative effects on attainable skill levels both by detracting from the time available for skill training and by establishing political priorities that reduce the skill return for the time that is devoted to it. The Soviets seem to feel that the pressure of political demands on individuals and on their "free time" provides for relatively cheap returns. But Soviet "cost-free" methods are far from being as cheap as some Soviet military planners probably believe. Negative repercussions on morale and concealed (and often open) evasion and resistance, with their demoralizing effects, limit results achieved and impose costs to effectiveness that are not easy to assess but are clearly substantial. The Soviet tendency to seek extreme gains leads to the use of extreme methods that create a whole set of new problems.

3. The importance of political criteria in the selection and promotion of officer and noncommissioned cadres must inevitably decrease the military effectiveness of units. There is no reason to suppose that a high correlation exists between military talents and a willingness and ability to exhibit the behavior and attitudes agreeable to Party officials and KGB informers.

4. Soviet military manpower and manpower budgets, especially for officer personnel, must be discounted to take account of the large number of officers having primarily political functions. These include especially the company political officers and the officer personnel in the political sections and political administrations at battalion, regimental, and higher headquarters. These officers are not without military skills, and indeed the four-year academies for company political officers stress the need for political officers to have military skills. Nonetheless, both selection processes and the nature of the daily duties of the political officer are almost certain to limit the retention and further acquisition of military skills, and this can lead to deficiencies when the deputy commander for political affairs takes on command functions or replaces his

---

[4] *KZ*, October 7, 1973, p. 2. Even at the highest levels, attitudes and sentiments induced by a lack of everyday familiarity with technological accomplishments manifest themselves. Speaking of his first view, in 1953, of a Soviet rocket, Khrushchev said: "I don't want to exaggerate, but I'd say we gawked at what he showed us as if we were a bunch of sheep. . . . We were like peasants in a marketplace. We walked around and around the rocket, touching it, tapping it. . . . Some people might say that we were technological ignoramuses." *Time*, May 6, 1974, pp. 41–42.

commander, a replacement or promotion that the Party seems increasingly to envisage.

The Party's program to provide political officers at the company (or equivalent) level throughout the armed forces could hardly be satisfied without, say, 15,000 new political officers. To what total this will bring the complement of officers having primarily political responsibilities cannot be estimated from our materials. In the first months of World War II some 100,000 "political fighters" were sent into the armed forces. Whatever their number may be today, it certainly is substantial and represents not only a reduction in the number of strictly military officers, but a subtraction from the military budget from the standpoint of the professional military man.

5. A further discounting of Soviet manpower, training, and operational time is required, at least in terms of most western military standards and practices, because of the use of troops (construction troops) in large-scale construction projects. Troops are also used on military farms to provide meats and produce for army mess halls. Garrisons in isolated or remote districts are especially encouraged to develop their own agricultural products. This do-it-yourself farming may be less resented than the need for military units to supplement Soviet farm labor in order to harvest and transport Soviet crops. This use of the military to solve or alleviate the crises of Soviet agriculture has long been resented by the military as an affront to its professional status. Nonetheless, troops were employed to harvest the crops in the crisis year of 1972 and in 1973. The use of troops for construction and farm labor may be advantageous from the standpoint of the economy's productivity, but it obviously has to be taken into account in assessing the *military* "output" of the Soviet forces. The time available for Soviet military training and exercises is also reduced by the severity of Soviet winters. Discussions frequently refer to training activities that the onset of summer once again permits. "As is known, summer is a particularly busy time for the troops."[5]

6. The Party's desire to control all sectors of the society creates special problems in the military, whose hierarchical organization with its strict subordination to the commander raises questions concerning the role of Party authority. We have seen that despite claims to the contrary, the principle of one-man command has clearly been violated by the Party (see pp. 296–298). Party writers do not hesitate to associate the political officers with the military leadership on a 50/50 basis. Party organs have the right to recommend, and it is the privilege of a political officer to caution the commander against making certain mistakes or rash decisions (see p. 299). In fact, political department "recommendations" are commands.

Apart from the effect this has on the morale of commanders, these am-

[5] *KVS,* no. 17, September 1973, pp. 48–57.

biguities and conflicts between military and political authority cannot exist without some deterioration in command effectiveness. The evasion of independent judgment, with its fear of responsibility and "creative" innovation, is only one of the crippling consequences of Party interventions in the command function. The need to bend training and operational routines to the exigencies of socialist competition leads to wholesale falsification of results in the military units and in the cadet academies and reduces the value to commanders of the otherwise valuable Soviet emphasis on constant testing of military performance. Getting "good marks" is more important than having a good unit. Good marks and operational effectiveness are far from perfectly correlated, as Soviet authorities are the first to acknowledge. Questioned as to why he used an ineffective procedure, a platoon leader replies, "That is how they will question them at inspection and that is how we train them."[6] A young flying officer complains that the young officers acquire certain skills but forget them in a month without practice. "The [flying] schedule is not set up for us but for inspection purposes."[7] In many units in order to safeguard performance ratings, an inexperienced small-unit commander "is replaced by a more knowledgeable comrade. . . . Thus . . . the individual with the greatest experience is able to improve . . . while the individual lacking experience becomes merely an observer."[8] In large-scale exercises regimental and higher commanders often show a lack of confidence in subordinate officers and the effect of their actions on the rating of the regiment. "As a result, battalion and company commanders are only concerned with moving subunits to the indicated lines and preventing accidents to combat and transport vehicles, while the superiors are left to worry about the 'enemy' and the execution of tactical missions."[9] A commander and his unit may get a rating of "excellent" in an exercise largely because the unit incurred no accidents, which are severely penalized by the Party, to a considerable extent out of motives of thrift.[10]

Finally, political interventions, including requirements for Marxist-Leninist study up to the highest command levels, compound harassment and the administrative burdens of the commander, whose deputy is often not so much an assistant as he is a rival and overseer. "The telephone rings from early morning until late at night in the commander's office. When something goes wrong it is to the commander that people appeal. By the end of the day his head is spinning. . . . But next door sits the deputy [political officer] . . . for some reason no one approaches him with papers."[11]

It is an interesting question whether the Soviet incentive system and the

[6] *KZ,* July 7, 1972, p. 4.
[7] Ibid., August 26, 1973, p. 2.
[8] Ibid., November 21, 1973, p. 2.
[9] Ibid., August 29, 1973, p. 2.
[10] Ibid., August 30, 1973, p. 2.
[11] Ibid, March 4, 1973, p. 2.

pressure exerted on trainees and cadres by the Party simply result from Soviet preferences in management methods and perspectives on human motivation, or whether in the military structure the failure to use constant surveillance and pressure would, in fact—despite the tremendous drawbacks of such surveillance—lead to a predictable drop in military effectiveness and/or political control. If, indeed, the Soviet training system must depend on the employment of an exploitative, coercive system, this would suggest its potential fragility, at least at the troop level. Concern for the reaction of the better-educated youth now entering the service, and the desire to soften, at least marginally, some of the harshness of the training system, indicate a Soviet perception of some aspects of the problem and possibly a growing conviction that winning internal assent may be a useful supplement to external pressure.

The Soviet military structure may not be totally dependent on a rigorous application of the present system. Some Soviet military writers show a hesitant interest in extending the prescriptions applied to the treatment of youth to commissioned and noncommissioned cadres as well. Military personnel have in any case developed protective measures against the system and some ability to defend themselves against the worst forms of exploitation. These defenses have two different consequences. For many Soviet Party and military leaders they seem to signal the need for even tighter methods of control, increased surveillance, greater pressure, and higher demands. These, of course, in their turn provoke more defensive responses. On the other hand, some military writers seem to show a desire to reduce demands in the face of the evasive measures of military personnel.

7. Despite the generous sums allocated for national security, one of the most striking features of Soviet military administration is its attitude of extreme thriftiness, not to say miserliness (see pp. 317–318). Thus, Soviet military authorities urge personnel to study for higher specialist certificates, but at the same time some units delay issuing the certificates, thus avoiding trivial bonus payments. In the manner of some wealthy men who spend large sums freely on major purchases but are penny-pinchers in lesser matters, the Soviet authorities are insistent on saving money in areas that do not *seem* crucial to military success. In the Soviet case the old adage is reversed, and it is a case of "pound wise and penny foolish." This often results in gross inefficiencies in training and operations and the need to spend inordinate amounts of time on makeshift procedures and materials. This excessive thriftiness is especially apparent in the failure to provide "minor" personal, training, and operational conveniences, especially for junior officers and recruits, whose time and energies are sapped (just as those of civilians are) by the need to improvise. The Party rewards thriftiness, and it is therefore not surprising that due to a "thrifty attitude toward property" some units have been able "to turn down scheduled deliveries of [bed] linens without detriment to provisions for person-

nel."[12] It does not seem to occur to the writer of this article that the discovery in a tank company inspection that thirteen soldiers had only one bed sheet among them might be related to these "thrifty attitudes" so sedulously cultivated by the Party.

Misplaced thriftiness also occurs in areas of considerable operational importance. A Soviet observer manifests his pride in the ability of Soviet military personnel, naturally without benefit of air conditioning or adequate insulation, to withstand temperatures up to 70° centigrade in the cabins of radar stations under conditions that blunt "all of the senses."[13] Perhaps this observer would have felt more alarm and less admiration had he been aware that Soviet military psychology had established a large rate of increase in the frequency of PVO operational errors with increases in installation temperatures.[14]

The assumption, often made in the West, that Soviet military goods are supplied under conditions that enable them to escape the deficiencies of the civilian production and distribution systems is by no means always correct, especially in the case of items that are provided not by special military production establishments but by the same enterprises that work for the civilian economy. Thus military skis have a habit of breaking just as frequently as those sold to civilians. And military insignia and matches may be just as difficult to procure on a military base or naval ship as are items in a civilian shop. Wrong measures, wrong weights, and overcharging "are causing great concern" in the military trade networks of the Kiev, Carpathian, and Ural military districts.[15] It is evident from Soviet discussions of the PX system that strenuous attempts at improvement, and incentives related both to professional military standards and to national security concerns, do not enable the military to escape all the difficulties and dilemmas of the national society and the national economy. It is not possible to calculate the costs to training, operational effectiveness, morale, and discipline of penny-pinching "thrift" in the military, but a close reading of Soviet materials suggests that they are indeed substantial.

8. Most Soviet officers and NCOs are handicapped relative to those of other military establishments, but more especially to those of the United States, by the lack of service under combat conditions. Some 70 percent of Soviet regimental officers have not served in wartime (p. 15), and the Soviet emphasis on military training and exercises under conditions of "combat realism" cannot entirely compensate for this inexperience.

9. One specific feature of a possible future nuclear war that concerns Soviet authorities has to do not so much with the destruction that may be caused by nuclear weapons as with the ability of nuclear weapons to overawe

[12] *KVS,* no. 13, July 1973, pp. 16–22.
[13] *Pravda vostoka,* July 19, 1973, p. 4.
[14] *KZ,* January 30, 1971, p. 2.
[15] Ibid., March 14, 1972, p. 4.

and frighten Soviet soldiers and the civil population, either in anticipation of their imminent use or, more especially in the event of their actual employment. It is likely that these concerns of Soviet analysts do in fact rest on a correct perception of existing attitudes of Soviet military personnel, especially recruits. The tone of these comments suggests that Soviet military personnel share the belief, apparently not uncommon in Soviet society, that a nuclear war is necessarily equivalent to the death of the society. The magnification of the power of nuclear weapons seems especially characteristic of societies without free access to outside information or which are still in large measure rural and technologically underdeveloped.[16] The preoccupation with nuclear weapons shown by Soviet leaders in their civil defense program might also help to account for the popular attitudes that alarm Soviet military writers. Nuclear war makes "particularly big demands on the morale of the troops."[17] General Yepishev, chief of the Main Political Administration, points out that nuclear weapons "undoubtedly will have an enormous and probably previously unknown effect on the minds of people. . . . This will involve the personnel of all branches and arms, because the diverse and very complex situations under which one must operate can happen to anyone. In this situation the military personnel undoubtedly will experience . . . at times very great mental and physical stresses. We must not . . . underestimate the tribulations of modern war. . . . We must constantly prepare people for these tribulations. . . . Psychological training of troops is one of the most important conditions for our victory."[18] The Soviet soldier must cultivate fearlessness "so that he will not tremble or become confused under any conditions, even when the enemy uses his most powerful and menacing weapons."[19] Nuclear attacks may induce "nervous shock," create great fear, and undermine the confidence of the troops.[20]

Rocket troops are, in the Soviet view, subject to a particular difficulty or stress. In the West, it is generally assumed that soldiers experience more resistance, morally and psychologically, to bringing destruction on human targets that are close at hand and visible to them than on those that are remote and not seen. In Soviet literature, however, the reverse assumption seems to be made. This is applied both to pilots who have to attack targets by following

---

[16] In 1951, I had the opportunity to study the attitudes toward and beliefs concerning nuclear weapons of Chinese and North Korean Communist soldiers. Their conceptions of the power of nuclear weapons went well beyond a reality already sufficiently horrendous. The popular imagination seems to outrun reality very readily when that reality embodies extremities that humans have rarely encountered. One senses in Soviet references to popular conceptions something akin to the extravagance of Chinese and Korean reactions. In any event, Soviet authorities are now trying to make attitudes toward nuclear weapons a lot more "prosaic" than they currently are in some sectors of the Soviet population. See chapter III, B.

[17] *KVS*, no. 24, December 1972, pp. 25–32.

[18] General Yepishev, in Badmayev [*An Important Factor of Combat Readiness*].

[19] *Nedelya*, July 10–16, 1972, p. 6.

[20] *KVS*, no. 6, March 1972, pp. 42–47.

ground commands and using instrument readings and to rocket troops. "Exceptionally high moral, political, and psychological qualities are demanded from rocket troops. They are entrusted with weapons having a tremendous destructive power. The employment of such weapons is characterized by the operator not seeing the target; they do not see the results of nuclear strikes; they do not see their enemies. Under these conditions, a great force of will is required."[21] It is indeed a striking position that is expressed here, namely that a lesser force of will would be required if the nuclear missile launch crew could see the enemy upon whom it is unloading its nuclear missiles. The Soviet view may not seem so strange to Soviet writers. Soviet indoctrination stresses the need to mobilize hatred of the enemy and to paint him in vivid, emotional colors to the troops. Perhaps the appearance of the enemy in flesh and blood is presumed more easily to release the hatred mobilized against him than does a distant, unobservable enemy. Perhaps involved here, too, is not the difficulty of attacking an invisible and therefore not entirely real enemy, as the Soviet writer seems to believe, but rather inhibitions stemming from a belief that to launch nuclear weapons is to participate in the destruction of the world, and one's self. Such views would, however, be more surprising in what one must presume are the technically trained and carefully selected launch personnel of the rocket forces than they would be in the ground forces.

10. In contemporary military establishments, reliability and consequently military effectiveness depend to a considerable extent on the dedication and skill of a group of highly trained, relatively young officer-engineers or officer-technicians. In the Soviet forces a nontrivial, although not specifiable proportion, of such personnel are reserve officers, many of whom resent their call to service, do not view themselves as professional military men, and are looking forward to their return to civilian life. The statement that "some of the young officers—including above all those called up from the reserves—did not always carry out their lessons well"[22] reflects these morale problems. Soviet military writers have shown a particular sensitivity to western references to difficulties arising from the sense of separation of the officer-technician from both commanders and the political officers.

11. Despite the emphasis on combat readiness, the Soviet training system cannot entirely overcome periodic variations in operational effectiveness caused by the biannual reception of new recruits in the late spring and autumn and the reception of new junior officers from the cadet academies that makes the autumn period especially difficult.[23] All military establishments with large numbers of draftees face similar problems. They are magnified somewhat in the Soviet forces by the twice-yearly disruption of operational routine and by

---

[21] Ibid., no. 21, November 1970, pp. 73–78.
[22] *KZ*, October 26, 1973, p. 2.
[23] Ibid., January 11, 1970, p. 1.

the early incorporation of the inductees into operational units rather than into training regiments (p. 91).[24]

Combat readiness is particularly demanded in the strategic rocket forces and in the PVO, and one is naturally led to ask to what extent the operational efficiency of these important services is affected by the Soviet induction and training process. One way of reducing the negative impact on operations caused by the periodic reception of draftees would be to employ a large proportion of cadres in the rocket forces, in the PVO, and in the nuclear submarine fleet. The high proportion of first- and second-class specialists in these services does, as a matter of fact, suggest a smaller number of recruits. Nonetheless, Soviet military literature makes such frequent references to recruits in the PVO that one must suppose, in the absence of other data, that a substantial proportion of PVO personnel is composed of draftees. In the strategic rocket forces references to the reception of draftees are less frequent, but not rare.

12. The increasing independence of youth and their antiestablishment attitudes may hardly seem, to an observer of the relation of western youth to western military establishments, worth including in this inventory of Soviet military problems. However, the preoccupation of Soviet military and political authorities with youth problems has to be viewed from the standpoint of the Party's habituation to and requirements for total conformity to its prescriptions. The Party authorities have been compelled by their anxieties about this matter to take hesitant steps to alleviate the strain between authoritarian dispositions and youthful aspirations. This has upset old military routines and practices and, for the time being at least, has imposed strains resulting from unfamiliar and undesired compromises.

13. Non-Russians in 1970 constituted 47 percent of the USSR's population. Although the Party likes to emphasize that these minority citizens are distributed among 100 nationalities, about 74 percent of the non-Russian population is accounted for by nine nationalities, Ukrainians (36 percent) being the largest group. The Soviet census of 1970 permits the calculation that 62 percent of the non-Russian population, that is, 29 percent of the USSR's population, do not speak Russian fluently. Unfortunately the census does not distinguish degrees of Russian knowledge in this nonfluent category. Since Russian is the sole written and spoken language permitted in instruction and command in the armed forces, one can anticipate that problems must arise, both in training and in operations, from the failure of a substantial number of recruits to have an adequate knowledge of Russian. And indeed Soviet military writings reflect substantial language problems that have led the military to push for increased Russian instruction in the schools of the minority republics and to institute special classes in the army (see pp. 186–189 and pp. 195–197).

[24] Ibid., October 13, 1971, p. 1.

These attempts to alleviate the military's language problem almost necessarily aggravate problems that derive from nationalist sentiments, whose strength is evidenced by the persistence with which most minorities have clung to their native languages and resist the introduction of Russian as the language of instruction in their schools.

It is hardly to be expected that ethnic divisions and anti-Russian sentiments that create major problems in the civil society are without a similar effect in the military forces. Naturally Soviet military writers refer only discreetly to tensions within the multinational units among which Soviet minorities are dispersed, but the need of commanders and political workers to "rally the military collectives"[25] explicitly refers to overcoming national divisions. Military collectives contain representatives of many nationalities, usually ten to fifteen in company-size units, and "the slightest hostility" among them can impair combat readiness (p. 188).[26] Propagandists are told that friendship among men of different nationalities can be strengthened by implanting a "burning hatred" of the enemies of the motherland[27] and by inculcating a "pan-national Soviet pride."[28] It is hardly likely that this will dissolve nationalist feeling or anti-Russian sentiments.

Nationality divisions are intensified by the religious differences with which they are sometimes associated. In 1970 there were in the Soviet Union 35 million persons of Moslem origin, who find religious sentiments easier to retain because of their nationalist associations, and who are increasing faster than the Russian population. But it is not only Moslems and believing and practicing Christians whose religious sentiments disturb the military forces. Nonbelievers in the military also show a surprising resistance to Soviet antireligious zeal (see p. 221).

The difficulties facing the Soviets reviewed above do not signify a profound weakness in the military forces of the USSR. They do not seem sufficient to prevent Soviet troops from performing their peacetime and wartime functions with a substantial measure of success.[29] There is, however, a tendency to view

---

[25] *KVS*, no. 24, December 1972, pp. 25-32.

[26] Ibid., no. 3, February 1971, pp. 70–77.

[27] Ibid.

[28] *KZ*, March 28, 1973, pp. 2–3.

[29] The adequacy of preparations for wartime functions will depend, of course, on the nature of the enemy. It is not inconceivable that the Soviet Union, in the event of a conflict with China, may find itself, particularly in a period of nuclear stalemate, overcommitted in its most technically advanced services and matériel and underprovided on the ground. An uneasy awareness of this may be reflected in the statement: "At the present time, the Chinese army, which is one of the largest in the world in terms of numbers, consists primarily of ground forces capable of close combat. According to information from the foreign press they comprise 90 percent of the armed

Soviet soldiers, both individually and collectively, and the Soviet military as an organization, as being qualitatively superior to most of their western counterparts—in short, to view the Soviet military as "10 feet tall." This view seems to stem from the impression made by the intensity of Soviet training, the importance attached to the military, the resources made available to it, and the reputation for excellence of Soviet matériel. The preceding review is intended to question this view and to draw attention to constraints on Soviet military effectiveness. The Soviets may score high on effort, but effort does not necessarily imply a corresponding degree of success. And difficulties and problems built into a system do not necessarily vanish at the command of the Party or of military leaders.

Western appraisals of Soviet society are generally alert to deficiencies and difficulties in the civil society, but apparently on the basis of a number of Soviet matériel and space accomplishments they are disposed to infer that in areas where high priorities are accorded these deficiencies are overcome. The materials in Soviet unclassified military journals on Soviet military life at the troop level provide impressions of foul-ups, inefficiencies, and individual, team, and organizational failures similar to those shown to exist in the civil society. One can, of course, assume that the supposed greater efficiency of Soviet military over Soviet civil life occurs primarily at "higher" and more important and, naturally, more secret levels. This may be true, but it is an assumption that should not be too lightly made. The study of social systems should make one suspicious of inferences that impute capabilities to a major sector of the system that are radically different from those known from the other sectors. Soviet administrative rigidity, the need to pursue conflicting goals with little or no compromise, and the insistence that all objectives and means are equally important cripple Soviet military and civil administrations far more than a casual observation is likely to reveal. It is possible by fiat to maintain a very high level of performance in the chess world because of the relative independence of this sector from most other sectors of the society, the longstanding *private* esteem for the game, and the small investment of resources and managerial talent required to provide the inputs and achieve outputs in this field. But a huge military establishment, consuming enormous resources and drawing on a great number of persons from every sector of society, is another matter, and it would be dangerous to take for granted that sharp qualitative differences exist between this sector and the civil sector. Particular segments of the military effort may indeed represent high levels of achievement, but the military forces as a whole are more likely to reflect the total nature of the society than do detached fragments of it. Hesitation to assume the existence

forces. They are given a major, decisive role in the plans of the military command." *KVS,* no. 20, October 1973, pp. 88–92.

of sharp qualitative differences for "high priority" sectors should be all the greater given the existence of high-priority programs in both the civil and military fields that have shown frequent failures—agriculture and the space program.[30]

In summary, then, we have no wish or intention to persuade the reader that the Soviet military is shot through with great weaknesses and subject to so many constraints that its operational effectiveness is seriously compromised. We wish only to caution the reader against accepting uncritically some current images of the Soviet soldier and the Soviet military and to provide him with some considerations that both explain observable deficiences and suggest the possible existence of others that are not so readily discernible.

[30] Concerning the Soviet space program, the reader's attention is drawn to Leonid Vladimirov's *The Russian Space Bluff* (New York, 1973), which is surely one of the more important documents from a credible Soviet source in throwing light on limitations to Soviet achievement in a high-priority program.

Soviet Journals
and Newspapers
Cited in the Text

Agitator
Aviatsiya i kosmonavtika
Bakinskiy rabochiy
Bloknot agitatora
Ekonomicheskaya gazeta
Istoria SSSR
Izvestia
Kazakhstanskaya pravda
Kommunist
Kommunistas (Vilnius)
Kommunist Estonii
Kommunist Tadzhikistana
Kommunist vooruzhennykh sil (KVS)
Komsomol'skaya pravda
Krasnaya zvezda (KZ)

Kryl'ya rodiny
Leningradskaya pravda
Leninskoye znamya
Literaturnaya gazeta
Literaturnaya Rossiya
Molodaya gvardiya
Morskoy sbornik
Moskovskaya pravda
Narodnoye khoziaistvo SSSR
Narodnoye obrazovaniye
Nauka i religiya
Nedelya
Neva
Novaya i noveyshaya istoriya
Oktyabr'

Partiynaya zhizn'
Pravda
Pravda Ukrainy
Pravda vostoka
Sel'skaya zhizn'
Smena
Sotsialisticheskaya zakonnost'
Sovetskaya Belorussiya
Sovetskaya Estoniya
Sovetskaya Kirgiziya
Sovetskaya kul'tura
Sovetskaya Latviya
Sovetskaya Litva
Sovetskaya Moldaviya
Sovetskaya pedagogika
Sovetskaya Rossiya
Sovetskaya yustitsia
Sovetskiy patriot
Sovetskiy voin
Sovety deputatov trudyashchikhsya

Soviet Life
Soviet Military Review
Sputnik
Sredneye spetsial'noye obrazovaniye
Starshina serzhant
Tekhnika i vooruzheniye
Trud
Uchitel'skaya gazeta
Vedomosti verkhovnovo soveta SSSR
Vestnik vysshey shkoly
Voprosy filosofii
Vospitaniye shkol'nikov
Voyenno-istoricheskiy zhurnal
Voyennyye znaniya
Voyennyy vestnik
Vyshka
Za rulem
Zarya vostoka
Zhurnalist
Znamenonosets

Index

Academy of Pedagogical Sciences, 73
Academy of Social Sciences, 253
Accidents, and guilt, 163
Activists, 95 n; and attitudes toward military service, 199; and attitudes toward Party right to supervise management, 278–279; and one-man command, 147, 298, 300; as Party elite, 284; and political indoctrination, 245; and solidarity, 178; and surveillance, 165–166
Address, modes of, 149, 179
Administration, 180, 201; ambiguity in, 311–314; and avoiding decisions, 311–314; burdens of, 326; "going through channels," 180; of mass military programs, 318–319; of socialist competition, 124
Aesthetics, in political indoctrination, 194
Age: and applications for military academies, 17; of extended-service personnel, 14; of

junior officers, 15, 19; and reserve status, 7–8, 12; of senior officers, 15 n; of women in Soviet forces, 10
Age differences, and solidarity, 182–184
Air Defense Forces, 106, 111, 120, 328; and combat readiness, 132, 331; and combat realism, 113; and lack of initiative, 101; personnel rivalry in, 177; and socialist competition, 117, 121; specialist ratings in, 96
Air Force: flight hours of pilots in, 108; pilot initiative in, 98; pilots self-satisfied in, 181, 183; specialist ratings in, 96; training in, 113
Alleluyeva, Svetlana, 219 n
Allende, 210
All-Union Central Trade Union Council, 78
All-Union Voluntary Society for Assistance to the Army, Air Force, and Navy. *See* DOSAAF

Selected Rand Books

Becker, Abraham S. *Soviet National Income, 1958–1964.* Berkeley and Los Angeles: University of California Press, 1969.

Bergson, Abram and Hans Heymann, Jr. *Soviet National Income and Product, 1940–48.* New York: Columbia University Press, 1954.

Canby, Steven L. *Military Manpower Procurement: A Policy Analysis.* Lexington, Mass.: D. C. Heath and Company, 1972.

Chapman, Janet G. *Real Wages in Soviet Russia Since 1928.* Cambridge, Mass.: Harvard University Press, 1963.

Davies, Merton and Bruce Murray. *The View from Space: Photographic Exploration of the Planets.* New York: Columbia University Press, 1971.

Dinerstein, H. S. *War and the Soviet Union: Nuclear Weapons and the Revolu-*

tion in Soviet Military and Political Thinking. New York: Frederick A. Praeger, Inc., 1959.

Dinerstein, H. S. and Leon Goure. *Two Studies in Soviet Controls: Communism and the Russian Peasant; Moscow in Crisis.* Glencoe, Ill.: The Free Press, 1955.

Dreyfus, Stuart. *Dynamic Programming and the Calculus of Variations.* New York: Academic Press, Inc., 1965.

Einaudi, Luigi R. (ed.) *Beyond Cuba: Latin America Takes Charge of Its Future.* New York: Crane, Russak & Company, Inc., 1974.

Fainsod, Merle. *Smolensk Under Soviet Rule.* Cambridge, Mass.: Harvard University Press, 1958.

Fisher, Gene H. *Cost Considerations in Systems Analysis.* New York: American Elsevier Publishing Company, 1971.

Galenson, Walter. *Labor Productivity in Soviet and American Industry.* New York: Columbia University Press, 1955.

Garthoff, Raymond L. *Soviet Military Doctrine.* Glencoe, Ill.: The Free Press, 1953.

Goldhamer, Herbert. *The Foreign Powers in Latin America.* Princeton, N. J.: Princeton University Press, 1972.

Goldhamer, Herbert and Andrew W. Marshall. *Psychosis and Civilization.* Glencoe, Ill.: The Free Press, 1953.

Goure, Leon. *Civil Defense in the Soviet Union.* Berkeley and Los Angeles: University of California Press, 1962.

Goure, Leon. *The Siege of Leningrad.* Stanford, Calif.: Stanford University Press, 1962.

Hammond, Paul Y. and Sidney S. Alexander. *Political Dynamics in the Middle East.* New York: American Elsevier Publishing Company, 1972.

Hoeffding, Oleg. *Soviet National Income and Product in 1928.* New York: Columbia University Press, 1954.

Horelick, Arnold L. and Myron Rush. *Strategic Power and Soviet Foreign Policy.* Chicago, Ill.: University of Chicago Press, 1966.

Johnson, John J. (ed.) *The Role of the Military in Underdeveloped Countries.* Princeton, N. J.: Princeton University Press, 1962.

Kolkowicz, Roman. *The Soviet Military and the Communist Party.* Princeton, N. J.: Princeton University Press, 1967.

Kramish, Arnold. *Atomic Energy in the Soviet Union.* Stanford, Calif.: Stanford University Press, 1959.

Leites, Nathan. *The Operational Code of the Politburo.* New York: McGraw-Hill Book Company, Inc., 1951 and Westport, Conn.: The Greenwood Press, 1972.

Leites, Nathan. *A Study of Bolshevism.* Glencoe, Ill.: The Free Press, 1953.

Leites, Nathan and Elsa Bernaut. *Ritual of Liquidation: The Case of the Moscow Trials.* Glencoe, Ill.: The Free Press, 1954.

Leites, Nathan and Charles Wolf. *Rebellion and Authority: An Analytic Essay on Insurgent Conflicts.* Chicago, Ill.: Markham Publishing Company, 1970.

Maullin, Richard. *Soldiers, Guerrillas, and Politics in Colombia.* Lexington, Mass.: D. C. Heath and Company, 1973.

Moorsteen, Richard. *Prices and Production of Machinery in the Soviet Union, 1928–1958.* Cambridge, Mass.: Harvard University Press, 1962.

Novick, David (ed.) *Current Practice in Program Budgeting (PPBS): Analysis and Case Studies Covering Government and Business.* New York: Crane, Russak & Company, Inc., 1973.

Novick, David (ed.) *Program Budgeting: Program Analysis and the Federal Budget.* Cambridge, Mass.: Harvard University Press, 1965.

Quade, Edward S. *Analysis for Public Decisions.* New York: American Elsevier Publishing Company, 1975.

Quade, Edward S. and Wayne I. Boucher. *Systems Analysis and Policy Planning: Applications in Defense.* New York: American Elsevier Publishing Company, 1968.

Rush, Myron. *Political Succession in the USSR.* New York: Columbia University Press, 1965.

Rush, Myron. *The Rise of Khrushchev.* Washington, D.C.: Public Affairs Press, 1958.

Selznick, Philip. *The Organizational Weapon: A Study of Bolshevik Strategy and Tactics.* New York: McGraw-Hill Book Company, Inc., 1952.

Sokolovskii, V. D. (ed.) *Soviet Military Strategy.* Englewood Cliffs, N. J.: Prentice-Hall, Inc., 1963.

Speier, Hans. *Divided Berlin: The Anatomy of Soviet Political Blackmail.* New York: Frederick A. Praeger, Inc., 1961.

Stepan, Alfred. *The Military in Politics: Changing Patterns in Brazil.* Princeton, N. J.: Princeton University Press, 1971.

Williams, John D. *The Compleat Strategyst: Being a Primer on the Theory of Games of Strategy.* New York: McGraw-Hill Book Company, Inc., 1954.

Wolfe, Thomas W. *Soviet Power and Europe, 1945–1970.* Baltimore, Md.: The Johns Hopkins Press, 1970.

Wolfe, Thomas W. *Soviet Strategy at the Crossroads.* Cambridge, Mass.: Harvard University Press, 1964.